When We Were Kings

The story of Athlone Town's
1924 FAI Cup triumph

Tadhg Carey

Published by Tadhg Carey

Contact: whenwewerekings@ireland.com

ISBN 978-0-9562111-01

Printed by Temple Printing, Athlone

For Finn and Eve

"And if you know your history,
It's enough to make your heart go whoo-oh-oh."

Contents

Acknowledgements

Work on this publication has been ongoing over a five-year period. During that time, hundreds of people have contributed to its development in a myriad of ways.

It would represent an impossible task to attempt to acknowledge all those who have assisted in bringing this work to print. However, equally, it would be extraordinarily remiss of me not to recognise those without whose contribution this work would have been markedly inferior or, in some cases, not possible at all.

The relatives and friends of the numerous players whose careers are related here were, almost without exception, eager to impart their personal stories. Particular thanks must go to Roy and Eileen Collins for their generous hospitality to me during a trip to England.

Thanks too to Peter Keenan whose initial enthusiasm for the project helped convince me there would be at least one reader for this work. Peter's own Athlone Town history collection was also a vital starting point as I scrambled around in the dark.

Other football historians and writers have generously shared their expertise, knowledge, information and memorabilia. From Sligo, Cork, Limerick, Dublin, Belfast, Mullingar, Walsall and Birmingham, they answered every plea for help without quibble. They know who they are.

In Athlone, Gearóid O'Brien, the touchstone for all things local, has been an invaluable assistance and has dealt with my rich variety of often offbeat and arcane questions with the infinite patience for which he is renowned. His generosity in providing photographs and other items for use during the research is also acknowledged.

The staff at the National Library of Ireland were consistently helpful and their colleagues in Athlone, Mullingar and Tullamore libraries similarly so.

The Westmeath Independent was probably the foremost research resource for this book and I am grateful to all who have ensured its continued good health over the last 163 years. This process taught me the true meaning of the old cliché that newspapers are the first draft of history.

Aston Villa FC belied the notion that football has lost its soul by providing me with a day-long work station in their Villa Park offices during a research visit.

My parents bore the appropriation of their study over the last three frantic months with remarkably good grace.

Thanks also to my brother, Seamus, who was co-opted as an honorary researcher on the Olympic Games in Paris during a study year in France.

As deadlines approached with frightening rapidity, Conor Small came to the rescue by provided crucial editing advice and proof-reading skills under strict time pressures. The sole responsibility for any remaining clumsy prose lies squarely with me.

I wish to record my appreciation to graphic designer Geraldine Greene whose work adorns the accompanying dust jacket and to Ann Hennessy and other photographers for generously permitting me to reproduce their images.

I also recognise the generosity of all the patrons of Athlone Town FC, whose financial backing kept the club afloat in these last few months. For some time, the prospect of producing a history book about a club that itself belonged to history appeared all too real.

Temple Printing served as both midwife and consultant for this labour of love, delivering the product and providing expert advice along the way. Particular thanks to Cathal Temple and Paul Breen.

And lastly, but most importantly, I acknowledge the support of my own family; Sinead, Finn and Eve, who have dealt with my mental journeys into 1920s Ireland with an equanimity that I did little to deserve.

My wife, Sinead, has treated my daydreams, night vigils and regular disappearing acts with boundless good humour. She has been a constant pillar of strength throughout this mammoth project.

Whilst I was engrossed in the past, she ensured the present was not neglected. None of this would have been remotely possible without her.

Tadhg Carey, Athlone, 2009

INTRODUCTION

Days when we knew no peers

It's a little known fact that Ireland's first two international football captains were Athlone Town players.

And it's probably even less well recognised that Athlone Town holds the record for fielding the most players from a League of Ireland club in a single Irish international match.

There are few too who could confirm that five Athlone Town footballers had the double distinction of being among Ireland's original international footballers and first Olympians.

This book tells the remarkable story of Athlone Town's 1924 FAI Cup winners and their unique place in Irish sporting history.

Published to mark the 85th anniversary of the cup final, When We Were Kings aims to introduce the 1924 cup campaign to a new generation of sports enthusiasts.

In the 122 years since Orlando Coote first established Athlone Town football club, there have been many glory days. Not least the league championship victories of 1981 and 1983, the forays into Europe and the visit of AC Milan, to name but a few.

But 1924 was, and remains, special. That was the year Athlone carried off the FAI Cup (or Free State Cup as it was then known) for the first and, to date, only time.

The scale of the achievement cannot be overestimated. With football in the Free State in its infancy, Dublin-based clubs reigned supreme. Athlone were newcomers to football's top table. And for a provincial side just out of nappies to seize the blue riband trophy from the very citadel of footballing power was unheard of.

That they defeated Shelbourne and Bohemians along the way left the Dublin football establishment bewildered.

That five of the winning team - Paddy O'Reilly, Tommy Muldoon, John Joe Dykes, Denis Hannon and Frank Ghent - would make history as the first Olympians to compete for the new Irish Free State later that same year in Paris only added to the fairytale.

The quintet were part of a football squad which was knocked out at the quarter-final stage. The intervening years have seen those Olympic Games internationals downgraded in the official history of football in this country. According to FIFA regulations, these were official Irish internationals – and the history of football in this State needs to be urgently revised.

This is not simply a matter of interpreting the past from the perspective of the present. There is ample evidence too that these Olympic Games matches were regarded as full internationals at the time.

My interest in the project began purely as an educational journey for my own benefit. But as I explored the subject, it quickly became apparent that this remarkable tale should be preserved before it drifted entirely from our shared memory.

The players themselves have long since passed away. Many of their families too.

And although the attendance at that cup final on St Patrick's Day 85 years ago remains a record figure for an Athlone Town fixture in Ireland, the folk memory of the occasion is becomingly increasingly endangered.

A unique set of circumstances has meant there is only one direct descendant of the seven South Westmeath players on the team remaining in Athlone. Strangely, four of the seven players had no offspring whilst another two emigrated.

The passage of time and this shortage of local descendants means the story of the men of 1924 has not faded from the retelling. In fact, in many ways, these men are forgotten heroes – an alternative working title for the book. Their feats are lost in the mists of time.

When We Were Kings aims to bring into sharp relief the achievement of these sporting pioneers and to restore them to their rightful place at the front rank of local sports history.

What is particularly inspiring is that nine of the eleven players were from Westmeath.

For a then small town like Athlone to seize the day with an effectively all-local side was a seismic shock to the football establishment of the day.

Athlone's success was also a critical factor in bedding down the new Football Association of Ireland (FAI) – and closing the door on the old discredited Irish Football Association (IFA) regime.

More than anything else, this is the story of eleven good men and true. Of explosions, shootings and unmarked graves; of goals and saves.

It's the story of a football club that's deeply embedded in its community.

This book has been long in the gestation. It follows a rigid structure with chapters on 15 players who featured in the cup campaign, alternating with themed chapters on various seasons and key matches.

Tracing the career paths of those who contributed to Athlone's cup victory has involved a wider focus on Athlone Town's first stint in the League of Ireland. In essence, the book charts Athlone's contrasting fortunes from their pre-League of Ireland days right up to their return to the junior ranks in 1928.

It finishes with the unique tale of Athlone's Olympic pioneers – the first sportsmen to fly the Irish flag aloft in an Olympic Games.

With a keen focus on the wider national picture, this publication is also aimed at those with an interest in general sports history.

Information was culled from a variety of sources, mainly contemporary newspaper reports. Modern-day sports reporting differs vastly from its predecessor of 85 years ago. Team line-ups were infrequently given and personal detail never revealed. Lengthy detective work was required to track information of all 11 players from the 1924 cup final team, shedding new light on their life stories.

This book is designed not only to commemorate the past, but to provide a springboard for the future. Our shared footballing heritage in Athlone should serve to inspire the next generation of sporting talent in our midst.

May the men of '24 soon be joined in the roll of honour by modern-day compatriots.

Footnote:

I have attempted throughout the text to use the terms 'football' and 'Gaelic football' to differentiate between the two sports.

Similarly, for consistency, I have opted to refer to the FAI Cup rather than to the Free State Cup as it was known for some years.

Chapter 1

John Sweeney

Taken out in his prime

John Sweeney at the 1924 FAI Cup Final

- *Scored Athlone's first FAI Cup goal*

- *Scored Athlone's first League of Ireland goal*

- *Scored Athlone's first League of Ireland hat-trick*

- *Captain Leinster Junior Cup winners 1921/22*

If anyone appeared destined to carve out a name for himself in the fledgling world of Irish soccer it was John Sweeney.

Boyish in both appearance and personality, Sweeney was a natural leader, a popular figure in footballing circles locally. His ready charm and cheerful disposition won him friends easily.

Sweeney's footballing apprenticeship was served as the dark shadow of both World War 1 and the Civil War hung over his native Athlone. As football began to reawaken following the formation of the new Free State League in 1921 and the restoration of some form of harmony, it was John Sweeney who captained Athlone's breakthrough side to victory in the 1921/22 Leinster Junior Cup final.

When Athlone's growing stature was recognised by an invite to compete in the first ever FAI Cup the same season, it was two goals from John Sweeney that helped them into the second round.

And when Athlone were elected in 1922 to join the League of Ireland in its second season, it was John Sweeney who made history with their landmark first League of Ireland goal. He continued making records with Athlone's first League of Ireland hat-trick.

His mould-breaking achievements didn't end with just Athlone. When a French club side broke the mould and recognised the pariah Free State

League in 1923, it was John Sweeney who featured on what could be called the first League of Ireland representative side.

When destiny called, Sweeney answered loud and clear. But on the night of Saturday, September 29th, 1923, destiny had a different hand to play.

From Sweeney's Corner

John Patrick Sweeney was born in 1887, the third son of James and Mary Sweeney (nee Gaffey). His father had been a Sergeant in the Royal Irish Constabulary, but had retired in 1906.

The Gaffeys owned a busy public house at No. 1 Castlemaine Street, Athlone, and when his mother died at a very young age, the property passed to the Sweeneys. The public house was the prime building in what, in the early part of the 20th century. was one of Athlone's poorer areas.

To this day, among an older generation of Athlone residents, the area is known as Sweeney's Corner. It was here, in the family pub, that John Sweeney forged a living. And it was here that his career was to be all but ended.

John Sweeney first featured in Athlone colours in 1916 in a series of friendlies against military selections stationed in the then British Army barracks in Athlone. Sport, like everything else in normal life, was badly disrupted by the Great War. And it was not until 1919 that competitive football returned to the country.

John Sweeney was to the fore of the resurgent sport: his role as centre-forward in the Athlone team that competed in the Leinster Junior Cup in 1919/20 and 1920/21 marked him out as the main goal-getter in the town. However, it was the following year that Athlone and John Sweeney really made their mark.

The first FAI Cup goal

The Free State League was formed in 1921/22 after senior clubs broke away from the Belfast-based Irish Football Association which had administered football on the island for years previously.

Athlone Town were among three clubs who qualified to join the eight league sides to take part in the original Free State Football Association of Ireland Cup (now known as the FAI Cup). In the new era of Irish soccer, Athlone made their bow in the Claremount Road grounds of Dubliners YMCA, then one of the original members of the Free State League.

Athlone had warmed up for the clash with their customary participation in the Leinster Junior Cup and centre-forward John Sweeney was in top form.

His goal from the penalty spot for Athlone, away to St Patrick's, Ringsend, in the first replay of the semi-final of the junior cup two weeks previously on December 31st had earned Athlone another bite of cherry, which they subsequently availed of.

And with history resting lightly on his shoulders, John Sweeney announced his arrival in Irish senior soccer on January 14th, 1922, with the opening goal inside two minutes against YMCA. Taking a pass from Dinny Hannon, John Sweeney slipped the two YMCA full-backs and finished neatly.

He had just scored Athlone Town's first FAI Cup goal – ensuring his place in the club's history.

The wait for his second took just 30 odd minutes, when, in an intoxicating see-saw encounter, John Sweeney converted from the penalty spot before the interval to level matters at 3-3. Athlone eventually emerged unscathed, by the odd goal in seven, to reach the second round where they were drawn away to Bohemians.

The Dalymount Park outfit had almost 20 years of senior soccer experience behind them in the IFA-run Irish League and had just finished runners-up in the inaugural Free State League. So it was no surprise that Athlone were out-classed and beaten badly (7-1), but it was John Sweeney who ensured Athlone made an impression on the score sheet with a second-half penalty.

A youthful captain

Athlone's growing status within Irish soccer was franked by their run to the quarter-finals of the Leinster Senior Cup that same season. With John Sweeney netting thrice, Athlone saw off Free State League sides Pioneers and Brooklyn on home soil, before going out narrowly in the quarter-finals to eventual winners St James's Gate.

John Sweeney

However, despite this promising start to their life in senior soccer, it was back in the junior ranks - and the Leinster Junior Cup in particular - where John Sweeney and Athlone were to enjoy their greatest success.

Although the competition remains in existence to this day, its honour and status have long since declined from its heyday in the years before and after the turn of the 19th century. Athlone had won the competition twice in 1894 and 1895. By 1921/22, with only eight teams competing in senior league soccer, it was next highest level available.

In 1922, soccer had yet to officially prosper outside of Leinster. The winners of the Leinster Junior Cup, therefore, probably merited the title of best junior club in the Free State.

Having seen off St Patrick's of Ringsend in the semi-final in the midst of their FAI Cup commitments, Athlone faced another Dublin side, Chapelizod, in the final in Dalymount Park on April 22nd, 1922.

That Athlone side featured Jim Sweeney, Joe Monahan, Frank Ghent and Norman Lyster - four who would make the jump to senior status and bring home the FAI Cup some three years later. Nonetheless, it was the relatively young John Sweeney, who had the honour of lifting the Leinster Junior Cup after Chapelizod were brushed aside.

With a Leinster Junior Cup medal in his pocket, the trophy on the pub sideboard and his goals in the FAI Cup to immortalise him, John Sweeney was ready for the 1922/23 season.

Making league history

On the back of their exploits in 1921/22, Athlone had been elected to join the Free State League for its second season.

Athlone prepared diligently for their first appearance in the top flight and John Sweeney was in fine fettle, scoring twice in a pre-season friendly against Midland Athletic, another Free State League side.

He continued that form into the season and recorded Athlone's first League of Ireland goal in the opening 3-1 home defeat to reigning champions St James's Gate. Again, it was his ability from the dead ball that proved crucial, a second-half penalty sparking a mini-revival.

John Sweeney was back on the scoresheet in the third game of the season, a 3-3 draw at home to Shelbourne Utd which earned Athlone their first league point. And he was also on the mark when Athlone recorded their historic first League of Ireland victory over Olympia on Saturday, October 14th, in the Sportsground, Athlone Town's then home.

After six games of the new season, he yielded his place as attacking pivot at centre-forward, mainly to his more robust brother Jim, who had previously held down the centre-half berth. John moved to outside-right and was to play much of the rest of the league season in that berth.

Not surprisingly, the move limited his goal-scoring potential and he managed just two more goals in the following eight games before returning to the centre-forward role with spectacular impact on St Stephen's Day.

Jim Sweeney had been called up to a Leinster selection to play Ulster the following day, so John took the opportunity to lead the attacking line in some style, netting a hat-trick in the 4-2 league victory over Rathmines Athletic in the Sportsground.

John Sweeney had added the honour of scoring Athlone's first League of Ireland hat-trick to his growing series of records.

Despite his startling impact spearheading the forward line, he was restored to the outside-right position for much of the remainder of the season. And it was in that position he was to receive representative honours for the new Free State League on April 1st, 1923.

Flying the Irish flag in a brave new world

Just as the youthful Irish Free State was struggling to gain international recognition in the political and diplomatic fields, the new Football Association of Ireland was also being blacklisted in the corridors of sporting powers.

The embittered IFA had rallied the London-based FA and the Scottish and Welsh Associations to its cause with the effect that the new association was not officially recognised by its closest neighbours.

Despite wielding significant power in the world game, the English FA was not, at that time, a member of FIFA.

As a result the Free State FA moved to exploit this weakness by focusing its energies on gaining admittance to FIFA and, in the process securing worldwide recognition for the new governing body of football in the Irish Free State.

In that world of sporting intrigue, the visit of then famous Parisien club La Cercle Athletique de Paris Gallia (La Gallia) to Dublin in April 1923 was a key moment.

La Gallia, who had been French Cup winners in 1920, played Bohemians in a friendly fixture on March 31st in Dalymount Park before meeting a Free State League side the following day at the same venue. The League side featured John Sweeney at outside-right as the sole player from outside Dublin on the team.

Despite significant pressure from the Belfast-based IFA, the French Association sanctioned the visit of La Gallia – and in one move pulled the rug from under the British-led boycotting of the new FAI.

Although the team was trumpeted beforehand as League of Ireland representative eleven, its name was changed on the day of the game to a Pioneers FC selected XI. The move, the Irish Independent reported, was to allow La Gallia conform with the terms of the permit from the French governing body.

Many saw the fingerprints of the IFA in the late difficulties imposed on the French. The newspaper Sport reported that the IFA had lobbied the French Football Federation to block the game, while simultaneously offering a larger purse to La Gallia to visit Belfast instead.

The IFA may have won a small victory by limiting La Gallia to playing what were, in name only, club selections from the unrecognised football association, rather than taking on a side representative of this blacklisted league. But in reality, it had lost a major battle in the war.

Indeed, the decision by the French football authority to allow La Gallia to play matches here at all was seen by the Evening Telegraph as representing a de facto recognition of the new league by the French Federation and, by implication, FIFA.

Keen to press home their advantage, the FAI treated the French to a diplomatic love-bombing; a special reception in the Shelbourne Hotel was hosted, nominally by Bohemians FC, with the justness of the FAI's application for membership of FIFA hammered home in speeches.

Both the Irish and French tricolours were flown aloft in Dalymount Park in a powerfully symbolic political and sporting moment. The French visitors were also met en route to Dublin by a delegation of FAI officials at Holyhead in Wales. The instinctive gesture of the Lord Mayor of Dublin after the game to offer both tricolours to the French players was noted with praise in French papers.

It was no coincidence that five months later the French were strong supporters of the FAI's successful application for membership of FIFA.

The entire dynamic changed with the granting of FIFA membership and the Free State FA was now in a position of strength, having outsmarted the IFA. The visit of La Gallia had been a pivotal moment in the process.

The football itself may have been dwarfed by the occasion's greater significance. But for the record, the match finished scoreless. Nonetheless, John Sweeney had played his small part in carving the name of the FAI on the consciousness of the international footballing world.

If that wasn't enough excitement for one season the 1922/23 campaign climaxed with Athlone's run to the Shield final. After the league and cup, the Shield was the third-ranked competition, and with league membership still small, the Shield served to provide footballing action beyond the new year.

The Shield was operated as a knock-out competition in the 1922/23 season, and Athlone needed two attempts to see off Pioneers in the opening round, with John Sweeney contributing three goals over the two games.

Victories over Shamrock Rovers and Shelbourne Utd in successive rounds led to a Dalymount Park final against Shelbourne, for which Sweeney was surprisingly omitted, having performed poorly in the penultimate round.

Indeed, Sport had referred to Sweeney in its build-up to the La Gallia games as "a nimble and hefty hustler" who "at one time showed great promise".

There were clearly some signs that Sweeney's youthful promise was not reaching full harvest.

Season of destiny

With League of Ireland selection behind him, John Sweeney must have entered the 1923/24 season with renewed enthusiasm.

Now 25, he was in the prime of his career – a swashbuckling attacker whose talents had been recognised across the country. And while there were still question marks as to whether he was fulfilling his true potential, a dawning season provided fresh opportunities.

Nonetheless, John Sweeney seemed poised to be in the front ranks of Athlone Town football for years to come.

However, all that was to change shortly after 10pm on Saturday, September 29th, 1923. On that fateful night, John Sweeney was cleaning up in his father's licensed premises having closed the pub.

When a knock was heard on the door, Sweeney asked the identity of the callers and received the reply: 'Military on duty'. He opened the door and admitted Lieutenant John Joseph Cosgrave, a Deputy Assistant Provost Marshall who was attached to the Athlone Command of the National Army.

Cosgrave was a military police officer and part of his duty was to ensure soldiers were not present in public houses. John Sweeney was not aware there were soldiers on the premises. However, the military officer proceeded to the kitchen, where he found two soldiers drinking at the table. The soldiers were ordered out, but one sought to finish a drink on the table before him. A brief verbal argument between the soldier and his superior occurred before the soldier's glass was smashed on the floor and a shot was fired by Cosgrave from a small revolver. The bullet struck the floor and ricocheted into a wall and for years later the pockmarks were visible close to the door of the pub.

The Sweeney family housekeeper, Mrs Kilroy, a Scottish native, remonstrated with the lieutenant, and threatened to report him. Lt Cosgrave was then confronted by John Sweeney and his father in the hall of the premises and asked why he had fired. Cosgrave threatened to shoot both men and backed out onto the street. He was followed by the Sweeneys and fired two shots into the ground in front of their feet.

The altercation had caught the attention of locals and a crowd had gathered outside the public house. When Cosgrave emerged he ran away losing his cap in the process. John Sweeney pursued Cosgrave down the street, apparently to report him to his superiors.

Cosgrave then fired two more shots, which he said were designed to disperse the angry crowd who had converged on the scene. One of the bullets struck John Sweeney on the left side of his chest, penetrating his lung. A local doctor, who tended to the stricken man, said his life was in danger.

However, after a month of medical care at St Vincent's Hospital, Sweeney recovered and was deemed to be out of danger. But his football career, although subsequently resumed, never reached the same heights again.

Sweeney escaped with his life but missed cementing his place in Athlone sporting history when his teammates won the FAI Cup six months later.

The incident shocked Athlone and prompted the Westmeath Independent, in an editorial, to demand a full public inquiry into the circumstances of the shooting.

"During the week a deplorable shooting affray occurred in Athlone. It was only one of many similar sad events which, for some time past, have been of rather too frequent occurrence in various parts of the country.

"Fortunately in the Athlone case, the shooting did not prove fatal – and we are glad to state that the young man – the son of a respectable trader – is making splendid progress towards recovery.

"The time has not yet arrived when our national soldiers can go about the streets of our town unarmed. It is necessary for them to carry arms in the discharge of their onerous and sometimes risky duties. But a day must soon come when they will be discarded. How soon that day comes depends on those people who have created the necessity for an army in this country.

"In connection with the unfortunate occurrence, we think there should be the fullest inquiry and that the public should be put in possession of the facts. It is in the interests of the army as well as in the interests of the public that there be the fullest public inquiry into the matter and we hope those in authority will recognise the necessity of satisfying the public mind by an investigation of this character. It will clear the air and set the army right with the public, whose servant it is."

Cosgrave was subsequently acquitted following a court-martial in Custume Barracks arising from the shooting. However, he also faced criminal charges and in January 1924 was sent forward from Athlone District Court for trial in the Dublin Commission Court on charges of shooting with intent to murder, shooting with intent to do grievous bodily harm and with wounding John Sweeney.

The jury decides

During a two-day trial on Thursday, February 28th and Friday, February 29th, 1924, the jury was told by prosecuting counsel that, when they heard the facts, they would agree that the accused was fortunate in not standing in the dock on a charge of murder.

The prosecution stressed the case was important for two reasons – firstly, because army discipline was involved and secondly, because it was necessary to impress on officers and privates in the army that they

SHOT AN UNARMED CIVILIAN.

CONVICTION OF FREE STATE OFFICER.

At the Dublin Commission yesterday, John Joseph Cosgrave, wearing the uniform of a lieutenant in the National-Army, was indicted for shooting at John Sweeney, in Athlone, on 19th September last, with intent to kill him. On another count he was charged with firing at and wounding John Sweeney, with intent to cause grievous bodily harm. He pleaded not guilty.

could only use firearms in the last instance and when their use was the only alternative. The jury was asked to show by their verdict that civilians must be protected against the wanton use of firearms by soldiers.

Under cross examination, Sweeney confirmed he had told Cosgrave that there were no military on the premises. He said he did not know they were there. He said a crowd had assembled on the street but they were not hostile to Cosgrave.

> ## USE OF A REVOLVER
> ### OFFICER FOUND GUILTY OF WOUNDING

Private Michael O'Connor, one of the soldiers who had accompanied Cosgrave to the premises, said he had heard the accused shout "Stand back! Stand back!" when he was confronted by the gathering on the street. There had been a crowd following Cosgrave but O'Connor had not seen them do anything.

Volunteer Thomas Tumulty, who was also present, said that he had heard Cosgrave tell the crowd, "he wanted no trouble" and to get back. The witness believed Cosgrave was in danger at the time.

Defence counsel said there had been much focus on army discipline but it was for precisely this purpose that Cosgrave and his colleagues had visited the pub, where on this occasion there was drinking going on after hours.

He said the Sweeneys wanted to draw a veil over their own offence of supplying soldiers and civilians during prohibited hours and to exaggerate the firing of a shot in the kitchen, which he submitted was accidental.

He added one would imagine that when Cosgrave fired on the street the crowd would have dispersed, but instead they closed in on the accused and were obviously in an ugly mood.

In response, the prosecution counsel said the crowd was not threatening or hostile. He pointed out that when Cosgrave was asked why he fired the shot in the kitchen, he did not apologise nor state that it was an accident as they were now told.

Summing up, the judge, Mr Justice Pim, said the firing of the shot in the kitchen was not the act of a soldier, but of a buccaneer. He did not believe the people gathered on the street were hostile because they made no attempt to disarm the accused or to attack him.

Eventually the jury returned not guilty verdicts on the charges of shooting with intent to murder and shooting with intent to do grievous bodily harm. Cosgrave was then convicted of the lesser charge of unlawfully and maliciously wounding John Sweeney.

On Monday, March 3rd, the defendant came before Mr Justice Pim for sentencing. Whilst finding that Cosgrave was entitled to enter the public house and order the soldiers back to barracks, the judge said it was not his duty, but was a wanton outrage, to fire a shot there.

"In this country, people expect that in the Free State Army, officers should behave as gentlemen. That is to say they should have forbearance, patience, courage and determination not to exceed their authority and have some consideration for the feelings of those with whom they come into contact."

He said Cosgrave's conduct was utterly unworthy of an officer and a gentleman. He had acted with a wantonness that had being brought on by being clothed in "a little brief authority". And the judge pointed out that Cosgrave would have been found guilty of murder, if the bullet had killed anyone.

Justice Pim said he had spoken strongly as he was going to mete out mercy. He had heard a good account of Cosgrave as being an active officer. Cosgrave was given a suspended twelve-month prison sentence and was bound to the peace for two years.

Recuperation and return

The timing of the trial was most inopportune for Sweeney's family, friends and former team-mates, not least his brother, Jim, who was captain of the Athlone Town team in 1923/24.

The trial had commenced the previous Thursday and Cosgrave had been found guilty on Friday but the case was adjourned for sentencing to the following Monday, March 3rd. In the meantime on Saturday, March 1st, Athlone faced Bohemians in the replay of the FAI Cup semi-final in Shelbourne Park.

With such a distracting backdrop, Athlone's victory over Bohemians was all the more commendable and the role of captain fantastic Jim Sweeney particularly so.

The shooting and the subsequent recovery period ruled John Sweeney out of the rest of the season and indeed nearly all of the 1924/25 campaign. And while he was selected as one of two Athlone substitutes for the FAI Cup final in 1924, the gesture was purely sentimental as no substitutions were allowed during the game.

Despite the immediate concern over his life and the longer-term impact on his health, John Sweeney returned to football and to the colours of Athlone.

But firstly, he eased his way back into the game with a stint with Mullingar during the concluding months of 1924. Mullingar played their football in Division Two of the Leinster Senior League and Sweeney joined up with the North Westmeath side around October 1924, shortly after the start of the 1924/25 league season.

Sweeney, with Martin Harkins, Arthur Enright and Mick Henry, was among a strong contingent of Athlonians who donned the Mullingar colours that year.

Despite his spell out of the game, Sweeney was soon back among the goals and having tested his nerve, health and fitness, it wasn't long before he cut his links with Mullingar and returned to Athlone.

The second coming

It's likely his first game back with Athlone Town was a narrow 1-0 victory over Pioneers in the Sportsground on December 20th, 1925.

And soon he was doing what he was best at: scoring goals. His first came the following weekend in a 3-0 victory over St James's Gate and he was on the mark in the next outing in the first round of the FAI Cup on January 10th, 1925, with a goal after just ten minutes as Athlone overcame Munster Senior League side Cork Bohemians 5-3 in the Ranelagh Grounds.

And just two months after returning to the fray with Athlone, John Sweeney faced his stiffest test –an FAI Cup semi-final against Shelbourne in Dalymount Park. Athlone were the holders and were expected to threaten Shelbourne with their usual blitzkrieg football.

Sweeney, though, was understandably ring-rusty and it was unfortunate that two clearcut chances fell to him in the opening minutes as Athlone attempted to swamp Shels with their high-tempo game. Having missed the early chances, the game slipped away from Athlone and they lost their hold on the FAI Cup in disappointing fashion, losing 4-0.

After the cup exit, Sweeney continued his rehabilitation, featuring in a number of end-of-season Shield games (the competition was run on a league basis that year).

The following season, he appeared to be back to his lethal self, scoring in four of the first six league matches, from his customary outside-right berth. But, in reality, he had never truly recovered from his horrendous experiences of September 1923.

Although he finished the 1925/26 season as Athlone's third-highest goalscorer, with a more-than-respectable tally of six goals from 18 league games, he was rapidly running on empty. He saw out the rest of the 1925/26 season, playing in the FAI Cup first and second rounds and in a number of Shield games, before hanging up his boots.

He did make a final once-off Christmas appearance the following season, 1926/27, when he lined out in a Shield game against Bray Unknowns in Athlone on December 27.

A premature death

Despite his enforced retirement, his passion for the game never dimmed and he was a notable figure in administration, particularly at underage level.

His obituary in the Westmeath Independent noted: "When failing health compelled him to take a less active part in his favourite sport, his interest in the game did not decline. He was one of the strongest stalwarts of the code locally."

Even as far back as December 1922, John and his brother James and a number of other football enthusiasts had decided to present a cup to the winners of a minor league in Athlone. And now that he was not wanted on the field of play, John Sweeney had more time to devote to developing the next generation of Athlone sporting talent.

In later years, he also took up the whistle, refereeing at a local level in an effort to retain contact with the game he loved.

However, the failing health which necessitated John Sweeney's retirement from football was to have tragic consequences within ten years.

On Friday, October 23rd, 1936, John Sweeney passed away at his home on Castlemaine Street, at the tender age of 38.

Officially he was the victim of a condition then and for many years the scourge of the nation until his fellow Athlonian and near contemporary Noel Browne acted to stem the tide of deaths. He had been suffering from tuberculosis of the lung since the summer of 1934 but his passing was hastened by severe asthma which had left him stricken for the previous month.

The bullet wound to the lung which had eventually ended his footballing career appeared to have taken an even greater toll.

He was buried in Cornamagh Cemetery on Sunday, October 25th, 1936. He was unmarried and the chief mourners at his funeral were his father, James, and two brothers, Jim and Thomas.

Fittingly, the game between his beloved Athlone Town and Home Farm in the Leinster Senior League Division One that same day was put back until after the funeral.

The Athlone players wore black armbands. Many, including the famous Paddy 'Ruby' Barlow and Tommy Farrell were involved in youth teams whom John Sweeney had assisted. Two minutes' silence was also observed in honour of one of the trailblazers of football in the town.

Chapter 2

First steps in a new footballing world

The split

The 1921/22 season was the year zero of League of Ireland football.

Up to then the Irish Football Association (IFA) in Belfast had governed the game across the 32 counties. Founded in 1880, the IFA administered both the Irish League and Irish Senior Cup.

Bohemians and Shelbourne had competed in the league since the early years of the 20th century along with the cream of Northern clubs. Both Dublin clubs had also regularly made their mark in the flagship knock-out competition, the Irish Cup.

However, in 1921, slowly-building pressures exploded across football in Ireland, shattering the game to its very foundations.

The pressure-points had been many. Over the years, there had been simmering resentment that international teams representing Ireland were heavily biased towards players from Northern sides.

There were concerns too that Dublin was not enjoying its fair share of flagship games.

In the context of a rising tide of nationalist sentiment sweeping the country in the wake of the Easter Rising and World War 1, it was no surprise that the IFA soon became seen as a symbol of British imperialism in Ireland.

Tensions were ratcheted up a notch when students waved tricolours at an amateur international against France in Paris. The IFA insisted the flags be removed.

It was only years later that it emerged that African students from the College of Surgeons were the guilty parties.

The final catalyst for the breakdown in relations was the IFA's refusal to fix a Dublin venue for the replay of the 1921 Irish Senior Cup final between Shelbourne and Glentoran. With the original game in Belfast having finished scoreless, it was accepted practice that the replay would be held in Dublin.

When the IFA instead ordered Shelbourne to revisit Belfast, citing security concerns due to the ongoing Civil War in the south, the Dublin club refused and the old IFA was no longer. Holders St James's Gate also withdrew from the Irish Intermediate Cup after the IFA reneged on a promise to hold the 1921 final in Dublin.

Instead, on June 1st, 1921, at a public meeting in Dublin, what was then known as the Football League of the Irish Free State was formed.

Attempts to heal the rift with the IFA dragged on for years with regular peace conferences taking place and potential compromises hatched. But the die was cast.

Athlone join the ranks

Athlone were quick to play their part in the nascent association in Dublin.

By September 1921, moves to establish an Athlone and District Association to affiliate with the new Football Association of the Irish Free State were already afoot.

Denis Hannon, the original Mr Football in Athlone, prominent referee Michael Broderick and Jim Sweeney, father of leading players Jim and John, were to the forefront of getting the association up and running. Hannon was chosen as the Athlone and District's representative on the council of the Free State Football Association.

And to highlight Athlone's crucial part in the development of football in the new Free State, it is interesting to note that only three district associations were affiliated that first year: the Greater Dublin-based Leinster Football Association, the Belfast Falls and District Association and the Athlone and District Association. It appears that the Munster Football Association did not enrol until the end of the first season.

The Leinster Football Association, which had been a constituent body of the IFA, continued in existence and its Leinster Junior Cup provided the first action in the new era for Athlone Town. The competition was regionalised – and its midlands' rounds run off in parallel with the Dublin section.

In October and early November 1921, Athlone emerged through their own region, having seen off local junior club, Riverside, Clara and another Athlone junior outfit, Strandville, along the way, with little difficulty. That brought them through to the last four of the competition and a semi-final clash with St Patrick's, a Ringsend-based junior club.

Prior to the draw, Athlone had applied to the Leinster Football Association to be allowed host the semi-final on home turf.

And with a myopia typical of much of the Dublin media, the Evening Herald commented: "The suggestion is a good one in the interests of the game but it is extremely difficult for a metropolitan club to get a team to travel."

Whether by the luck of the draw or by design, Athlone were fortunate to be nominated as the home side for the semi-final which was scheduled to take place on St Stephen's Day.

Although, Athlone had managed to hold sway in the matter of venue, there were more grievances voiced at the choice of a Dublin referee to officiate at the fixture. Athlone believed officials from Mullingar, Clara or Longford should have been considered.

This all appeared to point to an uneasiness between the sides and the subsequent encounter, when it did materialise, showed the signs were correct.

But in the meantime, Athlone had other fish to fry – in the shape of the FAI Cup qualifying competition.

The FAI Cup qualifying competition

Again, the Free State Football Association had organised the FAI Cup qualifying competition on a regional basis.

In total 37 teams entered, including members of the Falls and District League, the Leinster Football Association and the Athlone and District Association, as well as two teams from Tipperary.

With the Tipperary sides lumped in with the Dublin clubs, the winners of each of the three regional qualifying competitions were guaranteed entry to the FAI Cup first round, along with the eight existing Free State League sides.

Seven teams from the Athlone district entered the qualifying rounds, which were run off in November and early December.

After Longford conceded a walkover to Athlone Town in the opening round, victories over Mullingar side St Mary's (4-1) and Clara (2-0) in the final, ensured Athlone Town's entry to the first FAI Cup.

Back on the junior cup trail

And so with the attraction of a potential clash against some of the country's giants awaiting after Christmas, Athlone turned their attentions once again to the Leinster Junior Cup and that semi-final against St Patrick's.

Despite the pessimistic soundings of the Evening Herald, the Dubliners made the trip to Athlone on St Stephen's Day. As it transpired, Athlone too had to do their fair share of travelling – as the original contest ended 2-2.

The replay on December 31st, 1921, in St James's Park also ended with honours shared but Athlone were hugely unfortunate having gone ahead through a John Sweeney penalty before an undeserved late equaliser necessitated a third meeting between the sides, again in Athlone.

Johnnie Menton

Athlone were forced to play three quarters of the first replay with only ten men, following a serious injury to inside-left Johnnie Menton.

Menton, along with his brothers Mick and Joe who were from The Strand, had all played with Athlone. Indeed, Johnnie, the youngest of the three, was a survivor of the victorious Leinster Senior League Division Two champions of 1913/14.

Menton had been instrumental in securing Athlone's passage to the semi-final stage, having bagged at least three goals, including a brace in the defeat of Clara, along the way.

The Evening Herald noted there were passages of very rough play in the semi-final replay. And Menton sustained a broken leg which left him incapacitated and unable to work for over seven months, prompting a fund-raising dance in the Foresters' Hall in Athlone the following July.

He was never to play for Athlone again.

Johnnie Menton in the 1913/14 season

When Athlone met St Patrick's for the third time on January 7th, 1922, there was no doubting the superiority of the Midlanders, who coasted through to the final on a 3-0 scoreline.

However, the country's focus on that Saturday early in 1922 was not on sporting matters but on the vote the previous evening in Leinster House in which Dáil Eireann had accepted the proposed Treaty to end the War of Independence.

A 64-57 majority had brought to a close a violent and tempestuous period in Irish history but was to spark a new turbulent chapter: the Civil War.

It was in this nervous climate that Athlone's footballing pioneers made the regular trips to Dublin to further the growth of the game in the midlands.

The first foray in the cup

Having qualified for the first ever FAI Cup, Athlone were drawn away to Free State League strugglers YMCA.

The Dubliners, in what was to be their one and only season in the Free State League, had just finished at the foot of the league table with only three points from three draws to show from their 14 league matches. The game was played at Claremont Road in Sandymount, the venue to this day of the YMCA cricket club in Dublin.

Athlone's involvement piqued the interest of the national media. The week before, Sport, the popular weekly newspaper, hinted that "a couple of ex-internationals will assist them in this competition".

This presumably referred to Denis Hannon and Johnny McDonnell (of whom more later) but it transpired that only the former lined out with Athlone.

Hannon had been ineligible for the Leinster Junior Cup campaign – and with the FAI Cup qualifying competition taking place within the midlands and away from the focus of the national press - it was clear that this was the first inkling the papers had of his involvement with his hometown club.

If Athlone were apprehensive about their debut at senior level, their performance didn't betray any such signs. Instead, in a sensational opening, Denis Hannon created the opportunity for John Sweeney to register Athlone's first FAI Cup goal inside a minute.

In a tactic which Athlone employed to notable effect in other years, Hannon, nominally an inside-right, doubled up in defence to help his middle line.

The dramatic opening was the signal for a game played with typical cup-tie freneticism which featured goalmouth incidents aplenty as attacks flowed from end to end.

However, it was Athlone who added the second after some 20 minutes when inside-left Frank Ghent swept home after the YMCA defence had failed to clear an Athlone corner.

It was one of many crucial goals that Ghent would contribute for Athlone in a glittering career. The Athlone native was one of the leading lights of League of Ireland football throughout the 1920s; his marauding wing play combining speed with strength.

Burlace in the Town goal was single-handedly repelling the YMCA attack but he couldn't prevent the home side from deservedly opening their account five minutes later.

The floodgates well and truly opened at this stage and YMCA added two more goals within four minutes, to dramatically edge 3-2 in front.

However, almost immediately from the restart, John Sweeney levelled matters from the penalty spot after Ghent had been upended.

After such an intoxicating opening half, with six goals into the bargain, the second half was always unlikely to provide equal entertainment.

Although there was no let up in the passionate approach of both sides, the sole strike after the break proved to be winner.

It came courtesy of Athlone half-back Alan Smith, a Coosan man whose career with Athlone didn't stretch beyond the 1921/22 season.

Smith was better known for his exploits on the water. He was a former captain of

Alan Smith

28

Athlone Boat Club and all-round water enthusiast.

In 1921, he made a name for himself as part of the Athlone Boat Club crew which won the senior fours at the Carrick-on-Shannon regatta.

Smith, who lined out at right-half back, arrived on cue early in the second half to direct a Johnny McManus cross goalward. There appeared little danger for YMCA until a breakdown in communication between the home keeper and defence resulted in Smith's speculative effort finding its way to the net.

This time around, Athlone were not to let their advantage slip, despite being under the cosh for the majority of the second half.

After the game, centre-back Jim Sweeney, rover Denis Hannon and striker John Sweeney earned most of the plaudits. But it was keeper Burlace who took the lion's share of the credit for the victory.

Thomas Burlace

While the late 1910s and early 1920s in Ireland were a tumultuous period, then 24-year-old Thomas John Burlace had suffered more than most.

Before the war, the Burlace family of Castlemaine Street consisted of husband and wife Thomas and Mary and their two sons, Thomas and Patrick.

His mother, Mary, passed away in 1912 before the outbreak of the war and all three males subsequently enlisted. While Thomas returned from service as a driver with the Royal Field Artillery, his father and brother were not so fortunate.

Thomas Burlace in 1919

Private Thomas Burlace senior, 2nd Battalion, Connaught Rangers, died on September 9th, 1914, and his son, Patrick, 2nd Battalion, Leinster Regiment, lost his life while still a teenager on August 12th, 1915. Thomas senior is commemorated in the Beuvry Communal Cemetery, while Patrick, is honoured at the Ypres Memorial.

With his direct family wiped out, there would have been little to draw Thomas Burlace back to Athlone. Nonetheless, he returned and became active in the Comrades of the Great War Association, later to be known as the Legion of Ex-Servicemen.

The Comrades of the Great War Association, the first branch of which was formed in Athlone in April 1919, was designed to help discharged soldiers and sailors with pensions, employment and living conditions.

Set up as a campaigning alternative to what was seen as the more moderate British Legion, the Comrades eventually merged with the Legion in the mid-1920s.

Burlace's involvement with this pressure group might not, on its own, have signified a political radicalisation.

However, his family believe he helped to train republicans in weaponry skills during the War of Independence. At the time, the military expertise of war veterans was strongly coveted. Indeed, many ex-soldiers, disillusioned by the treatment meted out them by the British Government, had been radicalised to join the republican movement.

Burlace, though, was horrified to witness Irishmen fight Irishmen in the Civil War, having seen enough bloodshed in World War 1.

With no direct family ties remaining in Athlone, he opted to seek a new life in America. It was a path followed by many other ex-soldiers, who had been to hell and back on the battlefields of France and further afield.

Burlace was first-choice goalkeeper for Athlone throughout 1921/22, but only appeared in the FAI Cup and Leinster Senior Cup. His place in goal during the Leinster Junior Cup campaign was taken by William Bracken.

After the 1921/22 season, Burlace drifted out of the limelight and from the town. His last game for Athlone was in April 1923 against Pioneers in the Shield, one of only a handful of appearances that season.

He emigrated to America in early 1923 and settled down there as a railway worker, marrying a Donegal woman and having four sons – all of whom carried on a military tradition of some sort.

Despite integrating well into his new life, Burlace was always an Irishman in exile. Poignantly, after the death of his wife, he returned to Athlone for three years from 1966 to 1969, staying in a boarding house in the town.

His search for a spiritual home wasn't to be fulfilled, however, and he returned to live out the remainder of his life in America, before passing away in October 1990 at the age of 93.

Like many of his generation had who been through World War I, the ending of British Rule, the Civil War and emigration, the quest for a flag to salute was an important motif in his life.

The problem for Burlace was that, in the mind of others, he was an outsider. An Irishman who had fought for the British. An Irishman living in America. An American living in Ireland.

Burlace, more than most, encapsulated the shifting sands of Irish identity over the span of the 20th century.

World War 1 in Athlone

Irish soldiers had been promised that they would be treated as heroes when they returned from the front.

The reality was in stark contrast with many left to fend for themselves, at best forgotten, at worst betrayed and abandoned, and often in penury.

To make matters worse, unwanted by the British government, and viewed suspiciously by many in a changing Ireland, the veterans faced alienation on all sides.

In Athlone, the feelings of disillusionment must have been particularly acute, as the town had backed the war effort unstintingly. Indeed, Athlone was one of the foremost recruitment centres in the country for the British Army during World War 1.

A whopping 800 to 1,200 men from the town and hinterland are believed to have served in the British Army during what was known at the time as The Great War.

The Athlone branch of the Legion of Ex-Servicemen estimated in 1924 that 1,400 ex-soldiers were then living in the area from Kiltoom to Kilbeggan.

In September 1924, the same organisation, whilst on a deputation to members of the British parliament in Dublin, outlined that there was the very specific number of 1,257 demobilised British Army soldiers in Athlone.

In 1920, it was estimated that some 200,000 discharged and demobilised soldiers returned to Ireland. The legion

Irishmen!

What will you Do?

YOUR political leaders, your famous countrymen and particularly your brave Irish soldiers have asked you to do your duty to your country.

The need for more men is urgent. We must not merely win, but win handsomely. Half hearted measures will not suffice. Anything less than a supreme effort invites defeat. Germany is putting forth her full strength.

Every possible step has been taken to meet the wishes of Irishmen. They are trained together, and will serve together.

They are invited to select the regiments and divisions to which they would like to be posted.

To do nothing is to say "No." There are few considerations which justify a man of military age in refusing to come forward when his country is fighting for its very existence.

Full particulars of pay, of allowances to those who are dependent on you, and of pensions, may be obtained from any Post Office or Recruiting Office.

The response already received is an earnest of what Irishmen can do, but more and more men are wanted. If you are willing freely and voluntarily to respond,

SIGN THE FORM

A recruitment form published in the Westmeath Independent

itself had 120,000 members across the country at that stage.

Whilst figures of around 1,000 soldiers from the wider Athlone area may appear somewhat exaggerated, the Offaly Independent newspaper, in February 1917, listed 452 soldiers who had enlisted from the Tullamore urban district alone.

This suggests that Athlone's greater size and stronger military tradition could have resulted in an enlistment figure from the wider area in the region of 800 to 1,200.

Further evidence of the scale of Athlone's involvement was made clear when a local recruitment committee arranged the presentation of certificates of honour to families of the soldiers in late 1915 and early 1916. Some 360 made contact – and many more may not have wished to draw public notice to their family's war involvement. Plans for a third presentation evening never materialised - the Easter Rising probably intervening.

Official figures also showed that in late 1915, 407 people were drawing separation allowance, eligible to wives and dependants, at Athlone post office.

Taking into account the many single men who had joined up and who could not claim the allowance, and that recruitment would have continued for most of the war years, based on these figures, it's feasible that some 800 to 1,200 men did join up from the general Athlone region.

If these figures are hard to pin down, providing an estimate of the number of Athlone casualties is even more fraught with danger. One local historian has compiled a detailed, albeit incomplete, list of some 85 Athlone serviceman killed during World War 1.

Nationally, it's estimated that Ireland lost 35,000 of the 210,000 who fought in World War 1. A similar ratio of one death for every six would leave Athlone with a fatality rate of close to 150. At the very least, it would appear realistic that somewhere upwards of 100 men from this region lost their lives.

Whatever the dispute about exact figures, it's clearly evident that Athlone had made a major commitment to the war effort.

However, as is generally the case in wartime, that commitment was not spread equally across society.

The background of the soldiers was revealed in a comment in an editorial in the Westmeath Independent in July 1915. "There is scarcely a working class family in the town that has not one or more of its members at the front," the paper remarked.

In August 1916, of 47 pre-war members of the predominantly working-class Athlone Brass and Reed Band, 35 had joined up (of which three had lost their lives) and another three were working in munitions factories.

Contrary to popular myth, football in Athlone was not a garrison game – although the presence of the British Army in the town obviously helped to foster the game.

Instead, football in Athlone was a major working-class sport and for that reason there was significant involvement of footballers in the war.

Whatever about the socio-economic status of World War One soldiers, what is apparent is the high level of recruitment in Athlone.

So what factors were behind this staggering level of enlistment?

The town's established military tradition would have obviously helped, and the presence of the British Army barracks in the town made military life appear normal to townspeople. The grim poverty experienced in the early years of the war would also have encouraged many to volunteer. Soldiering at least offered a steady income.

Athlone was also a strong Home Rule town, providing many recruits to the Volunteer movement before the war. They probably stayed loyal and backed the volunteers' stance in joining the British fight in the War.

When the war was declared, the vast majority of the 180,000 volunteers agreed with John Redmond's support for the war and became known as the National Volunteers. A small more radical faction made up the Irish Volunteers.

The Redmondite view was supreme in Athlone and most of the volunteer movement would have favoured Ireland's participation in World War 1.

The urban council was dominated by the Irish Parliamentary Party - the old conservative nationalist elite, who were full square behind the war. The town's pillars of the establishment were also all Home Rulers.

These people were the backbone of a massive local recruitment campaign sparked off in 1915 to boost recruitment numbers.

Local recruitment committees were established in many towns across the country but the Athlone committee appeared particularly active. And a number of choreographed recruitment rallies were staged to generate interest.

A recruitment office is believed to have been located in Main Street close to the current day Sean's Bar

The chairman of the recruitment committee, and also then chairman of Athlone Town FC, Michael J Lennon, in some ways encapsulated the political stream of thought which was backing the war effort in Ireland.

A member of the urban council, a magistrate at Athlone court, Lennon, a Connaught Street publican, was the epitome of the middle class Catholic establishment which had found an economic and political niche in the empire.

Although an ardent nationalist, he believed Ireland's place was in the war effort.

Addressing one of a series of war rallies held in Athlone to enlist recruits, Lennon, in December 1915, said:

"Surely when this war is over, the rights of all nationalities will not be denied by the worldwide empire to this great nation of ours. In the future we must be an island within the empire."

Beside him on the platform was the local representative of the ruling imperial class the Right Hon Robert Arthur Handcock, Recruiting Officer for Athlone, and later to become Lord Castlemaine. He was happy to smudge over the real political question facing Ireland at the time – its status within the empire.

"As far as we are concerned politics as we know them are dead," he conveniently told the same rally.

From a conservative nationalist perspective, The Westmeath Independent was also fully backing the war effort. The paper had regularly urged Athlone men to join the fray in its columns, seeing Irish involvement as a necessity to ensure Home Rule, which had been granted but not enacted by the British, would be preserved.

Of course, in wartime propaganda and hysteria reach fever pitch and in an editorial published just one week before the Easter Rising, the then editor McDermott Hayes issued an amazingly shrill call for extra recruitment for the war.

"Athlone soldiers have the distinction of winning several distinguished conduct medals. It is true, unfortunately, that the town suffered a terrible holocaust in the war. Not only did it send more soldiers to the front that any other town in the country, but it had also a heavier mortality list – the melancholy pleasure of a lengthened roll of brave men who offered their lives fighting for Ireland in an Irish army of the empire."

Calling for more reserve volunteers, the editor continued: "There is no good in fathering an army if we do not maintain it in full fighting strength until the Hun is dished!

"It should be a matter of national pride to make this army of ours the free gift of a free people worthy of ourselves and worthy of the fight for freedom in which it is engaged.

"The aim of every man should be to lend a hand in the war. If the father of the family, the head of the house, cannot go, he should be represented by the son, or two sons, if they can be spared. If he had not a son, he may have a nephew. If he has neither a son nor a nephew he can spare for a few months, a sturdy workman.

"The Irishman who has no sons, relative, friend or workman as representing him in the war will not have much to say for himself when 'the day is fought and won'. He will find himself particularly small wherever he goes."

The paper's editor may have been reflecting the view of the majority of the townspeople - but he was clearly out of touch with a minority who were willing to fight for independence.

In later years, the growing levels of British repression and the rising movement for independence was also reflected in the paper's increasingly radical views, which eventually prompted the Black and Tans to silence the Westmeath Independent by burning down its premises and putting it out of business for almost 16 months.

Immediately after the Easter Rising, as the republican movement attempted to build up its strength, Athlone's urban core was still resistant to Sinn Féin and its allies for basic economical reasons.

David Daly, the officer commanding of the Athlone Battalion, explained that in areas like Irishtown, a hotbed of football, there was resentment to republican activities as wives and families feared the loss of their separation allowances if the war ended abruptly or Ireland disengaged.

Separation allowance was a crucial lifeline for many. Whilst their menfolk were being slaughtered in the fields of Belgium and France, those at home in Athlone did not have things all their own way either.

Indeed, prices of basic foodstuffs rose dramatically during the first half of 1915 due to the difficulty in accessing foreign supplies. During that same period, there was a scarcity of many commodities - resulting in what the Westmeath Independent described as "a certain measure of distress in Athlone amongst the very poor"

"The payment of separation allowance to dependants of men with the colours materially aided in relieving the hardships which must otherwise have been very acute for a large proportion of the population."

However, there were many who benefited too from the war that raged across Europe.

Before the outbreak of hostilities, the army barracks housed no more than a dozen youths undergoing training on top of its normal complement of staff.

But soon volunteers and recruits came flooding in, with every available inch of space utilised. Such was the demand that impromptu camps were erected in the Meadows, at Gallowshill and at the old Ranelagh Grounds, the one-time home of Athlone Town FC, close to where the current Athlone Extrusions building is located.

This, naturally, had an economic spin-off for Athlone. Traders who had struggled to keep afloat before the war suddenly found their businesses buoyant as the soldiers spent generously.

At the cessation of the day's work at 6pm until curfew at 10pm, Athlone became abuzz as thousands of recruits to the Royal Field Artillery (RFA) battalion swamped the streets nightly.

Taking into account that the Athlone woollen mills had also secured what must have been massive orders from the Russian Army during World War 1, it's clear that Athlone had a strong economic benefit in the war effort.

Having endured hell on earth, having survived conditions and sights that were beyond their own powers of description, having witnessed mass slaughter on an unimaginable scale and having completed all this in the name of Ireland, it must have been a traumatic experience for the returning soldiers to find Ireland had turned its back on them.

Four and five years previously these soldiers had left for the front as heroes, and now these Irish members of the British Army were returning to a changed political climate, where they were, at best, viewed suspiciously.

The Easter Rising, and more importantly, the British repression that followed, had helped to fan the flames of republicanism. To many newly-radicalised Irishmen and women, those returning in the uniform of the empire were representatives of that empire.

To make matters worse, the veterans could not rely on the British administration for support.

This was an experience shared by millions of returning soldiers of all nationalities - the rhetoric of creating nations fit for heroes proved to be hollow jingoism; nothing more than wartime propaganda. They returned to a life of unemployment and poverty - their sacrifices on the field of war forgotten.

The disillusionment must only have been heightened in Ireland, where the British administration had little motivation in providing succour to its Irish soldiers. It meant ex-British Army soldiers faced alienation on all sides in Ireland.

Many who simply wanted to return to civilian life found themselves caught up in a primal political battle.

In Athlone, the changing times were best exemplified by an incident on July 19th, 1919, which had been designated as Peace Day, a day in which parades were held throughout Ireland.

In Athlone, participants in the parade gathered in St Mary's Square to find a huge poster had been erected overnight bearing the inscription "Ex-soldiers, you have fought for freedom. Where is it?"

Similar writings were attached to Athlone bridge and a huge Sinn Féin flag had been hung on telegraph wires.

If the Republican movement was keen to politicise the war commemorations, so too were the British Empire.

Some 16 months later, in the lead up to Armistice Day on November 11th, 1920, posters with the following notice were plastered on shop fronts and walls throughout Athlone: 'Shopkeepers of Athlone are hereby ordered to close their premises on Armistice Day, November 11, in honour of the fallen heroes of the Great War and the police murdered in Ireland. This notice applies to all business houses and factories. And failure to comply with this notice renders destruction of said premises. (Signed) Black and Tans. God Save The King.'

This came just a few days after major reprisals by the British forces in Athlone, which involved the burning of a number of houses and the Athlone Printing Works and Westmeath Independent offices.

Although the Black and Tan notices were repudiated by the Brigadier General of what was then Victoria Barracks in Athlone, it's easy to see the impact this propaganda would have had on the public perception of ex-servicemen.

It was difficult enough at the best of time for republicans to distinguish between ex-serviceman remembering their colleagues and an imperialist faction manipulating these events for political purposes.

But with these posters, the Black and Tans were deliberately associating the World War 1 soldiers with the British military repression in Athlone. The murdered police who, in many cases, had been terrorising local communities, were lumped in with the ex-British soldiers. To have the Athlone remembrance commemorations hijacked by the Black and Tans in this overtly political way must have been a local nationalist war veteran's worst nightmare.

For many Athlone veterans, there were more practical concerns to be dealt with though, such as securing housing or employment.

One of the key complaints of ex-soldiers was the difficulty in acquiring promised housing units to be reserved for former service people. And despite £1.3m being allocated to a housing trust for Irish ex-servicemen nationally, just 19 houses in Cloghanboy had been constructed in Athlone by the mid-1920s.

In contrast 65 homes had been constructed in Mullingar, at a total cost of £50,000, despite the town having far less veterans.

In January 1924, the frustration bubbled over in Athlone with the hosting of a public meeting by the Legion of Ex-Servicemen in Ireland, seeking justice for its numerous members in the region.

Having been hailed as lions of the empire, the soldiers now found themselves fighting for crumbs.

Many settled back into civilian life, making the best of their lot. They slipped under the surface of Irish society; their stories excised from official history, their sacrifices forgotten. Others found the entire experience too much to handle and emigrated seeking to create a new life abroad.

Thomas Burlace was one such man.

A step too far

Fresh from their victory over YMCA, Athlone entered the Leinster Senior Cup with renewed optimism the following Saturday, January 21st.

The two Leinster Junior Cup finalists had qualified for a preliminary first round of the Leinster Senior Cup along with a number of top Leinster Senior League sides.

Athlone were drawn to play Pioneers, a club which had emerged from the Temperance movement in Dublin, and which was then a Leinster Senior League outfit.

This time, Athlone, with the added bonus of home advantage, were rampant. Although the home side only ran out winners on a 2-0 scoreline, the margin of victory could have been substantially more.

16-year-old Johnny McManus, from 69 Connaught Street in only his second competitive appearance for Athlone, opened the scoring with a beautiful strike before Frank Ghent added a second. Athlone also struck the crossbar on three separate occasions.

McManus was a loyal supporter of Athlone, but unfortunately, despite his promising debut with the Town, he was never provided with sufficient opportunity to showcase his talent.

Johnny McManus

And although he featured again in both the 1925/26 and 1927/28 seasons, it was with a struggling Athlone. McManus was destined instead to make his name firstly with Mullingar, then with Sligo Rovers and later on the international stage, in a career that stretched into the mid-1930s.

In a busy start to 1922, it was back to the main event, the FAI Cup the following weekend when Athlone travelled to Dalymount Park to take on the mighty Bohemians. The victories over YMCA (FAI Cup) and Pioneers (Leinster Senior Cup) on successive weekends had attracted the notice of the Dublin media.

And there were some wild predictions that Athlone might take the scalp of Bohs, who had just been pipped for the inaugural league title by St James's Gate. Unfortunately, reality bit and left its teethmarks all over Athlone.

For the game in Dalymount Park on Saturday, January 28th, 1922, Athlone made a number of changes from the side which had defeated YMCA in the previous round.

Young Johnny McManus was rested with Martin Harkins coming in at outside right in his stead. The flame-haired Harkins worked on the Midland and Great Western Railway line for many years as a ticket collector.

He continued playing in Athlone junior soccer for some years and had a spell with Mullingar in the Leinster Senior League in the mid-1920s. Harkins was also to feature in the Leinster Junior Cup-winning team later that season.

Joe Monahan, an experienced defender who had first played with Athlone around 1908, slotted in at right-full.

Monahan's family came from Connaught Street and were immersed in football in the town.

Alan Smith, despite his winning goal against YMCA, was left out with Hannon reverting to left-half against his former club. Into Hannon's place at inside-right came Patrick Colahan

Colahan, then just 23 years of age, was from a relatively well-off Newtown Terrace family. His father, David, was an insurance superintendent.   Born in Cavan, where his father then served as an RIC sergeant, Colahan later ran a public house in Mardyke Street.

Colahan had first featured for Athlone in the 1919/20 season, but his main involvement with the Bit of Blue was in the 1921/22 season.

A forward with the goal-getting knack, Colahan mainly featured at inside-right for Athlone, scoring three times during that season.

His one and only Free State League match for Athlone came in the third game of the 1922/23 season when he helped Athlone gain their first League of

Patrick Colohan

Ireland point in a 3-3 draw against Shelbourne Utd. He continued to feature in Athlone junior football circles for some further seasons, particularly with a local outfit called Riverside.

Despite the changes, Athlone were swamped, particularly in the second half, by a rampant Bohemians, who ran out winners by 7-1.

Although the diminutive Paddy 'Scratch' Flannery (another long-serving Athlone player, who had featured in the Town colours from as far back as 1913) was unlucky with a long-range effort early on and John Sweeney had two efforts chalked off for offside, it was the calm before the storm. Bohs were two up at the interval – but Athlone had been under serious pressure at the back.

After the break, Bohs added a further five goals while Athlone's sole response came from a John Sweeney penalty.

The Evening Herald reported it could have been even worse for Athlone, "if less individuality had been shown by the Bohemian forwards".

The same paper identified Athlone's half-back line of Hannon, Jim Sweeney and Paddy Flannery as the Town's main weakness.

It was no doubt a galling defeat for Dinny Hannon, who first played with Bohemians in 1906 and remained in their ranks up to 1919. Hannon had been for many seasons the Pied Piper of Dalymount Park, bewitching opponents with his footwork and leading defenders trailing in his wake.

After the ending of war hostilities, Hannon threw in his lot with his home town club, Athlone, where he then served as a solicitor.

In many ways if Orlando Coote was the founding father of Athlone Town, Hannon was its guardian angel, guiding the club through the choppy waters of the new league and acting as a surrogate father to football at all levels in the town.

Having opted to jettison Bohs for Athlone, the defeat must have highlighted to Hannon the chasm in quality between the top Dublin sides and the best provincial talent. However, it was a massive step up in class for Athlone, who had been more accustomed to meeting local rivals such as Clara and Longford and ad-hoc military selections from Athlone barracks in previous years.

Athlone did wreak revenge, of a sort, on their Dublin foes when Bohs visited the town for what had been an almost annual St Patrick's Day friendly later that year.

A 2-0 win in front of a surprisingly large attendance, though, was scant consolation for the FAI Cup trouncing in late January

Genuine revenge though was not to be long awaited with Athlone and Bohemians destined to meet again in the FAI Cup in two short years.

The Leinster Senior Cup

Meanwhile, Athlone had little time to lick their wounds and navel-gaze. Instead, they were back in action the following weekend, this time in the Sportsground, in the second round of the Leinster Senior Cup.

Another non-league side, Brooklyn, who had also qualified through the preliminary first round, were their opponents, but Athlone served notice, with a facile 4-1 victory, that, while they might struggle against the best of Free State League opposition, they could easily account for other non-league sides.

For that game Athlone made only one change in personnel from the side defeated by Bohemians with local businessman Norman Lyster making his first appearance in the new era of Irish soccer for Athlone at right-half.

It was Hannon who steadied the ship, opening Athlone's account in the first half after being set up by Ghent. Although Brooklyn equalised before the break, Athlone dominated the second half and Ghent was again the provider for John Sweeney to restore Athlone's lead.

Hannon showed typical opportunism to capitalise on an error by the visitors' goalkeeper for the third, before John Sweeney rounded up the sconng with his second for Athlone.

After such a busy baptism in senior football, Athlone enjoyed a few weeks' sabbatical before featuring in the third round.

In the meantime, one of the most momentous occasion in Athlone history had occurred with the takeover of the military barracks by Irish forces as a result of the treaty.

When Athlone returned to the field of play on March 11th, they faced a daunting task against St James's Gate. The Gate, who featured players employed with the famous Dublin brewery, had already won the inaugural Free State League and were due to contest the FAI Cup final some five days later.

A massive crowd of 1,000 people turned up in the Sportsground to witness the clash and they were not disappointed by the quality and excitement on offer.

Colohan, left off for the Brooklyn game, returned at outside-left in place of William Bluett, a winger of unknown background who had featured in the Pioneers, Bohs and Brooklyn games but who was never again to appear in the Athlone colours. Colohan justified his return with the lead goal on 40 minutes when he reacted quickest to net the rebound after John Sweeney's drive had struck the crossbar. The game may have ebbed and flowed for 40 minutes without score, but the last five minutes of the half produced three further goals, the first two from St James's Gate. John Sweeney did level matters before the break.

After the interval, Burlace produced stop after stop to deny the visitors who finally netted what was to be the winning goal through Kelly.

Post-mortems focused on the contrast between the smooth combination play of the visitors' forward line and the individual style of the homesters. It was to be a criticism of Athlone's approach that would be often repeated over the years.

If the heavy FAI Cup loss against Bohemians in late January had indicated the steep learning curve ahead of Athlone, the narrow defeat to the country's best side seven weeks later showed how quickly Athlone had become accustomed to the higher level.

With the exact same eleven which edged past Athlone, St James's Gate went on to win the FAI Cup after a replay. And the Dubliners also took home the Leinster Senior Cup, completing a hat-trick of titles that season.

The St James's Gate clash was to have a postscript the following season when the Dubliners lodged an official complaint with the Leinster Football Association regarding the distribution of the gate receipts from the tie.

After twice seeking a full statement from Athlone as to the income and expenses of the game, the LFA ruled that Athlone's deduction of half of the ground rent from St James's Gate share of the proceeds was unacceptable.

The first silverware

Despite the administrative hiccup, Athlone's dramatic improvement was obvious for all to see – and having qualified for the FAI Cup proper that season it was clear they were likely candidates for full membership of the Free State League the following season.

Victories over YMCA and top notch Dublin non-league sides Pioneers and Brooklyn marked them out as among the best outside the existing league. Success in the final of the top junior competition, the Leinster Junior Cup, would surely copper-fasten their reputation.

It was with this expectation that Athlone travelled to Dalymount Park on April 22nd, 1922, to meet Chapelizod in the final.

Athlone were without Denis Hannon, Jimmy Hope and Thomas Burlace, all of whom were ineligible for the junior ranks.

As had occurred throughout the junior cup campaign, William Bracken was chosen in goal. Hope's place at the back was taken by Jim Kennedy, a native of Bloomhill, Ballinahown, who operated a Mardyke Street public house. Kennedy had featured in local junior sides and irregularly with Athlone since the mid 1910s, alternating between full-back and goalkeeper.

Colohan retained his place in the starting eleven but moved to Hannon's traditional inside-right berth, while Arthur Enright slotted in at outside-left.

The Enright connection

Enright was born in 1894 to Limerick native, Thomas, and his wife Eliza. His formative years were spent in Glasses Lane (now Griffith Street).

A talented left-winger, Arthur Enright had featured prominently in Athlone colours as far back as the 1913/14 season.

In that year, Athlone were runaway champions of the Leinster Senior League Division Two, at the very first attempt.

Athlone also reached the final of the Edmund Cup, a separate knock out competition for the top four league sides, that season but lost out in the final at Dalymount Park to St James's Gate's second side.

Enright turned out at inside and outside-right throughout that season, alongside the likes of Jim Sweeney and Joe Monahan.

Arthur Enright

He featured with Athlone again in 1919, on the resumption of the game following the ending of the war. And he continued as one of the best players at junior level in Athlone, helping his club Strandville to the local junior cup in 1924.

When Athlone junior teams joined forces to compete in the Leinster Junior Cup under the umbrella Athlone Utd, Enright was one of the more prominent performers. He also played with Mullingar in the Leinster Senior League on a handful of occasions in late 1924.

Arthur Enright lived most of his life in St Columba's Terrace and died at almost 90 years of age in 1983.

Like many, he had fought in World War One, joining the Connaught Rangers in September 1915 and later being wounded in Mesopotamia (now Iraq).

However, Arthur wasn't the first, or indeed the most talented, Enright to feature with Athlone in the early years of the last century.

His brother, Joe, older by five years had stood out in the colours of local junior teams Rebels and St Mary's. He played with Athlone in the 1906/07 and 1907/08 campaigns, when the town team competed in the Irish Junior Cup.

Enright's exceptional displays as a nippy inside-forward were not slow to filter through to the capital and it was not long before he was snapped up by Shelbourne, as a professional.

By the summer of 1910, word of Enright's quality had spread even further afield and, along with wing half Mick 'Boxer' Foley, he was enticed cross-channel to Leeds City, an English Division 2 side.

Foley remained with Leeds until the 1919/20 season when the club was expelled from the English League after being found to have made illegal payments to players during the wartime leagues.

A few weeks later, a new club, Leeds Utd, was formed – and took up residence at Leeds City's old ground of Elland Road. Within a year, Leeds Utd were elected to Division Two of the league.

Meanwhile, during his own two and a bit seasons with Leeds City, Enright was a virtual ever-present, and notched a respectable goal rate of 23 in 77 league games. Enright's career continued with Newport County and Coventry City.

However, it was with Leeds City, that Joe Enright gained his greatest honour, a full Irish cap on March 16th, 1912, against Scotland in Windsor Park in the annual home nations tournament.

Enright featured at inside-left in a team that also included another Leeds City teammate Joe Moran and another Dubliner Patrick O'Connell who went on to manage Barcelona!

Enright's career was interrupted by the Great War – and after the hostilities ended he had spells with several other English clubs.

He returned to Ireland for a visit to his Athlone family in 1965 for the first time since leaving its shores.

The Enright connection with Athlone Town lives on as Arthur's grandson and Joe's grandnephew, Chris, is now assistant secretary to the club.

The Leinster Junior Cup final

Athlone travelled to Dublin on the 9.12 am train, on Easter Saturday, April 22nd, 1922, eager to carry home the trophy to the town for the first time in 39 years.

Athlone had previously won the Leinster Junior Cup, in the first two years of the trophy's existence, 1893/94 and 1894/95, while Chapelizod, the holders, were one of Dublin's best junior clubs.

However, the final in Dalymount Park proved to be a one-sided affair with Athlone running out easy winners by 4-1.

Athlone, playing down the Dalymount incline and with the wind in their backs, were well in control in the opening half.

They made the breakthrough around the half-hour mark when left-half Paddy Flannery fastened onto a clearance and smacked a long-range drive to the net

Prior to that beautiful strike, Athlone had an effort disallowed following a goalmouth scramble. Just eight minutes after Flannery's intervention, James Sweeney added a second as the half came to a close.

The side which won the Leinster Junior Cup in 1922.
Back row: Tom Ghent, Jim Kennedy, Patrick Colohan, William Bracken, Joe Monahan, Dinny Hannon.
Middle row: Martin Harkins, Paddy Flannery, John Sweeney, Arthur Enright, Alan Smith.
Front row: Frank Ghent and Jim Sweeney. Note: Alan Smith stood in for photographic purposes for Norman Lyster who appeared in the final.

44

If anything, Athlone bossed the second period even more comprehensively and another goal from Jim Sweeney and one from Colahan sealed a facile victory.

Monahan, Lyster, and Jim and John Sweeney were among Athlone's key performers, as was Arthur Enright, who took every opportunity to force the pace early on.

Match reports suggested Athlone's margin of victory, if anything, flattered Chapelizod, such was the Town's dominance.

A unifying force

The significance of the achievement in a town still torn apart by the War of Independence and Civil War was manifest in the joyous reaction of locals to the result.

Thousands carrying torchlights and headed by the Athlone Brass and Reed Band greeted the team as they arrived at the Midland and Great Western Railway Station that night.

Fog signals were exploded as the train steamed into the station, amidst scenes of wild celebration.

And members of the team were carried aloft to their individual homes as the town embraced its conquering heroes.

The Easter weekend may have contributed to the unbridled scenes of elation – but sport's ability to unify a divided people must also have been a factor.

Athlone, and Ireland, was slowly sinking into one of the most troubled periods in its history.

On another Saturday night just three weeks previously, another large gathering of 1,000 people attended at Athlone railway station. This time though they were there to pay tribute to Michael Collins.

Another indication of the deeply-scarred society in which football was being played came just three days later when Brigadier General George Adamson, Officer Commanding of the Free State Army in Athlone, was shot dead by anti-Treatyites in Irishtown.

It was one of the first shots of the Civil War.

Adamson, a native of Moate, was closely associated with the takeover of the barracks from the British Forces just two months previously.

Adamson, with his impeccable War of Independence credentials, had also fought with the British Army in World War 1 and had been awarded the distinguished conduct medal for his bravery.

On his return he joined the Irish Volunteers and was Vice Commandant of the Athlone Brigade of the IRA during the War of Independence.

Adamson is now remembered in the naming of Athlone Castle.

His death on April 25th, 1922, was the culmination of a slow racheting up of tensions between the pro and anti-treaty sections locally over the previous few months.

IRA activists in civilian attire had suppressed attempts to hold courts, under the jurisdiction of the Free State, in Moate and Mullingar in March.

There had also been a sensational split in the ranks of the army in Custume Barracks, as the treaty spawned a chasm within the armed forces.

The anti-treaty faction took up residence in the Royal Hoey Hotel – and an armed stand-off in March was only relieved by the intervention of an intermediary in the shape of a local Franciscan friar.

In such a deeply politicised society, not even sport could survive untainted by politics – and it's likely many of the conservative brand of Irish nationalists who were slowly bedding down in authority would have viewed football and those who played it, with suspicion.

But the large attendances at matches and the reaction to Athlone's victories displayed that the general public, at least, could leave their politics at the turnstiles when it came to sport.

In its own right, Athlone's Leinster Junior Cup victory produced obvious fruits; medals and a trophy to be cherished. However, it's greater significance can be gauged by the fact that Athlone, within five months, had been elected to the Free State League.

Having established their claims with their FAI Cup and Leinster Senior Cup exploits, the Leinster Junior Cup victory made Athlone's entitlement to full membership indisputable.

A writer in one of the Dublin sports papers said, in the wake of the Leinster Junior Cup victory: "Every club in Dublin is delighted they won the trophy. The hope of all is that it will prove to be a stepping stone to greater things."

It was a statement dripping in prescience.

Leinster Junior Cup final team:

Athlone Town: William Bracken, Joe Monahan, Jim Kennedy, Norman Lyster, James Sweeney, Paddy Flannery, Martin Harkins, Patrick Colohan, John Sweeney, Frank Ghent and Arthur Enright.

1921/22 season round-up

DATE	OPPOSITION		COMPETITION	SCORELINE	SCORERS
			(Athlone score first in all scorelines)		
October 16, 1921	Riverside	(h)	Leinster Junior Cup	5-3	?
October 29, 1921	Clara	(h)	Leinster Junior Cup	4-0	(Sweeney (2)*, J. Menton (2))
November 13, 1921	Strandville	(h)	Leinster Junior Cup	walkover	
November 19, 1921	Longford	(h)	Free State Cup qualifying	walkover	
December 3, 1921	St Mary's Mullingar	(h)	Free State Cup qualifying	4-1	?
December 17, 1921	Clara	(a)	Free State Cup qualifying regional final	2-0	?
December 26, 1921	St Patrick's Ringsend	(h)	Leinster Junior Cup s/f	2-2	(Sweeney** and Menton)
December 31, 1921	St Patrick's Ringsend	(a)	Leinster Junior Cup s/f replay	1-1	(John Sweeney)
January 7, 1922	St Patrick's Ringsend	(h)	Leinster Junior Cup s/f 2nd replay	3-0	(Colohan, Ghent and ?)
January 14, 1922	YMCA	(a)	Free State Cup	4-3	(Ghent, John Sweeney (2), Smith)
January 21, 1922	Pioneers	(h)	Leinster Senior Cup	2-0	(McManus, Ghent)
January 28, 1922	Bohemians	(a)	Free State Cup	1-7	(John Sweeney)
February 4, 1922	Brooklyn	(h)	Leinster Senior Cup	4-1	(Hannon, Blewett, John Sweeney (2))
March 11, 1922	St James's Gate	(h)	Leinster Senior Cup	2-3	(John Sweeney, Colohan)
April 22, 1922	Chapelizod (Dalymount Park)		Leinster Junior Cup final	4-1	(James Sweeney (2), Colohan and Flannery)

* Not known which Sweeney

** Not known which Sweeney

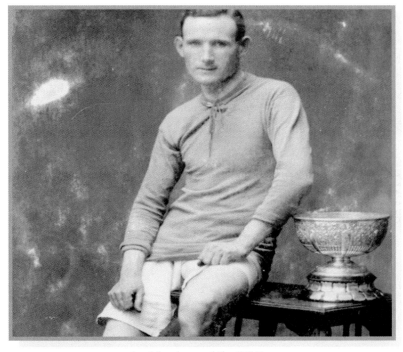

Joe Monahan and the FAI Cup.

Chapter 3

Joe Monahan

Twenty years of loyal service

One of the most satisfying aspects of Athlone Town's FAI Cup win in 1924 was that it represented just reward for many who had shown loyal and lengthy service to Athlone. The likes of Jim Sweeney, Frank Ghent, Jimmy Hope, Norman Lyster and Dinny Hannon had all toiled in the trenches in less glamorous times.

However, there was nobody whom the sporting gods needed to settle the tab with more than Joe Monahan.

The sturdy, passionate and no-nonsense defender had been a warrior on Athlone's behalf for longer than he would care to remember. His lengthy stint in the blue and black commenced in the old junior days of 1907/08 and lasted remarkably until 1927/28, when Athlone dropped out of the League of Ireland.

Son of Michael and Catherine Monahan, Joe was born into a family with a proud footballing pedigree.

His older brother John was a key figure in a previous era of Athlone Town football. Some 14 years Joe's senior, John was among the first wave of Athlone footballers to crash on the shore of the game in Ireland.

The elder Monahan featured, as an outside-forward, in both the victorious Leinster Junior Cup sides of 1893/94 and 1894/95 and in the Leinster Senior Cup final team of 1895/96. Like many of that team, he had defected from GAA in disillusionment with the treatment meted out to local team TP O'Connor's.

After Athlone's explosive entry to football had petered out, it was Monahan, as secretary of Athlone Town FC, who sought to reorganise matters towards the end of the 19th century.

His contribution to football continued after he finished playing at the age of 32 as he then took up the whistle and became a prominent referee for many years. An all-round sporting enthusiast, John Monahan was also an integral part of Athlone Boat Club.

John Monahan

Another brother, William also featured, at full-back, for Athlone in the latter part of the 1900s and the early 1910s. The paths of the three brothers crossed for just one season, 1907/08, with Bill at full-back, Joe (then aged just 18) at centre-half and John, at 32, up front.

Their younger brother Edward didn't follow in the family tradition when it came to playing with Athlone, but his wife Mary (nee Carr) was the team's medic during the famous cup run of 1924.

The Monahan family operated a public house in Connaught Street, then a real nursery for footballing talent. Their mother, Catherine, was a Hannon by birth, meaning that Denis Hannon, the famous Athlone international, and Joe Monahan were first cousins.

A fearless tackler

Of all the Monahans, it was Joe who was to enjoy the greatest success on the playing fields.

Born on September 23rd, 1889, Joe Monahan had his earliest schooling in Athlone. He was not dispatched to Summerhill College in Sligo, where his cousin Dinny Hannon was educated, as his family regarded him as not being strong enough to survive away from home.

But this apparent early physical weakness clearly didn't have any impact on Monahan's style on the field of play. As an out-and-out defender, Monahan's focus was to clear the ball from the danger area as quickly and as far away as possible.

His methods in blocking opponents were equally functional. The Dublin Evening Mail's description of Monahan captured his style of play nicely.

"A fearless tackler with a fine turn of speed, he proves a great obstructionist to forwards. Though his methods of the brusque type, while perfectly clean, often get him into trouble with spectators."

His daughter Kitty O'Neill, the only offspring of any of the eleven Cup final heroes to still live in Athlone, said a cousin of her father's had expressed concern about his welfare on Cup Final day in 1924. "What are you talking about, he'd take on four," was the immediate reply from family members. Joe Monahan knew how to look after himself on the football field.

It's no surprise either given Monahan's combative style of play that he conceded numerous penalties during his career.

From small acorns...

Joe Monahan first featured for Athlone as a fresh-faced 18-year-old centre-half in the Leinster Junior Cup campaign of 1907/08.

Although up front Athlone featured Johnny McDonnell and Joe Enright, two players who were later to earn full international caps, their campaign petered out early on.

Indeed, Athlone's progress as a club was sporadic until 1913/14. Before that, the club's only competitive action was in the Leinster Junior Cup or Irish Junior Cup campaigns.

But after a decision to enter the Leinster Senior League Division Two, 1913/14 transpired to be one of the club's most successful seasons.

In the league, Athlone couldn't have been more impressive with regular match practice helping to hone their competitive skills. So much so that they ran away with the division, with a side featuring a youthful Jim Sweeney, who was later to captain the Athlone Town FAI Cup-winning side of 1924, Paddy 'Scratch' Flannery and Michael Coyle, who also both featured in the Athlone shirt in the 1920s.

Joe Monahan only made a handful of appearances in the league campaign, but was a fixture in the side for the end-of-season Edmund Cup, a knock-out competition for the top four sides in the league table.

Joe Monahan 1912

The semi-final against Ulster - one of the most controversial games in Athlone's history - was tailor-made for Monahan. Ulster were a club for Ulstermen living in Dublin and tended to provide football for members of the Unionist ruling class.

It was a tempestuous and fractious encounter where will-to-win and guts were needed – and it was no surprise that it was Joe Monahan who starred for Athlone from the half-back line. After the visitors had opened up a two-goal advantage, it was Joe Monahan who rallied the troops, with a fine display at half-back, capping it off with the crucial first Athlone goal which helped them on their way to securing a replay.

The equaliser came amidst a frenzy of excitement with almost the last kick of the game. In fact, the concluding stages of the game were played in a heightened atmosphere and so exercised were the crowd that they encroached on the field of play.

The conduct of the Athlone spectators was strongly criticised by some of the national media. The Evening Herald said "this unruly body" would not serve to further the cause of the midland club as visiting teams would not care "to run the gauntlet of what Ulster were treated to on Saturday". Taking their cue solely from reports from the Ulster team, the Evening Herald also claimed that the last-ditch equaliser had been scored by a spectator!

Ulster also claimed that the players and referee (who incidentally travelled by car down from Dublin with the Ulster team) had to be escorted from the ground to their hotel. This claim was denied in the national media by

Athlone, who themselves pointed to a horror tackle on Jim Sweeney in the final minutes as a cause of the crowd's excitement.

Reports had also reached Athlone before the game of political provocations and cheering from the Ulster cavalcade as it made its way through the midlands for the match. Athlone also claimed they had information that the Ulster team had fielded a series of ringers.

In any event, when the sniff of cordite in the air had disappeared, Athlone saw off the visitors on their own Dublin turf in the replay and went on to face St James's Gate second team in the final.

Monahan, who remarkably never scored during Athlone's six-season stint in senior football between 1921/22 and 1927/28, was on a scoring streak that season. He converted a late spot kick for Athlone in the Dalymount Park decider, but it was too little too late and the Town were overcome by the odd goal in five.

With the heavy expense of travelling to Dublin fortnightly for the Leinster Senior League, it was decided not to contest the Leinster Junior Cup. Instead, a local team, St Patrick's League, obliged, featuring eight or nine of Athlone's regulars, including Joe Monahan, Paddy 'Scratch' Flannery, Michael Coyle and Jim Sweeney.

Captained by Coyle, at centre-forward, St Patrick's League somehow contrived to lose the final to Dublin junior league champions Clarence in Shelbourne Park on Good Friday, April 10th. An early goal, which had all the appearances of being offside, put the Dubliners in front and although St Patrick's dominated, they couldn't find the equaliser and Clarence secured the victory with a last-minute break-away goal.

The Evening Herald said the lead goal was "palpably offside" and deemed Athlone to be unfortunate, although they had contributed to their own misfortune by failing to avail of chance after chance. Again, Monahan impressed in this cup-tie atmosphere; the Westmeath Independent described him as "a big and sure kicker, and the right sort for a cup tie".

Eight years would elapse before Joe Monahan would have a second chance to secure a Leinster Junior Cup medal.

By the end of the 1913/14 season, Athlone, as Leinster Senior League Division Two champions, were aiming to compete in the top division of that league the following season. At 24, Joe Monahan had matured as a footballer and was now one of the first names on the Athlone team sheet. However, his career, like that of all of his contemporaries, was to be effectively put on hold by the outbreak of World War 1.

Rhyming with Hope

Monahan competed in the rare football occasions that took place during the war years but at the conclusion of the conflict in November 1918, football began to slowly dust off the cobwebs. By 1921/22, the creation of the Football League of the Free State provided a launching pad for the game in Athlone.

The season also witnessed the creation of a new defensive pairing for Athlone in the shape of Joe Monahan and Jimmy Hope, a full-back duo who were to soldier through thick and thin and enjoy glory and honour for Athlone in the coming years. Monahan was predominately right-footed and so naturally slotted in at right-full, while Hope took the left-full berth.

Footballing formations were entirely different in the early part of the century. Teams fielded two full-backs, the last line of defence, three wing-halves, including the pivotal centre-half and five forwards: a centre-forward, two flank players (outside-left and outside-right) and two inside-forwards. It was a 2-3-5 or even a 5-5 formation.

Full-backs were purely defensive-minded players whose task was to block the opposition attacks. The most sought-after quality in a full-back was kicking – in other words the ability to clear their lines. Tackling was obviously another necessary trait, though this was equally required in the protective wing-halves.

The ineligibility of Jimmy Hope for the Leinster Junior Cup, due to an involvement with Bohemians the previous season meant Monahan forged a partnership with Jim Kennedy at full-back for the Leinster Junior Cup campaign of 1921/22.

Monahan and Hope though restored their link up for all the senior games that season, including the Leinster Senior Cup and the 7-1 FAI Cup defeat to Bohemians.

However, Monahan missed out on Athlone's historic first appearance against YMCA in the FAI Cup.

Monahan also added to his medal cabinet, featuring in the Leinster Junior Cup final win against Chapelizod, a belated revenge for the defeat to Clarence eight years previously.

The Evening Herald said Athlone had been brilliantly served by Monahan, among others. Indeed, he produced a display that seemed to suggest he had been waiting for this day in order to erase the memories of the defeat against Clarence. The win meant it was the third Leinster Junior Cup medal to be secured by the Monahans, following his brother John's winning medals in 1893/94 and 1894/95.

Missing out on history

Monahan had the unfortunate knack of missing out on historic occasions though. Having already not featured in Athlone's first FAI Cup team against YMCA, he also wasn't included as Athlone began their League of Ireland life the following season, 1922/23.

Whether through injury or otherwise, Joe Monahan was absent for the opening half-dozen games of Athlone's first League of Ireland campaign in 1922/23. However, he was back for the 4-0 defeat of Dublin Utd in the seventh game and generally retained his berth at right-full for the remainder of the season.

The highlight of the 1922/23 campaign was reserved for the season's end, though, as Athlone won through to the final of the Shield. Monahan featured throughout this run at right-full and was a member of the Athlone side that went down, a mite unluckily, in the final of the competition to Shelbourne on May 19th in Dalymount Park. His restored pairing with Jimmy Hope was deemed a complete success by commentators.

Season of glory

And so it was to the 1923/24 season where Monahan and Hope were again almost ever-present in the last line of defence for Athlone. And for the first time they were fronted by a more settled half-back line

It was Athlone's most successful league campaign in their seven-season membership, as they finished fourth of the ten teams competing.

Considering the disadvantages Athlone, as the only non-Dublin club in the league, faced in travelling to Dublin every second game, it was a commendable performance.

Monahan was an ever-present, with Hope, in the five FAI Cup games on their way to the historic triumph in 1923/24. Their defensive partnership was the foundation for Athlone's victory.

And with Paddy O'Reilly in goal behind them and the likes of John Joe Dykes and Tommy Muldoon offering protection in the half-back line, it was no surprise that Athlone went through the 450 minutes without conceding a goal.

Later that summer, Monahan was among a provisional list of players submitted by the Football Association of the Irish Free State to take part in the Olympic Games representing Ireland. It subsequently transpired the association had misunderstood the deadlines and a trial process was undertaken from which a separate squad was compiled. Monahan did not take part in the trials nor did he participate in the Olympics.

Keeping the faith

Having cemented his partnership with Hope during the 1923/24 season, the duo were rarely absent for Athlone the following year. Defensively that season Athlone were quite solid, but without Jim Sweeney, who took a break for most of the year, they had severe difficulty in finding the net, managing just 15 goals in 16 league games played.

Athlone by now were seasoned league campaigners and the novelty of playing weekly against the best of the Dublin clubs was beginning to wear off. The club's travel itinerary was a distinct disadvantage and it was almost impossible to contemplate a challenge for the league title given the financial and logistical pressures involved.

Instead, the focus of the 1924/25 season and even more so the following year was the FAI Cup. The cup levelled the playing field somewhat – and Athlone's distinctive style seemed to suit cup football.

Monahan did duty in the 5-3 victory over Munster Senior League outfit Cork Bohemians in Athlone in the first round and was also at his customary position in the eleven that defeated Drumcondra in the second round.

And he played in the cup semi-final against Shelbourne that season. Unfortunately, Athlone's single-minded cup focus was insufficient as they slumped to a 4-0 defeat in the semi-final played in front of 13,000 people in Dalymount Park.

The Westmeath Independent noted the soft ground conditions had hindered both Monahan and Hope, neither of whom produced their normal form.

Until the bitter end

In his younger years, Joe Monahan worked as a clerk in the offices of P. Lyster & Sons, the family firm of his 1924 cup-winning team-mate Norman. He also worked in Athlone Workhouse and in later years, he was a rent collector and rates collector with Athlone Urban District Council.

Joe Monahan married Catherine Walshe of Chapel Street, Athlone, in 1929. He resided in mature life in St Paul's Terrace. He passed away in May 1947, aged just 59 years old.

Around the start of the 1925/26 season, Joe Monahan celebrated his 36th birthday. Time was catching up on him and nippy inside-forwards were no longer as easily collared as in the past. Monahan took time out from the game and only featured no more than three times in the league campaign that season.

He had returned to line out in a number of games in October before apparently falling out with the club. The Evening Herald noted he had walked from the pitch in the game against Fordsons in Athlone in October 1925 "presumably through injury". However, it commented a week later, mysteriously: "Athlone were without their right full-back and it is rumoured that he may not be seen assisting them again."

Family lore indicates that on one occasion in his career, riled up by his own supporters' criticisms, Monahan had deliberately scored an own goal. Incidentally, one of the Fordsons goals in a 5-2 victory was attributed by the Football Sports Weekly thus: "One of the Athlone defenders presented

Fordsons with a free gratis, by putting through his own goal." It may have been the case that Monahan stormed off after the own goal and opted out of football.

Whatever the reason, Monahan was not seen in Athlone colours for some four months. In his stead at right-full came Barney Connaughton, a youngster who had emerged through the junior soccer ranks locally, and who had featured, albeit intermittently, since 1923/24

Monahan did return to the side for the Shield campaign at the end of the 1925/26 season. His partnership with Jimmy Hope, though, was not restored, as the Mullingar man was tried out in the half-back line.

If Athlone fans thought Monahan's infrequent appearances during the 1925/26 season represented a slow fade out to retirement they were mistaken. Instead, with enthusiasm renewed, Monahan launched into the 1926/27 campaign. From the outset, he retained his spot at right-full, joining mainly Connaughton, though on occasions his old sparring partner Hope lined up beside him, in the full-back line.

Monahan appeared in the FAI Cup first-round defeat to Shelbourne that season – his second last bow in the Blue Riband event and he even participated in the end-of-season Shield campaign, a competition Athlone had usually only used to try out new players.

Maybe Monahan was attempting to squeeze every last game from his ageing frame. Whatever the reason, he opted to continue playing into the 1927/28 season at the ripe old age of 38. He was joined later in the campaign by his nephew John Monahan, a Garda officer and son of his older brother John.

It was a disastrous season for Athlone, with many unwanted records established. Monahan and Connaughton were again partnered at the heart of the defence – and both were in the side which succumbed to the heaviest league defeat in Athlone's history: 9-1 to Shelbourne on August 27th, 1927, in Shelbourne Park.

Poor early season form saw serious changes in personnel throughout the campaign but Monahan had returned in time for the 9-3 defeat to Drumcondra in the FAI Cup – the worst cup defeat in the club's history. It's likely his last game for Athlone was in a Shield clash in the early months of 1928 – over 20 years after he had first pulled on a competitive shirt for Athlone.

A lost medal

Although Monahan's tenure with Athlone ended with the club's departure from the League of Ireland, he, more than many, had some silverware to show for his efforts.

A series of medals from the successful 1913/14 campaign, a Leinster Junior Cup medal from 1922, a Shield runners-up medal from 1923 and, most gloriously of all, a 1924 FAI Cup medal had been pocketed.

Unfortunately, for Joe Monahan, there was to be no 1924 FAI Cup medal to cherish through his later years.

A year after his success with Athlone, Monahan was checking bait in the River Shannon with his medal and an old gold watch attached to a chain, which was in his vest pocket. Bending down to collect his bait which he had left under the water in an old sweet can, he watched in horror as the neck chain, watch and medal disappeared into the waters of the river.

Despite desperate searches, with even the services of a diver from Belfast being utilised, the items were never found.

Chapter 4

1922/23 season

Slow, but steady, progress

Spreading the gospel

Athlone's entry to the League of Ireland for the 1922/23 season was an eleventh-hour move.

By the time of the AGM of the Free State League on August 17th, Frankfurt and YMCA, two of the eight clubs which had competed in the inaugural season of the league, had withdrawn.

It was decided to operate a ten-team league meaning there were four vacancies for which there were seven applicants: Shamrock Rovers, Midland Athletic, Pioneers, University College, Shelbourne Utd, Rathmines Athletic and St Paul's Swifts of Belfast.

All seemed resolved when the first four of the above seven were given the nod at the AGM.

Rovers, who had reached the previous season's FAI Cup final while playing in the Leinster Senior League, were an obvious choice. Midland Athletic and Pioneers were two other Leinster Senior League sides while University College were something of a surprise choice, though the league may have been attempting to build a base in the third-level colleges.

There was discontent that Shelbourne Utd and Rathmines Athletic had been omitted and their applications were reconsidered a week later after the resignation of University College. Newspapers had previously warned that this particular student-based club would need to display a better record of fulfilling its fixtures if it was to make a contribution at top league level. And when it emerged the club could not field a team until October, the writing was on the wall.

It seemed as if either Shelbourne Utd or Rathmines Athletic or, indeed, both would now be added to the league but a meeting to ratify further members held the following week deferred a decision in order to allow the league's grounds committee examine both club's proposed pitches.

The difficulty was that Shelbourne Utd had proposed to play at Anglesea Road, Donnybrook, on a pitch already being used by Dublin Utd. At that stage, the proposed starting date for the league of September 9th appeared impossible and fixtures were deferred for a further week.

In the meantime, Shelbourne Utd and Dublin Utd played a friendly on their jointly-run Anglesea Road surface. The set-up was evidently found to be satisfactory by the ground inspectors as the former were accepted as a new member of the league at another meeting on Monday, September 4th. Rathmines Athletic's ground was also passed, allowing them to be accepted. But out of the blue, Athlone also joined the ranks making it an even dozen clubs.

The inclusion of Athlone had not even been hinted at previously and obviously a late application had been submitted by the club.

Nonetheless, the decision to spread the league outside Dublin was hailed in many quarters. The influential weekly Sport said Athlone's inclusion was "the best piece of football business ever done by the Dublin clubs and will do more to clinch the severance from Belfast than anything previously attempted. The more the game spreads the less prospect there will be of the IFA ever again bossing football in Ireland".

Although regarded as a surprise by many, Athlone's inclusion in the firmament of Irish football should have been a mere formality. The first AGM of the FAI itself just a few days later provided clear evidence of Athlone's exalted position in the new regime.

The AGM heard the FAI had a membership of 206 clubs, spread across four divisional associations, Athlone, Leinster, Munster and Belfast and District. Athlone was a growth centre for the game – a hub of the sport in the provinces.

Swimming with the big fish

With their League of Ireland debut set for just twelve days time, Athlone moved quickly and arranged a friendly with fellow newcomers Midland Athletic for the following Saturday, September 9th.

Midland Athletic derived their personnel from the ranks of the Midland and Great Western Railway Company based at Broadstone in Dublin. The rail connection with Athlone was to prove a conduit for more than just trains as many former Midland Athletic players subsequently played in the blue of Athlone – thanks to their ability as railway staff to find cheap and easy passage to and from the midlands town. Many also ended up working on the railways either in Athlone or Mullingar.

Athlone warmed up in encouraging fashion for their debut in the league dismissing the Railwaymen 2-0.

A week later in the Sportsground, history was made when Athlone took part in their first League of Ireland game. The opposition could hardly have been tougher. St James's Gate were reigning league, FAI Cup and Leinster Senior Cup champions. Their eleven showed only one change from that which defeated Athlone in the FAI Cup the previous season on the same ground.

For Athlone, all eleven were broadly-speaking 'locals' – Mullingar's Jimmy Hope being the only non-Athlonian.

A local line-up

William Bracken featured in goal and was a fixture between the posts for most of the season.

Bracken, who originated from Brideswell Street, had earned a Leinster Junior Cup medal with Athlone the previous season but had played second fiddle to Thomas Burlace in the senior FAI Cup and Leinster Senior Cup games.

By the start of the 1922/23 campaign, it was Bracken who was in possession of the No. 1 jersey.

William Bracken

Ironically, in a time when there was little, if any, crossover between the sports, due to the infamous ban, Bracken was a keen hurler and had also played Gaelic football locally as a member of the Sinn Fein McBrides Club

His last appearance for Athlone Town came early in the following season.

His brother, John, remembers attending the FAI Cup final in 1924. John, who died in recent years, was a stalwart GAA player and administrator in his own right.

The full-back line comprised Jimmy Hope and Jim Kennedy while the half-backs were Paddy 'Scratch' Flannery, left, Jim Sweeney, centre, and Norman Lyster, right.

At outside-right was Tommy Muldoon, making his first appearance for Athlone, not long after returning from British Army service in India. Muldoon was the son of a shopkeeper based at Main Street, Athlone, and had began to make his mark in the local junior scene with St Patrick's. He was to experience a startling rise to fame.

At inside-left was Mick Rafferty, an old reliable who had played with local junior sides as far back as 1912, but was making his senior debut in the first league game.

32 years of age, Rafferty was one of a vast battalion of west-side Athlonians who staffed the Town's soccer team in the 1920s.

Brought up in Abbey Lane, Rafferty had featured with the St Patrick's side for many years at junior level along with his older brother John.

Rafferty was a trade union activist. A wool weaver, he was also prominent in the Labour Party and ran for the organisation in the 1928 local elections. Although he failed to secure election, he was later co-opted after the death of one of the serving councillors. At that time

Mick Rafferty in 1913/14

he was living in Chapel Street, although in later life he resided at St Francis Terrace.

Although the name Rafferty was a fixture at inside-left for the first ten games of the league campaign, there's a strong suspicion that Rafferty, particularly in away games, was pseudonym for a ringer.

Indeed, there were numerous national newspaper references to 'Rafferty' – the not-so-subtle quotation marks being the method used at the time to indicate that was the player's given name on the day.

The front five was completed with the three by now well-known names of John Sweeney, Dinny Hannon and Frank Ghent.

As it turned out, the fixture was a real baptism of fire for Athlone who, despite playing reasonably well, found themselves three down to the visitors in the early part of the second half.

It was the lively John Sweeney who pulled one back late on from the penalty spot in the process earning himself a place in the history books by registering Athlone's first league goal.

To give the tie even further local flavour, the referee was Michael Broderick, one of the most experienced whistlers in the Irish game and a resident of Athlone.

Michael Broderick

Michael Broderick

Broderick, a baker by profession and a member of the famous Broderick family, had a seminal role to play in Irish football history as he officiated at the first two FAI Cup finals, between St James's Gate and Shamrock Rovers in 1921/22 and Alton Utd and Shelbourne in 1922/23.

The love of the whistle obviously ran in his family. Local football administrator and referee assessor Breffini Rowan is his grandson.

Broderick was also a member of Athlone Town Council, representing Labour; and his brother, Harry, was the first Labour TD in the Longford/Westmeath constituency.

Michael was probably the most highly-regarded referee of his day and was a key figure in the development of the game both locally and regionally, chairing a meeting in 1925 to structure the game in the midlands. He also took a keen interest in the promotion of schoolboy football and helped to organise minor competitions in the late 1920s.

He officiated at numerous representative and inter-provincial games as well as the Free State Junior Cup final of 1926.

Refereeing was hardly a valuable pastime either as Broderick told a newspaper

Breffni Rowan with his grandfather's whistle.

in 1926. He pointed out he had left Athlone at 9am one morning to referee a league match in Dublin, returning home at 9.30pm that night – and all for twelve shillings and sixpence and expenses.

In some 20 years of refereeing, he only once experienced violence; in a game between Shamrock Rovers and Dundalk in the Louth venue in November 1927. He complained he was struck when surrounded by spectators.

A newspaper reported: "This is the first time in his lengthy period of activities that he has been the object of a hostile demonstration."

Despite his Athlone origins, he was the regular referee for the Town's home games during their league membership and officiated at Athlone's final game in their first stint in the league at the end of the 1927/28 season.

The weekly grind

Bohemians away presented an equally stern test of Athlone's credentials the following week and the side showed a few changes from that which had plunged headlong into the new era the previous week.

The game was notable for the inclusion of Tommy Robertson at right-half in place of Norman Lyster. He was the first of many Dubliners to hitch their wagon to the Athlone cause.

Again it was probably the Midland Athletic connection which yielded Robertson, as he had played with the Railwaymen prior to joining Athlone.

During his career he was a regular on Leinster Senior League representative sides and he returned to Midland Athletic after a one-season stint with Athlone and later turned up with Frankfort in the Leinster Senior League.

The Athlone Town team which met Bohemians in Dalymount Park in September 1922.
Back row, from left: Paddy Flannery, Jim Kennedy, Willie Bracken, Jimmy Hope, A.N. Other, Frank Ghent, A.N. Other.
Front row, from left: Dinny Hannon, A.N. Other, A.N. Other, John Sweeney, Jim Sweeney.

Athlone struggled to contain Bohemians and went down 2-0. The opening goal was netted by Albert McLoughlin who was later that same season to turn out for Athlone.

Two games in, two defeats. But Athlone refused to panic and stuck with their playing personnel, probably conscious it would take some time to find their feet at this exalted level.

The paper Sport, although advising Athlone to adapt their style of football, was confident they would fit into the league.

"With some experience that should accompany practice, ability will be seen on their side. They are rather a team in the making than the finished article. Steadier and more accurate passing would serve them. Their present methods are too much on the kick-and-rush principle.

"More than most clubs they have plenty of scope for improvement and with a little effort they should attract the best talent in the western province, which is a terra incognito to the clubs in the metropolis. They may unearth some gems, who can tell?"

The first victory

A fine opportunity to show their potential came in their very next match when they were due to meet fellow newcomers Shelbourne Utd on home turf. The visitors, though, had rattled off two wins in their opening two fixtures and would prove difficult opposition.

This was to prove a cracker of a tie with Athlone twice taking the lead through Rafferty and a John Sweeney penalty before on each occasion being pegged back. And with time running out it was Shelbourne Utd who edged in front before Frank Ghent sealed Athlone's first point in the League of Ireland with a late equaliser.

On the team front, Patrick Colohan made his sole appearance in full league action for Athlone at outside-right, while relatives Paddy and Joe Flannery filled the wing-half berths.

The Flannery family originated from Shannonbridge and Joe's mother Teresa operated a public house and shop in Irishtown during the late 1910s and early 1920s.

Buoyed by their first point, Athlone went in search of a breakthrough win but had to wait two weeks until their fifth match against Olympia on home soil on October 14th, 1922, for the historic occasion.

It was fitting that three of the Athlone stalwarts, Denis Hannon (2), John Sweeney and James Sweeney were on target as Athlone ran out 4-0 winners in a victory that moved them from the foot of the table.

Having broken their duck and established their credentials, Athlone rattled off three more wins on the trot, against Pioneers and Dublin Utd away and Midland Athletic at home.

The triumph in Clontarf's Tudor Park against Pioneers represented Athlone's first League of Ireland win away from home. Pioneers had taken a fortunate one-goal lead into the interval after Bracken had misjudged the flight of a shot and could only watch as it entered the net off the post.

But Athlone tore into the home side after the break and goals from Ghent and Jim Sweeney sealed the victory. The second half represented a duel between the Athlone forwards and the home defence and both Ghent and Sweeney also struck the bar.

Dinny Hannon was rested for the following away game against Dublin Utd, which Athlone comfortably won 4-0, with goals from Jim and John Sweeney, Ghent and John McNulty.

This was a game in which Athlone were castigated for their over-physical approach. Their dangerous jumping and charging caused injury to two of the Dublin Utd players, it was reported.

And Athlone completed four wins on the trot the next weekend, albeit narrowly, at home to Midland Athletic. After the game Midland Athletic objected to Athlone's refusal to admit more than 16 club members into the game free of charge. They claimed league rules indicated that 25 should be facilitated.

The switching of Jim Sweeney from the backline to an attacking position helped in this run of form as the versatile player bagged two of the eight goals, including the winner against Pioneers. But it was Frank Ghent's scoring streak - four goals in the three games - which propelled Athlone up the table.

Bizarrely, Ghent appeared on none of the team sheets and instead was replaced by the mysterious T. Browne. This Mr Browne had made his debut for Athlone in the second game of the season against Bohemians in Frank Ghent's customary outside-left position. The apparent newcomer was described in one of the Dublin papers as 'Brown', another hint that he was not who he seemed.

And it's almost certain that Brown or Browne was in fact Frank Ghent as the duo never featured in a single game together, despite the fact that Browne appeared some dozen times or so that season.

A club official Teddy Browne – a close friend of Ghent – seems to have lent his initials and surname to this imposter.

It was the Dublin Evening Mail which let the cat out of the bag, as it named Ghent as scoring the equaliser against Pioneers. Ghent was not listed in any team sheet for the game and every other paper attributed the strike to the unknown Browne.

However, there was no logical pattern to Brown's appearances or to why on occasion Ghent was forced to subsume this new identity, bar perhaps that he was under suspension at the time. The solution to the mystery is lost in the mists of time.

Finding their level

In any event, Athlone's winning run was brought to a halt by league leaders Shamrock Rovers in the Sportsground on November 11th, 1922. In a real ding-dong tussle, Rovers, who only lost their opening fixture in the 22-game league that season, were forced to go all out to secure a 1-0 victory, the winner coming just 15 minutes from the end.

Athlone gave a home debut to John McNulty at centre-forward in this game. The striker was unfortunate not to earn a late penalty. McNulty was from the border region and subsequently played with Newry Town before returning to the Leinster Senior League.

In the run-up to Christmas, Athlone's form was topsy-turvy, winning three games including a special 2-1 victory at home to eventual third-placed finishers Bohemians, drawing one (at home to league runners-up Shelbourne) and losing two away from home.

The first of the three wins came with a victory away to Jacobs – a team connected with the W & R Jacobs biscuit factory on the South Circular Road.

The last of the three victories took place on St Stephen's Day in Athlone. This game was notable for the first ever hat-trick by an Athlone player in the League of Ireland as John Sweeney netted thrice to help his side to a 4-2 victory over Rathmines Athletic.

Come the turn of the year, Athlone could now reflect on a relatively positive start to their time in the league. Aside from the opening four games in which Athlone took time to settle, the Town had more than held their own. In fact their record of seven wins in their previous eleven games was impressive form.

A marathon battle

In the early months of the New Year, the attention switched temporarily away from the league as Athlone became embroiled in a remarkable four-match tussle with St James's Gate in the Leinster Senior Cup.

The sequence started on December 30th in St James's Park in Dolphin's Barn. Denis Hannon put Athlone ahead inside a quarter hour before the home side equalised from the penalty spot following a Jimmy Hope handball.

The replay in Athlone a fortnight later, in front of 1,500 people (for a Leinster Senior Cup game!), ended scoreless and it was back to Dublin on the following Tuesday night.

This time, Athlone were delayed by more than 90 minutes after train tracks had been torn up on the Midland and Great Western Railway line at Streamstown in an incident connected to the Civil War. Armed raiders had twice within three days hijacked trains travelling on the Mullingar-Athlone-Clara lines and then deliberately derailed the wagons by sending the trains speeding into the section of removed track.

It was a singular reminder of the social unrest being experienced across the country.

Unsettled by the delays following the removal of part of the train line, Athlone were quickly two down but rallied to level matters before half-time.

However, the late kick-off meant darkness descended early in the second half and the game had to be abandoned.

The Evening Telegraph noted the referee had no alternative but to declare the game null and void as the teams would not agree beforehand to a shortened duration.

With their passage home uncertain, Athlone players stayed overnight in Dublin, with some taking in the concert perforamnce of a certain Count John McCormack in the Theatre Royal that night.

Before Athlone and St James's Gate could renew rivalries, there was further proof, and closer to home, of the vicious civil war breaking out in Ireland. On January 20th, 1923, five young republicans were executed in Custume Barracks by the Free State government. Included among the quintet was young Bogganfin man Thomas Hughes.

Life and sport went on, despite the chaos encircling the country, and on the following Saturday, again in Dublin, Athlone came through their marathon contest thanks to a single John McNulty goal just after the hour mark.

This game, too, was not without its own mini-drama as Athlone fielded with only ten players for the entire first half. An eleventh player had to be obtained by club officials when Robertson, one of the eleven chosen, failed to arrive. It was common practice for Athlone, when travelling to Dublin, to secure the emergency services of a local, often, junior footballer.

Including the abandoned game, which was stricken from the records, the St James's Gate saga was finally concluded after almost five hours and thirty minutes of football.

The four-match tussle with St James's Gate had only added to Athlone's already burgeoning reputation and the Evening Telegraph noted during this period that the team continued to improve.

"It is now upsides the best in the metropolitan area, which when the genesis of the club and its many handicaps are considered, borders on the miraculous".

The dreaded Rovers

In the midst of all this, Athlone were drawn at home to Shamrock Rovers in the FAI Cup first round.

Having narrowly lost to the mighty Hoops in the league, Athlone entered the tie with some confidence.

1,200 turned out for this one and watched another close encounter.

Hope was absent as he had played with his native Mullingar against Athlone junior side St Patrick's in the qualifying rounds, thus making himself ineligible. Jim Kennedy took his place at left-full. Along the same flank, Tommy Muldoon filled in at left half-back, the first time he had featured in a position he was to make his own and from which he would later carve out a career cross-channel.

Athlone employed bustling methods – a buffeting style of play that would become their Cup trademark – in an attempt to unsettle their opponents.

However, after shaking up Rovers early on, the visitors settled and forced their own brand of football on the game. A lead goal was not long in coming and Rovers incurred the wrath of the home crowd by slowing down play and booting the ball out of play at every opportunity in an attempt to defend this lead.

Although Athlone dominated the first 15 minutes after the break and equalised through McNulty in a goalmouth scramble, it was Rovers who found the crucial second as the game ebbed and flowed from end to end.

With the FAI Cup campaign over for another year, Athlone refocused on the Leinster Senior Cup and their second round clash with the same Shamrock Rovers. By this stage, Jim Kennedy had taken over instead of Bracken between the posts and would remain the first-choice custodian for the remainder of the season.

Having overcome St James's Gate in the marathon first-round contest, Athlone were not willing to give up the ghost easily and it took Rovers two attempts to see off the midlanders.

Athlone came from two down in the opening game in front of almost 2,000 spectators in the Sportsground to force a replay. The excitement reached fever pitch as Athlone strove for a late winner and the large crowd had to be prevented from entering the pitch, such was their enthusiasm.

The comeback was all in vain as they lost 2-0 in Milltown the following Saturday in a performance which merited at least a goal. Out of the Leinster Senior Cup despite their Herculean efforts, Athlone returned to league action the following week against, as luck would have it, Shamrock Rovers. It meant the two clubs had met for the third successive weekend – and including the FAI Cup match five weeks earlier, for the fourth time in quick succession.

Again, though, there was no joy for Athlone, who lost 4-2 in an amazing game in which they had led 2-0 with 17 minutes remaining, before conceding three goals in as many minutes.

New faces

Two Sligo players, John Joe Dykes and Frank Tiernan, appeared for the first time in the Athlone line-out in Milltown as did Tommy Collins, a Moate native.

Dykes. had been an accomplished junior footballer in his native Sligo. In just over a year he was to make the spectacular transition to the level of Irish international. It was a stratospheric rise to prominence for Dykes who was snatched from relative obscurity by Athlone.

A measure of Athlone's immediate confidence in Dykes was his selection in the pivotal centre-half role in his debut against Shamrock Rovers.

Tiernan had also featured in Sligo junior circles with Sligo Celtic.

Both may have come to prominence thanks to their roles in Sligo Celtic's FAI Cup campaign that same season. The men from the shadow of Ben Bulben had emerged from the Connacht and District pre-qualifying rounds to take their place in the FAI Cup proper against Dublin Utd.

Dykes and Tiernan (2) were the scorers as Sligo Celtic emerged with honours intact from a 3-3 draw in the capital. A 0-0 draw followed in Sligo, before the Dubliners finally ended the resistance of the non-league outfit in the second replay.

That latter game took place on January 28th, 1923, and it was only 20 days later that Dykes and Tiernan first pulled on an Athlone shirt.

The duo were also tried out a few weeks later against Shelbourne in Dublin and on St Patrick's Day, Athlone visited Sligo to play a local selection and possibly to secure the services of Dykes.

Tiernan, on the other hand, didn't make the grade with Athlone, but went on to enjoy success as a regular goalscorer for Mullingar in the 1924/25 and 1925/26 seasons when they competed in the Leinster Senior League Division Two.

He finished on the losing side in Leinster Junior Cup finals in both years despite scoring three goals in the two deciders.

He also dabbled with GAA and featured on the Sligo squad which won the 1922 Connaught Championship but was disqualified and lost the replay

The day after the Leinster Junior Cup final defeat in 1925/26, Tiernan took the emigrant ship to America. As medals were often formally presented months after the relevant occasion, Tiernan never received his runners-up medal. Instead, it remains in private ownership in Mullingar to this day – a souvenir of one of the strongest periods of Mullingar's football history.

The mystery of the missing goalposts

Regular, albeit narrow, defeats to Shamrock Rovers were no embarrassment. Although, like Athlone, only in their first season in the league, the Hoops had quickly established themselves as the pre-eminent team of the era.

They had competed in the 1921/22 FAI Cup final as a Leinster Senior League outfit, before taking the league and Leinster Senior Cup crowns in their first season as league members. The Rovers of 1922/23 included such talents as Bob Fullam, the foremost player of his generation.

Fullam was a national sporting hero, in an era when media focus on celebrity was almost non-existent. Renowned for his powerful shot, Fullam scored 27 goals for Rovers in their league campaign in 1922/23.

The catchphrase Give it to Bob –
designed to encourage his teammates, if
all else failed, to find their talismanic
striker - became common currency in
dance halls up and down the country,
taking on a life of its own.

Fullam's playing stints in America
were followed closely by the sporting
media at the time, such was his fame.

Alongside him up front were John Joe
Flood and Jack 'Kruger' Fagan. Known
as the Three Fs, they wreaked terror on
opposing defences. After an off year in
1923/24, Rovers were back with a bang
in 1924/25 sweeping everything before
them in a remarkable treble.

A contemporary cartoon depicting Bob
Fullam and the trademark phrase.

The league, FAI Cup and Shield all went to Milltown as Rovers remained
unbeaten in 31 competitive games in a season in which League of Ireland
sides did not compete in the Leinster Senior Cup due to a dispute.

After losing out to Shamrock Rovers in that dramatic 4-2 game, Athlone
finished off their league fixtures in some style, winning four of the remaining
five games – the only exception being an away defeat to Shelbourne.

In the other games, Athlone showed their improvement was ongoing
throughout the season, winning impressively 5-0 at home to Pioneers, 6-1 at
home to Dublin Utd and in the last league fixture, 4-0 away to Midland
Athletic.

Dykes and Tiernan featured against Shelbourne, the former this time at
right-back and the latter at inside-left.

Tommy Collins had also been blooded in these relatively inconsequential
end-of-season league ties and had registered Athlone's only goal in the 3-1
defeat to Shels.

Athlone were due to play Olympia the following day and arranged
overnight accommodation after the Shelbourne game. But the game never
took place as the goalposts were stolen from Olympia's grounds. The
Freeman's Journal speculated it may have been connected with a campaign
of protest over increased ticket prices to the FAI Cup final.

Despite this mishap, Athlone were notified after the Shelbourne game on
the Saturday evening that the following day's match against Olympia would
take place. However, when they arrived at the venue the following
afternoon, their opponents never put in an appearance. Despite an
abandonment that was clearly the home team's fault, the points were
officially shared.

Athlone and later Dundalk, as non-Dublin clubs, were often at the butt of such unusual league decisions.

What a first impression

However, all in all it had been a promising inaugural league season for Athlone. Despite the handicap of having to travel to Dublin every second weekend, despite an abysmal start which saw them register just a single point in the first four games, Athlone finished in mid-table, sixth of twelve, and only behind fifth-placed St James's Gate on goal difference.

If that final fixture against Olympia had been fulfilled, the likely victory would have propelled Athlone into fifth behind only the big three of Shamrock Rovers, Shelbourne and Bohemians and the surprise packets Shelbourne Utd.

More than anything else it was a season of progression; senior status had been cemented and the experience of playing weekly at the highest level had strengthened the side.

The end-of-season Shield competition, run in 1922/23 on a knockout basis, would show that Athlone had made the jump from Leinster Junior Cup winners the previous year to serious contenders for senior cup honours.

Perhaps most significantly of all, some key personnel had emerged during the season. The half-back line, the Achilles heel of the side, had been changed beyond recognition thanks to the arrival of John Joe Dykes at centre-half and the realisation that Tommy Muldoon's natural position was left half-back.

Jim Sweeney was now firmly entrenched as the line-leader up front – rather than as a stop-gap measure at centre-half.

Sweeney and the likes of Norman Lyster had filled in at centre-half and Paddy Flannery, Joe Flannery Jim Kennedy and Robertson had all toiled manfully in the half back line at various stages during the season but until Dykes and Muldoon became regulars, it remained Athlone's weak point.

Elsewhere Tommy Collins had provided a solution to the difficult inside-left berth – another position which had plagued Athlone for the past two years.

The pieces of the jigsaw were beginning to fall into place but first the 1922/23 season provided one more opportunity for glory: the Shield.

1922/23 season round-up

DATE	OPPOSITION	COMPETITION	SCORELINE	SCORERS
			(Athlone score first in all scorelines)	
September 16, 1922	St James's Gate (h)	League	1-3	(John Sweeney)
September 23, 1922	Bohemians (a)	League	0-2	
September 30, 1922	Shelbourne Utd (h)	League	3-3	(Rafferty, John Sweeney, Ghent)
October 7, 1922	Rathmines Athletic (a)	League	0-2	
October 14, 1922	Olympia (h)	League	4-0	(Hannon (2), John Sweeney, Jim Sweeney)
October 21, 1922	Pioneers (a)	League	2-1	(Ghent, Jim Sweeney)
October 28, 1922	Dublin Utd (a)	League	4-0	(John Sweeney, Jim Sweeney, McNulty, Ghent)
November 4, 1922	Midland Athletic (h)	League	2-1	(Ghent (2))
November 11, 1922	Shamrock Rovers (h)	League	0-1	
November 18, 1922	Jacobs (a)	League	2-1	(Hannon, Jim Sweeney)
November 26, 1922	Shelbourne (h)	League	0-0	
December 2, 1922	St James's Gate (a)	League	1-4	(Joe Flannery)
December 9, 1922	Bohemians (h)	League	2-1	(Joe Flannery, John Sweeney)
December 16, 1922	Shelbourne Utd (a)	League	1-3	(Jim Sweeney)
December 26, 1922	Rathmines Athletic (h)	League	4-2	(John Sweeney (3), Hannon)
December 30, 1922	St James's Gate (a)	Leinster Senior Cup	1-1	(Hannon)
January 6, 1923	Shamrock Rovers (h)	FAI Cup	1-2	(McNulty)
January 13, 1923	St James's Gate (h)	Leinster Senior Cup	0-0	
January 16, 1923	St James's Gate (a)	Leinster Senior Cup	2-2	(Muldoon, Jim Sweeney)*
January 27, 1923	St James's Gate (a)	Leinster Senior Cup	1-0	(McNulty)
February 4, 1923	Shamrock Rovers (h)	Leinster Senior Cup	2-2	(Ghent, McNulty)
February 11, 1923	Shamrock Rovers (a)	Leinster Senior Cup	0-2	
February 17, 1923	Shamrock Rovers (a)	League	2-4	(Ghent (2))
February 25, 1923	Pioneers (h)	League	5-0	(?)
March 4, 1923	Dublin Utd (h)	League	6-1	(John Sweeney, Jim Sweeney + ?)
March 10, 1923	Shelbourne (a)	League	1-3	(Collins)
March 25, 1923	Jacobs (h)	League		(Jim Sweeney (2))
April 15, 1923	Midland Athletic (a)	League	4-0	(?)

*Game abandoned and scratched from records
Game away to Olympia league not played. Points shared.

Chapter 5

Tommy Collins

Moate's gentlemanly little cup fighter

Tommy Collins

Out of India

Tommy Collins was probably the youngest of the Athlone Town heroes of 1924.

Born in September 1901 in Nasirabad, India, where his father was a Colour Sergeant with the Connaught Rangers, Tom came from a well-established Moate family, which survives in the region to this day.

In a family immersed in Gaelic games, his dalliance with football marked him out as a bit of a renegade.

Indeed, his younger brother, Louis was a driving force behind the foundation of Moate All Whites, and was captain when they enjoyed their first success, winning the Westmeath GAA Junior Football Championship of 1923. Ten years later, when they won the senior title for the first time, Louis Collins was again the triumphant captain, in the first county final to be played in Cusack Park.

But it was not just Gaelic football that was in the family blood; soldiering too was a Collins condition. And it was no surprise that Collins joined the British Army towards the end of World War 1, having come of age. Fortunately, he didn't see any service but he remained in England from 1918-1922 working with the Royal Flying Corps.

It's likely his footballing talent was honed while in England; his family hold a medal dating back to that period. And it was here he fine tuned his boxing skills, competing at the featherweight level in army tournaments.

His time with Athlone: short but sweet

Returning to Ireland, Collins settled back in his home region and secured employment as a draper's assistant in Athlone, where he showcased his new-found footballing skills with Athlone Town.

The lure of England was too strong to resist though and Collins returned to London at the close of the 1923/24 season, ending his Athlone Town career in the process.

Although his stint with Athlone spanned only a season and a bit, it coincided with the highpoints of Athlone's initial foray into the League of Ireland.

It was not until February 1923, that he first lined out for Athlone, appearing in a 4-2 away defeat to Shamrock Rovers in the league. However, he quickly made an impression, cementing a starting berth in the team, at either outside or inside-left.

He scored again away to Shelbourne in the third last game of the league season and became a fixture in the side during the exciting Shield campaign which saw Athlone reach the final in 1922/23.

Nippy, quick-witted and incisive, Collins formed a formidable left-wing partnership with Frank Ghent. Ghent was a formidable operator at outside-

left, his speed, strength
and determination prov-
ing a potent mixture.
However, he required the
right service – the ball in
front of him coaxing him
forward on one of
his trademark dashes.
Collins, at inside-left,
was his supplier and the
two were a lethal
combination and it's no
surprise that Ghent's
best form with Athlone

*Bohemians keeper Keogh saves ahead of Tommy Collins
(on goal-line) during the 1924 FAI Cup semi-final.*

probably coincided with Collins' time at the club.

Collins, in his own right, made no small contribution to Athlone's cup
success.

An ever-present in the five-game cup run, Collins played through the pain
barrier to assist Athlone in their first round game against Midland Athletic in
the Sportsground on January 5th, 1924.

According to the Westmeath Independent: "Early in the game, in trying to
head the ball which was coming rather low, he gave his neck a slight wrench
but with commendable pluck carried on until he collapsed on the field."

This occurred within a few minutes of the end of the match and at the final
whistle Collins was assisted out of the ground "amidst the victorious
cheers".

Collins knew that the FAI Cup final would be one of his final games in
Athlone colours and produced a stunning performance in the final. It was he
who released Frank Ghent down the left wing to produce the cross from
which Dinny Hannon netted the vital score. And it was Collins who made
the most of the extra room available as Fordsons defence concentrated on
restraining Athlone's danger man, centre-forward Jim Sweeney.

Tommy's impending departure to England was common knowledge
before the showpiece decider and the Westmeath Independent in its match
report on that historic occasion expressed the hope he would return.

"In hoping that the connecting link between Moate's gentlemanly little cup
fighter and Athlone Town is only to be severed temporarily I know I am
voicing the innermost thoughts of all those who have had the undoubted
pleasure of meeting Collins. Furthermore, it will gladden the hearts of his
myriad of admirers to know that if at all practicable the redoubtable Tommy
will appear in his customary place when the Shannonsiders take the field for
the Leinster Senior Cup final on Easter Monday."

In fact, Collins didn't make the final on Easter Monday as Athlone failed to overcome the small matter of a semi-final in the meantime! But he did feature in that last-four clash against non-league Brideville, having apparently returned from London for the game.

When the game went to a replay, Collins was back in the English capital. He was never again to feature with Athlone.

The London years

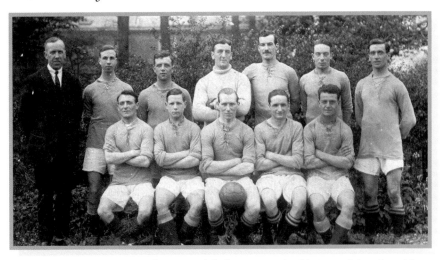

Tommy Collins is pictured extreme right bottom row in this team picture from his London days.

Cross-channel his footballing career continued, albeit, without the fanfare.

On his arrival back in London, according to his family, he secured a trial with Tottenham Hotspur. However, it was not to be and instead he continued playing with various London league sides up to at least 1932, initially at senior amateur level before playing at intermediate and subsequently junior levels.

One keen fan of the Athlone Town team jotted down his recollections of the players some 50 years later, around the time AC Milan were visiting Athlone.

The big game naturally sparked reminiscenses of Athlone's previous glories, particularly of the 1924 Cup final team. Amidst much nostalgic exaggeration, the writer penned a somewhat jaundiced assessment of the Athlone eleven.

His view of Collins was that he was "just about able to hold his place on a senior amateur team in London".

Tommy married Jessie in London in 1926.

Collins was again in the British Army during World War II and saw service in North Africa and Italy as a Bombardier with the Royal Artillery.

He came through the experience unscathed, unlike his brother Alfie, who was held in a Prisoner of War camp and required six months hospitalisation afterwards.

Tommy subsequently worked as a clerk on a farm outside London and as a pub landlord for a few years before living out the remainder of his days in London.

Throughout his life Tommy kept in touch with the happenings on the Athlone football front through contact with his family in South Westmeath.

In 1971 he returned to Athlone and paid a visit to St Mel's Park for a league game against Shelbourne.

He was cordially welcomed home over the loudspeaker – a returning hero. Less than two years later, on May 20th, 1973, Tommy Collins passed away

To this day, he has one son and one daughter living in England. Tommy's FAI Cup medal and Shield medal remain in the family's possession.

Chapter 6

A first final

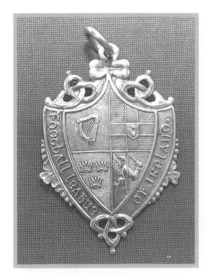

Shield Medal - front and back

Having finished the league campaign so impressively, it was no surprise that Athlone entered the season-closing Free State Shield competition with considerable anticipation.

The shield was the premier trophy after the league and cup. The competition continued in existence up to 1973 when it became the League Cup. The more recent First Division Shield bears no relation to the earlier Free State Shield competition.

The fact they were drawn at home in the first round to Pioneers, whom they had already beaten home and away in league action, must have only added to their optimism.

However, at half-time on April 22nd, 1923, Athlone found themselves two down to the impressive Dubliners. On the verge of a first-round exit it took a major second-half revival to keep Athlone in the competition. Even still, Athlone were dependent on a late John Sweeney penalty to level matters after Pioneers keeper Paddy O'Reilly had stopped two previous spot-kicks.

Athlone's loyal fans may have played their part too. The Evening Telegraph noted that the players' movements had been restricted by crowd encroachment across the touchline in the second half.

O'Reilly's amazing performance caught the eye of all in the ground, not least the Athlone selectors, and sure enough within a few months he was in Athlone colours.

But for now, O'Reilly and his Pioneer counterparts had to be overcome and on the following Sunday in Jacobs' ground, Athlone duly obliged with goals from Hannon, Albert McLoughlin and John Sweeney (2) resulting in a 4-2 victory.

McLoughlin was a vastly experienced and versatile centre-forward who saw service with both Bohemians and Shelbourne in the League of Ireland as well as with a host of non-league outfits. Earlier that season, he had scored for Bohemians against Athlone in the Town's first ever away league game in September 1922. But he returned to Leinster Senior League action with his former club Glasnevin for a couple of months before joining Athlone in late April 1923.

His stint with Athlone was equally short-lived, although it coincided with the Town's participation in the 1922/23 Shield final in May 1923. After a few appearances in the early part of the league campaign of 1923/24 he decamped to Shelbourne, was soon back with Glasnevin, before again appearing with Shels the following year.

McLoughlin was one of three Athlone players to feature in the annual charity match, the Herald Hospitals' Cup, which took place on May 20th, 1923, the day after the Shield final.

McLoughlin and Robertson were in the Leinster FA X1, which met a Free State League side featuring Tommy Muldoon in the annual fund-raising match for Irish hospitals. Originally played for in 1906, the cup, which is still in existence, is one of the oldest trophies in Irish football.

A major shock

After overcoming Pioneers, Athlone faced Shamrock Rovers in the quarter-final of the Shield the following weekend.

The Evening Herald speculated: "It is hardly likely they will spring a surprise by taking the match though they may force a replay."

In reality, it was unsurprising that Rovers were the hot favourites, despite having to travel to Athlone. The form guide was well and truly in the Hoops favour. The sides had met five times already that season, including in the FAI Cup and twice in the Leinster Senior Cup, and Athlone had only managed to eke out one draw. However, of the three games on Midland soil, Athlone had lost narrowly in two and drawn the other.

Indeed, there was bad blood between the sides – not helped by the fact they had met each other four times in five weeks in three different competitions in January and February of that year.

Athlone had a score to settle having been frustrated at the antics of the

Rovers fans and players in Milltown when the sides met in the Leinster Senior Cup replay in January. For their part, the Rovers contingent had been unhappy with Athlone's behaviour the previous week.

In any event, when the sides met in the Shield quarter-final, the Westmeath Independent noted: "It speaks volumes for the people of Athlone that they didn't stoop to the antics employed by the crowd at Milltown and that they preserved their decorum and did not allow themselves to be carried away with the excitement prevailing."

As it was, Athlone were to have their vengeance in some style, seeing off the famous Rovers, who had already carried off the League and Leinster Senior Cup trophies that season, by a two-goal margin.

The combative Jim Sweeney opened the scoring in trademark fashion, bundling ball and goalkeeper into the net, setting Athlone on their way to a 2-0 victory.

The result in what, according to all newspaper accounts, was a cracking game, shocked the Dublin papers and left the Evening Herald stating if the defeat of Rovers by Bohemians B in a Dublin cup game the previous season was a big surprise, it was mild in comparison to the reverse they suffered at the hands of Athlone. As ever the excuses were quickly available; apparently Rovers were tired after a long season.

Regardless, Athlone marched on to the last four where they encountered Shelbourne Utd the following Saturday, May 12th, on neutral territory in Shelbourne Park.

For this one, Athlone had Kennedy in goal, the familiar pairing of Hope and Monahan in the full-back berths and Muldoon, Dykes and Lyster in the half-back ranks. McLoughlin was outside-right with Hannon inside while John Sweeney led the line at centre-forward, with Ghent and Collins combining on the left-wing.

Although, Athlone were forced to wait until five minutes before the end to secure the victory, it was well merited as they entirely bossed the second half.

After the break, and with the wind on their backs, Athlone had taken control and put the Shelbourne goal under concerted attack. A Ghent header was tipped onto the crossbar by the Shelbourne Utd keeper; Hannon twice came close with potshots while Sweeney fizzed another effort by the post.

Shelbourne United struck the crossbar in a rare sortie forward but the pressure finally bore fruit for Athlone when Muldoon smacked back a poor clearance to the net off the butt of the post with a stunning 18-yard volley.

Athlone were through to meet Shelbourne in the final. The Dubliners won the other semi-final after St James's Gate walked off the pitch, with the score 1-0 in their opponents' favour, in protest at a refereeing decision.

Athlone's journey to the final met with strong praise. The Evening Telegraph noted: "They have now demonstrated beyond all cavil that they are a team of quality and quite capable of putting up a game worthy of the best of our local combinations."

However, as ever, resentment at the rapid emergence of Athlone was not far from the surface. The Telegraph also revealed: "What the feelings of the older established clubs may be on seeing the winners of last year's Junior Cup figuring in the final of the Irish Shield against the veteran Shelbourne club is difficult to say but those who desire to broaden the sphere of the game's activities the contemplation of this fact must bring unalloyed pleasure."

It said other provincial centres should take Athlone's lead. "What Athlone have achieved is within the power of other centres to emulate or excel as soon as they make up their minds to wade in."

The more progressive football officials knew that promoting the game outside Dublin was critical for its future health and growth, particularly with Gaelic games gaining prominence nationally.

Gaelic games in Athlone in the 1920s

Gaelic games in Athlone had been vibrant since the early years of the association.

Indeed, a short-lived team from Athlone named T P O'Connor's had won the Westmeath championship in 1890. In 1892, they were refused affiliation by the Westmeath Gaelic games authorities and switched allegiance to Roscommon.

They represented Roscommon and Connacht in the All-Ireland senior Gaelic football semi-final against eventual champions Dublin (Young Irelands) that same year.

That game was notable for an incident in which John Monahan, brother of later Athlone Town FAI Cup-winner, Joe, was assaulted. A Dublin player, it was said, ran the length of the field and struck Monahan, almost breaking his jaw. Athlone objected, but Dublin were allowed to keep their victory.

Interestingly, given the rivalry between the sports, Tom Hunt, in his fascinating study 'Sport and Society in Victorian Ireland: The Case of Westmeath', has pointed out that virtually the entire TP O'Connor panel deserted to Association football in 1893 after becoming disillusioned with both the North Westmeath bias of the Westmeath GAA scene and the uncertain rules of the game in those early days.

The influx of such new blood was a real shot in the arm for Association football in Athlone and many of the former Gaelic footballers helped Athlone to win the Leinster Junior Cup in 1893 and 1894. Indeed, the aforementioned John Monahan was a crucial force in driving Athlone Town forward.

Up to 1910, Gaelic football was very much alive in Athlone, with a local club, St Mary's, contesting the county final in that year. However, interest ebbed and it was not until March 1916 that moves began to re-establish a formal club in the town. This club St Ciaran's was intended to cater for both Gaelic football and hurling.

The club was to have an immediate impact, particularly in Gaelic football, winning the 1916 junior crown in March 1917, after a typically convoluted saga over their second-round victory against Castletown Geoghegan.

No Athlone Town player appeared in the subsequent final against Kinnegad but soccer enthusiasts Denis Hannon, Jim Kennedy, John Begadon and Michael Coyle were among those listed in squads for friendly games and may have lined out in earlier more low-key rounds.

Most, if not all, of Athlone's local 1924 heroes had at some time tried their hand at Gaelic football, particularly in the popular local street leagues held in the later years of the 1910s. Names like Frank Ghent, Jim Sweeney, John Sweeney, Paddy Flannery, Joe Monahan, Jim Kennedy, William Bracken and Paddy Colohan were regularly seen on team sheets in these local events.

Up to the early 1920s at least, football and Gaelic football were not seen as mutually exclusive.

However, as the political situation worsened, the GAA more and more began to be seen as the sole repository of Irish manhood – and by implication, rival sports, in particular, the suspiciously British football, a threat to the new Ireland.

In Athlone there was a more diverse sporting tradition, mainly due to the strength of football in the town.

The provision of the new Sportsground was a contributing factor in the revival of Gaelic games and led to Athlone hosting significant inter-county fixtures, including the Croke Cup, a competition for the beaten provincial championship finalists, in early 1916.

Even by early 1916, before the Easter Rising, sport was already becoming politicised. The focus of the rising Gaelic revival movement in emphasising the Irishness of native games and the emergence of the infamous ban made sure of that.

In Athlone, the decision, in October 1916, of the British authorities to effectively scupper one of the biggest local sporting occasions also meant that Gaelic games was granted a veneer of radicalism and became a focus of rebellion.

Up to 15,000 were expected at the All-Ireland hurling and football semi-finals in the Sportsground between the Connacht and Munster champions; Cork v. Mayo and Tipperary v. Galway in Gaelic football and hurling clashes respectively. However, the British military authorities moved to cancel trains destined for Athlone at the eleventh hour, a move which slashed the attendance to a miserly 1,000.

The action sparked outrage and did much to send young men in the Athlone area into the arms of rebellion against British rule.

With its managing director Thomas P. Chapman, also the MD of the limited company which ran the Sportsground, it was no surprise that the Westmeath Independent reacted angrily to the development.

The paper's editorial, presumably written by then editor McDermott Hayes, thundered: "It was, we can only regard it as, a deliberate act of provocation intended to inflame, not allay, the present disturbed state of the country. It was utterly unjustified and uncalled for. It was an attack directed at a little local enterprise - in the success of which everyone is greatly interested.

"For many years back, we have all been lamenting the absence of a suitable athletics ground in Athlone. When the opportunity offered, the sporting public took advantage of it, with the result we now have in Athlone, a general sportsground unsurpassed by any city or town in Ireland."

It continued: "The greatest athletic event Athlone ever witnessed was made through this disgraceful officialism largely a fiasco. It was devoid of reason, if it had not, as we believe, the reason to exasperate many thousands of people.

"It will not be forgotten by the young men of Ireland. English stupidity in dealing with Ireland is colossal."

The GAA stuck by Athlone and awarded it the right to host the 1917 All-Ireland Gaelic football semi-final a year later.

By 1918, there were at least four Athlone town-based GAA clubs, Sean Costelloes, Sinn Féin Sean McBrides, St Ciaran's and St Patrick's, the first two at least having nationalist identity in their names if nothing else.

And although Gaelic games was becoming the preferred sport of the up-and-coming Irish nation, in Athlone, football retained its primary position.

Indeed in the early 1920s, interest in Gaelic games in Athlone again lapsed and the sport suffered from administrative disorganisation. By April 1923, the Westmeath Independent was noting "the lack of enthusiasm about Gaelic games".

The comparative strength of football in Athlone to Gaelic games helped to ensure that those who preferred football were not seen as outsiders playing a foreign game. The common support for the 1924 cup winners also showed that the game had deep roots in Athlone and the ban was less likely to be enforced by a weaker GAA.

In 1925, the Connacht GAA Council debated a motion at its convention to adopt Athlone as a central venue for Gaelic football in the province. The motion was deferred with one speaker remarking: "Athlone is at present a hotbed of foreign games."

Contrast the situation to that which prevailed in Offaly where in January 1927, the Offaly GAA convention unanimously passed a motion banning jazz music from all GAA dances. The Daingean delegate said: "It was up to Gaels to put down not alone foreign games but foreign dances as well and particularly immoral dances."

That narrow definition of Irishness thankfully didn't prevail in Athlone in the 1920s.

However, the pendulum swung back towards Gaelic games in Athlone shortly after the resignation of Athlone from the League of Ireland in 1928.

Another revival in Gaelic games combined with chaos in the local soccer scene in the latter years of the 1920s shifted the balance away from fraternal respect.

By January 1930, the chairman of Westmeath County Board, Liet P. Cowen, was feeling confident enough to taunt: "Soccer is dead in Athlone".

It prompted an immediate rebuttal from local junior enthusiasts and the first clear shots in a public power struggle between the sports in Athlone had been fired.

Although the changed political landscape in a maturing republic has taken the heat out of the rivalry between the sporting bodies, they are still battling each other to attract the best young sporting talent everywhere.

The Shield final

Athlone may have been seen as ambassadors for the game outside Dublin but now it was the far more practical challenge of the Shield final that was on the club's mind.

The game was set for Dalymount Park on May 19th.

Special trains were put on to facilitate Athlone supporters who travelled in large numbers to witness what one newspaper described as "a great game, devoid of end-of-season weariness".

Some of the media indicated their preference for a Shelbourne victory in the Shield as the Dubliners had reached the FAI Cup final only to be surprisingly beaten by Belfast non-leaguers Alton Utd.

The Evening Telegraph commented: "It will be a bitter pill for Shels to swallow if they are forced to play second fiddle to the winners of last year's Junior Cup in this very important competition.

"If Athlone beat Shels, no greater sensation could be possible. To staunch supporters of the Reds a reverse for their favourites is what is called unthinkable," the paper wrote.

However, in the rapidly changing environment of Free State soccer, some commentators were quicker to adapt to the new realities than others.

Athlone showed just one change from the side which had defeated Shelbourne Utd in the last four; Jim Sweeney replacing his brother, John, as leader of the attack. John Sweeney, the Sunday Independent said, had been disastrously slack in missing two simple chances against Shelbourne Utd in the previous round.

Athlone started brightly and both Tommy Collins and Sweeney spurned early opportunities before Shelbourne took the lead after about ten minutes when Sammy Wilson broke free onto a through ball from Foley and finished confidently with an excellent cross shot.

There were chances at both ends in a free-flowing opening half in which Shels had longer periods of pressure but Athlone equal chances.

In the second half, Athlone attacked with greater aggression but were left to rue some poor finishing. They came close when Hannon, receiving a pass from Collins, tore through the heart of the Shels defence. As he bore down on goal, a last-ditch tackle from a Shels defender took the sting from his shot, allowing the keeper to save.

At the other end, Athlone had a fortunate escape when Val Harris's 20-yard blast struck the face of the bar and dropped into the unknowing hands of Kennedy between the Athlone posts.

Soon, Shelbourne were awarded a dubious penalty – conceded after Dykes' arm and Wilson's head came into contact as they closed in on a cross. The referee deemed Wilson to have been pushed and Connell scored from the spot.

The decision to award the penalty was greeted with a hostile reaction, according to the Sunday Independent. It left Athlone with a stiff task although another penalty, this time unquestioned, provided a lifeline with Muldoon converting after Sweeney had been upended while bursting through on goal.

There was a frantic and exciting ending to the game as Athlone pressed manfully for an equaliser, and, of course, left more gaps at the back themselves.

Although, there were narrow escapes at both ends the game ended without further score and with Shels as narrow winners.

The Evening Herald said the game was up for grabs throughout and with a little bit of luck could have gone Athlone's way. The same paper credited veteran Denis Hannon and newcomer Tommy Muldoon with the honours of the losing side.

Hannon, as was now his wont, divided his time between defence and attack, despite his nominal starting role up front as inside-right.

Muldoon, who had only nailed down the left-half berth in the weeks prior to the final, again proved himself a real talent. Muldoon's rapid emergence was confirmed when he stayed over in Dublin after the Shield final to line out with the Football League selection in the Hospitals' Charity Cup final the following day.

Elsewhere, there was less flattering comment reserved for goalkeeper Jim Kennedy who was described as a "real laggard". His slowness in clearing, according to one paper, caused nervousness in his defence of Hope and Monahan, who, nonetheless, performed with credit. Dykes, McLoughlin and Ghent also showed up impressively.

Shelbourne attacking lynchpin Sammy Wilson was gaining a little revenge – he had been part of the YMCA team which had been summarily dismissed from the FAI Cup by non-league Athlone Town in 1921/22.

The Evening Telegraph lamented Athlone's misfortune: "With a small slice of luck, Athlone might have equalised."

However, it remarked: "Athlone did not play a combined game and were very disjointed at times. But their energy was irrepressible and their forcefulness overpowering."

The general feeling was summed up by one national daily: "The Midland team will, in due course get its turn of a trophy or two". The slow but steady progress was now being noticed elsewhere.

Shield final team:

Jim Kennedy, Joe Monahan, Jimmy Hope, Norman Lyster, John Joe Dykes, Tommy Muldoon, Albert McLoughlin, Denis Hannon, Jim Sweeney, Frank Ghent, Tommy Collins.

1922-23 Shield round-up

DATE	OPPOSITION	COMPETITION	SCORELINE	SCORERS
		(Athlone score first in all scorelines)		
April 22, 1923	Pioneers (h)	Shield	2-2	(John Sweeney, Ghent)
April 29, 1923	Pioneers (a)	Shield	4-2	(Hannon, McLoughlin, John Sweeney (2))
May 5, 1923	Shamrock Rovers (h)		2-0	(Jim Sweeney, ?)
May 12, 1923	Shelbourne Utd (a)	Shield semi-final	1-0	(Muldoon)
May 19, 1923	Shelbourne (Dalymount Park)	Shield final	1-2	(Muldoon)

Chapter 7

Paddy 'Scratch' Flannery

An injury-prone acrobat

The Flannerys

The name Scratch Flannery was a familiar one to local football fans in the late 1910s and early 1920s.

The diminutive Paddy (better known as Scratch) was from a family who originated in the Shannonbridge area of Offaly.

But he was not the only Flannery to feature in Athlone colours during that same period. Joe, a younger member of the same extended clan, was another occasional performer for the Town.

Born in 1898, Joe Flannery had been educated at the Marist Brothers School, in Athlone, before training to be a teacher at the Drumcondra Training College for two years.

Paddy Flannery

His first posting was to Crookstown NS in Ballytore near Athy, Co. Kildare, in January 1923 – and he remained there until April 1939. He was then appointed principal of Kilkea National School at Mageney near Castledermot in Kildare. Joe married Portarlington woman Rose Lalor in 1939 and the couple had one daughter.

He passed away at the young age of 55 in April 1953.

His remains were buried in Killinard Cemetery in Portarlington alongside those of his wife Rose, who had predeceased him.

Joe was one of five children of Shannonbridge native John and his wife Teresa (nee McGlynn). The family settled in Athlone in the last few years of the 19th century, operating a pub and grocery on what is now Sean Costello Street.

John, one of the elder children, worked in the book binding department of Athlone Printing Works. Formerly of St Paul's Terrace and Beechpark, he moved to Cork where he passed away in 1972. The siblings also included Kieran and two sisters, Peg and Molly.

The family owned a provision shop and an adjacent private dwelling in Irishtown for many years in the vicinity of where the Westmeath

Independent and Moran's public house now stand. They also operated a pub close to the existing Potters' premises on the same street.

Crowd-pleaser

Paddy Flannery first featured in the Athlone side just before the war. He lined out briefly in the forward line at inside-left for the side which won the Leinster Senior League Division 2 title in 1913/14.

Paddy Flannery was also a member of the St Patrick's League side which lost out to Clarence in the Leinster Junior Cup final that same season.

As the years went by, Paddy Flannery was more likely to be found in service in the half-

A young Paddy Flannery

back line. And it was in this line of defence that he appeared in the two FAI Cup games of 1921/22 against YMCA and Bohemians as well as in the victorious Leinster Junior Cup team of that same season. Flannery was particularly impressive in that final, scoring the opener as Athlone coasted to victory.

Small in stature, Flannery played with exuberance and a joie de vivre. A quirky liking for overhead kicking was another notable feature of his play.

He was also a talented dribbler – a trait that made him a sure-fire crowd-pleaser. The Evening Telegraph reported in early 1923 that Dublin spectators always enjoyed watching Flannery and Frank Ghent on their visits to the capital.

Despite, or maybe because of his small frame, Flannery was not shy in mixing it physically. In the FAI Cup game against Shamrock Rovers in the 1922/23 season, the Sunday Independent noted his over-robust style of play.

The other Flannery, Joe, first began to appear in Athlone teamsheets in 1919 in friendly matches with local military sides.

When competitive fare was revived in 1920 after the cessation of hostilities, Joe Flannery appeared regularly at half-back.

His studies to become a teacher in Dublin meant he was generally unavailable for Athlone during those formative years of 1921 and 1922.

It was not really until the winter of 1922 that, freed from the demands of education, he began to make his mark and emerge from the shadow of his relative. He also featured on the local junior scene, playing for Strandville.

However, when Athlone joined the League of Ireland, it was the elder Flannery who was a regular starter.

Paddy was in the Town eleven for the first League of Ireland game against St James's Gate in September 1922 and for the following contest, the first away game against Bohemians.

For the third game of that historic first league season, he was joined by his namesake, Joe, in the half-back line for the 3-3 draw against Shelbourne Utd.

The duo played together on a few occasions. When only one was selected, he was usually referred to as Flannery, making it difficult to identify whether it was Paddy or Joe who featured.

However, it seems that Paddy Flannery was a virtual ever-present in the league line-outs for the 1922/23 season, with Joe making occasional appearances, including as a goal-scoring outside-right against Bohemians at home in the Sportsground on December 9th, 1922.

Neither were in the line-ups for the end-of-season Shield campaign which culminated in a showpiece decider against Shelbourne.

The year of the cup

By the start of the new season, Paddy Flannery was in at left half-back for the second game of the season against Shelbourne. During the following week's game, away to St James's Gate, he sustained an injury that kept him out of the first-team reckoning for three months.

He returned in late December, and managed to fit in a couple of league appearances before the cup campaign started on January 5th, 1924, against Midland Athletic.

Scratch, possibly because of his robust approach and small stature, was prone to injury. And he was consigned to another spell on the sidelines with the most unfortunate timing when he picked up a knock against the Dubliners in the first round of the cup. The Westmeath Independent said he had sustained superficial injuries to his knee early on but persisted in seeing out the game.

However, the injury subsequently necessitated a stay in St Vincent's Hospital and the paper reported he was expected to remain under medical care for at least a fortnight.

It was an injury that was sufficient to seriously hinder his involvement in the campaign. Having missed the cup quarter-final dismissal of Shelbourne, Flannery was included in the pre-selected line-up for the trip to Dublin for the semi-final against Bohemians. However, he had obviously not fully recovered and did not take up his place.

Two weeks later, on March 1, he finally returned, in the semi-final replay, in what was an unaccustomed inside-left role. Again, he had been pre-selected in his more regular left-half berth, However, he was shifted to the forward line at inside-left in a last-minute reshuffle caused by the unavailability of another of the selected eleven.

The Westmeath Independent was complimentary of his performance. "To his credit, Scratch Flannery was called upon to occupy the inside-left position a role which might well fill many another purely half-back with awe but not so in the present circumstance. To his credit, Scratch undertook the difficult ordeal and in so doing proved himself of very high order, an able lieutenant of Ghent's, fast, tricky with a fine combination game. It is never a mean performance to undertake a duty of this kind and still greater credit is due because of Flannery's absence from the playing pitch for some considerable time past."

Despite the kudos winging their way to him, he was omitted from the final eleven – but was reintroduced to the side for the Leinster Senior Cup semi-final replay about three weeks later. This time, Flannery's old knee wound split early in the second half, rendering him useless and requiring another hospital visit.

By this stage, his susceptibility to injury was becoming a real disadvantage as, with substitutes not permitted, he was liable to leave Athlone short-staffed during games.

The end of service

The close-season break permitted Flannery to recover from what was described as "a serious knee injury". And although he was back in the team for the third game of the 1924/25 season in September, it was only followed up by one other league appearance at the very conclusion of the campaign the following April.

It was a similar situation in 1926, when he was again listed in the pre-season squad and then selected for the away trip to Bohemians in the second game of the season.

Again, though, the injury jinx struck and he limped off during what was to be his final game for Athlone.

Scratch Flannery was one of the more naturally gifted of this golden generation of Athlone footballers. However, his physical size in a team which laid great emphasis on sheer strength limited his involvement.

His weak knee was also, on too many occasions, an injury waiting to happen.

Chapter 8

1923/24 season

The pieces fall into place

Preparing for the season ahead

At the conclusion of the 1922/23 season, the club held its AGM at which it presented medals to the vanquished Shield finalists.

Chairman Michael J. Lennon noted it was the first time the club had reached the final of a senior competition in 28 years.

Lennon was reappointed as chairman with the following officers and committee elected: Hon Sec: W. Tormey; Hon Treasurer: D. J. Hannon; Chairman on working committee: J. Huban. Committee: M. Farrelly, F. Ghent, E. Browne, P. Boushell, J. Galvin, J. McDonnell, J. Sweeney, T. Ghent, G. Gaylard and S. Dolan.

A selection committee, appointed to choose the team, was comprised of D. Hannon, J. Sweeney, J. McDonnell, T. Ghent, E. Browne, P. Boushell and G Gaylard.

Membership subscription amounted to 10s.

Lennon was a publican who traded from 10 Connaught Street, a premises later run as Maguire's.

A staunch nationalist, he had been a member of Athlone Urban District Council and a Justice of the Peace for many years. Initially a member of the Home Rule Irish Parliamentary Party, he first began to flirt with Sinn Féin policies from 1906. He then became the first president of Sinn Féin when a branch was established in Athlone in March 1909. Having quit the party seven months later, he

Michael J. Lennon

subsequently became, ironically, a key member of the local World War I recruitment committee in Athlone.

A keen swimmer, Lennon was chairman of Athlone Town for many years and his devotion to the furtherance of the game locally was well-known.

Preparing for the league

The build-up to the new season continued apace with a narrow 3-2 victory in a pre-season friendly with Dublin junior side Seaview in the Meadows in late August.

Among those who had joined the fray for 1923/24 was an army officer, Captain Hamilton, who may well have been stationed in Athlone at the time.

He was one of the few new faces to feature during the season as Athlone built on the gradual stepping stones laid over the previous two seasons.

A week before the big kick-off, the Westmeath Independent noted the interest of the committee in getting the players "thoroughly fit" for the coming campaign.

Whether there was more to this pre-season training initiative than one friendly is difficult to ascertain.

The paper went on to credit an "admirer of the team" for a number of hints which it published, in the belief that it would produce "beneficial results".

"When the goalkeeper has been beaten, the players should note there is no necessity to break the net – it will be required for other matches," the paper remarked cattily.

"When tackled the player should part with the ball to the best advantage – any goal scored is for the honour of Athlone and not for the individual."

And the paper stressed the spectators had a role too in assisting the team to success. Not by increasing the scale of their support, but, instead, ironically, by controlling their enthusiasm, it said.

"It is to say the least rather surprising that spectators should require to be informed that they should not encroach on the playing pitch in the matches which take place in the Sportsground. To anyone who knows the meticulous exactness with which almost all of the city teams observe this particular rule, there certainly appears good grounds for stating that objections will very likely be made in the coming season if those who take an interest in the local team do not use their best endeavours to prevent the malpractice."

However, comments included in a review of the league campaign in the same paper four months later at the end of December, served to indicate that talk of pre-season fitness was nothing more than wishful thinking on behalf of the reporter.

"It has been remarked that the real reason why our team had not come out on top in the league this year is their utter disregard of the necessity for all-the-year-round practice. The first few matches of the present season should have been so many presents for the home eleven, if they had been prepared," the Westmeath Independent stated.

The big kick-off

Despite this subsequent criticism, the home side did unwrap its first gift of two home points with little discomfort when Athlone opened the season promisingly with a 3-0 victory at home against Pioneers. However, three defeats in a row quickly followed.

The losing streak began at home against Shelbourne in a narrow 3-2 defeat – a game notable for what appears to have been a trial for Tommy Muldoon with Shelbourne.

Dykes missed a penalty and a goalkeeping error by Kennedy gifted Shels the winner in a tightly-contested encounter.

Athlone lacked the combination work of Shelbourne (a regular criticism of the team in those days) and, according to the Westmeath Independent, were in need of a little more care and a little less selfishness on the part of some individual members of the team.

The following weekend, a 4-0 away defeat to St James's Gate was a real blow, although an understrength Athlone were further compromised by the loss early on of Paddy Flannery through injury.

The following weekend's defeat by the odd goal in three at home to Shamrock Rovers, watched by a crowd of 1,000 people, can be effectively discounted.

It occurred just a day after the shooting of John Sweeney and in the words of Sport: "It would be as well to regard the match as little more than the fulfilment of a fixture".

In the midst of all this regular travel to Dublin, there was the need for constant fundraising and weekly practice dances were being held in the Longworth Hall by the club in the early part of this season to help offset the running costs.

Feeling hot, hot, hot

The defeat to Shamrock Rovers was the third loss on the trot, but Athlone then embarked on an amazing 22-match run, during which they were only beaten by Bohemians (albeit on two occasions). The hot streak culminated in the famous 1924 cup win.

It all started away to Midland Athletic who were put to the sword 2-0, thanks to goals from Jim Sweeney, who had returned to the team after his brother's shooting, and Muldoon from the penalty spot.

Bohemians did intervene to prevent a completely unbeaten record, overcoming Athlone 1-0 at home on October 13. This was a game in which Athlone excelled and their narrow defeat was attributed to misfortune (the third successive home defeat by a single goal to significant teams – Shelbourne, Shamrock Rovers and now Bohemians).

In the Bohemians game, Willie Bracken, who had not featured for some time, returned between the posts for a close encounter against the then league leaders, and eventual champions.

A tight game was decided by "the softest goal which the Bohemians have scored during the season" in the first minute of the second half.

And Athlone's attempts to fashion an equaliser were not helped by the time-wasting tactics of the honourable amateurs of Bohemians, who according to the Westmeath Independent, sent the ball over the touchline as often as possible.

Despite the defeat, it was now apparent, as the Irish Independent noted, that Athlone were displaying greatly improved form in recent games.

This improvement continued in the 2-1 away victory over Jacobs (Jim Sweeney and Tommy Collins scoring).

Athlone were unhappy with the approach of the home side in this contest.

"In one instance, Collins of Moate was held by one of the Jacobs players until another Jacobite split his ear with a thump."

It was a repetition of the regular mistreatment which the Westmeath Independent said Athlone players suffered in Dublin. For that reason, the club was reluctant to utilise young local junior talent in away games in the capital.

The upsurge in form – and the fact Athlone had run league leaders Bohemians so close – led a hopeful Westmeath Independent to suggest that a continuation of these performances could leave Athlone fighting it out at the top of the table come the end of the season.

And indeed, Athlone did improve, and with the exception of one more defeat away to Bohemians, finished the final twelve league games without further loss.

A home draw to Shelbourne Utd (1-1) – where again a lack of combination prevented Athlone from notching at least the three goals which their play merited – was followed by a 2-0 away victory over Dublin side Brooklyn.

It was the first of three successive games away in Dublin the latter a commendable 0-0 draw with championship-chasing Shelbourne.

However, in between, was one of the more embarrassing moments in the club's history – when just six players travelled to take on Pioneers.

The Dubliners themselves were a club in chaos; conceding a massive 97 goals in 18 league games that season.

They too had failed to field a full team on a number of occasions – and perhaps complacency took over in Athlone.

With cutting sarcasm the Westmeath Independent noted: "Supporters of the Athlone football team will be pleased to know that for the important league match in Dublin last Sunday as many as six of the team travelled to play Pioneers. This was very encouraging – to Pioneers. Though the result of one goal each might actually have been different if say, a seventh man could have been induced to go."

"The moral is of course that it will not do for any smaller number than six to try to beat eleven Dubliners. A local wit has suggested five, but Sunday's result does not justify this charge."

The report went on to say that a large crowd attended the match after it was circulated that Athlone were going to play with six men with the fixed intention of winning "a new innovation in soccer".

Thankfully, Athlone's enterprising six were assisted by an unusual source of reserves, members of the crowd. "Athlone were able to gather, after making a diligent search of every spectator on the field, a few youngsters to help them.

"The youngsters worked hard and deserve, at least, to be allowed to get into togs and to see a football for the second time in their lives."

In its post-match analysis, the Westmeath Independent did not pull any punches.

"It would appear that there are several – perhaps five – players on the Athlone Town team who desire a rest. They should have it. After all it is not to be expected that they would feel the exertions of going through a soccer season with all its ups and owns without wishing to be exempted now and again."

The six that did appear were Sweeney, Hannon, Ghent, Hope, Dykes and Connaughton.

Bizarrely, this half dozen, with the assistance of those press-ganged into service from the crowd, managed to secure a draw, thanks to a second-half own-goal by a Pioneers player.

As we have seen, the core of the 1924 Cup-winning team had been built up over previous seasons, most notably in the last campaign.

It meant there were few personnel changes for the 1923/24 campaign, although the Pioneers debacle did prompt a rethink for the next game away to Shelbourne.

The most notable arrivals during the year were Paddy O'Reilly and Terry Judge, two players who were to capture cup medals later that season,

O'Reilly, who had signed from Pioneers, helped to solve the dilemma between the posts – as Athlone had failed to settle on a regular, preferred netminder.

He may have first lined out with Athlone in the third game of the season, the 4-0 away defeat to St James's Gate. Details are sketchy for team line-outs at the start of the season, but O'Reilly was a fixture between the post from the Shelbourne game onwards.

Judge lined out at right-half in the cup final, having been plucked from neighbouring Mullingar.

Both were featured in the very next game away to Shelbourne, as Athlone unsurprisingly rounded up the available talent to ensure a full team was dispatched to Dublin.

It was Judge's debut for the Town, although it's likely that O'Reilly had featured in a few of the preceding games in the 1923/24 season.

Norman Lyster made what was probably his seasonal bow in the Shelbourne contest too.

On the outgoing column, forward Albert McLoughlin left Athlone after a handful of league games at the start of this season.

O'Reilly was in stunning form, proving an impenetrable barrier to Shelbourne, while Athlone defended in wonderful fashion, securing a 0-0 draw. The result lifted the spirits of the Westmeath Independent which more charitably noted that the draw "proved beyond doubt that the material is at our disposal".

It continued: "The players in general only need to be reminded now and again of their duty towards their supporters and also of the necessity for upholding the reputation which Athlone always had in the soccer world."

Two impressive victories (at home) over St James's Gate (3-2) and Midland Athletic (6-0) sandwiched an equally commendable 3-3 draw away to Shamrock Rovers.

The impressive Muldoon, who was steadily growing in stature, was the "outstanding player on the pitch", according to the Irish Independent. Athlone survived after Rovers had failed to convert two penalties.

Having enjoyed an eight-game unbeaten run, Athlone succumbed away to champions elect Bohemians on December 15. The 4-1 scoreline was deceptive, however.

The Freeman's Journal reported that there were passages of the game worthy of a cup final and the paper regarded it as the best game of the season. The performance of Dykes, who scored Athlone's sole goal, was deemed particularly worthy of comment.

The Evening Telegraph said the result conveyed no idea whatever of the struggle that the winners had to save the points.

It noted how early in the second half, following Dykes' equaliser, Athlone were bowling all over the Bohemians like nine pins and the ball was travelling everywhere and anywhere at the same time. "It was the first time that the many present saw Bohemians fighting for their laurels. Most of their wins have been effortless."

The nature of the game was a warning of what was to come when the two sides renewed acquaintances during the cup run. "Athlone played a wonderful, dashing, rousing, bustling, hustling game," one paper noted.

They had twice come within inches of taking the lead when the game was in the balance and only a lack of finer touches, nimbleness and cohesion in the forward line prevented them from lowering the Bohs' flag, the paper felt.

The Sunday Independent struck a discordant note when it claimed that Athlone's testing of the home defence was "of an uncouth order and blessed by the leniency of the referee".

It somewhat churlishly added: "The visitors would be well advised in future games to play the rules.

It was now clearly apparent that Athlone were on an upward curve – a fact confirmed by the remaining league results, a 3-1 victory at home to Jacobs, a 1-1 away draw on St Stephen's Day to Shelbourne United and a 4-1 home win over Brooklyn in the final league match on December 30.

An impressive league campaign

Athlone finished the league campaign on 21 points in fourth position, three points behind third-placed Jacobs, and seven behind runners-up Shelbourne.

It was to be their highest league position achieved until the second-placed finish in 1974/75 which qualified the club for the UEFA Cup and an eventual meeting with AC Milan.

Only the losing streak of three games at the very start of the campaign and the odd mishap mid-season (such as the six-player fiasco) prevented the Town from jostling with Shelbourne for the runners-up spot.

Considering the impact of the fortnightly trips to Dublin – a burden not shared by any other side – it was a fine achievement.

More importantly, the side had built up a habit of not losing, a tendency and a trait that would stand them in good stead in the FAI Cup campaign that was just around the corner.

And there was a growing realisation of Athlone's strongest eleven. Dykes had bedded down at centre-half, O'Reilly was inspirational in goal.

On the other hand, Muldoon was as likely to feature in the forward line as in the half-backs, while Connaughton had nailed down a starting berth in the forward line towards the end of the season, even at centre-forward in the final game against Brooklyn.

There was obviously still some fine-tuning to complete, but the club that would lift the FAI Cup some three months later was now in the ascendancy and its personnel were falling neatly into place.

And parallel to the improvement in quality on the field, came a growth in interest in the game locally.

Athlone had always been a stronghold of the game but there were growing indications of the rising popularity of the sport locally.

The Westmeath Independent noted in February 1924 of dissatisfaction with the practice of playing football on certain streets in the town.

The paper said juveniles and others who could not be regarded as being any longer in that category, were indulging in the sport on the principal streets of the town.

The issue had obviously not been resolved as the paper returned to the subject in May, noting that there were plenty of open spaces near the town where the game could be played without causing annoyance to residents, whose windows, in some cases, were being broken.

Another sign of the increased popularity of the game was the growth in the number of junior clubs, many of whom even had their own private club rooms.

A local junior league had been established – and regular representative friendlies were taking place between the junior league and other leagues.

A Midland League was also up and running, though it went into abeyance relatively quickly. The plethora of junior clubs meant there were calls for some form of governing body in the town to help ensure the better junior players would graduate to senior level with Athlone Town.

Athlone Town, conscious of the need to develop new talent for the future, also presented a special challenge cup for contesting by the town's junior clubs. It became known as the Athlone Junior Cup and was first played for in 1924.

Of course, the tortuous internal politics of football meant that this gesture backfired.

In response, members of the local junior committee penned an angry letter to the local paper complaining at the action of the Athlone Town committee in removing posts from the Sportsground ahead of an important junior match planned

The committee claimed the act was a form of revenge on a number of junior clubs which did not enter the Athlone Town competition.

It transpired the junior leagues had been planning their own cup competition and were peeved at what they interpreted as a pre-emptive strike by the senior club.

"It was hardly fair for some of these senior committee members to try and take those junior teams under their jurisdiction, having done nothing whatsoever in the past to encourage them."

Whatever about this unseemly squabble, it was clear that there was a massive public support for the game in Athlone.

Snubbed by international power-brokers

Athlone's rise through the ranks of football may have helped to bed down the sport – and more importantly, in the short term, its fledgling new association.

However, there were still battles to be won on the international diplomatic front.

The same day as Athlone were being edged out in the Shield final in May 1923, the association itself was being rebuffed at a meeting of the International Football Federation in Geneva.

In fact, its application for membership was turned down by a huge majority, with members adopting the attitude of the English FA that the IFA, with headquarters in Belfast, was the governing body of the game in Ireland

and that matters must be resolved between the two bodies before recognition could be considered.

It meant the Free State Football Association was effectively persona non grata in the world of international football. As Athlone prepared to take Irish football by storm, there were uncertain times ahead for the game south of the border.

1923-24 League round-up

DATE	OPPOSITION	COMPETITION (Athlone score first in all scorelines)	SCORELINE	SCORERS
September 8, 1923	Pioneers (h)	League	3-0	(?)
September 16, 1923	Shelbourne (h)	League	2-3	(Sweeney*, ?)
September 22, 1923	St James's Gate (a)	League	0-4	
September 30, 1923	Shamrock Rovers (h)	League	1-2	(Muldoon)
October 7, 1923	Midland Athletic (a)	League	2-0	(Jim Sweeney, Muldoon)
October 13, 1923	Bohemians (a)	League	0-1	
October 21, 1923	Jacobs (a)	League	2-1	(Jim Sweeney, Collins)
October 28, 1923	Shelbourne Utd (h)	League	0-0	
November 3, 1923	Brooklyn (a)	League	2-0	(Jim Sweeney (2))
November 11, 1923	Pioneers (a)	League	1-1	(own goal)
November 17, 1923	Shelbourne (a)	League	0-0	
November 24, 1923	St James's Gate (h)	League	3-2	(Muldoon, Jim Sweeney, Collins)
December 2, 1923	Shamrock Rovers (a)	League	3-3	(Jim Sweeney, Muldoon, Dykes)
December 8, 1923	Midland Athletic (h)	League	6-0	(Jim Sweeney, Ghent, ?)
December 15, 1923	Bohemians (a)	League	1-4	(Dykes)
December 23, 1923	Jacobs (h)	League	3-1	(Dykes, Ghent, Muldoon)
December 26, 1923	Shelbourne Utd (a)	League	1-1	(Corr)
December 30, 1923	Brooklyn (h)	League	4-1	(Ghent, Jim Sweeney (2), Hannon)

* Not known which Sweeney

Chapter 9
Tommy Muldoon
A class apart

Tommy Muldoon in an official Aston Villa photo.

A rapid ascent to the footballing pinnacle

Tommy Muldoon was one of the most successful of the 1924 Athlone Town FAI Cup heroes.

When Athlone triumphed on St Patrick's Day, 1924, he was a relative newcomer to top-class Irish senior football. A year earlier, he was confined to local junior football, having hardly featured with Athlone.

Within another three months, he would represent his country in the Olympics and in two subsequent internationals against USA and Estonia.

And by Christmas, 1925, he would be lining out in front of 50,000 to 60,000 people in England with one of that country's premier clubs.

Muldoon carved out a professional career, drawing a wage for his sporting talent for seven years cross-channel, albeit, in an era when football was far from the lucrative pursuit of modern days.

It was a spectacular ascent to the top echelon of sport for the young man who spent his formative years in Main Street, Athlone.

His early days

Tommy Muldoon's story began in Granard, Co. Longford, around the turn of the century.

He was one of two sons born to Christopher and Bridget Muldoon.

After retiring from the Royal Irish Constabulary, Christopher left Granard in the early 1900s and brought his family to Athlone, where he operated a shop on Main Street.

There is an air of mystery about Tommy's date of birth, but he received his education in Athlone, attending Deerpark NS and St Mary's Intermediate School.

He developed his interest in the game on the streets and pitches of Athlone and his skills were further enhanced during his years of service with the British Army.

The war years

In around 1916, Muldoon joined the Leinster Regiment – which had its base at Crinkle near Birr. He trained at The Curragh and subsequently saw 22 months service in France, during which time he rose to the rank of sergeant.

His wartime exploits included sleeping on a bed of riches, as he explained in an interview with a Birmingham newspaper in 1925.

"My billet was in an old barn attached to a modest and quiet little farm kept by an aged man and his wife. They had saved ten thousand francs. When the war broke out they decided upon their own way of saving it and banking it. Instead of putting it into war bonds or war saving certificates, they simply buried it in the barn.

"When I took up my abode in the barn I made my bed on the very spot where the pieces were buried. I often noticed that the aged couple were ferreting around my bed but take it from me I had no suspicions of the value of my pillow. And apparently they had no qualms about my honesty or should I say ignorance.

"The great upheaval came on the very day the Armistice was signed. I was away from my "cot" very early in the morning and when I returned I found my bed disturbed and the ground opened. I saw the money unearthed and carried away by the aged couple. They left me without a franc reward for taking care of it!" he told the Sunday Mercury.

After the end of the war, Muldoon served for a further two years in India and then returned with his unit to The Curragh to be disbanded.

Back in Athlone, he found work in the Woollen Mills, resumed his footballing career and married Athlone woman Frances Henry, sister of Mick and Pa, who featured for Athlone in the League of Ireland, and John, who lined out in the blue and black in the 1930s.

Developing with Athlone Town

Tommy Muldoon first featured in Athlone footballing circles with junior team St Patrick's League.

Indeed, even in the throes of the run to the Shield final in May 1923, Muldoon was centre-half and captain of his local club in the Midland League of 1922/23.

His first involvement with Athlone Town came in the opening game of the 1922/23 league season, against St James's Gate. Athlone had difficulty finding Muldoon's natural berth and on this occasion he lined out in the forward line. Indeed, he made more than a half-dozen league appearances that campaign, predominantly up front.

But it wasn't until he moved to the half-back line towards the end of season that his special talent became more apparent.

By May, in the Shield semi-final and final, he was Athlone's starring player. In an indication of his growing importance he had also been assigned penalty-taking duties – a task he successfully discharged in the final.

Ten months after his debut, he was now clearly one of the team's senior players. And he already was building up a steady fan club among the legions of journalists who covered the matches.

He was a tower of strength in the quarter-final win over Shamrock Rovers, according to the Westmeath Independent. In the semi-final against Shelbourne Utd, he gave "a splendid display throughout" according to the Evening Telegraph. The same paper said he won extra admirers for his excellent play in the final.

His selection to appear in a Free State League XI in the Hospitals' Herald Cup charity match against a Leinster League selection at the end of that season was further indication that he had well and truly arrived on the national football scene. This was a distinction usually only conferred upon those who moved in the right circles in the Dublin footballing world.

And it indicated that Muldoon already knew how to further his own career by putting himself in the shop window.

A season to beat all seasons

After such a phenomenal rise from football obscurity, Muldoon would have been forgiven for thinking that the 1923/24 season could never match what had gone before. But instead, he continued where he left off.

Muldoon weighed in with five league goals that season, including two penalties, often from an attacking half-back role.

He guested for Shelbourne on their visit to Athlone for the second game of the league in a clear sign that he was already attracting the interest of top clubs.

Muldoon, though, paid the price for his versatility, as he was forced to line out in a whole series of different positions during the league campaign.

Nonetheless, wherever he played he generally caught the eye. The Irish Independent noted he was "the outstanding player on the field" in Athlone's 3-3 draw with Shamrock Rovers in Milltown in November.

It was not until the turn of the year, and the start of the first round of the 1923/24 cup against Midland Athletic, that Muldoon featured in what was clearly his best position of half-back.

He missed the quarter-final victory over Shelbourne, but was reinstated at left half-back for the two semi-final games against Bohemians and the final itself against Fordsons.

And again he earned rave reviews, with a real starring role in the drawn cup semi-final game against Bohemians. He was the most cultured of the Athlone backs according to the Irish Independent. Sport said he was the star performer on the Athlone side.

In the final, Muldoon was his classy self, cool, collected and in the words of the Westmeath Independent "unequalled in style, effectiveness, shrewdness, reliability".

The exertions took their toll as Muldoon contracted "a severe chill" and missed the next game.

He saw out the season with Athlone, lining out in the remaining Leinster Senior Cup and Shield games, before heading off on the historic trip to Paris with the Irish Olympic team.

Muldoon's prominent role in the cup voyage and in the Parisien adventure was to ensure the 1923/24 season was his last for Athlone.

His final appearance was probably in a Shield game away to Shamrock Rovers in May, where he played at full-back in the absence of the ill Jimmy Hope.

To Villa Park

A whole new life opened up for Muldoon in September 1924.

Initially, newspapers had reported that he was set to join Shelbourne, the club he had guested with almost a year previously. However, there was a sudden u-turn and it was indicated that he would now remain with Athlone. But then came news that Muldoon had secured a month's trial with Aston Villa.

Muldoon himself gave an interesting account of background to his departure in a piece written in a Birmingham newspaper in 1925.

"While in Paris, Mr Dennis Hannon, the former Bohemians and Irish amateur international sounded me about making a bid for higher fame and suggested joining Aston Villa. I believed Mr Hannon had met an Aston Villa representative at an England V. Irish match at Derby and most likely the Villa man had expressed himself as not adverse to a bit of Irish in his team."

Like any modern-day professional footballer, Muldoon knew how to play to his new side's fans. He told the Sunday Mercury: "In my boyhood days, spent mostly in Athlone, Aston Villa's name was a footballing inspiration. We talked of them as the greatest football team on earth and it was about the last thing imaginable for an Athlone boy to talk about playing for them."

Although, Muldoon was clearly massaging the egos of the Villa fans, it remained the case that the Birmingham club were then among the giants of the game, having been beaten FA Cup finalists just months before his arrival. In addition, they had finished in the top six in Division One (then the top flight) in each of the previous three years.

He added: "I want to tell you straight away that Irishmen regard English football as the best in the world and the Irishman who can hold his own in English football is regarded as somebody good, somebody exceptional. A young man with my foot on the ladder of fame, I have yet to prove myself somebody good, somebody exceptional. If the flesh is good enough the spirit is and my desire is to prove myself a worthy Irish member of Aston Villa's team.

"I dare not hope to be as useful an Irishman to Aston Villa, as Gillespie has been to Sheffield United, Hamill to Manchester City, Harris to Everton, Kirwan to Spurs and Chelsea, Lacey to Everton and Liverpool and McCracken to Newcastle Utd but given health and strength, I am going to try and maintain the good reputation of those distinguished men from the Emerald Isle."

The secret of youth

Muldoon arrived in Birmingham in late September 1924 and fitted in some matches with the third team, the Aston Villa Colts, before securing a contract.

Aston Villa records give Muldoon's date of birth as February 1901, meaning he was still a relatively youthful 23 when he signed up.

However, his real date of birth was in fact July 27th, 1897, revealing he was 27 when he signed his first contract with the Villa.

His little lie about his age was clearly designed to lengthen his potential career, though it created difficulties when relating his life story to the Sunday Mercury.

In particular, given his false date of birth of 1901, he was hard pressed to explain how he joined the army in 1916. The best way of covering up one untruth, though, is with another – and so Muldoon simply claimed he was underage when he joined the British Army, neatly solving the dilemma of his army service at such a youthful age.

"At the age of 15 – I told a lie about my age – I enlisted in the Leinster Regiment. We trained at The Curragh and in 1917 I found myself with the regiment in the thick of the fighting at Ypres," he explained.

His relatively mature years for a new professional footballer, however, was an insignificant issue compared to the scale of the challenge facing Muldoon in Villa.

When Muldoon joined ahead of the 1924/25 season, Villa already had some nine half-backs on their books. Included among his rivals were Aston Villa captain Frank Moss (the first man to captain England at Wembley) and George Blackburn, who had played in the cup final with Villa the previous season.

Muldoon lined out with the reserves in a half-dozen matches over October, November and December, often in front of significant crowds of five or six thousand supporters. By late October he was adjudged to have passed his trial and was given a one-year contract.

Within weeks, he was called unexpectedly into first team action for an away game against Preston North End on December 13th, 1924.

Such was the scale of the injury crisis, the Villa half-back line included three players who had a total of just five Villa league games between them under their belts. The Villa News, the club's own programme, said the half-back line was "not at all successful".

Muldoon understood his spot of luck. "I don't mind confessing that I joined Villa's camp at the right moment for opportunities. Owing to accidents, illnesses etc, Villa wanted players and I got no fewer than 18 games with the first team in my first season at Villa Park," he wrote in the Sunday Mercury in September 1925.

"Accidents have given me my chance this season and while I am sorry for the men who are on the casualty list, I must not look a gift horse in the mouth."

His second opportunity arose during a congested Christmas fixture list which saw Villa thumped 6-0 away by Leeds Utd on Christmas Day. Bizarrely, the two sides met again, a day later, in Birmingham, with Muldoon drafted in to line out at half-back in front of 50,000 people - Villa's second biggest home league gate of the season.

This time he was more impressive, but nonetheless, he returned to the reserves for two games, before nailing down a first-team berth for the next nine league games.

During this extended run, in late January, he was the best of the half-backs against West Ham, while he was the only half-back to impress in a 4-1 defeat to reigning league champions, Huddersfield Town.

But probably his best game for Aston Villa came in the FA Cup second-round victory away to Swansea on January 31st, 1925. The Birmingham Daily Post said Muldoon had taken his chance with both hands.

"His tackling was admirable and his placing, considering the state of the ground, was excellent."

The paper said he had marked the Swansea right-wing with grim determination and "so fine was his conditioning that he was playing as strongly at the finish as at the start. He was one of the successes of the match".

The club's own programme, the Villa News, remarked: "When Villa arrived the ground was dry enough, but between the time of arrival and the start of the game, rain fell in torrents." The downpour turned the pitch into a mudbath. "Muldoon particularly soaked up the mud, for he fairly wallowed in it," it remarked.

Despite his role in this 3-1 victory, Muldoon was omitted in favour of the now fit Frank Moss for the next-round cup clash against neighbours West Brom.

Moss, exacerbated his injury in the replay, and was out for the rest of the season, opening the door once again for Muldoon. He completed his run of nine successive league games, including a run-out in front of 60,000 people in Villa Park against Birmingham.

After a poor performance away to Everton (in a game in which the famous Dixie Dean scored on his home debut for the Toffees) he was dropped for the next fixture at home to Arsenal.

But, he was back in the starting line-up a week later and as the season came to a close, Muldoon managed to register six appearances from the remaining eight games.

In recognition of the fact that his progress was ahead of schedule, Muldoon was given a new contract before the end of the season.

He was also clearly a popular figure around the club. He had acquired the less-than-inspired nickname of Patsy and was spoken of as a genial, cheery sort of player.

In his first season, he lined out on 17 occasions for the first team in the league and once in the FA Cup. He had also a dozen second-team games under his belt as well as a number for the third team.

However, it was a horribly disappointing campaign for Villa as they finished a lowly 15th of 22 teams. The injuries and absences had hit Villa hard and the enforced volatility in selection (13 different players were tried out in the half-back line) was a real difficulty.

Second season success

An Aston Villa squad picture from 1925. Tommy Muldoon is seated on extreme right of front row.

Despite the fact that Villa had faltered badly, they evidently had a great deal of faith in Patsy's ability.

In fact, he started the new season in flying form and was now clearly more attuned to the demands of regular first-team football. Muldoon was a fixture from the start, featuring in the opening eight league games, in the process earning rave reviews. His form in the opening 10-0 annihilation of Burnley was "an eye-opener".

He was the star player in a 2-2 draw with Newcastle – with one commentator noting that he "had improved by leaps and bounds".

Against Bolton, the Daily Chronicle said that he stuck to his forward with terrier-like determination.

Indeed, Villa themselves were on a roll, losing just once in that opening eight games. The Villa News said he shone in his endeavours against Bolton.

It remarked that sections of the crowd had criticised his mistakes in the game. By the end, they were cheering him for his pluck and persistence.

An injury setback

However, there was misfortune just around the corner.

On October 3rd, 1925, during a 1-1 draw with local rivals West Bromwich Albion in The Hawthorns, Muldoon was badly injured in the final minute.

"Taking a flying kick at the ball, he was blocked by an opponent and his instep and ankle were injured," said The Villa News

The club programme said he would be out of action for a month or two and was hobbling around with the aid of sticks but was "a cheery sort of cripple".

Although, there was early optimism that he would return quickly, it was not until December 12th – more than two months later – that he did return to the field of play, in a trial match with the Villa Colts.

The Villa News reported he came through the game with no ill effects.

But it was a slow road to full recovery and it was not until late January that he was tested with the reserves.

"He does not like being on the sick list … he himself will be the happiest man in the ground," it was said ahead of his reserves reappearance against Preston on January 23rd, 1926.

By late February, he was reported to have retained his old form and he was reintroduced to the first team on March 6th – five months after his injury.

"Muldoon reappeared and he played in a manner indicative of a return to the vigorous form that made him such a favoured player in the early days of the season," said The Villa News.

He played in five of the next seven games, but again the return of Frank Moss from injury meant Muldoon shuffled back to reserve team duty for the end of the season.

Having missed 21 league games through injury, his final tally of 14 first team appearances was admirable. Villa finished in 6th place in the league.

The close-season witnessed Villa embark on a continental tour of Scandinavia, taking in Sweden and Norway.

A disappointing campaign

Again Muldoon was retained on a new contract in time for the 1926/27 schedule. However, this was to be Muldoon's most disappointing campaign for the Villa.

The Sports Argus, in reviewing the season ahead, had pointed out that although Muldoon had improved rapidly, it would still be a surprise if he kept Frank Moss out of the side.

Again, Muldoon lined up in the opening game away to Newcastle Utd. A 4-0 defeat meant there were four changes for the following game, with

Muldoon among those jettisoned.

He was to line out just once more, against Bury in mid-September, but was effectively consigned to the reserves, for whom he was almost ever-present, often featuring at centre-half.

Ireland's call

The Irish team that took on Italy B in Lansdowne Road in 1927. Tommy Muldoon is extreme right bottom row, with Christy Martin second from left.

The season was not a complete write off though.

In April 1927, Muldoon was called back to Ireland to wear the green against Italy B in what, at the time, was regarded as a full international. The same day the Italian first eleven played France. FIFA does not recognise a match between a country's first-choice team and the opposition's second-string eleven as a full international. As a result, the match should not be in the record books.

Despite their second-string status, Italy fielded a strong line-up, including three players from each of Juventus, Inter Milan and Bologna

Although the game has been wiped from the records, it is still listed in many quarters as Ireland's first home international. And it was a feeling shared by many at the time.

The Evening Herald described the match as "what may be truly termed the first international match in which the Free State has engaged in its own soil since the Saorstat became a separate and autonomous entity in the management of soccer affairs takes place tomorrow".

It was also the first time that players from English clubs were released to play in the green of the new Ireland. Muldoon was not the only player with

Athlone connections on the team, according to contemporary newspaper reports.

Christy Martin

Centre-forward Christy Martin of then Scottish club, Bo'ness, was born in Athlone. The slightly-built Martin had been plucked from the Glasgow Junior Leagues by Bo'ness, a club based in Borrowstounness, a town in the Falkirk area of Scotland.

In April 1927, Martin had just helped his club to promotion to the First Division However, Bo'ness's stay in the top flight was limited to just one season, as they suffered immediate relegation. Martin also featured with Brooklyn Wanderers in the American Soccer League, as well as Falkirk, before returning to Bo'ness, where a fractured skull ended his career.

Martin has the distinction of being the first player to line out with both the IFA and FAI sides after the split.

He had been selected by what is now known as Northern Ireland in 1925 against Scotland, two years before his involvement in the Irish Free State's game against Italy.

Injury strikes Muldoon

In the game against Italy B in Lansdowne Road, Muldoon started brightly and prevented a certain goal in the first half by throwing himself in front of an Italian player in the act of shooting.

However, injury was once again to blight Muldoon as he was laid low early in the second half in a game which the Italian B side surprisingly won by the odd goal in three. The injury necessitated his departure and when he returned, he was clearly a passenger and was shuttled out to the outside-left position. The Evening Herald noted: "He was clearly shaken by the accident, just at a point when he was about to get to grips with the game and promised to do well."

Muldoon's incapacity did highlight a strange anomaly in the rules, as the Italians had utilised the services of a substitute after one of their defenders, Zapello, was knocked out cold by a Bob Fullam piledriver.

The Evening Herald noted the inconsistency and said there would have been nothing wrong with Ireland acting similarly in the circumstances. Still it was to be 7 years before Fred Horlacher became the first substitute used by Ireland in an international match.

English clubs had agreed to release players for the Lansdowne Road game. It was a position they had not adopted for Ireland's visit to Italy the previous season – nor would they repeat the offer for the next international away to Belgium. It hardly helped Muldoon's international career and the Italian game in Dublin was to be his last call-up.

The Italian visit to Ireland had renewed memories of Ireland's voyage in the opposite direction 13 months previously.

Writing in the Evening Herald in the week leading up to the Lansdowne Road game, one of the official party recalled some amazing scenes in Turin.

The writer claimed that more than 20,000 Italians were waiting outside the train station when the Irish players and officials arrived.

The writer continued: "As though the whole proceeding had been especially organised and rehearsed, it divided itself into two sections on the extensive square or plaza in front of the railway terminus, leaving a human avenue along which the Free State team and officials passed to the charabancs waiting to convey the party to their hotel.

"Dead silence prevailed amongst the monster assembly until the Irishmen were seated and the drivers were ready to set off. Suddenly, into the human avenue, referred to sprang a huge figure of a man, who , waving his broad brimmed black felt hat, uttered a few Italian words in a stentorian voice. At once the huge crowd composed of men and women of the best type of Italian citizens broke into vociferous applause."

Heart-warming as the anecdote may be, one would have to query its legitimacy, particularly when it later transpired that only 12,000 turned up for the game itself a few days later!

Spurred on to leave Villa

Despite his absence from the first-team in the 1926/27 campaign, Muldoon was retained by Aston Villa for one final season, 1927/28.

However, he again failed to register on the first-team radar. Indeed, he slipped well down the ranking order and was only chosen for the reserves with increasing irregularity. Again, injuries proved a handful and he sustained a troublesome cartilage problem, which eventually required an operation.

His time with Villa was at an end, but Spurs, who had just been relegated from Division One, offered him a lifeline ahead of the 1928/29 season.

The Spurs programme noted that he had enjoyed success with Villa, but injuries had meant he was not re-engaged. "He is now thoroughly fit. Muldoon is spoken of in the highest terms by good judges of players," the club optimistically declared.

Again, Muldoon didn't register on the first team with the White Hart Lane outfit, Having made just two league appearances in the three seasons from 1926 to 1929, his career seemed almost at an end.

In his small number of Spurs reserve games, Muldoon lined out occasionally at left-full, though, mostly, at half-back. Early in 1929, he again was on the treatment table having sustained a serious knee injury.

Walsall offer new hope

The Walsall squad for the 1929/30 season.
Muldoon is pictured on the extreme left of the back row.

It was from Birmingham that a chink of light emanated from amidst the ever-darkening clouds that were encircling Muldoon's career. In the summer of 1929, Muldoon headed back to the general Birmingham area for a month's trial with Walsall, then in the 3rd Division South.

It was a journey he could well have made some five years earlier, it transpired, as Walsall were the first club to be alerted to his talent. When he arrived in Walsall the story emerged that a local teacher, who was visiting Ireland in or around 1923 or 1924, had seen Muldoon play for Athlone.

"He was so impressed that he at once wrote to Walsall telling him of his discovery and offering to enter into further negotiations on the club's behalf." The teacher apparently could "recognise a real footballer when he sees one". The matter, though, was not dealt with promptly, and, in the meantime, Aston Villa stepped in.

Now in August 1929, there was optimism that Muldoon could still be a valuable recruit. The Walsall Observer noted: "Tommy Muldoon, the former Aston Villa half-back has been signed. He should prove to be a useful acquisition if he can reproduce the form he showed whist he was at Villa Park."

Muldoon's injuries were still an issue – and he was initially given a month's trial to ensure that the question of his fitness was settled.

The club programme, the Walsall Football News, noted his arrival with a lengthy introduction outlining his career to date cross-channel. It added that Muldoon was well thought of in Villa – but that the effect of a serious injury which happened against WBA back in 1926 had hampered his development.

"When he had recovered sufficiently to resume playing, he was allowed to depart to Tottenham Hotspur where he spent last season but there remained some doubt about him being thoroughly sound," it said.

Obviously believing Muldoon was 28, instead of 32, the Walsall club said: "He should have years of football left in him." On the positive side, it also reported that he was rapidly recovering his confidence and something like his old form. It also commended his good use of the ball, noting that his passes were invariably placed to the advantage of his forwards and were always on the ground.

Muldoon featured in the opening game of the 1929/30 season, but clearly still had to be nursed along as the club deliberately rested him for the following midweek game. It was an understandable precaution particularly in a year when the hot, late summer had left grounds "baked almost to the hardness of concrete".

His early-season appearances were erratic and he did not again feature until the seventh league match, at home to Southend.

An injured thigh sustained in that game ruled him out for the next three fixtures. He returned on October 11th for a run of 32 successive league appearances right up to the season's end in May. The cup also brought some joy to his stay with Walsall. In his two seasons with the club, Muldoon played in all eight of the club's FA Cup games.

Taking on Villa

The undoubted highlight of his stay in Walsall was a fourth-round FA Cup clash in January 1930 with neighbours Aston Villa. A massive 74,626 attended the game, which was played in Villa Park after Walsall agreed to cede home advantage. Another 5,000 were locked out.

It remains the biggest attendance ever at a Walsall match and was a then record attendance at Villa Park. The game had obviously extra significance for Muldoon, who was returning to his old stomping ground.

The cup had provided some much-needed relief to Walsall that season as they had been on a horrible league run of seven games without a win. During that winless league streak, Walsall had shown some form in the cup, having overcome Exeter City, Newport County and Swansea Town to secure their fourth-round berth.

A section of the 74,626 people who watched the Aston Villa v. Walsall cup tie of 1930.

A page from the programme of the same game.

Finally, the week before the Villa game, Walsall overcame Exeter in the league but the renewed form was hardly like to paper over the stark reality: Villa were fifth in the first division, Walsall struggling in Division 3. Despite the gap in standings though, Walsall fought tigerishly and were unfortunate to lose.

The game was played with the usual fury associated with such derby cup ties, but Villa's class finally told.

Muldoon found the going tough, particularly as his direct opponent, Eric Houghton, ran the show, producing left-wing crosses for two of Villa's three goals.

The eventual 3-1 scoreline was somewhat unfair on Walsall, who were striving manfully for an equaliser late on when Villa broke for the final goal.

Houghton went on to become a Villa legend, managing the team to a cup win in 1957, playing for England, and later sitting on the board of both Villa and Walsall.

The game is recalled in Birmingham for the remarkable crowd scenes.

An attendance of some 60,000 had been expected, but the extra thousands caught organises by surprise

Many fans walked seven or eight deep along the eight miles from Walsall to Villa Park, blocking the Birmingham Road, as they made their way to the game.

Walsall's little resurgence in form came too late for manager Sid Scholey who was sacked the week after the Villa game. A new coach was appointed, but no manager was put in place for another nine months.

The club secretary, Joseph Burchell, had previously acted as manager for five years from 1921-26 and appears to have stepped into the breach again in the interim. It appears as if Burchell or the new coach rated Tommy as he continued as an ever-present at right-half up to the end of the season.

It had been a mediocre campaign for Walsall, despite the cup highs. They finished a lowly 17th of 22 teams in the 3rd Division South. The Walsall Observer's review of the season simply described Muldoon as "an average half-back".

The final hurrah

A number of new players were brought in during the close season, including a new right half-back. Tommy Godfrey, a Scot, had played with Stenhousemuir and in a small number of games for Stoke City, but was clearly signed as first-choice for his position.

Indeed, even in pre-season games, Muldoon was consigned to the reserves. After being omitted from the opening few games, Muldoon was placed on the transfer list at his own request.

But there were clearly no takers and when he did get an opportunity in the eighth match of the league, his performance was poor, as Walsall slumped to a 4-0 home defeat to Torquay Utd. He was promptly dropped again.

He was clearly out of favour. An injury to the first choice left-half, Bill Bradford, soon after, resulted in players who were specialists in other positions being utilised to shore up the half-back line.

In October 1930, in the middle of an eight-match losing streak, a new manager Peter O'Rourke was appointed. And within a few weeks, Muldoon was back in favour as O'Rourke opted to play the Irishman in his preferred position of left half-back.

Before Muldoon's first game under O'Rourke away to Luton on November 15, Walsall were bottom of the 3rd Division South. Coincidentally or not, results immediately improved with Walsall embarking on an eight-game unbeaten run (including five draws). Muldoon missed just one of these eight games (one of two in successive days over Christmas).

His resurgence coincided with the 1930/31 cup campaign and Muldoon again played in all four of Walsall's cup ties that season.

In the third round, Walsall were drawn away to Division One side Blackburn Rovers and emerged with a surprise 1-1 draw. Muldoon was one of the stars of the show.

The Walsall Times reported: "The pitch was in a deplorable condition, being ankle deep in mud. Walsall seemed to revel in it. Whilst the stalwarts floundered about in all directions, the muddier the Saddlers got, the more they seemed to enjoy it. Muldoon had the distinction of being one of the best half-backs on the field as well as the muddiest player."

The fairytale did not continue in the replay as Blackburn overturned Walsall on their home ground by 3-0.

By this stage, a new threat to Muldoon in the shape of left-half John Archer had emerged and for the cup game and the reminder of his appearances, the Irishman reverted to right half-back.

In total, Muldoon played 17 league games that campaign, along with the four cup appearances. His run of first-team games ended after an embarrassing 6-1 away defeat to Brentford on February 28, 1931.

The Walsall Times reported he had been ill – and it was not until late April that he reappeared on reserve team duty. It was his last game for Walsall.

Little is known of Tommy Muldoon after the ending of his football career.

He worked in a labour exchange in Walsall in the 1930s and he died in Selly Oak Hospital in Birmingham, from bronchopneumonia, on October 12th, 1989, aged 92 years. His body was cremated.

Members of Muldoon's extended family continue to live in the greater Birmingham area.

Chapter 10

FAI Cup first round

Sending the Railwaymen back down the tracks

The end of the 1923 calendar year would have been an opportune time to take stock of Athlone's progress in their second season in the new Free State League.

And take stock the Westmeath Independent did, noting that the team's manifest lack of fitness and conditioning in the earlier rounds of the league had left them with too much of a hurdle to climb.

"It has been remarked that the real reason why our team had not come out on top in the league this year is their utter disregard of the necessity for all-the-year-round practice. The first four matches of the present season should have been so many presents for our home 11 if they had been prepared.

"Indoor training is not the thing, there must be so many evenings of work – winter and summer – given over to practice on the Sportsground, where a worthy lot of opponents picked from the other local teams, should appear also and the full 90 minutes played as if it were a cup or league competition.

"Only by this means can we hope to see the next year's struggles entered upon with any degree of confidence in the Town's ability to lift one of the most coveted prizes," the paper said.

In a separate piece in that week's edition, the same writer, presumably, had no qualms in labouring the point.

"The right material is there, and has been always, and it only requires a little more interest and determination on the part of each player to do what was done 30 years ago by their predecessors who in their day made the name of Athlone at once feared and respected in soccer circles throughout Ireland.

"Judging from the talent available in Athlone at present, it would not appear too erratic to expect that both junior and senior trophies be captured in 1924 – systematic practice would bring the two within the realm of possibility and probability."

Whilst the writer appeared to be looking towards the 1924/25 season which would commence after the summer months, he also pointed out that the Shield, to be played for in the Spring, would provide Athlone with a prospect of silverware.

"The reason that our eleven are being spoken of as probable winners is because they are a much more dogged, determined and skilful lot when fighting issues of this kind than they are in league football."

But before the Shield competition could get underway, there was the opportunity to prove Athlone's knock-out credentials in the more prestigious FAI Cup.

That season, Athlone joined the other nine league sides and three non-league outfits in the hat for the first round of the cup. The three additions were comprised of Fordsons and the winners of qualifying competitions in Leinster and Munster. Fordsons, a factory works team attached to the famous Ford plant in Cork, had reached the last four of the cup the previous year and had been invited to partake again.

Five first-round ties were fixed, with the three remaining teams receiving byes into the second round.

The respected weekly Sport was one of the few to foresee Athlone's tremendous impact in the Cup. Previewing the Town's first-round match against Midland Athletic, the paper's correspondent predicted not only an Athlone victory but a lengthy cup run.

"The next round should be of tremendous interest and when it arrives with Athlone in it, I look forward to seeing some of the high fancied goods receiving the rudest shock of their lives. It is to be hoped the luck of the next draw will put Athlone up against the best of them, when they will have to hop to it with some purpose. Athlone are nothing if not cup fighters. They are just the team to play ducks and drakes with the methodical footballers. I am given to understand, with a view to upsetting a lot of smug egotism, they are going into special training for the Cup games."

Midland Athletic's players were drawn from the ranks of the Midland and Great Western Railway Company which had its base in Broadstone, Dublin.

Among the Midland Athletic eleven which took the field in Athlone was goalkeeper Paddy Sherlock who would line out with Athlone later in the 1920s.

The game against the Railwaymen took place in the Sportsground on January 5th, 1924, and according to the Westmeath Independent was favoured with tolerably fine weather.

Unfortunately, details are somewhat sketchy regarding Athlone's first step on their voyage to cup glory.

The game was notable, in the eyes of the Westmeath Independent reporter at least, because of injuries sustained by three players which resulted in a number of disruptions.

A relatively short match report provided few details of the action and instead focused on this element of the game.

The two goals were covered succinctly and uninformatively thus: "After an interval the game again resumed and during play in which the home team had it practically all their own way, netted the leather twice."

The goals came shortly after the visitors had been reduced to ten men; one of their half-backs was forced to withdraw with head injuries. The Westmeath Independent explained the incident occurred when Frank Ghent, in attempting to head the ball, came into violent contact with Lynch, who sustained injuries to the back of his head.

Lynch was seen to by a local doctor and subsequently returned to Dublin by train. What impact this collision had on Ghent is not recorded.

There were injuries on the Athlone side too. Paddy Flannery sustained a superficial knee wound but remained on the field of play and needed medical treatment for a couple of weeks.

Tommy Collins too was in the wars, a neck injury sustained early on resulted in his collapse on the pitch in the final minutes. He recovered quickly though - buoyed no doubt by the actions of the Athlone crowd who assisted him from the ground amidst victorious cheers at the final whistle.

Elsewhere, Jim Sweeney was credited with a fine performance while the defence of Hope and Monahan was virtually impregnable.

Apparently, the Westmeath Independent reporter or correspondent was also on duty for the various national papers as the few scant reports which appeared in either Sunday's or Monday's nationals were more like health updates than sports reports.

The scorers of Athlone's two goals were not recorded anywhere for posterity.

Elsewhere, Bohemians, St James's Gate and Bray Unknowns all secured their passage through to the second round of the cup in the other three first-round ties played that day.

The remaining tie, due to feature the winners of the Munster qualifying competition at home to Shelbourne Utd, was not played for over a month due to a remarkable and titanic struggle within the Munster qualifying competition.

Of the ties completed, the most eagerly anticipated featured league champions Bohemians against Shamrock Rovers. Bohs had been beaten in a meaningless final game of the league campaign the previous weekend by Shamrock Rovers. They gained swift revenge with a narrow one-goal victory over the Hoops in Dalymount Park. The contest was attended by over 7,000 and was refereed by Athlone whistler Michael Broderick.

That game was notable too for the theft of a sizeable portion of the proceeds from the turnstiles. The culprit, a steeplejack, was subsequently arrested as he attempted to leave for Manchester on a steamer and was jailed for three months.

In the other ties, the brewery side St James's Gate kept their season alive, but only just in a five-goal thriller against lowly Pioneers who had finished second from bottom in the league.

Leinster Senior League side Bray Unknowns who had reached the Cup proper having won the Leinster qualifying competition, sprang a mild surprise by travelling to defeat league outfit Brooklyn by the odd goal in three.

Elsewhere, there was drama aplenty to be played out in the sporting fields of Cork and Tipperary as the Munster qualifying competition continued to fascinate. In fact, it required a staggering six games to separate Tipperary Wanderers of the North Munster section and Cork side Barrackton Utd in the Munster semi-final. The marathon struggle caught the imagination of sporting fans in the province of Munster, where football had been slow to recover after the war.

The sides had drawn for the fourth occasion in Tipperary on January 6th but apparently - and bizarrely - had agreed the match could be decided on corner kicks won. The referee, therefore, awarded the game to the Tipperary outfit, but the Free State Association, stating that no such rule existed, stepped in and ordered yet another replay.

That too, in Turners Cross, failed to separate the teams, but eventually the following weekend in Tipperary, the home side prevailed after an unbelievable six games spanning over eleven hours of football!

After all that, it was a real anti-climax when the Tipperary men failed to reach the cup proper despite a home draw in the Munster qualifying competition final. They were comprehensively defeated by another Cork side Clifton Utd. In their turn, Clifton's involvement in the cup was to be short-lived as they came a cropper in the first round at home to league side Shelbourne Utd.

Of course in the meantime the competition had continued on regardless. The second-round draw produced the following pairings: Bray Unknowns v. Bohemians, Shelbourne v. Athlone Town; Jacobs v. Fordsons and St James's Gate v. the winners of the Clifton/Shelbourne Utd game.

The newspaper Sport had its wish. Athlone had their chance to mete out the rudest shock of their lives to the mighty Shelbourne and on their own turf. Now, it simply remained to be seen whether they could pull off the victory.

The Evening Telegraph's preview described Athlone as certainties and said the home side were "likely to hand it out thick and hairy to much stronger sides than Midland Athletic".

Team V. Midland Athletic

Paddy O'Reilly, Joe Monahan, Jimmy Hope, Paddy Flannery, John Joe Dykes, Tommy Muldoon, Barney Connaughton, Dinny Hannon, Jim Sweeney, Frank Ghent and Tommy Collins.

Chapter 11

Terry Judge

Mission Accomplished

From Mullingar to Athlone

On January 5th, 1924, when Athlone Town's cup run began against Midland Athletic, Terry Judge was otherwise engaged.

The then 28-year-old Westmeath man was playing instead for his native Mullingar in the Leinster Junior Cup semi-final against Chapelizod in Dublin.

Mullingar lost that semi-final, the second time in successive years they had succumbed at the penultimate hurdle in the blue riband junior event.

By then Judge had already worn the blue of Athlone, making his debut during the league campaign of that same season -1923/24.

Terry Judge

But it was with his hometown club that he lined out that day in early January.

Terry Judge was born in Mullingar on May 1st, 1895, son of Leitrim native Francis and his wife Catherine

He was the second youngest of seven children, six brothers and one sister, and spent his formative years in Patrick Street, Mullingar, before the family later moved to Mount Street.

His father was a shoemaker and it was a trade continued by many of Terry's older brothers. Terry himself worked in the business for nine years before the war.

The premises Francis Judge and Sons had locations in Mount Street, Mullingar, and, for a period, in Castletown Geoghegan. Two of his siblings, James and Joseph, continued running a shoemaker's business in Mullingar for many decades from their premises in Mount Street.

Buried in at Ypres

Terry's immersion in football began as far back as 1913 as a callow 17-year-old with a local Mullingar junior team. However, as for so many others, the Great War intervened.

Judge joined the Irish Guards in Mullingar in December 1914 – a few months after the outbreak of the war, and was immediately dispatched to Caterham Barracks in Surrey, south of London.

He was called up to the British Expeditionary Force in August 1915 as the war effort intensified and spent some two years and four months on the front with the Irish Guards. In March 1917, he was promoted to Lance Corporal.

Judge saw much service along the Western Front with the 2nd battalion of the Irish Guards – and was twice admitted to army hospitals with shell shock. The latter occasion, in June 1916, was the more serious of the two – and arose following the slaughter that was Ypres. Although he subsequently resumed service in the field, the impact of his experiences in Ypres remained and he was again hospitalised in Le Havre and finally, in late December 1917, posted back to regimental headquarters in Warley.

There he was assessed by a medical board and deemed to be permanently unfit for war service. He was discharged in May 1918, debilitated from his experiences of being buried in at Ypres.

Thousands of Allied soldiers died in similar circumstances as buildings in which they sheltered collapsed around them in a hail of German shells. Judge survived – probably having been dug out by his colleagues.

His symptoms were testament to the toll of war; he was anaemic, suffered slight tremors of the heart and endured shakiness, increased knee jerks and tremors of the fingers.

War had wreaked a terrible price from Terry Judge.

Trying to rebuild a career

Discharged from the army in June 1918, Judge returned to his trade as a shoemaker and joined the family business in Mount Street, Mullingar.

His elder brothers were the main beneficiaries of the business, however, and Terry was left to pick up the crumbs, employed only when there was sufficient work.

He married a Mullingar woman Bridget (Delia) Cooke in November 1919, just 16 days after his brother James had married Delia's sister, Rose. As a married man, and reliant on a small army disability pension, Terry set out to open his own store on Patrick Street.

In a highly-competitive market where shoemakers were among the main advertisers in Mullingar's local newspapers and in the midst of the War of Independence, it was a brave move.

By March 1920, he too was advertising his Patrick Street premises in local newspapers.

Judge had gambled he would be able to source funds from his old army regiment and in January 1921, he wrote to the Irish Guards seeking a contribution to help him establish his own business. The matter was referred to the local War Pensions Advisory Committee in Mullingar.

However, as his disability did not prevent him from resuming his pre-war trade, he was not eligible for the main source of resettlement grants for ex-soldiers. Instead, he was advised by the local committee to lodge an application for a grant to buy tools. This was sent to the then Ministry for Labour and was rejected after six months of consideration.

An ad from the Westmeath Examiner.

After persistent recommendations from the local war advisory committee, Judge was finally given two grants totalling £15 from Irish Guards regimental funds. These grants, the first of £5 and the second of £10, enabled him to purchase leather to establish the store.

However, the business faded away during the mid to late-1920s leaving Terry and his wife to contemplate emigration.

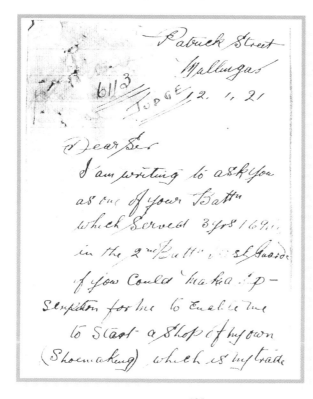

Terry Judge's initial letter to the Irish Guards seeking funds.

Back on the field of play

In the midst of attempting to build a business, Judge recovered his energy and passion for sport and helped his beloved Mullingar in the 1922/23 Leinster Junior Cup campaign

Athlone had won the Leinster Junior Cup the previous season, a victory that helped propel them into the League of Ireland. Their fellow Westmeath side, Mullingar, were also serious contenders for the prize during the later years of the 1920s. In fact, Mullingar reached the semi-final in five successive years, losing two finals on the trot, before eventually capturing the elusive silverware in 1926/27.

By that stage, Judge's football career was in abeyance, but when the five-year pursuit began in 1922/23, he was at the core of the Mullingar side, featuring in the lynchpin centre-half position. It was an involvement that probably eventually brought him to Athlone's notice at the end of that same season.

During that campaign, he had rapidly established a reputation as one of the finest half-backs in the junior leagues.

Judge had featured in two Midland League sides which played challenges against Dublin Junior selections in Clara and Mullingar in March and April 1923.

And it was probably in these contests that he came to the notice of the Leinster selectors who included him in the side for a junior interprovincial against Connacht in Sligo on May 20th, 1923.

It was a signal honour as Leinster in those days simply meant Dublin. For a player featuring in the Midlands with lowly Mullingar to be plucked from such obscurity ahead of the Dublin junior players, meant that he possessed a special talent.

Similarly, football in Connacht was confined to the Sligo District and so it was a team solely composed of players from Sligo clubs which represented the western province. For the record, Leinster won 2-1.

John Joe Dykes, the most talented product of the town in the shade of Ben Bulben, was unavailable for Sligo, having played the Shield final in Dublin with Athlone against Shelbourne the previous day – although a young relative Freddie Dykes did feature. Also among the Sligo eleven was Anthony 'Gully' McKenna, who would also line up with Athlone later in the 20s.

The presence of such a promising half-back just 25 miles away would have surely stimulated Athlone's interest come the start of the 1923/24 campaign the following September.

And if Athlone's sources didn't register Judge's ability, Jimmy Hope, Mullingar's other footballing son, would surely have brought him to their attention.

Their playing days together dated back as far as 1913 when both featured with Mullingar St Mary's in the Irish Junior Cup; Hope in his customary full-back position alongside one of the other Judge brothers, with the youthful Terry at inside-left. And the duo had more recent shared history as both played for Mullingar, alongside Athlone native Martin Harkins, against leading Athlone junior side St Patrick's in the 1922/23 FAI Cup qualifying competition.

Mullingar had beaten Clara in the first round and then saw off a St Pat's side featuring Tommy Muldoon and Barney Connaughton after a replay. They then lost out at the final qualifying stage to Sligo Celtic, who proceeded to the first round of the Free State Cup proper.

Of course, Athlone Town, as a league club, went straight into the hat for the first round proper but were knocked out by Shamrock Rovers, in a game in which the ineligible Jimmy Hope didn't feature but the equally ineligible Muldoon did.

Stepping up a grade

The Leinster Junior Cup campaign was the main focus of the Mullingar football year. As we have seen, Mullingar reached the last four of that competition in the following season, 1923/24, but were knocked out by Chapelizod.

The defeat at the semi-final stage had a silver lining for Athlone as it freed up Judge to pull on the blue of Athlone Town again.

For his native Mullingar Terry Judge filled the centre-half berth but for Athlone, he was to slot in at right half-back. Like so many of the final components of Athlone's cup-winning side, Judge fell into place by accident.

Although Athlone were only in their second season in the league, the fortnightly journeys to Dublin during the 1923/24 campaign had already become a serious impediment to their progress.

The frequent voyages placed inordinate pressure on the club's finances but also tended to demotivate players.

A run of four away games in five during the dark and dreary months of October and November was always likely to be a source of aggravation for the club. It was in the fourth game away to Dublin side Pioneers that the cracks began to show – with Athlone forced to call up volunteers from their supporters to make up the numbers. It's no coincidence then that Terry Judge made his debut for Athlone in the very next fixture – an away trip to Shelbourne – as Athlone began to cast around for players to supplement their obviously meagre playing resources.

Judge was only a bit-part performer for the remainder of the league campaign and didn't really nail down his place in the side until the cup quarter-final against Shelbourne. He was to retain the right-half berth for the rest of the cup campaign, climaxing on that famous occasion in Dalymount Park on March 17th, 1924.

For an ex-solider, called into service for a specific campaign, this was mission accomplished.

An enthusiastic player

Due to the logistical difficulties the league provided, Athlone had always earmarked the cup as their target – and having attained their objective so quickly after their arrival on the scene, the following league campaign of 1924/25 was always going to prove a difficult challenge.

But Judge was an enthusiastic recruit and when some of the others displayed less commitment to the cause, the Mullingar man was a virtual ever-present during that season.

Standing over 5ft 10 inches in height, Judge was slim with dark hair and hazel eyes. Although the vast majority of his games for Athlone were at right-half, his height enabled him to fill in at centre-half and he even occasionally played at right-full.

His style of play was energetic, enthusiastic and whole-hearted and that approach was reflected in the manner of his involvement with both Athlone and Mullingar.

The jaundiced analyst who had compiled his assessment of the various 1924 players years later remarked of Judge: "What he lacked in skill, he made up for in energy."

During that 1924/25 season, Judge also featured with his native Mullingar in the Leinster Senior League.

Despite having won the ultimate prize in cup football in the State with Athlone the previous year, Judge's ties with Mullingar remained strong and it was in the amber and green of the North Westmeath team that he played in the FAI Junior Cup that season.

Athlone had stressed their focus was mainly on retaining the FAI Cup that year and Judge was ever present in the half-back line during their quest, which ended at the semi-final stage against Shelbourne.

The following year saw Judge again registered with Athlone, but his appearances were limited to just one or two league games at the start of the campaign.

1925/26.

An injury in a league game against Jacobs in September 1925 may have ruled him out of contention for the rest of the season. Judge's career with Athlone was all but ended.

However, he did answer the call on one further occasion in the 1927/28 season lining out in a 5-2 defeat to Brideville in the Ranelagh Grounds.

In a strangely neat twist, Judge's last appearance for Athlone on September 3rd, 1927, like his debut some four years previously, was necessitated by one of the club's lowest ebbs.

In 1923, Judge had first pulled on the Athlone colours a week after an incident in which the team had been badly short of players.

Now his final appearance in 1927 immediately followed Athlone's worst league defeat in their history – a 9-1 thrashing away to Shelbourne.

Having been recalled from oblivion for the game against Brideville, he faded back out of the reckoning soon after.

The emigrant ship

Judge slipped quietly away on the emigrant boat to New York in early 1928. A short note in the Westmeath Independent of February 4th, 1928, marked his departure.

"Mr Terence Judge who played with Athlone Town when they won the Free State Cup a few years ago left for New York on Thursday morning to the regret of his many friends."

Judge was one of an avalanche of young Irish men and women seeking to flee these shores in search of a better life. His local paper the Westmeath Examiner reported in April 1928 that 1,100 emigrants had left on the boats from Cobh to the United States the previous Saturday.

"They were from all parts of the Free State. Most of them are lost to Ireland forever. The tide of emigration is as full as it has been here for many years. In fact, it is on the increase."

By 1930, Judge was living in Queens area of New York with his wife Delia. He was working as an elevator conductor.

He died in December 1963, some eleven years before his wife, who passed away in May 1974.

Distant family relatives, descendant from his only sister, remain in Mullingar today but have no memory of Terry Judge himself and few of his brothers who stayed on in the town

Judge himself never set foot in Ireland again. However his surviving grandnieces recall a visit by his only child, probably also called Terry, to the town in the 1960s.

The whereabouts of his direct family ancestors in America, if indeed there are any, are unknown, as indeed is the location of his precious FAI Cup medal.

Chapter 12

FAI Cup quarter-final

Entering the lions' den

Personnel changes

Two weeks after the victory over Midland Athletic, Athlone travelled to Shelbourne Park in Ringsend to take on the home side, Shelbourne. The team that took to the field on Saturday, January 19th, 1924, showed three changes in personnel from the side which had seen off the Railwaymen in the previous round.

With Paddy Flannery missing from the right-half berth, due to the knee injury received a fortnight previously against Midland Athletic, and Muldoon absent, a major reshuffle of the half-back line was required.

Jim Sweeney, who had switched between centre-forward and centre-half for much of his career, was a natural choice to fill one of the vacant defensive spots. He was selected at left-half. On the other wing, Lyster had filled in for Flannery in the previous week's Leinster Senior Cup game against St Paul's.

However, for the cup clash with Shelbourne, it was Mullingar native Terry Judge, who took the right-half jersey. Judge had played with his local club Mullingar in the Leinster Junior Cup final the same day Athlone played Midland Athletic.

With Sweeney missing from the front line, Tommy Collins stepped in as the leader of the attack. Frank Ghent moved from outside-left to inside-left to replace Collins, leaving a vacancy at top of the left. Bizarrely, the selection committee opted for the experienced Jim Kennedy.

Kennedy had last played with the team four months previously; but, in goal. The tall gangling player had a strong association with Athlone, stretching back as far as 1913 but in all those years had never played in any forward position.

Although primarily a goalkeeper, Kennedy had also seen service in the full-back and half-back lines. His selection as a forward, on the face of it, was a bolt from the blue.

An impossible task?

The reshuffle only served to compound what appeared an almost impossible task for Athlone as Shelbourne were generally regarded as unbeatable on their home turf. And the statistics showed why.

Earlier that season, Shelbourne had been pipped for the league title by Bohemians. However, in ten home league games, Shelbourne had never been beaten, winning nine and drawing just one (incidentally with Athlone). In the Shield, Shels were unbeaten at home in seven games, while the Ringsend side were later that year to win the Leinster Senior Cup, with four victories on home soil in the process.

Shelbourne's overall record at Shelbourne Park for the 1923/24 season excluding the cup match against Athlone read as follows: Played 21; Wins 18; Draws 3; Defeats 0.

Athlone, though, were not without confidence. After the game against St Paul's the previous weekend they had told Viator, the football correspondent with the newspaper Sport that they would beat Shelbourne. In fact, they had earmarked the cup as their source of silverware from the off, making no secret of the fact that it took priority over the league.

Nonetheless, the previews foresaw a Shelbourne win. Even Sport, which had championed Athlone's cup prospects, was now getting cold feet.

"It will be a gruelling experience for the Reds who must play with consummate coolness to win. Athlone will use every artifice to put them off their game, and they have the ability to put many teams off their game. Shels are not novices in the art of cup fighting, and when the occasion arises, they have shown before now that they can produce a blend of cup-fighting tactics and good football which in the long run is what will be required to overcome Athlone. Provided they infuse life into their movements, their superior football capacity should win them the day. But as already stated they may prepare themselves for a rare old buffeting."

The Evening Telegraph gauged the game as a case of craftsmanship versus speed and relentless endeavour.

The Freeman's Journal predicted a similar struggle but anticipated a Shelbourne victory on the basis the home side would be prepared for a tussle and would go all out from the off.

As it turned out, it was Athlone who stamped their style of play on the game from the first whistle. Over 5,000 were in attendance to witness Athlone's foot-perfect display of vigorous and speedy football.

It was a thrilling encounter, brimming with goalmouth incident and retaining the interest from start to finish. "A game which will be remembered for some time by those who saw it," the Dublin Evening Mail reported.

Shelbourne had a distinguished eleven. At centre-back was Val Harris, one of the most decorated players of his generation. He had played 20 times for Ireland and enjoyed a lengthy stint with Everton. He was captain of the first Dublin team, Shelbourne, to win the Irish Senior Cup in 1906 and also captain of the first Irish team to beat England in 1913. In later years, he coached Ireland and managed Shelbourne to a cup win in 1939.

A thrilling away victory

By 1924, Harris was 39-years-old and Athlone showed him no respect. Within the first minute, Frank Ghent had harried the centre-half out of possession and released Denis Hannon, who speared a rocket low drive just past the butt of the post.

It was a sensational opening and one which set the tone as Athlone harassed and harried the Shels players, while attacking at a break-neck pace when the opportunity arose.

In contrast, Shelbourne stuck to a short-passing game which played into their opponents hands, particularly in the heavy ground conditions.

It was the Midlanders who enjoyed the majority of chances for all but the final ten minutes of the opening half. They were helped by a facial injury sustained midway through by Shels right-half Mick Foley in a collision with Ghent.

Foley, another Irish international who had a decorated career cross-channel, was in a dazed condition and did not return to the field of play until 20 minutes after the interval. His absence left Shelbourne down to ten men for over 40 minutes.

To add to Shelbourne's woe, right-full Daly had failed to fully recover from an ankle injury sustained the previous weekend and was badly hampered throughout.

The elements conspired in Athlone's favour too with the strong wind undermining Shelbourne's more measured approach.

Athlone were ebullient and Collins, in his unaccustomed centre-forward role was creating havoc, heading just over from a corner before being taken out of it when clean through soon after.

Shelbourne too had their chances and Paddy O'Reilly, who was deemed to be man of the match by most judges, was at full stretch to tip over a goal-bound header from just under the angle of crossbar and post.

In the final ten minutes of the half, Shelbourne rallied and O'Reilly was called into action to foil what appeared to be goalbound efforts from Shels forwards Jock Simpson and Frank Rushe. And with Simpson striking the crossbar in the dying moments of the half, it appeared as if the tide was turning.

As Shels had a strong wind at their backs on the resumption, Athlone's failure to find the net while on top appeared fatal. But, again, it was Athlone who opened the better, with Collins, now operating at outside-right, after a switch with Connaughton, firing over. Shels came even closer to taking the lead when a Rushe effort skimmed the crossbar.

Then ten minutes into the second half, Athlone forced the vital opener.

The move began when Judge released Hannon down the inside-right channel and he switched the point of attack allowing left-winger Kennedy to swoop inside the stricken Daly and drive home a rising shot past the stranded keeper. It was one of the few contributions the out-of-position Kennedy was to make to the victory.

Athlone, though, didn't attempt to sit on their lead and there were chances at both ends in a thrilling encounter. O'Reilly scrambled low to block a Harris piledriver at the foot of the post soon after Foley had reappeared.

Although Shels were now restored to the full complement of players, the game was practically put beyond their reach on 70 minutes when Ghent received a pass near the half-way line and outpaced the Shels defence before beating the keeper from 18 yards.

Shels piled on the pressure in a valiant attempt to recover the game but O'Reilly produced a goal-keeping masterclass, calmly gathering everything directed at his goal.

The home side forced umpteen corners but also found Monahan and Hope in typically resilient form. And when Monahan conceded a penalty in the final quarter, O'Reilly watched as Paul O'Brien drove the spot kick well wide of the posts.

Boosted by the let-off, Athlone went back on the attack and Jim Kennedy should have added a second after being fed by Ghent but struck the post.

A litany of heroes

SURPRISE FOR SHELBOURNE
Athlone's Brilliant Performance at Ringsend

Post-match plaudits were concentrated on O'Reilly whose goal-keeping was described as masterly and absolutely great. One paper gushed: "His was undoubtedly the best exhibition of goalkeeping seen in Dublin this season."

Dykes was the pick of the defence, ably assisted by Hope and Monahan and, in the second half, Sweeney. Ghent too was described as the best forward on view, his turn of foot constantly troubling a one-paced Shels rearguard, while Hannon's energetic contribution was also noted.

Tactically, Athlone's bustling style of play had won the day - and Sport censured Shels for failing to blend their passing game with cup-tie tactics.

Viator had rediscovered his faith in Athlone and now tipped them to go all the way.

"On Saturday's play, Athlone would beat any of the city clubs left in. They are, without a doubt, the best cup fighters, whatever else they may or may not be in the country.

"This may sound rank heresy to those pure blind followers of some of our city clubs, but the fact is that the style of play by the best of the latter contrasted with what Athlone, for instance, can show would put donkey's years on one."

It remained the case, though, that Athlone's attacking prowess was entirely dependent on moments of individual skill and enterprise. Teamwork and combination play were absent up front. However, in contrast to Shels' "easy-going short-passing tactics", Athlone's dashing style of play easily won over.

Elsewhere on the same day, Bray Unknowns conceded home advantage and opted instead to play their quarter-final against Bohemians at Dalymount Park, rather than their home ground of Woodbrook.

The decision was obviously made to help maximise their share of the gate revenue. Despite the disadvantage, the Leinster Senior League side put up a brave performance. In what was a poor game, marred by treacherous weather conditions, Bray made the league champions fight all the way to secure a narrow victory courtesy of the only goal of the game.

The heavy rain was sufficient to force the postponement of the third quarter-final between Jacobs and Fordsons, which had been due to be played on Sunday, January 20th, the day after Athlone's defeat of Shelbourne. Fordsons too had been sounding confident notes from their Cork base. A representative of the club told Sport at Christmas that if Shels and Bohs represented the best of the Dublin clubs, the cup was as good as won by the Cork club.

When the teams did meet on Sunday, January 27th, the Munster men justified their confidence with an impressive display. A goal in each half from left-winger Denis Collins ensured a 2-0 victory, although they also required two full-length saves from their international keeper Willie O'Hagan to see off the Dublin side. After the game, their captain Harry Buckle sounded out a defiant message to the remaining clubs left in the cup: "The team that beats us will have to play."

The fourth quarter-final did not take place until Sunday, February 17th, the day after Athlone's semi-final.

Another Dublin voyage

In the meantime, the draw for the semi-finals of the cup had thrown up the following ties: Fordsons V. Clifton or Shelbourne Utd/or St James's Gate; Bohemians V. Athlone.

For Athlone, it was a draw which pitted them against their closest friends in League of Ireland football. Bohemians had helped to foster the game in

Athlone by regular pilgrimages over the years. During the late 1910s and early 1920s, a Bohemian eleven paid an annual St Patrick's Day visit to Athlone.

The Dalymount Park club were always warmly welcomed to Athlone – and the long list of Athlonians that paid loyal service to the Dublin side only ensured the fraternal relations were reciprocated.

The draw, coincidentally or not, averted a major crisis, after Bohemians had dropped a bombshell days before by indicating their refusal to travel to Cork if drawn away to Fordsons. Such a high-handed move would be inconceivable in modern times but only served to underline the developing nature of football administration in the country.

Meanwhile, St James's Gate had been waiting patiently to re-enter the cup fray since their first-round tie on January 5th.

When the interminable Munster qualifying competition had finally resolved itself, Shelbourne Utd emerged as their opponents. A sizeable attendance of up to 6,000 turned out in Dolphin's Barn, knowing the prize of a trip into the unknown to Fordsons' Cork home awaited the victors.

Gate were slow off the blocks and found themselves one down early on, but two replies, both before half-time, ensured victory. Shelbourne Utd had numerous second-half chances to secure an equaliser and a deserved draw, but left their collective shooting boots at home.

The victory consigned St James's Gate to a trip to Fordsons on March 2nd, with a place in the 1923/24 FAI Cup final at stake.

The semi-final line up was now complete and left open the tantalising possibility of an all-provincial final between Athlone and Fordsons.

Chapter 13

Paddy O'Reilly

The life of Reilly

- *Five FAI Cup winners' medals*
- *Three Leinster Senior Cup winners' medals*
- *Three international caps*
- *Two representative appearances*
- *Two league titles*

Paddy O'Reilly

A decorated career

Of all those who filled the teamsheet for Athlone in the 1924 cup journey, it was Paddy O'Reilly who enjoyed the most subsequent success in domestic football.

For O'Reilly, the cup victory was the first of five FAI Cup medals he was to secure in a glittering career.

In an era when brute strength and swiftness in dispatching clearances was the accepted hallmark of goalkeepers, O'Reilly was before his time. Instead, he was marked out by his agility and cat-like reflexes.

That natural ability was undermined, though, by a tendency to worry and a lack of self-confidence which left him prone to nervous displays.

Nonetheless, his contribution to the Athlone cup win of 1924 would be difficult to exaggerate. In fact, he was particularly proud of his feat of not conceding a goal en route to cup glory. It was an achievement that would not be repeated for another 34 years.

After his first cup success with Athlone, O'Reilly departed soon after to Shamrock Rovers, with whom he added another cup medal the following year, becoming the first player to win the cup in successive seasons. He added three more winners' medals for Rovers in 1929, 1930 and 1931, and was on the losing side in the 1926 final.

Athlone's cup triumph also catapulted O'Reilly onto the international scene and he won three caps during Ireland's memorable Olympic adventure that summer.

The path less travelled

A Dubliner, O'Reilly's first port of call was Pioneers, a side he served from the early 1920s.

He was snapped up by Athlone ahead of the 1923/24 season, on the back of two penalty saves for Pioneers against the Town in a Shield game at the end of the previous season.

Indeed, throughout his career he had an uncanny ability to stop penalties.

It's likely that he made his debut for Athlone in the third match of the 1923/24 season, away to St James's Gate. However, it was not until later in that league campaign that he became a fixture between the posts.

In fact, in total, he probably only played between 25 and 30 games for Athlone but his contribution was, nonetheless, critical to Athlone's cup success.

According to the Westmeath Independent, Athlone could have won the league campaign that season but "for the fact of being fatally handicapped by not having their invincible, brilliant, outstanding goal-keeper – their idol and talisman – Paddy O'Reilly".

During the cup run, his displays against Shelbourne and Bohemians were top class and he also produced crucial saves in the final against Fordsons. Indeed, his penalty save from Bohemians' Dave Roberts in the first semi-final was vital while his display against Shelbourne was "masterly" in the eyes of some commentators.

Over the entire cup campaign, it's arguable that O'Reilly was Athlone's best player.

His eligibility for the Olympics indicates that he served as an amateur with Athlone and it was not until someway through his career with Shamrock Rovers that he turned professional.

And it was probably his performances on Olympic duty in Paris, in the wake of his cup heroics for Athlone, that secured him a move to the Hoops and back to his home city.

Hoop Dreams

His decision to link up with Shamrock Rovers brought his career to an altogether higher level. Within a year, he was back in Dalymount Park on St Patrick's Day becoming the first player to win two FAI Cup medals.

Rovers overcame Shelbourne by 2-1 in the final – after the latter had knocked then holders Athlone out in the previous round.

The first season was undoubtedly the highlight – with Rovers winning the treble of league, cup and shield, without defeat.

O'Reilly was a fixture during this glorious run of 31 unbeaten games. The stunning success prompted O'Reilly to sign up as a professional in March 1925.

The Shamrock Rovers side which won the treble in 1924/25 with O'Reilly third from left in back row.

But the following 1925/26 season was something of an anti-climax for the Hoops who turned from bride to bridesmaid.

There were question marks over O'Reilly's goalkeeping with occasional hints during the season that his place was in jeopardy.

With the race for the league title going down to the wire, O'Reilly saved a penalty in a key clash with Fordsons, but it wasn't enough to take the crown from Shelbourne.

The art of penalty-saving was one he had clearly mastered and he again ruled the roost in the FAI Cup semi-final against Jacobs, denying the Biscuitmen from the spot.

Rovers finished second in both the league and shield and were thwarted in their attempt at winning two FAI Cup finals in a row by Fordsons. For O'Reilly, it meant he missed out, for now, on adding a third successive cup winners' medal to his trophy board.

1926/27

A number of reports towards the end of the 1925/26 fixture list appeared to suggest that he would be with Drumcondra come the start of the new season. These rumours served to highlight that O'Reilly was not necessarily flavour of the month with the Hoops.

Although he started the 1926/27 campaign as first-choice netminder, he soon lost his place to Charlie O'Callaghan. During this period, he missed out on the official opening of Milltown, Shamrock Rovers' famous former ground.

O'Reilly returned to the fray after his replacement hurt his thumb but then found himself out of action over Christmas though injury. However, he regained his place when a third stand-in keeper failed to impress.

The season ended with O'Reilly collecting another league title as Rovers went through the 18-match schedule unbeaten. Shield and Leinster Senior Cup winners' medals completed another fantastic campaign.

1927/28 + 1928/29

By the following season, he had regained his old panache and was deemed to be in brilliant form by the newspaper Sport. His resurgence was recognised in March 1928 in his selection for a representative match against the Irish League in Dublin.

"O'Reilly is showing greater confidence now, has improved a lot of late and is the most agile of all of our custodians," Sport declared.

Unfortunately, by the end of the season, another shaky spell had once again left his future uncertain. In fact, throughout his career, O'Reilly was afflicted by regular periods of nervousness, during which his goal-keeping confidence deserted him.

Sport reported in August 1928 that O'Reilly was one of only two players from the previous year's Rovers' squad who had not been retained.

A few weeks into the season, the same paper remarked on O'Reilly's continued presence with Rovers. It explained he might not have been signed, but for a lapse in form of his rival for the number one jersey.

In October 1928, O'Reilly secured further representative honours when he lined out with the Free State League against the Welsh League in Dalymount Park. In a 3-3 draw, Sport said O'Reilly was very good and "saved a couple of shots by his wonderful agility that hardly any of our other goalies would have got to".

That 1928/29 season saw O'Reilly win his third FAI Cup winners' medal. This victory was the first in a three-in-a-row for O'Reilly and the start of an amazing sequence of five cup wins on the trot for the club. However, that fragile self-confidence was again remarked upon, with the Irish Independent describing his performance in the first game of a replayed cup final as "nervous but good".

Rovers overcame Bohemians after a replay and were also forced to play two games before sealing the Leinster Senior Cup with victory over Dundalk.

1929 onwards

O'Reilly repeated the FAI Cup and Leinster Senior Cup double with the Hoops the next season. And in 1930/31, his last season with Shamrock Rovers, he completed a hat-trick of successive FAI Cup medals.

This time, though, he missed out on much of the campaign through injury, including the cup final against Dundalk.

Billy Behan, who was later a famous Irish-based Manchester Utd scout, took his place, but performed poorly (the occasion proving too much for him, according to the Irish Independent).

When the decider went to a replay, O'Reilly, back from injury, was reinstated for the 1-0 victory. It was O'Reilly's last heyday with the Hoops. He missed out on much of the following campaign, before appearing in the colours of St James's Gate towards the end of the league.

He guarded the nets for the Brewery side the following season, before then dropping out of league football.

O'Reilly later featured with Drumcondra in the Leinster Senior League, turning out until at least the 1935/36 season.

In later years, O'Reilly worked in the technician's section of the Post and Telegraphs and as a church sacristan on the southside of Dublin.

A gentle, quiet and unassuming man, O'Reilly freely earned the respect of his footballing peers during a decorated career.

A six-month spell with Athlone had been the catalyst for an improvement in his fortunes and acted as a launch pad for a highly-successful club career.

Paddy O'Reilly's family continue to reside on Dublin's southside.

Chapter 14

FAI Cup semi-final

A game of demonic intensity

Having seen off Shelbourne, one pillar of the old Dublin elite, Athlone were given the task of demolishing the entire edifice, when they were drawn to play Bohemians, the other historic Dublin club, in the semi-final.

Although the semi-final was nominally to be played on neutral territory, undoubtedly the choice of Dublin's Shelbourne Park would have suited Bohemians far more than it did Athlone, particularly with the considerably more onerous travel arrangements of the 1920s.

Dalymount Park was the traditional venue for showcase games but was ruled out on this occasion due to the presence of Bohemians in the semi-final. It meant elaborate arrangements were required in an effort to adapt Shelbourne Park to accommodate the massive crowds expected.

Chief among those was the provision of touchline seats all around the ground. New turnstiles and gates were also constructed in the week leading up to the contest, while Shelbourne players and officials were also engaged to assist in stewarding the expected throngs.

Charabancs (a type of motor coach, often open-topped, which were used for works outings) were organised to link O'Connell Street to the ground before and after the match. A special tram service was also arranged from Nelson's Pillar to add to the regular services which came near the ground.

The upgrading was entirely necessary as a sizeable crowd of 11,000, a then record for an FAI Cup semi-final, thronged the ground. Despite the numbers, the match passed off successfully, proving, according to the Evening Herald that, with more temporary accommodation, Shelbourne Park was more than adequate for cup games.

Although Athlone's comprehensive dismissal of Shelbourne had left commentators loath to write them off, the consensus view of the Dublin papers was that Bohemians would prevail, albeit with the mandatory struggle over the valiant, but less talented, Athlone. The script was already written and in cold storage for the next day's match reports.

The Evening Herald warned that any side that defeated Shels on their home turf in the cup, and shared the spoils with them in the league, must be treated seriously. But it predicted: "Considering that the Bohemians are the better balanced and more methodical side, I see no reason why they should not follow up their double league success, though the margin in their favour will be small."

The Evening Mail also pointed to Bohemians' two wins over Athlone in the league that season.

The choice of the Dalymount Park side as favourites was unsurprising given that Bohemians were the league champions for the 1923/24 season, having been crowned the previous December. Later that season they would also win the Shield.

The Evening Telegraph bucked the trend, and predicted that if O'Reilly could repeat his goalkeeping heroics against Shels, Athlone could spring a surprise. It cited Athlone's advantage in physical strength and stamina as the key factor.

Both teams nominally had a fortnight's rest from competitive action as all games had been cancelled the previous weekend to facilitate the first inter-league match between the Welsh League and the new Free State League. However, with four Bohs players included in the representative eleven, Athlone may have had the advantage in this regard. This was an historic encounter, the first time the fledgling Free State League had been given any form of recognition.

The Welsh League had long participated in an annual fixture with the old IFA. However, in a fit of pique in response to news of the inter-league clash in Dublin, the IFA cancelled all future arrangements with the Welsh.

The game in Dalymount Park attracted much attention, providing as it did the first opportunity for the new league to test its mettle against outside forces. The occasion was also greeted with real interest by football supporters. Letters poured into the newspapers analysing the selected side, which had been announced over two weeks prior to the game.

Disappointment with the team chosen was widespread, so much so that the editor of the Evening Herald was eventually forced to bring a halt to the stream of correspondence. The main criticism was that selectors had wallowed in sentimentality by including a number of veterans long since past their best.

Athlone's growing status in the game was reflected in almost universal calls from the letter writers for the inclusion of John Joe Dykes at centre-half, while Jim Sweeney also had his supporters. The criticism surrounding the choice of certain players was only part of the problem. There was also an unpopular reaction to the decision to select eleven Dublin-based players representing just four clubs.

When the controversy died down, the game itself played in front of a significant crowd of some 15,000, ended in a 3-3 draw.

The attendance the following week in Shelbourne Park for the Bohemians V. Athlone clash was also sizeable, indicating the eagerness with which the tie was anticipated.

Athlone, on their visits to play Dublin teams, were often taken to the hearts of supporters of rival capital outfits.

And the Bohemians game was notable for the presence of a huge Up the Blues flag exhibited by the Shelbourne team in support of Athlone. Local rivalry with Bohemians and a desire to see their conquerors in the last round progress were probably equal motivations for the flag.

Athlone lined out as follows: O'Reilly, Monahan, Hope, Judge, Dykes, Muldoon, Connaughton, Hannon, Sweeney, Collins, Ghent.

The actual team involved one change in personnel from that selected prior to the contest with Judge joining the eleven instead of Flannery. According to the preselected side, Hannon was due to play at right-half, Flannery at left-half and Muldoon at inside-right.

It's likely that Flannery still hadn't shaken off the effects of a knee injury sustained against Midland Athletic. His unavailability meant Muldoon was switched back to left-half. Hannon reverted to his traditional inside-right berth, allowing Judge, who had impressed against Shelbourne in the previous round, to retain his right-half berth.

After the thrilling encounter with Shelbourne in the previous round, it was probably too much to expect a repeat. Indeed, Athlone, if anything, over-exaggerated their bustling tactics, to such an extent that they were accused by many of ruining the game as a spectacle.

Kick and rush was the favoured style of play with Athlone spraying the ball in all directions in an attempt, successful as it transpired, to put the more cultured Bohemians off their game. According to the Freeman's Journal, the wilder they played, the wilder became the work of Bohemians.

Physical strength was another integral part of Athlone's gameplan and they managed to lure their more skilled opponents into a battle of muscle.

"Bohs should have resisted all temptations to give as much as they got in the matter of being knocked about," said the Evening Telegraph.

Although cultured football was at a premium, the high-tempo, pressurised game which Athlone adopted ensured a high degree of excitement.

"Easily the liveliest game of the season," Sport declared – in contrast to its colleagues.

Granted it ebbed and flowed with play proceeding at a fast and furious pace throughout but quality football was conspicuously absent, with the ball spending lengthy periods in the air and out of play.

All in all, it was a game for the passionate partisan and not the disinterested neutral.

The Westmeath Independent reported: "The play itself could not be classed as finesse, but it was, oh yes it was, typical cup-tie football with not an uninteresting moment or slackness of pressure from beginning to end."

Pictured prior to the semi-final against Bohemians in Shelbourne Park were back row (players only), from left: Denis Hannon, John Joe Dykes, Terry Judge, Paddy O'Reilly, Joe Monahan and Jimmy Hope. Front row (from left): Barney Connaughton, Tommy Muldoon, Jim Sweeney, Tommy Collins, Frank Ghent. This picture adorned the walls of the Royal Hoey Hotel for many years. It was mistakenly described as the cup final winning team.

Both sides fought demonically for the breakthrough in a frantic game played with relentless intensity. And although there were a few heart-stopping goalmouth incidents, there was nothing like the volume of thrills which kept the crowd on the very edge of their seats in the previous round against Shelbourne.

Athlone again attempted to set out their stall from the start and Tommy Collins produced a stinging shot early on which the Bohemians' keeper did well to block. Bohemians' main danger man in the opening half was their outside-left Mick O'Kane, who produced a series of dangerous crosses.

Keogh, the Bohemians' netminder, also displayed his bravery, blocking at the feet of the in-rushing Jim Sweeney after clever combination work between Frank Ghent and Collins had unhinged the Bohemians defence. The collision left both Keogh and Sweeney momentarily injured.

Jim Sweeney heads clear.

Eventually, Bohemians got to grips with the rushing tactics of the Athlone forwards and began to put together a few passing movements of their own.

O'Kane had their clearest chance of the half, but lifted over the crossbar, with only O'Reilly to beat, from a position which the Sunday Independent declared was "palpably offside".

Possession was evenly shared but a weakness at Athlone's outside-right, where Barney Connaughton featured, spoiled many movements. Connaughton was later to forge out a stellar career with Athlone as a defender, but his performance as a winger in the semi-final prompted subsequent calls for his replacement.

Towards the close of the half, Athlone again enjoyed the better of the fray and Jim Sweeney did find the net with a fast daisy-cutter, only to have the effort ruled out for offside. The decision infuriated the Westmeath Independent which declared afterwards that Athlone would have won but for the failure of the referee to carry out his duties in an impartial manner.

Five minutes before the interval, Bohemians lost the service of their right-back Bertie Kerr, who had his jaw broken and lost teeth in a collision with Sweeney. However, despite the numerical disadvantage, it was Bohemians who played much the better after the interval and enjoyed the upper hand.

O'Reilly was again needed to come to Athlone's rescue, turning away efforts from Harry Willets and Christy Robinson. At the other end, early in the final quarter, former Aston Villa amateur Dave Roberts, who had represented the new League the previous week against the Welsh League, was denied from the penalty spot by O'Reilly. The save was greeted with a deafening roar by the crowd.

In the final ten minutes, Athlone again took the initiative and only brilliant work from Keogh prevented Sweeney from scoring with a close-range drive. The keeper also twice came to Bohemians' rescue in a goalmouth scramble following a Muldoon corner.

Despite putting Bohemians to the pin of their collar to save the game, Athlone didn't receive the majority of the post-match plaudits. Instead the Dublin club's achievement of remaining in touch, whilst playing with ten men for the majority of the second half, earned them the credit. Nonetheless, a draw was generally perceived as a fair result in the circumstances.

Bohemians' wide men had provided a string of crosses throughout the match, but the failure of their inside men to capitalise was a significant factor in their inability to close out the game. It was a defect they were to attempt to remedy for the replay.

Although many commentators were openly critical of Athlone's style of play, they also grudgingly admitted it had been more than effective.

The Irish Times said the Athlone tactics were employed to such effect that "not only did they avert a defeat that seemed inevitable, but gave their rivals more than enough to do to save the match".

Athlone's prime spoiler was inside-right Denis Hannon, whose links with Bohemians stretched back to 1906, when he first pulled on the famous red and black stripes.

His return to Dalymount Park was a sub-plot of some interest, particularly as he was more than just a player with Athlone. In effect, he was their spiritual leader. Although technically gifted and a fine dribbler, Hannon had been the brain behind the unorthodox tactics employed in their cup run thus far.

As ever, he was everywhere on the field, helping out in defence when required and attempting to prod his fellow forwards into action when the opportunity arose.

However, Athlone's ragged attack generally disappointed; Sweeney, although prominent, played only in patches, while Ghent, admired as one of the best technicians in the Athlone side, was hard pressed to escape the attentions of his marker.

Connaughton, though, was the failure of the line, and without naming him the Westmeath Independent was in no doubt what was needed.

"Hannon, ubiquitous, was handicapped by not having a partner. If he had a good winger with him, the result would have been an outright win for Athlone. This solitary defect in the team must if possible be remedied before the replay."

Dykes and Judge were busily effective, mainly in defence, while Hope was the better of the full-backs, Monahan's tendency to boot the ball out of play at every opportunity came in for particular negative comment from some quarters. Muldoon, deemed the most cultured of the Athlone eleven, was the star performer, alongside the ever-reliable O'Reilly in goal.

The Westmeath Independent took comfort and pride from the wonderful appreciation shown to Athlone by the attendance.

"No matter how the replay goes, the 90 minutes' play on Saturday last will ever remain indelibly imprinted on those who were fortunate enough to be there."

It said the match had also convinced football fans of the idea that a provincial team was more than capable of holding its own against the top teams in Ireland.

The announcement some weeks previously of the visit by the Welsh League had been quickly followed by news that the famous Glasgow Celtic, then as enthusiastically supported in Ireland as now, were also to take on a Free State eleven.

That game took place on the Saturday following the cup semi-final draw, meaning the replay was instead scheduled for two weeks later, Saturday March 1st, again at Shelbourne Park.

The busy schedule meant that close on 50,000 people attended the Welsh League game, the and Glasgow Celtic friendly, or one of the three semi-finals,

Over £1,250 was taken in gate receipts for the two semi-final clashes between Athlone and Bohemians and the other semi-final between Fordsons and St James's Gate.

The cup revenues were divided in five between the FAI and the last four sides remaining. Athlone netted an estimated £250.

Athlone Town:
Paddy O'Reilly, Joe Monahan, Jimmy Hope, Terry Judge, John Joe Dykes, Tommy Muldoon, Barney Connaughton, Denis Hannon, Jim Sweeney, Tommy Collins and Frank Ghent.

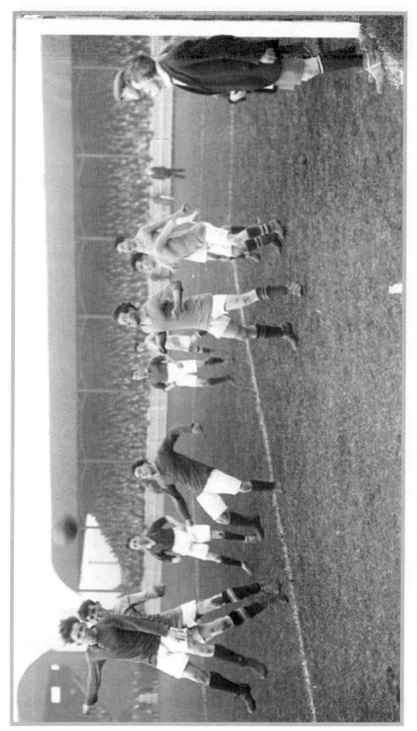

Action from the semi-final as a Bohemians player gets in front of Jim Sweeney to flash a header goalwards. Note position of referee at the near post.

Chapter 15

John Joe Dykes

Are there more at home as good as you?

John Joe Dykes on his wedding day.

A shooting star

Many of Athlone's players experienced a dizzying rise to prominence during the club's cup final success in 1924.

None more so than Sligo native John Joseph Dykes.

In January 1923, Dykes was performing quietly in a newly-developed junior scene in his home town – unknown but to the most astute football enthusiasts in the region.

Eighteen months later, he was at the pinnacle of his career captaining Ireland on foreign shores with a cup winner's medal safely secured back home.

Unfortunately, Dykes' career was to end in similarly rapid fashion. Eight months later, he was fortunate to escape with his life, although, his football career was effectively at an end.

A football family

Born in 1898 in Sligo, Dykes was soon to immerse himself in the reorganised football scene in Sligo, following the end of World War One.

In 1919 when football was administered across the island by the Belfast-based IFA, Sligo Rovers (not the current League of Ireland club which was not founded until 1928) reached the quarter-final of the Irish Junior Cup.

A young JJ Dykes was a key player at centre-half. His footballing prowess had, however, been recognised from a younger age. In the early 1910s, Dykes embarked on a visit to Scotland, with two uncles and a number of other relatives.

The group joined in a kickabout with some local Scottish adults who were astounded by the ability of the young Dykes, who was then no more than 14 or 15-years-old.

"Are there more at home as good as you?" the impressed Scots asked. They weren't to know that in later years Dykes was to prove that the correct answer would have been: "Very few".

A formal junior football league was only established in Sligo in May 1922 and it was not until early January 1923 that the name JJ Dykes became known to any degree outside Connacht. Within Sligo, though, by then the Dykes family name was deeply entrenched in football circles and remains so to this day.

One of his descendants, Kevin Dykes, was a former chairman of Sligo Rovers and another, Gavin, was the victorious captain of the club's treble-winning 1994 side, which took the FAI Cup, First Division trophy and Shield back to the Showgrounds.

Other members of the extended Dykes family have played with Sligo Rovers, Longford Town and Athlone Town. A relative, Freddy, won a League of Ireland championship medal with Sligo Rovers in 1936/37, a year after playing with Athlone Town.

Indeed, after Athlone Town's FAI Cup win in 1924, the newspaper Sport gave an intriguing insight into the extent of the Dykes family immersion in football.

"All the Dykes were always footballers and the family can boast of something which will take a lot of beating. It would be surprising if there is or ever was a parallel to it in the whole football world and it is this: At one time, not so very long ago, there was a soccer team in Sligo, to which the Athlone Dykes belonged and the name of every single player was Dykes. What do you think of that?"

He has no equal in the country

Just as Athlone had emerged from their regional qualifying competition to play in the FAI Cup proper the previous year, it was Sligo Celtic who came out on top in the Connacht district in 1922/23.

With Athlone having automatically qualified for the first round as a Free State League member, St Patrick's were left as the sole Athlone

A Sligo junior team from 1919. Dykes is extreme right in bottom row.

representatives in a competition which included seven teams from across Connacht and the Midlands.

After defeating Mullingar in the regional qualifying final, it was Sligo Celtic who qualified for the FAI Cup proper.

The victory paved a way for a visit to Dublin and an FAI Cup first-round clash with then League of Ireland outfit Dublin United. It was the first time in many years that a Sligo side had played in Dublin and the visit was eagerly anticipated by both the simply curious and the proselytisers alike, the latter hoping that Sligo's rise would help to spread the gospel of the new League of Ireland across the Shannon.

Sligo Celtic were real dark horses – but it was not only some anonymous Scottish football enthusiasts who were privy to the secret of the Westerners' star half-back John Joe Dykes.

The talent hidden west of the Shannon was also known to Athlone's Mr Football, Denis Hannon.

Previewing the cup clash, the Evening Telegraph said Sligo Celtic might not be able to reach Dublin for the game as train tracks were regularly being blown up during the ongoing Civil War.

"If they do come many will go to see them. I am told that one of their half-backs has no equal in the country. Denis Hannon raves about him."

As it was Sligo came, saw and very nearly conquered. 3-1 up at the interval thanks to goals from Dykes and Frank Tiernan (2) - who was also to subsequently feature with Athlone - Sligo succumbed to a second-half fightback from their hosts who did enough to secure a replay.

Sligo were unable to find a way past Dublin Utd in the scoreless rematch on home soil in the Showgrounds and were finally defeated in the second replay in Dublin by 3-1. Dykes again played a prominent part; his deflected shot found the net for Sligo's sole strike.

Whether Hannon made his way to Dublin to witness this new phenomenon isn't clear, but what is known is that within a month of Sligo Celtic's cup run coming to an end, JJ Dykes was playing with Athlone.

Joining Athlone

His debut for Athlone came in the league game against Shamrock Rovers in Milltown on February 17th, 1923. Alongside him in the Athlone line-out was fellow Sligo Celtic player, striker Frank Tiernan.

Details of Athlone's matches in this period are sketchy. However, three weeks later, both Sligo men appeared in another Athlone line-out, this time against Shelbourne in Ringsend

Dykes featured at full-back. Tiernan evidently didn't do enough to impress and his stint with Athlone was not extended but Dykes certainly did.

A week after the Shelbourne game, Athlone visited Sligo on St Patrick's Day for a friendly against the pick of the local junior sides.

Athlone's visit was described in one national newspaper as having a "missionary" purpose. But it may simply have been part of an agreement to sign Dykes – the equivalent of the more recent set of jerseys 'transfer fee'. Alternatively, Hannon, in the words of the Scots, may have been visiting Sligo to check whether there were more as good as Dykes.

Whatever the reason for the visit, Athlone were more than happy to accept Dykes into their ranks and he immediately settled into the side in the centre-half position.

Two months later, at the tail end of the 1922/23 campaign, he featured prominently in the Athlone side which reached the Shield final against Shelbourne.

Dykes received compliments for his performances against Shelbourne Utd in the semi-final and Shelbourne in the final, although the likes of Hannon, Muldoon and Ghent were the recipients of more extensive praise.

Having cemented his place in Athlone's ranks, John Joe Dykes had quickly acclimatised to senior football. He was beginning to vindicate his high reputation.

The pundits' favourite

The 1923/24 season saw John Joe rapidly improve as he clocked up more experience in the League of Ireland. A regular at centre-half from the opening league game of that season, Dykes also highlighted his ability to weigh in with goals, scoring at least three in the league campaign.

By late January, some nine months after he had made his debut for Athlone and after possibly less than ten appearances before the Dublin soccer public, Dykes had made such an impression that his omission from a League of Ireland selection to take on the Welsh League was heavily criticised by a flood of letter writers to the Evening Herald.

The Irish league team was chosen after Athlone's defeat of Shelbourne in the FAI Cup quarter-final in Dublin. The side was heavily biased towards veterans who had seen service in the old days of the IFA and the selectors were accused of sentimentality.

It was the first representative game in which the new league had participated and interest was at an all-time high, prompting close scrutiny of the chosen eleven.

Dykes was the most popular choice of the detractors, one of whom remarked: "I am not the only one who cannot understand why Dykes of Athlone was passed over. He certainly is the best centre-half we have, is young and by his masterful displays has won the admiration of many football enthusiasts both here and across channel."

Almost without exception the critics chose Dykes. Another letter writer said: "Having seen all the teams play I would unhesitatingly plump for Dykes as our best centre-half." The Evening Herald itself poured fuel on the fire by suggesting that Dykes' non-inclusion was "a first-class blunder".

The public support for Dykes was all the more surprising as it represented an implicit criticism of the centre-half chosen, Shelbourne veteran Val Harris, a sort of footballing institution who had been capped 20 times for Ireland under the old IFA.

And all of this public reaction was for a centre-half, Dykes, who had probably some 20 games in senior football under his belt.

A couple of weeks later, Athlone were still not represented on a new League of Ireland selection to play Glasgow Celtic in a friendly.

Considering by that stage that Athlone had held Bohemians to a draw in the first cup semi-final, the omission of Dykes and his colleagues could now only be interpreted as simply Dublin centrism.

A pivotal role in the cup success

Dykes was now a critical component of Athlone's team – and he duly played a key role in the progress to the 1924 cup final triumph, playing in four of the five games en route to the trophy.

Dykes deserves a large share of the credit for the fact the Athlone net was not breached in the 450 minutes of football during that cup-winning campaign. His most notable contribution was possibly in the quarter-final victory over Shelbourne, a game in which Athlone scored early and late and in between were subjected to periods of sustained pressure by the Dubliners.

Dykes was at the heart of the resistance. The Evening Mail said he was "a splendid pivot, powerful both in attack and defence".

In the drawn semi-final against Bohemians, Dykes was again a staunch defender for Athlone, although the frenetic atmosphere in which this game was played also seemed to have affected the centre-half. "Dykes got through a tremendous afternoon's work, but his passes were not always well-placed," said the Irish Independent.

For the replayed semi-final though, Athlone had to cope without their main defender, after Dykes missed his train from Sligo!

The centre-half was never the most reliable; he also failed to show at a trial for the Olympics Games later that summer; and also missed an international against USA due to injury.

However, the Sligo man was too crucial for Athlone to ignore and although a reshuffled team saw off the Bohs in the replay, Dykes was back for the final itself against Fordsons.

After that game, the hyperbolic analysis by an excitable local reporter read as follows: "Dykes is simply a marvel, versatile, brainy, powerful and accurate and admirably suited to the peculiar style of play which the Town adopt in cup-tie football." His inclusion in the team "infused abject terror into the hearts of his opponents".

To travel back and forth from Sligo to Athlone and, for away games, to Dublin, must have been a major chore and the Westmeath Independent noted that Athlone would never forget "the sacrifices so frequently and freely made by him".

On occasions, Dykes would often stay before or after a game with the Sweeneys in Castlemaine Street.

On the presentation platform after the cup final was football enthusiast Alex McCabe, a TD for Sligo, dressed in the blue of Athlone.

He was there to support Athlone and to offer congratulations to his fellow townsman, Dykes.

Dykes turned out the following weekend for a low-key Shield contest against Midland Athletic but may have been regretting his commitment when he sustained an injury which kept him out of the next few games.

That night, Dykes also missed a major ceremony to hail Athlone's cup heroes. What was quaintly known as "a smoking concert" was hosted by the Ancient Order of Foresters. His injury necessitated him staying in a Dublin hospital with team trainer George Gaylard, who was also chief ranger of the Foresters.

Dykes returned to the fray in the Leinster Senior Cup semi-final replay against Brideville less than three weeks later. It's likely he wasn't quite ready, though, as he was soon absent from the team again before making a second comeback against Shelbourne a month later in a Shield game.

Even still, the Westmeath Independent's comments that he wasn't his old self indicated the lingering effects of the injury had still not been shaken off.

Normally, games towards the latter end of the season were increasingly unimportant as it became a case of simply fulfilling fixture obligations. An injured player like Dykes would normally have been in no rush to return to the fold.

But this season, Dykes was in a race to ensure he was back to full fitness in time for the Olympic Games. He made the squad for Paris and lined out in the two competitive games against Bulgaria and Holland.

And he then had the distinction of captaining the side in a friendly international against Estonia in Paris, becoming Ireland's second captain.

Inter-league honours

By the start of the following season, Dykes was working in Athlone as a carpenter in Custume Barracks.

His reputation had been solidified by impressive performances in the Irish shirt.

Dykes, like many of his Athlone team-mates, was somewhat tardy in returning to the fray in 1925. His first appearance was in the third game of the league campaign.

His involvement was only intermittent during the 1924/25 league campaign but he was back at his customary centre-half berth for most of Athlone's attempt to regain the cup.

Dykes was in place for the quarter-final victory over Leinster Senior League side Drumcondra, before taking on Shelbourne in the semi-final in mid-February.

Dykes was Athlone's best player in a 4-0 defeat. He was "the most prominent figure" said the Evening Herald.

Having impressed in Paris, when the time for the second annual inter-league match against Wales came around, there was be no repeat of Dykes' controversial absence of the previous year. This time, he took the pivotal centre-half berth, alongside four players from Shamrock Rovers, two from Bohemians and Shels and one from St James's Gate and Fordsons.

Previewing the contest, the Evening Herald said Dykes was a player for the big occasion. "Dykes is big in every sense. Physically, he is well endowed for the position of pivot," the paper said. "He has not reached his best yet."

Although the League of Ireland lost 2-1 in front of 17,000 people in Dalymount Park on March 14th, 1925, the Evening Herald described Dykes as "the ablest defender" on the Irish team. However, it added: "He was of little use to those in front of him with passes that were far ahead of the forwards".

A dream dies

Dykes' performance, in the inter-league test, combined with the favourable impression he had given in Paris the previous summer, was enough to prompt the interest of Aston Villa. The Birmingham club, of course, had already secured Tommy Muldoon, another half-back from the victorious 1924 Cup team, on their books.

Two weekends later, Dykes tied up details with the Birmingham club. Apparently, a deal was agreed – and it's believed a house owned by the club was to be available to him for a period.

Villa had been attempting to secure his services for some time, it later emerged.

After the deal was struck, Dykes returned to work in Custume Barracks the next day, Monday, March 30th, 1925.

At about 12.30pm, Dykes was putting felt on the roof of a large storage shed, which contained planking, felting, old metal and debris while two army privates were engaged inside.

An Athlone labourer James Kearney was also working in the shed, having been employed by the army's engineering section as a carter.

Amidst this everyday scene, tragedy struck when a mine which had been abandoned in the shed from the days of the troubles exploded, claiming the lives of his three colleagues and leaving Dykes badly wounded.

Although there were no eye witnesses to the accident, it's believed Kearney may have inadvertently discharged the mine.

It had been encased in a two-foot long cylinder, which had a diameter of some nine inches. Both sides of the container were closed by a cap and held together by a bar inside.

The cylinder was left behind after the end of the Civil War and War of Independence and was deemed to be harmless – however, events that Monday revealed it to be a fully-charged mine.

Local anecdotes indicated the mine had been seized by the Free State military near Kilgarvan Bridge between Ballinahown and Athlone after one of a series of bombings on railway lines.

According to the Westmeath Independent one of the ends of the mine slackened, and Kearney, it would appear, had either by unscrewing the cap, or allowing it to make contact with the concrete floor, set off the explosion.

Kearney died instantly with his head and both legs below the knees blown off. Army privates Daniel Tighe from North Westmeath and Joseph Hoey from Tullamore, who were also working in the shed, also lost their lives. Hoey survived for five hours before passing away.

Dykes had a miraculous escape, having been sent hurtling some 30 yards through the air from the roof by the force of the explosion.

He told the Westmeath Independent: "All I know of the explosion is that I suddenly found myself on the ground a good distance from where I had been working. I thought my legs were blown off and stood up to see that it was not really the case."

The Irish Independent quoted him as saying: "I recovered sufficiently from the shock to be able to get up and look back with horror at what had happened."

It was a horrific scene with three fatalities, a mangled shed and contents strewn around the barracks yard. Half the roof was blown away but somehow Dykes lived to tell the tale.

His daughter Gretta recalled that the initial telegram from the military authorities was worded in such a way to lead her mother to believe John Joe had been killed in the explosion.

Such was the force of the blast that it was heard some considerable distance from Athlone, while maps on the walls of the former boys' national school beside St Mary's Church were blown off.

And while Dykes survived, his football career was effectively over; his dreams of joining Aston Villa blown away.

The aftermath

There were early indications that Dykes could make a full recovery.

By the start of the 1925/26 season, he was re-signed by Athlone and the newspaper Football Sports Weekly reported he had experienced "a wonderful improvement after the well-nigh tragic explosion".

However, both the physical and mental impact of the horrific explosion could not be wiped out that quickly as a court case subsequently indicated.

In November 1926, Dykes claimed compensation in the Circuit Court after his ordeal. The court heard that Dykes had been working in Sligo for some ten years, before his employment in Custume Barracks.

He had been conducting repair jobs throughout Athlone barracks and had been there for some three months, earning £4 a week. After the explosion, he was brought to the military hospital in Custume Barracks where he attended for six weeks before being sent to St Bricin's Hospital in Parkgate Street in Dublin.

Dykes remained as a patient there for some 13 to 14 weeks. He had sustained injuries to his hands and stomach and was suffering from shock. His feet were injured and he had been confined to bed for a month as he could not walk. His legs were also burned at the back, down to his calves.

The court heard he now had no movement from his right wrist down – and could not flex his fingers at all.

Since the accident, he had been paid 35 shillings a week, the maximum allowable under the Workmen's Compensation Act for those deemed to be totally incapacitated.

The military authorities then sought a report from a Sligo-based doctor and brought Dykes back to St Bricin's Hospital where he was examined and x-rayed. As a result, compensation was paid up to mid-September.

At that stage, the military authorities threatened to stop the compensation, but after Dykes had engaged a solicitor (his old teammate Denis Hannon) the payments continued. Meanwhile, a Sligo doctor told the court that Dykes' grip was very feeble, due to his injured wrist. He thought it problematical that Dykes could do any work. He also stressed that the patient was still suffering from nervous shock.

However, a Dublin specialist at St Bricin's Hospital, claimed that although Dykes could not move his wrist, movements were present in the wrist when manipulated. The specialist said Dykes had 75% reflexion and extension.

He believed Dykes was genuine when he could not move his wrist. The fact was possibly due to nervous fear.

The specialist said Dykes was fit for some work. He had a 60% capacity to work and with the removal of a bone at the back of his wrist, he would have full movement.

Judge Wakeley, in ruling, said his own medical assessor had indicated that Dykes was suffering from nervous stress.

"There was no doubt at all that Dykes was suffering from shock. He was a fine looking fellow and one could see by looking at him that he was still suffering from nervousness," the judge said.

The military authorities had claimed Dykes was not due compensation as he had only been in casual employment; and since September 19th was recovered from the accident and no longer incapacitated.

Ruling, Judge Wakeley said it was clear to anyone in court that Dykes right arm was injured and that his wrist was quite stiff.

His own assessor Dr Keelan had been unable to move Dykes' hand. "He did his best to do it but he could not. I think that Dykes is perfectly bona fide," the judge said.

Judge Wakeley said Dykes was at a terrible loss due to his decline in earnings, down from £4 a week to 35 shillings.

"This is a fearful loss. I am satisfied that this is a perfectly genuine case. I am surprised that he is not totally incapacitated. I do not know how he can work. He has never been brought up to do anything else except carpentry work."

He awarded Dykes 35 shillings a week and a lump sum of £14 and 10s for the eight weeks during which the payments had stopped.

Less than three years later the matter returned before the Circuit Court, with the army again seeking to have the compensation revised. This time, a full and final settlement of £750 was made to Dykes.

While undoubtedly a large sum, it was effectively equivalent to less than four years wages.

The short-lived comeback

Aged 32, Dykes did make a short-lived return to the playing fields with Sligo Rovers in the 1930/31 campaign.

Four-and-a-half years out of the game, Dykes returned in November 1930 to line out with Sligo in the Free State Qualifying Cup campaign against Dublin side Rossville.

He had featured in a practice game the week before but was thrust straight into the action, in the unusual position of centre-forward.

It was an interesting side, composed of three Athlone natives, Johnny McManus, Michael Dowling and Mick Henry. In its report of the game which Sligo Rovers lost 2-1, the Sligo Champion noted, charitably, after the game: "Dykes, good footballer as he is, would have been of greater assistance in the half-back division."

The Sligo Independent remarked that Dykes had "worked hard, but did not do justice to himself". It also said, promisingly, that Dykes was "not finished yet".

However, as a footballer, he pretty much was.

Family lore indicates that at some stage in his career he played with Bangor in Northern Ireland, but it's likely to have been earlier, possibly in the late 1910s or early 1920s. The Dykes family say he was once kidnapped at gunpoint at a Bangor game and forced to play Gaelic football in Casement Park the following day.

Unfortunately, as the Custume Barracks explosion would later testify, it was not the only occasion that weapons intervened in Dykes' career.

Over the years, Dykes was always welcomed back like the prodigal son to Athlone - with many tales of him being liberally refreshed by supporters on his pitstops in the town.

He retained a fond place in his heart for the Town too.

He died on June 25th, 1976, in Sligo General Hospital and despite the fact that it was over 51 years since he had lined out with Athlone Town, his death notice referred to him as being 'late of Athlone Town FC'.

His FAI Cup medal was stolen from the home of his daughter Gretta some seven or eight years ago in Sligo.

Chapter 16

FAI Cup semi-final replay

Another one bites the dust

Athlone Town would have needed little motivation ahead of the replay of their FAI Cup semi-final against Bohemians on March 1st. But if any extra inspiration was required, the sight of their stricken talismanic striker, John Sweeney, in the witness box in a Dublin court would surely have provided the extra incentive.

Sweeney had been badly wounded in a shooting incident in his family pub in October 1923. And five months later, an army officer, Lt John Joseph Cosgrave, was tried in connection with the incident.

The trial had commenced the week prior to the replay, and Cosgrave had been found guilty, on the day before the match, of a lesser charge of wounding John Sweeney. However, sentencing was adjourned to the following week, meaning the Athlone players, and, in particular, their captain Jim Sweeney, brother of John, had much to ponder ahead of the game.

A silent vow to overcome the Bohs in honour of the missing John Sweeney is likely to have passed many lips as they trotted out onto the Dalymount Park turf that March Saturday.

Teams reshuffled

The first Athlone V. Bohemians cup clash had been preceded by a storm of controversy over the absence of any Athlone players from the Free State XI which drew with their Welsh counterparts.

And despite Athlone holding their gloried opponents, the Free State XI selected to meet the famous Glasgow Celtic the following weekend was also devoid of Athlone representation.

The visit of the Bhoys meant Athlone's replay against Bohemians was fixed for the following week, March 1st.

The up-and-coming Fordsons were represented in the person of goalkeeper Bill O'Hagan, but the remainder of the side were again plucked from Dublin-based clubs. Bohemians' representation was reduced to a single player, full-back Jack McCarthy.

Glasgow Celtic triumphed easily by three clear goals against a very nervous Free State XI, in front of a crowd of 22,000 in Dalymount Park. Without any involvement in the Glasgow Celtic game, Athlone concentrated on their rematch with Bohemians and the club selectors announced their team in the week leading up to the game.

The preselected team was: O'Reilly, Hope, Monahan, Judge, Dykes, Flannery, Muldoon, Hannon, Jim Sweeney, Collins and Ghent.

The selectors had moved to alleviate the ineffectiveness of the right-wing which had been harshly highlighted in post-match comments following the original clash between the sides.

It was Muldoon, a player equally at home at left or right, who was selected instead of the unfortunate Barney Connaughton at outside-right. That may have been partially down to the renewed availability after injury of Scratch Flannery for the left-half berth. His return freed up Muldoon to fill the vacancy in attack.

Judge, after his impressive displays against Shelbourne and Bohemians, retained his right-half berth.

However, all the selectors' tinkering in the week leading up to the game came to naught on the morning of the match when news filtered through that John Joe Dykes had missed his train from his native Sligo. It forced Athlone into an eleventh-hour reshuffle.

Jim Sweeney was brought back to fill Dykes' vacancy at centre-half with Tommy Collins, as in the game against Shelbourne, filling in at centre-forward.

With no real left-wing players available to fill Collins' original inside-left berth – Jim Kennedy despite his goal against Shelbourne was obviously regarded only as a crisis option in attack – Flannery was the sole option.

His move from his pre-selected berth of left-half to inside-left, meant Muldoon returned to his natural left-half position and Lyster came in at outside-right.

The changes seemed set to undermine Athlone. Flannery and Lyster were press-ganged into a hotch-potch forward line, where Collins was playing out of position in the key centre-forward role. In defence, the absence of Dykes was also expected to be a major factor.

Bohemians too had made a number of changes as Bertie Kerr was unavailable following the injury sustained in the original game.

In a move designed to pep up their forward line, Ned Brooks was introduced for his first game of the season at centre-forward. Brooks was a highly-regarded attacker who had previously played with Shelbourne, Linfield and briefly cross-channel with Stockport County.

But his introduction came as somewhat of a surprise as he had been playing Gaelic football and had not featured with the Dalymount Park outfit that season. Brooks was later to spend two productive seasons with Athlone, writing his name into the club's history books in the process.

Lowering the Bohemians flag

Over 9,000 people braved Arctic weather conditions to witness the replayed semi-final, which was again held in Shelbourne Park. Much of the game was played in heavy snow showers, until a pallid wintry sun

BOHEMIANS' EXIT FROM CUP

Athlone's Great Victory in Semi-final Replay

shone towards the end of the encounter.

Athlone once again opened with all guns blazing and Frank Ghent was frustratingly thwarted by the referee's whistle in the opening minutes when clean through with only the Bohemians keeper to beat. His annoyance must only have been enhanced when it became clear that an injury to a Bohemians defender had necessitated the stoppage.

Athlone were quickly on the offensive again and Tommy Collins shot wide when presented with a clear-cut chance by Hannon soon after.

But the Midlanders did not have to wait long for the opening goal which arrived after just twelve minutes play. Norman Lyster fed Collins, who attempted to find space to shoot goalwards. His eventual effort was weakly hit, but full-back McCarthy and keeper Keogh both hesitated in the absence of proper communication. And when Keogh eventually attempted to gather the loose ball, Ghent, dashing in, got there first and flashed the leather to the net.

With Athlone's tenacious doggedness, the lead goal was always likely to prove crucial and the Westmeath Independent reported: "'The one goal dearly purchased and superbly accomplished was the winning effort. Athlone never looked back, nor was there any need to, for Ghent had sown the seed of victory, well merited, richly deserved, absolutely decisive and without a moment's warning."

Bohemians enjoyed the better of the remainder of the half, but found the Athlone defence in typically resolute mood. Buoyed by the goal, and with an advantage to defend with their lives, Athlone deployed extra resources at the back, with Hannon, as usual, assisting his defenders.

Despite this rearguard action, O'Reilly, in goal, was still summoned to save a number of stiff shots. In particular, he had to be vigilant to prevent a low Brooks effort from finding the net.

Athlone also threatened on the break courtesy of the pace of Ghent, who forced Keogh into a save.

But play was mainly confined to the Athlone half. Despite their level of possession, Bohemians' chances were limited, thanks to the stonewall defending of the Athlone backs.

When the Bohemians' forwards did break through O'Reilly was in unbeatable form – his two saves from Roberts and Willets before the break being nothing short of miraculous, according to the Westmeath Independent.

The Dubliners' clearest opportunity of the half came in the dying moments when Brooks and Willets got in each other's way and the chance went abegging.

The second half was similarly intense though Bohemians' play improved somewhat and towards the midpoint of the half they seemed to have the Athlone defence seriously shaken.

O'Reilly saved brilliantly from an overhead kick by McIlroy, while simultaneously being charged in possession by Brooks.

After withstanding a full 20 minutes of concerted pressure, Athlone rallied and began to ask questions of their own of the Bohemians' rearguard.

And with seven minutes remaining, Athlone secured the vital second following an attack down the left. When the raiding menace, Ghent, crossed, he found Norman Lyster on space on the far wing. Cutting in from the right, Lyster carried the ball forward and fired home from 12 yards for the clincher.

The victory was confirmed and the large Athlone contingent in the 9,000 plus attendance celebrated wildly.

The Evening Mail noted: "The big Athlone following almost got out of hand when the second goal was scored, but the stewards dealt with the incident."

The jubilation in Dalymount Park was matched by that at home in the midlands where the team was met at the train station by a joyous crowd. The players were guided by a torchlight procession of fans back to the Foresters' Hall where celebrations continued no doubt long into the night.

The players

O'Reilly had again been in unbeatable form, but this time, the real honours of the game went outfield where Hope, Monahan, Judge, Sweeney, and Hannon defended as if their lives depended on it.

Hannon's ability to be everywhere and anywhere was again remarked upon. His effectiveness in closing down Bohs forwards and in forcefully kick-starting counter attacks was a crucial element in Athlone's masterplan.

Showing typical bravery, despite the ongoing court proceedings, captain Jim Sweeney proved a more than sufficient stand-in centre-half in the absence of Dykes. Indeed, the Sunday Independent conferred the honours of the game to Hannon and Sweeney.

The Evening Herald said Hannon's leadership had a startling effect on his colleagues. According to the Westmeath Independent, Sweeney was an inspirational captain – leading by both example and encouragement.

Ned Brooks charges Paddy O'Reilly between the posts with Tommy Muldoon, Joe Monahan and Jimmy Hope looking on.

"Great in his simplicity, unostentatious in his greatness. An ideal captain in every way, possessing as he does the ability to transfer enthusiasm into all his comrades without ever allowing that enthusiasm to be counteracted by impatience, an indispensable attribute in every capable, efficient leader," the paper reported.

Maybe, it was his brother's trials and tribulations, maybe Sweeney sensed the moment, whatever the reason, he had the game of his life, according to the Westmeath.

Other papers were particularly praiseworthy of O'Reilly, Hope, Judge and Monahan.

The Sunday Independent captured Athlone's energy and enthusiasm well: "When under pressure there were times when it was hard to believe they had only eleven men operating."

Despite their territorial dominance, Bohemians displayed a notably blunt edge up front.

And indeed the Sunday Independent said it would not have been a surprise if Athlone had added a further couple of goals to their total, as their attacks, albeit fewer in number, proved much more dangerous than those of Bohemians.

Athlone's display was received in more complimentary terms than two weeks previously. This time, they had combined their bustling and swamping defence with a speedy, incisive counter-attacking style.

But once again, Bohemians had failed to adapt their style and their insistence on attempting to pass their way tidily through the packed Athlone defence was a fatal strategy.

Up front, Collins and Ghent, and, to a lesser extent, Flannery, carried off most of the plaudits. Collins again turned in a respectable performance as a makeshift centre-forward. The Sunday Independent said he worked hard, although his methods were crude.

Lyster's goal capped an impressive second-half display, which helped to redeem a poor first-half performance.

Athlone had seen off Dublin standard-bearers Shelbourne and Bohemians, along with Midland Athletic, on their cup adventure. Now, they were secure in the knowledge that their place in the St Patrick's Day showpiece final was assured. All that remained to be resolved was the identity of their opponents; the remaining Dubliners, St James's Gate or Cork's flagship eleven, Fordsons.

Another provincial triumph

The replay of Athlone's semi-final with Bohemians had allowed the other side of the draw to catch up – and the second semi-final was played on Sunday, March 2nd, the day after Athlone had booked their final spot.

Theoretically the game should have been held at a neutral venue, but in an era where the only real facilities capable of hosting such a crowd were in Dublin or Cork, it was a Hobson's Choice for the FAI.

Wisely, they finally opted to play the game in Cork, to help promote the sport in the Southern region. They needn't have worried. Interest in the game was huge and a large crowd of up to 12,000 turned up at the Mardyke, the University College Cork rugby grounds, for the clash, which was refereed by Athlone's Michael Broderick.

It was a then record attendance at a soccer game in Cork and Fordsons had agreed to rent the Mardyke for the occasion to facilitate the expected large crowd. Special excursion trains were organised from Dublin by the Free State Football Association – and such was the interest that some 2,000 tickets had been booked for the trains by the Wednesday preceding the game.

It was the second successive year that Fordsons had reached the last four of the cup and their rise had sparked a wave of interest in the sport Leeside.

Although Saturday had been taken up with snow showers in Cork, the day of the game itself was fine and bright. It was an auspicious omen for the Cork side as they easily accounted for a disappointing St James's Gate on a one-sided 4-0 scoreline.

The opening half hour was evenly contested but two goals from Denis Collins before the break put Fordsons firmly in the driving seat. St James's Gate had a more than even share of possession throughout but their forward play was abysmal and when they did manage to carve out an opening, they found Bill O'Hagan in irresistible mood between the posts.

Fordsons clinched the contest with two further strikes, one from Laurence Pinkney and, just before the end, the fourth from Collins, as he concluded his hat-trick.

The peerless Harry Buckle had created two of the four goals. Dubbed Peter Pan due to his seemingly eternal career, Buckle was one of the founding fathers of football in Cork. He was now in the dying days of a career that had seen him capped at international level for Ireland, play in England and also enjoy a stint as manager of Coventry.

St James's Gate had been forced to play some of the second half with just ten men after one of their starting eleven left the field of play through injury. But in reality the game was well-beyond them at that stage.

How Athlone helped to save the League of Ireland

The pairing of two provincial sides, Athlone and Fordsons, in a major final for the first time, had sparked varying responses from the football family. To some it was an impertinent shot across the bows of the Dublin clubs, others wallowed in the novelty value, ignorant of the wider implications and a few simply begrudged.

But some astute commentators could see the positive implications. Sport, which had declared its desire to see an Athlone/Fordsons final from the very start of the competition, voiced this view most clearly.

"Of all the achievements of the Football Association of the Irish Free State, none is more remarkable than this. None is calculated to fill the members with more pride and none is more likely to further its interests than that these two clubs, Athlone and Fordsons, should clash in the cup final."

It attributed the growth of both clubs directly to the establishment of the Free State Association. "But for the creation of the new body, Athlone would still be playing junior football and Fordsons would not have been heard of in any grade of football whatsoever."

Indeed, it was also reported that more clubs had joined the Free State FA in the first year than had previously existed in all Ireland.

The cup final was being held amidst a series of 'peace conferences' between the new FSFAI and the old IFA. There was optimism in the air, mainly from the Northern side, that a rapprochement was imminent

In this climate, the very future of the new League of Ireland was uncertain. There was talk that two Dublin clubs, probably Bohemians and Shelbourne could be considering returning to the IFA, while also playing in the Free State League.

The move would have effectively led to a downgrading of the status of the Free State League.

As ever, it was left to Sport to spell out the real significance of the Athlone V. Fordsons pairing. The paper asked: "What will become of Athlone?"

"If the sequel to the settlement of the international question means the passing from the Free State League to the Belfast 'Irish' League of two of its present clubs, what would become of Athlone?" The paper asked if Athlone could be expected to revert to junior football having beaten Bohemians and Shelbourne on the way to the cup final. On the other hand, if a Free State League was to continue could Bohemians and Shelbourne hold their own in that, at the same time as playing in an expanded Belfast-centred Irish League?

"To be worthy of its name, any future Irish League must embrace the best teams in all Ireland, and not confine itself to Dublin and Belfast. Travelling facilities do not permit of regular weekly interplay for a season between Belfast, Athlone, Dublin and Cork."

Arguing that Athlone and Cork were now equal in footballing terms with Dublin, Sport said that similarly talented teams might emerge from other centres outside Dublin the coming years.

The only way to continue the development of the game outside Dublin was through the existing league.

Sport had no doubt where the solution to these quandaries lay; the Free State FA must retain its total independence.

"The maintenance and extension of the Free State League under its present football government alone can call them into being. Anything likely to impair the Free State League or to narrow its operations can have but a stunting and deterring effect on the future," it declared.

It may not be an exaggeration to say that the emergence during 1923/24 of Athlone and Fordsons was a crucial factor in the survival of the Free State League.

For the moment, though it was the achievement of the present that was being celebrated in Athlone, even in verse.

The Battle of Shelbourne Park

What though the ground is coursed white and chill the morning air,
Athlone shall field a team to win and little do they care
We'll win the Cup! We'll win the Cup! We'll make it all our own
We'll never let down the dear old town, the honour of Athlone
(II)
And see again how round the goal they press with might and main
And though the backs stand manfully, their strength is all in vain
Keogh falters, reels and drops the ball, like hawks upon its prey
In rushes Ghent and scores, hurragh!
Athlone has won the day
(III)
Not yet for backward comes the ball and onwards press the Bohs,
Full bitter waxed the second half between the friends and foes
But staunch, and still with iron will, Athlone withstand the charge
And Lyster e'er the game is o'er the victory will enlarge

(IV)
Ah awful 'tis to think they cry that just a country team
Should beat the great and famous Bohs, or is it just a dream
But Athlone Town shall lower down the colours highly flown
A thousand throats shall raise the shout, the war cry "Up Athlone"
(V)
See Reilly staunch sentinel ward off the fierce attacks
See Monaghan and trusty Hope the ever-ready backs
The halves and gallant forward line with Dinny at their head
Ah tell tell me where you'll find a country team instead.

(VI)

An onward then ye gallant men, the race is now quite o'er
'Tis but a coward that doubts you'll do as you have done before
What though they call ye bogmen or villagers unknown
You'll win the Irish Senior Cup and then 'tis Up Athlone

Athlone Town:

Paddy O'Reilly, Jimmy Hope, Joe Monahan, Terry Judge, Jim Sweeney, Tommy Muldoon, Norman Lyster, Denis Hannon, Tommy Collins, Paddy Flannery and Frank Ghent.

Chapter 17

Norman Lyster

A fine sporting pedigree

The Lysters

Norman Lyster was a member of one of Athlone's most prominent business families for the greater part of the 20th century.

The Lysters were a powerful family who originated in Curraghboy. Over the years, they relocated to Athlone.

Norman's grandfather Patrick established a builders' supply firm based in King Street (now Pearse Street) in the 1850s. The business prospered and Lyster grew in wealth and influence, becoming chairman of the town commissioners.

His obituary in the Westmeath Independent in 1889 said he hailed from the Baylough area.

"Mr Lyster was educated and reared in the town and here he married and started a business as a carpenter and builder. Times were favourable some 40 or 45 years ago for building in this part of Ireland and Mr Lyster received a profitable proportion of this contracting and by this means amassed a considerable income which he spent with no niggardly hand in the education of his family and for charitable and religious purposes in the town."

After his death the business continued. A sawmill had been established on Excise Street in 1887. By the late 1930s, Norman and his brother, Lionel, were directors of the firm.

The business originally catered for the building trade, but widened its range to stock everything from hardware to homeware. The Lysters were also large property owners on the west side of town.

Norman Lyster's father, Joseph Lyster, was a justice of the peace who died in 1913, while his uncle, John, who was Bishop of Achonry, died in 1911.

Born in June 1893 to Joseph and Roseanne (nee O'Connell) of King Street, Lyster dabbled in football when a boarder in Dublin's Castleknock College in the early years of the last century.

A wide sporting interest

Of all those associated with Athlone Town in the 1920s, Lyster was probably the most active in other sports, most notably as an accomplished hockey player.

He was also a keen yachtsman and served on the committee of Lough Ree Yacht Club for several years. He captained Athlone Golf Club, was a member

of Athlone Boat Club, and both a bridge fine player
and administrator.

His involvement with Athlone on the football field
was irregular, but his contribution was, nonetheless,
significant.

Lyster's first appearance with Athlone Town came
in 1915 when he lined out in a Leinster Senior Cup
match at full-back. By 1919, he was more likely to be
found at half-back, appearing in the Leinster Junior
Cup ties of that season.

By 1921/22 season, Athlone had been accepted
into the FAI Cup, but Lyster was absent for the
historic first game against YMCA.

Norman Lyster

During the 1920s, Lyster alternated between
football and hockey, playing each to a competitive level.

Provincial honours

On Saturday, January 28th, 1922, when Athlone travelled to Dublin to meet
Bohemians in the FAI Cup, Lyster was on the Connaught men's senior
hockey team that was overcome by Ulster in the interprovincial series in
Dublin's Park Avenue. A day previously, he had also lined out for Connaught
in a defeat to Leinster.

*Norman Lyster, second from left back row, is pictured with the Connaught and Midlands
hockey team in 1926.*

The interpros were traditionally used as selection trials for the Irish national team, but players from Connaught or Midlands effectively made up the numbers – and were rarely, if ever, selected for national honours.

Lyster appeared in the interprovincials for Connaught in 1921 and 1922, for Midlands in 1923 and for a combined Connaught and Midlands side in 1925 and 1926, earning probably 15 interprovincial 'caps' in the process.

Chasing hockey medals

On the club scene, he lined out as a half-back for Athlone hockey club at a time when they were making an impression on the national scene, albeit at a more modest level than their football counterparts.

In 1925, the Athlone team reached the semi-final of the Irish Junior Cup, a competition founded in 1895 that is still played today.

They met Ennis at the semi-final stage in a game held in conditions that were nigh on unplayable.

In the circumstances, hockey of the hit and rush variety was a necessity and the game evolved into a test of endurance and adaptability to the underfoot conditions.

"Certainly under normal conditions, it was highly probable that Athlone would have won without a great deal of difficulty," the Times reported. As it was, having gone ahead through Norman's brother Lionel in the first half, Athlone were pegged back by Ennis after the interval.

And 40 minutes of extra time eventually saw the Munster men through 2-1. Ennis were beaten the following day in the Irish Junior Cup Final by Railway Union B.

Hockey – Junior Cup despair

In 1926, Athlone again reached the Irish Junior Cup semi-finals as the Connaught representatives.

On Friday, March 5th, they overcame Ulster junior champions Belmont and on the following day in Serpentine Avenue, Athlone crossed sticks with Leinster kingpins Pembroke Wanderers B who had defeated Waterford Bohemians in the other semi-final.

It was Athlone's first and only Irish Junior Cup hockey final appearance.

Unfortunately, it was another tale of what might have been for Athlone, who were unfortunate to have to meet the Dubliners on their home ground of Serpentine Avenue. In a marathon contest, two spells of extra time comprising four ten-minute periods were added to the regulation match time in an attempt to separate the sides.

In the end, the Dubliners emerged victorious, though by all accounts, undeservedly. The Irish Times reported that Athlone had numerous chances – with penalty corners in particularly not being availed of.

For the record the Athlone team was: W. Reid, A Carroll, P. Dolan, J. Corcorcan, N. Lyster, W. H. Strong, F. Duffy, K. Coghlan, L. Lyster, P. Kelly and R. O'Brien.

It was, effectively, to be Lyster's hockey swansong.

Football: Junior Cup triumph

Having been absent for the cup defeat to Bohemians, Lyster returned for the remaining three games of the 1921/22 season, culminating in an appearance at right wing-back in the victorious Leinster Junior Cup final team.

According to the Evening Herald, he produced a "brilliant" performance.

Although never an ever-present, Lyster always had the happy knack of being selected for the crucial games – a sign perhaps of his experience and reliability, even if he was not the most talented of footballers.

Norman Lyster was tremendously shy and rarely appeared in any post-event photographs. A special picture of the Leinster Junior Cup winners staged some time later in Athlone was notable for his absence, with Alan Smith listed as standing in for Lyster in the caption.

In fact Lyster was only likely to be photographed in a team picture on the pitch before the match.

This personality trait also meant he opted out of the celebratory homecoming procession for the FAI Cup winners through Athlone.

Helping Athlone in its debut season

Still whether captured on film or not, he was there, again, at a key moment of history, in Athlone's first League of Ireland side which played St James's Gate in the opening game of Athlone's debut 1922/23 season, again at right half-back.

He perhaps featured more in this season than any other in Athlone colours, with most of his appearances coming at the key centre-half position.

The season culminated in the Shield final defeat to Shelbourne and by this stage John Joe Dykes had entered the reckoning so Lyster lined out at his more customary right-half position.

1923 was a busy sporting time for Lyster, as he was also captain of Athlone Golf Club that same year.

For some reason, he missed out on interprovincial hockey honours in 1924 – but instead helped Athlone to bring home the Blue Riband.

Having played only a handful of league games that season, Lyster was not selected for the opening-round cup game against Midland Athletic in January 1924.

Late addition to cup run

An injury sustained by half-back Paddy Flannery meant Norman returned for the following game against St Paul's in the Leinster Senior Cup. And although team sheets are not available for some of the other Leinster Senior Cup games which took place in the run-up to the cup final, it's clear that Lyster was very much part of the 14 or so players in line for a berth in the crunch FAI Cup games.

Strangely, it was to be in the entirely unaccustomed outside-right role that Lyster would make a vital contribution in the cup semi-final replay and final.

After Athlone had drawn with Bohemians in the semi-final, most of the post-match criticism focused on the performance of Barney Connaughton at outside-right. In a major reshuffle, Lyster was called into the side to fill that weak spot.

A square peg in a round hole, Lyster strove manfully – and was central to the two key moments of the match.

After just 12 minutes, he was involved in the move which led to Ghent swooping for the opener. And then six minutes from the end, in a counter attack, he received a ball from the opposite wing in space, dribbled towards the goal and dispatched a fine shot past the Bohemians keeper.

Despite the valuable contribution, Lyster's overall performance in the unaccustomed forward-line role was less than impressive.

The Evening Herald remarked on his poor display, oblivious to how he had come to Athlone's aid in filling a clearly unsuitable role. He had missed a clear-cut chance in the opening few minutes and was under par for the opening half, the paper said.

It added he had "made amends for a hitherto poor display" with the late second goal.

Despite not being ideally suited to the role, his replay goal ensured he was retained for the cup final against Fordsons on St Patrick's Day at outside-right.

Winding down his playing career

Having claimed the country's highest footballing honour with Athlone, Lyster, at the age of 31, began to wind down his footballing involvement.

He did not feature at all the following season, and probably only twice in 1925/26, initially midway through the league campaign at home to Bray Unknowns and then at right half-back in the FAI Cup first-round victory over Brideville.

It was likely to have been his last game for Athlone, though he remained, as he had always been, a key financial backer of the club.

Norman Lyster was married to Annie (nee Coen). The couple had no children and he died unexpectedly on August 14th, 1968, at Portiuncula Hospital in Ballinasloe. He is buried in Cornamagh Cemetery.

Chapter 18

Fordsons

Introducing the Tractor Men

The origin of Fordsons

If Athlone's success in reaching the FAI Cup final had taken the footballing world by surprise, the arrival of Cork upstarts Fordsons was an upset of equal proportions.

Fordsons were a works side attached to the famous Ford factory, which had been established on the site of the former Cork Park Racecourse in 1919.

In its heyday, some 1,800 people were employed at the plant. The factory was originally envisaged as a production line for Fordson tractors. In the 1930s, that element of the business was relocated to Dagenham in Essex, with many workers following their jobs. Dagenham became known as Little Cork and if, and when, they returned to Cork, the workers were labelled "Dagenham Yanks".

On the football front, Fordsons, by 1924, had only been in competitive action for about two years. They had, nonetheless, improved rapidly, poaching talented and experienced players from near and far to fill out their ranks.

When assessing Athlone's progress, prejudice often clouded judgements. And for Fordsons too, there were none so blind as those who would not see. For observers willing to accept that Dublin was not the be all and end all, the signs of Fordsons' emergence would have been clearly evident.

The team began life as Fords FC in 1921 and took part in an inaugural four-team South Munster League, which was held over a few months in early 1922. The Cork-based South Munster League was accompanied by a Tipperary/Limerick North Munster League. Both had emerged in the early months of 1922 as the enthusiasm prompted by the establishment of the Free State Football Association and League swept the south.

Among the key evangelists for the new football administration was Belfast native Harry Buckle, whose experience as a player and manager cross-channel and in the North spanned 20 years.

Buckle, with a couple of other enthusiasts, arranged a public meeting seeking to recruit teams to the South Munster League in January 1922.

As well as sowing the seeds of the new league, Buckle, a Fordsons player, had also been the driving force in the establishment of that club. Therefore, to avoid the potential conflict of interest inherent in being involved in the administration of a league in which his club was a member, Buckle opted to take office in the sister North Munster League.

In February 1922, he was elected the first president of that league. And he was also the first vice president of the Munster Football Association, which was reformed in March 1922.

Making an early impression

By 1922/23, Fords had changed to Fordsons and the South Munster League had expanded to nine teams. After a mediocre first campaign, Fordsons made a real impression in 1922/23, winning the Munster Senior Cup and qualifying for the Free State Cup proper. Non-league Fordsons' journey to the Free State Cup followed a similar route to that travelled the previous season by Athlone Town.

The Athlone and District Association had been formed in time for the 1921/22 cup competition, allowing Athlone Town, as the winners of the local regional qualifying rounds, to enter the first-round draw. Similarly in 1922/23, having came unscathed through the local qualifying competition, Fordsons reached the first round as the representative of the Munster FA.

A walkover against Rathmines Athletic and a victory over Dublin Utd, both league members in that 1922/23 season, saw the Cork novices into the cup semi-final.

That visit to the capital to meet Dublin Utd represented a little piece of sporting history as Fordsons became the first Cork side to play a club game in Dublin.

The victory qualified them for a semi-final clash against Northerners Alton Utd. Although Alton Utd were only a junior club playing in the Falls League as part of the Belfast Divisional Association, they had an impressive pedigree, having won the IFA Irish Junior Cup in 1920.

In the semi-final, the Northerners conquered the Southern representatives 4-2 with Buckle and Jack O'Sullivan scoring for the Cork outfit. Alton went on to spring a surprise by defeating red-hot favourites Shelbourne in the final.

Fordsons did have explanations for their mediocre display. They could only have been unnerved by an horrific experience on their journey to the semi-final when the train in which they were travelling came under fire for five minutes near Blarney. All the windows were smashed and the players were forced to lie on the carriage floors to escape the hail of bullets.

Despite the incident, Fordsons displayed their sense of sportsmanship with the unusual gesture of meeting their opponents Alton Utd on their arrival by train in Dublin. The Evening Telegraph admitted that Alton Utd would be "unaccustomed to demonstrations of that kind from opponents".

Fordsons also showed their true character by issuing what the Evening Telegraph described as a "rousing cheer" for the victorious Belfast outfit in the dressing rooms after the game.

Further development

Fordsons' trip to the semi-final had highlighted their abilities and their arrival in the final the following season against Athlone represented a further step forward.

During that 1923/24 season, Fordsons had continued to develop and progress, totally dominating what was now known as the Munster Senior League. By the time of their appearance in the cup final, they had already wrapped up the league championship, losing only one game in the process.

As a works team, Fordsons had the advantage of being able to attract footballers of talent and repute from far and wide with the offer of good employment. And once they had established their earnestness as a football club, the recruits came thick and fast.

Following their exploits in the 1922/23 cup campaign, Fordsons were exempted from qualifying for the 1923/24 FAI Cup and a place was reserved for them in the cup proper. A bye in the first round and victories over Jacobs and St James's Gate this time saw them through to the final.

Such was their dominance in the Munster senior league that the club had not undergone any training for most of that season. After their victory over Jacobs, that omission was remedied ahead of their semi-final clash with St James's Gate.

The team that lined out against Athlone on St Patrick's Day 1924 included six who had succumbed to Alton Utd at the penultimate hurdle the previous year: O'Mahony, Millar, Maher, O'Sullivan, Buckle and Pinkney.

The full line-out for the cup final against Athlone was: William O'Hagan, Jeremiah O'Mahony, Daniel Millar, Leo Maher, Jack O'Sullivan, Paddy Barry, Frank Hunter, Laurence Pinkney, John Malpas, Harry Buckle (captain) and Denis Collins.

Only four were to eventually get their hands on the FAI Cup two years later: O'Hagan, O'Sullivan, Buckle and Barry.

FAI Cup winners 1926. Back: Paddy Kelly, Mal McKennie, Denny Driscoll. Centre: Sally Connolly, Barney Collins, Bill O'Hagan, Jimmy Carabine, Jack Baylor, Jock Finn. Seated: Billy Hannon, Jack O'Sullivan, Frank Brady, Harry Buckle, Dave Roberts and Paddy Barry.

THE PLAYERS

Bill O'Hagan

Goalkeeper Bill O'Hagan was an experienced campaigner, whose presence between the sticks was a crucial factor in Fordsons' 1923/24 successes.

Born in Buncrana in 1890, O'Hagan was a member of a prominent Irish sporting family; his uncle Charlie had been capped eleven times for Ireland. O'Hagan, himself, was twice capped by the IFA in 1920 in the home internationals against England and Wales.

O'Hagan started his career with Derry Guilds, then one of Ireland's strongest junior clubs in the later years of the 1900s and with whom he won the Irish Junior and Irish Intermediate Cups in a three-year spell.

After impressing in an Irish junior international in Scotland in 1910, he was snapped up by St Mirren, with whom he remained until the outbreak of World War 1.

O'Hagan saw service at Gallipoli, Salonica, Egypt and France but returned home in mid-1918 and briefly joined Linfield, before returning to St Mirren. Spells with other Scottish clubs Third Lanark and Airdrie continued before he made 53 appearances over the best part of two seasons with Norwich City in Division 3 of the English League.

When he first returned from the battlefields of Continental Europe, O'Hagan had initially been stationed at the military training camps in Fermoy and it was back to Cork he travelled for the 1923/24 season, hitching his talents to the Fordsons' bandwagon.

O'Hagan headed cross-channel for one last stint playing a single season, 1924/25, with Welsh club Aberdare Athletic, who were then in Division 3 of the English League, before returning again to Cork where he resumed with Fordsons. He had a pivotal role in securing the FAI Cup for Fordsons in 1925/26, saving a late penalty in the dramatic cup-final decider with Shamrock Rovers.

Proof of his status within the game was provided in February 1923 when he was chosen on the Free State League XI to play Glasgow Celtic, despite his club playing in the Munster Senior League at the time.

O'Hagan enjoyed 34 years service with Ford, at their plants in Cork, Trafford Park, Dagenham and Liverpool, where he died in 1972.

Jeremiah O'Mahony

At right-back was Jeremiah (Jack) O'Mahony, who was later to become a trainer of Fordsons. He continued putting Fordsons' successors, Cork, through their paces in the early 1930s.

O'Mahony gained representative honours as a player with Munster in 1923 and continued to play in the Munster Senior League up to the end of the decade, featuring mainly with Fordsons.

Jeremiah O'Mahony

Daniel Millar

Left-back Daniel Millar was one of the non-locals in the side. From Northern Ireland, he had featured with Belfast Celtic prior to his arrival in Cork. He had been attached to Fords since their entry into the South Munster League in early 1922 and had gained representative honours for Munster against Leinster that same campaign.

Although he was to continue plying his trade with Fordsons and other Cork clubs well into the late 1920s, he was not fortunate enough to secure a second chance at an FAI Cup winner's medal. By 1925/26, when Fordsons finally won the cup, he was mainly confined to the Fordsons B team in the Munster Senior League. He continued to make irregular appearances for the Fordsons' first eleven up to the 1926/27 season at least, before joining Cork Celtic and later Cobh Ramblers in the Munster Senior League.

Leo Maher

Leo Maher was a Cork man who played at right-half during the 1922/23 and 1923/24 campaigns for Fordsons, before slipping out of the limelight.

He won a Munster Senior Cup medal in 1925/26 as Fordsons B beat Cork Bohemians in the final.

Jack O'Sullivan

At centre-half was Jack O'Sullivan; one of Cork's most famous footballing sons.

Born on Spike Island, Haulbowline, O'Sullivan shares the distinction with another of the 1924 cup side, Paddy Barry, of being the first Cork man to be capped by Ireland.

Jack O'Sullivan

O'Sullivan was equally talented at Gaelic football and won county senior football medals with Cobh as well as inter-county honours with Cork.

He also played with the legendary Belfast Celtic side. Having returned to his native Cork after the war, he was lined up to emigrate to the United States before Fords came calling in early 1922.

In the 1922/23 campaign, O'Sullivan lined out at centre-forward and scored a hat-trick in the quarter-final victory over Free State League side Dublin Utd as well as weighing in with another in the 4-2 defeat to Alton Utd in the semi-final.

By the following year, he had switched to the centre-half position and it was in this role he was to enjoy great success.

Jack 'Hatcher' O'Sullivan's part in Fordsons' progress was recognised by the Irish selectors in 1928 when he was chosen at centre-half on the Irish team that defeated Belgium in Liege by 4-2. O'Sullivan scored from the spot in that victory, becoming the first Cork-born player to score for his country.

O'Sullivan had also been chosen as a reserve for what is generally and incorrectly regarded as Ireland's first international in Turin against Italy in 1926. However, he was unable to travel. He also captained Fordsons to their FAI Cup victory in 1925/26 and was the first man to bring the cup home to Cork.

O'Sullivan later worked in the Cork Flower Mills and continued his playing career with Fordsons right up to their demise in 1929/30. He also continued turning out in the colours of their replacement, Cork, in the League of Ireland into the early 1930s.

He was on the losing side with Cork B in the 1931/32 FAI Intermediate Cup final and again, in 1936, tasted defeat in the decider of the same competition when lining out in the colours of another Munster Senior League side, Great Southern Railways.

O'Sullivan gained representative honours with Munster on many occasions, notably against Leinster and the Welsh League, both of whom made a number of visits to the Southern capital during the 1920s.

O'Sullivan also twice represented the new Free State League against the IFA in 1927 and 1930 as part of the series of annual representative games which resumed in 1925/26.

Paddy Barry

At left-half was Paddy Barry, who was also capped by Ireland, thanks to his exploits with Fordsons.

From Glanmire, Barry had learned his football while on service with the British Army in India. He too featured with O'Sullivan in the 1928 clash with Belgium and retained his berth for the return game in Dublin thirteen months later.

Barry's place in Cork sporting history was ensured in the 1925/26 season when he was moved to the left-wing during the cup campaign. It was an inspired change and in the final Barry weighed in with two goals, including a last-minute winner, in the 3-2 victory over Shamrock Rovers.

He too represented Munster in interprovincial games during the height of his career. Barry played on with Cork as far as 1932/33 and lined out in the 1932 Intermediate Cup final.

He is believed to have died in England, having moved there to work in the Ford plant in Dagenham in the 1930s.

Frank Hunter

Frank Hunter, another Cork man, played at outside-right. From Grange, Hunter had tied down a starting berth during most of the 1923/24 season, but was generally confined to the Fordsons B team in future years.

In that capacity, while many of his teammates from 1924 were competing in the Free State League, Hunter represented the Munster Senior League against the Leinster Senior League in 1925/26 – a year in which he also won the Munster Senior Cup with Fordsons.

Laurence Pinkney

Laurence Pinkney was another who had been associated with Fords since their arrival on the scene in early 1922. Like many of his colleagues, he won interprovincial honours for Munster in his early years with Fordsons.

Another Corkonian, Pinkney began as an attacker with Fordsons, and played inside-right in the 1924 final against Athlone. A versatile player, by 1926/27, he had been converted to a half-back or full-back, although he still turned out occasionally in the forward line too.

He too featured with both the Fordsons first team and reserves up to the end of the decade but did not share in the 1925/26 cup final glory.

John Malpas

Centre forward John (Jock) Malpas was probably Scottish. He had previously featured with Mostend in the North Eastern League. His stint with Fordsons' first team appears only to have lasted the one season. He was consigned to the reserve side from then on, featuring in the Munster Senior League up to 1926 at least.

Harry Buckle

At inside-left was Fordsons' most glittering star, Harry Buckle. Coach, administrator, key player, Harry Buckle was Fordsons and Fordsons was Harry Buckle. Born Henry Redmond Buckle in Belfast on March 6th, 1882, he began his career as an amateur with Cliftonville in 1899, whilst serving his time in the shipyards of his native city.

During the 1902/03 season, he was snapped up by Sunderland, who were the reigning English League champions at the time. During a three-year stint with the Black Cats, he played 43 games scoring 14 goals from the outside-left position.

While with Sunderland, Buckle received his first cap in 1904 in a game against England played at Cliftonville. From Sunderland, Buckle moved south to join Portsmouth in May 1906. He remained at Fratton Park for a solitary season, making 15 Southern League appearances and netting three goals.

Harry Buckle

Buckle then transferred to Bristol Rovers in the close season of 1907. It was then he earned his second and last cap, against Wales, again at outside-left.

His arrival at Coventry's Highfield Road in 1908 coincided with their election to the Southern League. His first campaign at the club was spent in a side struggling to make their mark at the higher level. Buckle was an immediate hit, though, finishing the season as top scorer with 17 goals from 39 league appearances.

By the start of the following season, Harry Buckle had been made player-manager. Again he was top scorer, netting 17 goals from 38 games. And he weighed in with two goals in Coventry's run to the quarter-finals of the FA Cup, beating First Division opponents Preston North End and Nottingham Forest along the way. It was at this time that he played for the Southern League against the English League. He finished his three-year association with Coventry with a respectable tally of 46 goals in 126 league and cup games.

In the summer of 1911, he returned to Ireland to join Belfast Celtic as player-manager. He moved to Glenavon in 1914 and to Belfast Utd in 1917, where he was player, manager and club secretary.

On arrival back in Ireland from England, Buckle had taken employment as a shipbuilder with Harland and Wolff. During the World War, there had been a large influx of Catholic workers, like Buckle, into industries which formerly had been almost exclusively Protestant.

As the impact of the War of Independence down south spilled over into the north, conditions for those Catholic workers deteriorated rapidly.

In July 1920 Protestant workers, aided and abetted by the Orange Order, drove thousands of Catholic workers out of the factories of industrial Belfast, particularly the shipyards.

Buckle had an iron bolt fired in his face on one occasion and was forced to swim across Belfast Lough on another to escape his pursuers.

His footballing renown may have saved him from a worse fate – but even that couldn't protect him indefinitely from the gathering tide of sectarianism. And eventually like hundreds of his colleagues, he was forced out of employment, moving initially to Wales and eventually to Cork.

By the Lee, he initially took up employment as a shipbuilder before moving to the new Ford plant sometime in 1921.

Finding no serious football organisation in Cork, Buckle took it upon himself to attempt to rejuvenate the game in the region. He became the first chairman of the Munster Football Association, was vice chairman of the North Munster League, acted as a referee and linesman for games in that league, and, of course, was the driving force behind Fordsons.

During the 1923/24 campaign Buckle was captain and coach of Fordsons. According to the newspaper Football Sports Weekly: "Without Buckle, there would be no Fordsons, and without Fordsons, the other Cork and Munster clubs, highly efficient and formidable as very many of them are today would be floundering in a muck of mediocrity."

During his lengthy career, Buckle finest moment came in 1926, when, as player-manager, he steered his beloved Fordsons to the cup at the ripe old age of 44!

At the start of that same season, it had generally been assumed that his days as a senior player were over and he was omitted from the line up for the opening two league games. But with the younger talent not meeting expectations, he was drafted in for the third game and scored a hat-trick in the 5-1 defeat of Shelbourne – the only time the Dubliners, who went on to be crowned league champions, were beaten that season.

Later that season, his longevity was rewarded with a cup winner's medal just weeks after his 44th birthday. Buckle continued playing during the following league campaign before finally hanging up his boots.

In retirement, he continued to take an active part in the game, remaining as vice president of the Munster FA for many years. He also excelled at pitch and putt in his later years.

Aside from the legacy of his involvement in the administrative side of football, the Buckle name continued to resonate on the playing fields of Cork for some time too. In 1934, his son Bobby followed in his father's footsteps in winning a cup medal with Cork.

Harry and Bobby then became the first father and son pair to win cup medals. The Buckle family connection to Cork sport continued in the shape of Dave Barry, who is Harry's great grandson.

Harry Buckle died on January 2nd, 1965.

Denis Collins

Making up the eleven for the 1924 cup final was Denis Collins at outside-left.

Collins was a Cork native who had been coaxed from the Gaelic football fields to soccer just over a year previously. In that short spell, his development was amazing.

Soon after signing with Fordsons, he was selected for Munster for the 1923 interpro with Leinster. And the next season, he was the dynamo for Fordsons' cup run. Two goals in the 2-0 victory over Jacobs in the quarter-final and a hat-trick in the semi-final thrashing of St James's Gate said all that needed to be said. By that stage, his talent had been well and truly signposted and scouts from

Denis Collins

Middlesboro and Chelsea were in attendance at the semi-final.

However, Collins was never to fully realise that early glittering potential. A paltry return of 14 league goals over the next four seasons told its own tale. Although he featured with Fordsons in the League of Ireland until the 1927/28 season, Collins too missed out on cup glory in 1925/26. Having played and scored in the first round-draw against Shelbourne, he was dropped for the replay, with the selectors instead opting to experiment with Paddy Barry at outside-left.

The Fordsons line-up for the cup final was: Bill O'Hagan, Jeremiah O'Mahony, Daniel Millar, Leo Maher, Jack O'Sullivan, Paddy Barry, Frank Hunter, Laurence Pinkney, Jock Malpas, Harry Buckle, Denis Collins.

These were the eleven men, clad in green and white vertical stripes, who represented the pride of Cork on that day Spring day in 1924.

Belfast conference fails to make the peace

Just a week before the cup final, the latest attempt at a peace agreement between the old IFA and the FAI had taken place in Belfast. There had already been two conferences, in Dublin and Liverpool, in a bid to hammer out an agreement between the warring factions.

The FAI had been admitted to FIFA membership in August 1923 and given responsibility for administering the game in its territory. As a direct result, a conference between the English FA, the Scottish FA, the Welsh FA and the two Irish Football Associations was organised for Liverpool in October 1923 in order to resolve the outstanding issues.

The Freeman's Journal reported the next day: "The long fight waged over a period of 18 months by the Free State FA for recognition by the cross-Channel bodies has ended."

It said the decision by the FIFA a few months previously had placed the IFA and the English, Welsh and Scottish Associations in an awkward position.

The conference accepted the IFA and FAI had administrative control over their own territories and also agreed the associations would recognise suspensions in each other's areas.

The other cross-channel associations agreed to recognise the FAI and its clubs. This ended the boycotting of the FAI by the English, Scottish and Welsh associations and paved the way for matches to be held between member clubs or representative teams of the two sides.

Whilst the agreement effectively permitted the Free State FA to select its own 'international' team, it failed to facilitate the development of an all-Ireland international side.

A proposal by the FAI that the two governing bodies on the island join "in setting up an (international) selection committee with equal representation from the two Associations" was rejected out of hand by the IFA. So too was the proposal that home international games be alternated between the North and Free State. The IFA believed that the Free State, "as a dominion", now having their own international team had no claim for involvement in the selection of an Ireland side. The IFA believed this was their prerogative.

Attempts to resolve this sticking point dragged on into 1924, and the two associations met again in Belfast on March 8th – just nine days before the cup final.

There were now growing indications of a rapprochement between the sides in the run-up to the Belfast conference.

It was in this backdrop that the 1924 cup campaign was being fought out.

At the conference, the IFA made significant movement on the one remaining issue from the previous talks; the make up of a selection committee for a 32-county international side.

They agreed to the notion of a selection committee made up of equal representation from both associations. However, they added the rider that the chairman of the IFA would remain chairman of the selection committee.

This ploy was accompanied by an offer of an equal management committee to run the Irish Senior and Junior Cups on a 32-county basis.

Along with another pledge to give equal representation to the southern association on one body governing football in Ireland, this concession was clearly designed to entice the Free State clubs back into an Irish League of old. The IFA was wiling to incorporate the new proposals into its constitution at its AGM in May and was eager for a swift response.

However, the FAI would not waver on the need for an alternating chairman on the international selection committee. Some forces with the FAI were also not keen to relinquish the Free State League - and to subsume themselves back into one governing body for the game in the island.

The potential peace accord was dead in the water and the chance of restoring a 32-county Irish international side went with it.

The question of an All-Ireland team had become entwined with broader issues of the development of the game in provincial locations.

In the end of the day, the emergence of Athlone and Fordsons had come in the nick of time and prevented the return to an 'All-Ireland League' that was anything but that. The notion that there was more to football in Ireland than Dublin and Belfast had won the day.

The League of Ireland as we know it today was copperfastened and secured – and clubs like Waterford, Limerick, Sligo Rovers and Longford Town were all given the opportunity to flourish and develop in later years, thanks in no small part to Athlone Town.

The pre-match build-up

In the run up to the final, Fordsons had been confidently asserting their expectations of bringing home the cup.

Before Christmas, one of their officials told a newspaper that the cup was as good as won by the Cork side, if Bohemians or Shelbourne represented the cream of Dublin talent. After the quarter-final defeat of Jacobs, captain Harry Buckle also voiced the same view: "The team that beats us will have to play."

Such was Fordsons superiority in the Munster Senior League that they had not trained. Following their qualification for the semi-final and with their sights now set on FAI Cup glory, the club set about training in earnest.

The build-up to the final continued apace with the Munster Football Association organising a special excursion train from Cork on the morning of the match Thousands of Southern football enthusiasts availed of the service to Dublin.

In Athlone too, anticipation was growing. The Athlone Trades Council postponed a planned public meeting scheduled for St Patrick's Day which was to have been addressed by top Labour Party personnel. A special train running via Mullingar left Athlone, bound for both the Free State Cup final and Baldoyle Races

Newspapers predicted some 3,000 Cork fans would travel north, with over 1,000 Athlonians expected to make the trip. A week and a half before the game, the Free State FA Council announced the officials for the decider; referee: J.J. Kelly; linesman: J. Galloway and J. Roe. Dalymount Park was the venue with a 3.30pm kick-off.

As the game neared, newspapers began to assess the merits of the various sides. The consensus: Fordsons were slight favourites.

The Evening Herald praised their delightful style of play and said the general opinion was that a Cork victory was likely. But it warned that the Munster men must be prepared to face the Athlone tactics.

"If the Corkmen allow themselves to be bustled like Shelbourne and Bohemians, it is quite on the cards that a second match will be necessary," it declared confidently.

The Evening Telegraph hedged its bets: "It is claimed for Fordsons that they are the better footballers and for Athlone, that they are the best cup fighters in the country. Form students claim that the record and performances of Athlone entitle them to the position of favourites as by defeating Shelbourne and Bohemians they have accomplished something greater than Fordsons, who in Jacobs and St James's Gate, had lesser foemen to vanquish. On the other hand, it is held that neither Jacobs nor St James's Gate fully extended Fordsons whereas Athlone were all out to defeat Dublin's two premier teams."

Wounded pride gave way to curiosity on the part of the Dublin footballing public with the vast bulk of the 22,000 attendance from the capital.

Sport feared "the holding capacity of Dalymount Park will be taxed beyond its power".

The Cork side arrived in Dublin on Saturday and took in a Shield game between Jacobs and Shelbourne Utd that day. Athlone, meanwhile, travelled up on Sunday evening.

The Evening Telegraph, if a little over-exuberant, captured the sense of anticipation before the game.

Predicting an attendance equal if not larger than the massive crowd which gathered for the Glasgow Celtic game, it warned its readers: "Come early and secure a good position. Come late and you will regret it all your life."

Chapter 19

Denis Hannon

A Bohemian rhapsody

- *The first player to win senior cup medals under both footballing jurisdictions in Ireland*

- *A member of the first Irish team to beat England in a full soccer international*

- *Eight full caps for Ireland – two after the creation of what is now the FAI*

- *Five amateur caps*

- *Captained the first Republic of Ireland international football team*

- *A member of the first Irish Olympians*

- *Winner of four Leinster Senior Cup medals*

A sporting passion

Born in January 1888, Hannon was the fourth child of a relatively well-to-do family from Athlone's Connaught Street where they operated a public house and general store.

His father, William Hannon, a town councillor, passed away when Denis was a young boy, leaving his mother, Kate, to bring up six children.

His father had been involved in Athlone Town from its formation and was listed as attending the 1894 AGM of the club.

Denis was initially educated in Athlone and later at Summerhill College in Sligo, at the same

Denis Hannon in 1929

time that another famous Athlonian, John 'Count' McCormack, was a student there. Hannon played local junior football with a side called Connaught Wanderers in Athlone and also in Sligo.

In 1906, he made his way to the capital to study medicine before settling on a career in law. He initially played a few friendly games for University College Dublin, before joining Bohemians that same year. It was a connection with the famous old Dublin club that was to continue for some 14 years.

Hannon had an abiding interest in horses too, and enjoyed the odd flutter. He was a member of the committee of Lough Ree Yacht Club and a steward at Garrycastle Races but football was his passion and he retained an interest in the sport until his death.

As a footballer, he possessed a distinctive, inimitable style, which didn't always please the pundits. He wasn't afraid to run with the ball and seemed to have little interest in remaining in his given role on the pitch. In his early years, his enthusiasm meant he was prone to overdoing the trickery and he often failed to avail of team-mates in better positions.

But as the years went by he became much more conscious of his team duties and learned to curb his individual style of play. By 1923, the Irish Independent reported: "Hannon now does in one touch what he used to do in many."

However, his roaming tendencies became even more pronounced as the years went by. It meant he was as likely to be heralded for his all-round contribution and his defensive involvement as he was to be criticised for what was sometimes perceived to be a neglect of his attacking duties.

Athlone cleverly utilised Hannon's versatility by regularly adding defensive half-back duties to his normal attacking responsibilities. This gave him licence to roam, but harnessed his natural inclinations for the best interest of the team.

Equally at home in the half-back line as in his more regular inside-right berth, Hannon was akin to the modern third midfielder in Gaelic football, an attacker who could help shield his defence when required.

It was a role he adopted with relish for Athlone in the vital cup wins over Shelbourne and Bohemians – adding an extra man to the half-back line, while helping to launch sweeping counter-attacking raids.

Although he didn't actually feature for Athlone until eight years after first fielding for Bohemians, Hannon was always intimately bound up with football in his native town. His commitment to the game continued through his involvement with Athlone Town right up to his death, a connection that spanned close on 50 years.

It was entirely fitting that he was present to witness his old club rejoin the League of Ireland in 1969, having been the driving force behind its original affiliation in 1922, some 47 years previously.

Linking up with the Bohs

Hannon's introduction to Bohemians came whilst studying in Dublin to become a solicitor.

In his student days he turned out more regularly in the Dublin club's colours than in later years.

Indeed, while based in the city, Hannon was a regular in Bohemians' first eleven – playing in all the major competitions, the Irish League, Irish Cup and Leinster Senior Cup.

Travelling to regular away games in the North militated against Dublin teams' prospects of competing at the upper end of the Irish League. And during Hannon's early years with Bohemians the club struggled in the league, finishing bottom of eight in 1907/08 (before relegation was introduced).

Later on, while undergoing his apprenticeship in Athlone, or when working as a fully-fledged solicitor in his home town, the logistics of travelling to and from Dublin for weekly games hampered the level of his involvement. Indeed, in the later years of the 1910s, he generally only lined out with Bohemians in the more important Irish Cup and Leinster Cup games

1906/07 – Serving his football apprenticeship

In a matter of months, he quickly climbed though the ranks of the Bohemians sides, from their D team which played in the Leinster Junior League, right up to the first team.

Hannon helped the Bohemians C team win the Leinster Senior League Division Two title in 1906/07 and around that time played his first senior game for Bohemians B against Trinity at College Park in Dublin in the Leinster Senior League.

Hannon concluded his opening season with the Dalymount Park outfit with a small number of appearances in the first team at the end of the season. Notably, he appeared in a charity fundraiser for Bohemians first team against Shelbourne in early May 1907.

1907/08 – A season of triumph

By the start of the following season, he had nailed down a starting berth and, indeed, scored in the first game of the 1907/08 Irish league campaign against Glentoran.

Despite his small stature – Hannon was 5'5" - he lined out as pivot, or leader of the forward line in that game.

The Westmeath Independent reported that the general opinion in Dublin footballing circles was that he would get an international cap by the end of the season. Indeed, his international bow did come that year but it was in the amateur ranks.

Amateur internationals at that time had almost the same lustre as their professional equivalent as the game was still beginning to emerge from the gentleman's code practised by the likes of Corinthians in England. These internationals were an annual affair between the Irish amateurs and their

English equivalents and were normally played in the final two months of the year.

At full international level, an annual series of games involving England, Scotland, Wales and Ireland had been ongoing since 1884. This series in which each side played each other once was usually conducted in February and March and both professionals and amateurs were eligible for selection.

The 1907/1908 season saw Hannon turning out at both amateur and full international level.

The match in the autumn of 1907 was just the second amateur international between England and Ireland. Proof of the high level of public interest came when up to 10,000 witnessed the match in which Ireland were comprehensively defeated 6-1 at Tottenham's White Hart Lane. Strangely, Hannon featured at inside-left. Reports stated he was one of the better performers for Ireland and it was his shot that was spilled by the English goalie for Ireland's only goal of the game.

Denis Hannon's amateur cap from the 1907 game against England

The 1907/08 season continued impressively for Hannon as he assisted Bohemians to their first Irish Cup success that year. Bohemians defeated Glentoran, Linfield and Belfast Celtic on their way to meeting Shelbourne in an historic first final between two Dublin teams. Strangely, Bohemians required replays in each round of the competition before earning the trophy.

Indeed Hannon played a crucial part along the way, scoring in the replay victories over Glentoran and Linfield before stamping his mark at the semi-final stage against Belfast Celtic. That game in Belfast on February 1st came a fortnight before the Ireland v. England full international of 1908.

Fortunately for Hannon, he reserved one of his best performances ever for the occasion. In a game which ended in a 2-2 draw, Hannon scored the first goal with a low shot that had crossed the line before being scooped out by the Belfast Celtic keeper. And he nearly added a stupendous second with a move that his team-mate Willie Hooper recalled some 50 years later in a newspaper interview.

Hannon was cheered to the echo for taking the ball from the centre through the Celtic defence single-handedly before slipping his effort past the goalkeeper, but agonisingly just the wrong side of the post. The Irish Times recorded that he was "undoubtedly the best forward on the field". Years later, Hannon would still recall this game as the most vivid in his memory.

As the team for the full international against England was chosen that night, the performance secured Hannon's place.

"Hannon can be said to have played himself onto the team on Saturday as after his display in the amateur international in London, his chances appeared remote of receiving the highest honours," said one newspaper.

The replay proceeded the following Saturday in Dalymount Park and Bohemians prevailed by 2-0, thus qualifying for their fourth Irish Cup final, with the Athlone native again prominent.

Hannon's attention turned to the international arena the following Saturday, February 15th, 1908, when he played his first full international game for Ireland against England in Cliftonville.

The game was overshadowed by the refusal of Newcastle Utd full-back Billy McCracken to play for Ireland in a row over payments. The Belfast native demanded £10 in addition to his expenses – the same rate being paid to the professional members of the English team rather that the two guineas on offer for the Irish professionals. McCracken was blacklisted – and only played for Ireland again some eleven years later. It was a sporting sensation at the time as McCracken was one of the most prominent footballers of his day. He went on to rack up a then massive 377 games for Newcastle over a 19-season run.

Ireland were dressed in blue, their original colours, instead of green in what was to prove a sensational debut for Hannon.

After just eleven minutes Hannon, at full stretch, converted a right-wing cross for an Irish equaliser four minutes after the English had gone ahead. Soon after he went close to a second with an audacious overhead kick.

Ireland held on to that equaliser until six minutes from time but within that last half dozen minutes England scored twice to ensure their undefeated run of 26 international matches against Ireland continued.

The Evening Herald claimed Ireland's physical inferiority, particularly up front against robust English defenders, was the cause of their downfall. "Forward was the weak spot of the side and although Hannon scored and played a vigorous game in the opening half, it was really asking too much of him to take part against such a robust side as the English one."

Hannon was only 5"5" in height and probably weighed around 9 stone.

Despite fading in the second half of his debut against England, he did enough to be one of eight players retained for the next international game, this time at home to Scotland in the familiar surrounds of Dalymount Park on Saturday, March 14th, 1908.

However, the Scotland game was to be instantly forgettable as Ireland suffered an embarrassing 5-0 defeat. Again, Ireland were outmuscled and outclassed and Hannon sustained his share of the criticism. "He found the

The 1908 Irish team which met England in February. Hannon, making his debut, is pictured second from left in the front row.

company he was opposed to altogether too good for him and not to his liking."

Still, attention had to be swiftly refocused as Bohs, with Hannon in their ranks, lined up against Shelbourne in the Irish Cup final the following Saturday in Dalymount Park in front of close to 10,000 spectators. It was the first time two Dublin sides had met in the decider.

Shelbourne were contesting the final for the fourth successive year, while Bohemians were seeking their first win after three previous unsuccessful final appearances.

In a cracking game, Shelbourne were in control of the opening exchanges but had the wind dramatically taken out of their sails when Bohemians' keeper Jack Hehir saved two first-half penalties.

Hannon had been well-marshalled in the early periods but came more and more into the game as the match progressed, wielding a major influence by the end of proceedings. It was Bohemians who edged in front before the break, from a penalty, before a resilient Shels rallied and secured an equaliser midway through the second half. In its post-match analysis, the Evening Herald praised the contribution of Hannon. "Whether it was in defence or attack, he was always to be found eager to accept an opening."

In the replay, the following Saturday, Bohemians prevailed by 3-1, with Hannon prominent after a nervous start. When he did regain his confidence, the Irish Times said he combined with great effect with the outside-right Willie Hooper.

The victorious 1908 Irish Cup side, with Hannon front row on left.

It was an historic victory; Bohemians' first in the Irish Cup, a trophy that is still played for in Northern Ireland today.

Sixteen years later, Hannon added an FAI Cup medal and became the first player to win both.

Despite his performances in the Bohemians shirt, the 5-0 defeat against Scotland meant it was no surprise that Hannon was among those not retained for the last full international of that year, against Wales. It was to be another three years before he could pit his wits again against the top English professionals.

1908/09 – *More amateur caps*

In November 1908, Hannon earned his second amateur cap in a 5-1 defeat by the old enemy in Dalymount Park. He was one of only three Irish players to retain their places after the 6-1 thrashing by England the previous year.

Amateur sides were mainly chosen from the two senior amateur clubs in the country, Bohemians and Cliftonville, supplemented by the odd amateur with other clubs.

Hannon was somewhat erratic, missing a clear chance before half time. The game played on a heavy, greasy pitch in a strong wind and amid rain showers suited the physically stronger visitors. In particular, the conditions tended to make life difficult for the smaller Hannon, whom the Evening Herald said "could not be excelled for trickery" but who did not possess the strength necessary for the contest.

In the same year, Bohemians were beaten in the Irish Cup final after a replay by Cliftonville. After a 0-0 draw with Cliftonville in an almost underwater Windsor Park, the Belfast side prevailed in front of 13,000 people in Dalymount Park on a 2-1 scoreline.

Bohemians' valiant attempt to retain the trophy had come unstuck at the last hurdle.

Hannon again featured at inside-right, with fellow

Amateur International.
IRELAND   v.   ENGLAND.
Dalymount Park, Dublin.   21st November, 1908.   Kick-off 2.30.

→ IRELAND. ←

The programme for the 1908 amateur international. This is possibly the oldest extant football programme in the state.

Athlonian Johnny McDonnell at centre-forward. Hannon had introduced his fellow Athlonian to Bohemians and their relationship would strengthen in future years when they married two Naughten sisters from Athlone.

1909/1910 – Leinster Senior Cup success

In 1909, Hannon did not feature at amateur international level as Ireland drew 4-4 with England in Leeds. His clubmate and fellow Athlonian Johnny McDonnell was on hand to fly the local flag.

In total, McDonnell earned four full and four amateur caps in his time with Bohemians, as well as Irish League representative honours on five occasions. A dashing centre-forward, whose direct style unhinged defences, McDonnell was a goal-scoring machine for Bohemians in the late 1900s and early 1910s.

During the later years of the first decade of the 20th century and the early years of the second, Bohemians played in both the Irish League and the Leinster Senior League – though Hannon rarely featured in the latter, which was effectively a second team, although often featuring first-teamers.

In 1909, he only made his debut in the Irish League for Bohemians two days after Christmas, scoring twice to help Bohemians to a draw against old rivals Shelbourne. This was effectively a

Johnny McDonnell

warm-up for Hannon ahead of the important cup games early in the new year.

There was to be some silverware at the end of the season for Hannon when he won the first of three successive Leinster Senior Cup medals from a career haul of four by assisting Bohemians to victory over army side Inniskillen Fusiliers. The competition was then far more reputable than it became in later years.

1910/1911 – Bovril and the first international victory over England

The season was notable for Bohemians' relegation from the Irish League, after they finished bottom in the eight-team division. However, as was now becoming increasingly more common, Hannon had little involvement in Bohemians' league travails. As was now his wont, he reserved himself more and more for the crucial cup games which occurred in the first few months after the turn of the year.

His first appearance of the season came in late September when he scored twice to help Bohemians to a 2-0 win over old rivals, Shelbourne. "The Athlone lad may be said to have been responsible for the failure of Shelbourne to annex full points, for he scored both goals for his side and his dashing display had a wonderful effect on the home forwards, particularly in the second half, when they required someone to lead them," the Irish Times noted.

He was present again for the annual amateur international in November 1910, when he helped to create a little bit of footballing history. In that month, Ireland secured their first victory over England at the amateur international level, thanks to a 3-2 triumph in Cliftonville's Solitude ground.

Hannon, at inside-right, was accompanied by Johnny McDonnell who lined out at centre-forward. The duo, were "superb", according to the Evening Herald, completely overshadowing the English defence.

After England had taken an early lead, Ireland initially equalised from the penalty spot following a foul on Hannon. When the visitors again edged in front, Hannon equalised before McDonnell scored the historic winner. The Irish Times said Hannon was the best forward on the field – some praise considering some of the English amateurs were regarded as the top players in the world at the time.

In what must be the world's first example of product placement, the Evening Herald, somewhat tongue in cheek, attributed the victory to an unlikely source: Bovril!

It reported: "If one could pat a member of the Irish Association team on the back and ask him what gave him the brilliant victory over England … he would probably say the way we kept it up during the second half … At half time, both teams were offered Bovril. The English team, thinking the Bovril would make them thirsty, preferred tea. But the Irishmen, one and all, drank Bovril and scored for the first time a win against an English team."

The Irish Senior Cup campaign followed in the early part of 1911 and Hannon was back in harness.

The cup run saw Bohemians meet Glentoran. Hannon was at the centre of controversy before the game when the Northerners lodged a protest against his possible inclusion, stating that he was ineligible under Rule 5 of the Irish Challenge Cup rules. This related to the need for a player to live within ten miles of his team's ground for a period of four weeks.

According to the Irish Times, Bohemians were "perfectly satisfied that Hannon is eligible in accordance with the rule referred as he has not played in an Irish Cup tie for any club other than the nearest or most convenient catered for in the competition". The Evening Herald described the objection as "contemptuous and ridiculous". In any event, Hannon played and, possibly too intent on making his own personal point, overdid his inimitable trickery.

Glentoran won, but ironically, Bohemians on appeal were subsequently awarded the tie. They had protested that Glentoran had included a player who was not listed on the official roster of 22 which by rule had to be sent to the opposition by registered post in advance of the game. And although the player's details had been subsequently telegraphed by Glentoran, the appeal was upheld and Bohemians were deemed to have qualified for the next round. The decision sparked uproar in the North and spilled over into unsavoury threats.

In the meantime, Hannon was soon concentrating on the international front as a week after the Glentoran game he was back on full international duty for Ireland. After playing two of the three full internationals in 1907/1908, he had been forced to wait a further three seasons before securing another international cap, this time against England in February.

His involvement in the victorious amateur side probably helped to bring him back into the full international fray. Ireland had lost their opening match of the 1910/1911 season against Wales in Belfast by 2-1. Ireland's sole score had been registered by another Athlone native, Willie Halligan, then with Derby County, a centre-forward who was making his international debut in that contest.

Halligan had risen from the junior ranks in Dublin, before travelling north to play with Belfast Celtic and Distillery in the Irish League. He later pulled on a jersey for Leeds City, Derby County, Wolves and Hull, amongst others in England.

He was twice capped for Ireland – the second appearance coming against England the following year.

Despite scoring on his debut, Halligan was one of three players dropped for the next international against England. The newspaper Sport reported that he had at least three fine chances to add to his goal but missed opportunities that no man of his experience should have squandered. He was replaced in the green shirt for the game against England by another Athlone-born centre-forward, Johnny McDonnell, a rare feat!

Hannon was also brought into the inside-right berth, meaning two Athlone players lined out in the Irish forward line for this full international.

The game itself was played in front of 25,000 supporters in Derby and despite being one of Ireland's better performances, the home side prevailed by the odd goal in three.

According to the Evening Herald the right-wing partnership of Hannon and Liverpool's Billy Lacey was Ireland's strongest point of attack. While Johnny McDonnell was closely marshalled by the English defence and created few chances, he did link the play well and the Herald argued should be retained for the next international against Scotland in March.

However, before that, Bohemians had the small matter of an Irish Cup semi-final against Cliftonville in Belfast to get through.

Bohemians' decision to protest against Glentoran's victory in the previous round, coming on top of Glentoran's pre-match attempt to exclude Hannon, had created a hostile atmosphere.

And the Evening Herald reported that there were rumours as to what would happen Bohemians which it hoped would prove to be nothing more than "the idle talk of a few hotheads".

Despite being named on the original selection, Hannon was a late absentee - possibly for safety reasons given the controversy that proceeded the game. According to Sport, he was "much missed" as Bohemians struggled to a draw in Belfast.

However, he returned for the replay, which was held in Dublin, where he played a starring role not as inside-right but as right-half in a 2-2 draw. Hannon had previously only occasionally played at right-half back, but it was now to become a regular enough position for him.

The second replay finally saw Bohemians come through in Belfast thanks to a double from McDonnell with Hannon again featuring. Ironically, the Evening Herald noted that Hannon had to be brought from Athlone for the midweek replay – maybe Glentoran had some grounds for protest after all!

Before Bohemians could take on old rivals Shelbourne in the Irish Cup final, Hannon featured in the Irish professional eleven to take on Scotland, again at inside-right alongside centre-forward McDonnell who was also retained from the England game.

This time Ireland were less impressive, losing 2-0 to the Tartan Army in Glasgow in front of 30,000 people. Again the Hannon/Lacey right-sided partnership worked a treat and they were reported to have terrorised the Scots defence in the opening half. However, Hannon was deemed to have spoiled matters as the game went on by endeavouring to do too much. A first-half injury curtailed the contribution of McDonnell, who up to then had been the best forward on the Irish team.

McDonnell and Hannon had no time for post mortems, and were back in harness for Bohemians for the Irish Cup final against Shelbourne in Dalymount Park the following week.

Hannon again turned out at right-half, although the Evening Herald said he was "so capable an exponent of the game that he could fill any position with credit to himself and the club". The same paper said he was "one of the finest players to work an opening for his team." The contest ended scoreless in front of some 17-18,000 fans. Hannon was impressive, giving a "fine exhibition" and his "brilliant half-back play was a feature of the game", according to Sport.

Bohemians eventually lost the replay by 2-1 despite another sterling display by Hannon in the half-back line. Sport said he was the best player on the losing side. It was his third and last Irish Cup final appearance following the win in 1908 and the defeat the following season.

There was to be some little consolation for Hannon and Bohs, though, as they defeated Shelbourne in the Leinster Senior Cup final by the only goal of the game.

1911/1912 – Athlone in the international limelight

After relegation from the Irish League, and with only the Leinster Senior League to provide week-in, week-out action, Hannon made a late start to the 1911/12 season, exemplified by the fact that he passed up on selection for the annual amateur clash against England in November 1911.

Despite the late start, he was soon back in the full international limelight having been selected for the final international of the season against Wales in Cardiff in Spring 1912. Ireland had slumped badly in the earlier games against Scotland and England, as had Wales – so this was a wooden-spoon decider.

Again in all three internationals that season, Ireland included at least one Athlone forward.

For the opening 6-1 defeat to England, William Halligan featured at centre-forward. The second Athlone forward to play for Ireland that season was Joe Enright who was inside-left in the 4-1 loss at home to Scotland.

Neither Halligan nor Enright was selected for the final game away to Wales, on April 13, 1912 – two days before the sinking of the Titanic, but the Athlone representation was maintained as both Hannon and McDonnell featured for the first time that year.

Despite going two down early in the second half away in Cardiff, Ireland rallied to win by 3-2, thus avoiding bottom place in the table. Hannon, according to the Evening Herald, played "a serviceable game" but wandered far too much from his inside-right berth and was "really a better defender than attacker".

The season ended with another Leinster Senior Cup medal for Hannon in a 3-0 victory over the Manchester Regiment.

1912/13 – Bringing home the bacon!

The first Irish team to beat England in a full international. Hannon is third from right in the middle row.

Hannon gained his fourth amateur cap in October 1912 when he lined out in Belfast for the annual clash with English amateurs. The strength of the English side was evidenced by the fact that ten of the starting eleven had been on the team that won the Olympic Games soccer tournament in Stockholm a few months previously.

For the second time since the amateur internationals began in 1906, Ireland emerged victorious, claiming what was a significant scalp. Again there was a considerable Athlone involvement, with Hannon at his traditional inside-right role and McDonnell leading the line as centre-forward.

Ireland raced into a three-goal lead with the energetic McDonnell bagging two in his trademark bustling style – and although England rallied, the home side held on for another famous win.

Both Hannon and McDonnell earned inter-league honours later that month when they represented the Irish League against the English League in Belfast.

Four months later, at the other side of the year break, Hannon was to return to haunt the old masters, England, this time as part of the first Irish eleven to overcome the English at the full professional ranks.

The day Saturday, February 15th 1913, in Windsor Park, Belfast, was a day that to its own generation was akin to the Giants Stadium in New York on June 18th, 1994, or Stuttgart on June 12th, 1988.

It was the day that Ireland slayed the footballing giant next door for the first time. A day when David finally put paid to Goliath.

The scale of the achievement can be measured by the fact that for the previous 31 internationals against Ireland, England had remained undefeated.

Indeed, in the subsequent 21 internationals between England and what is now the Republic (8 more up to and including 1921 under the IFA umbrella and thirteen completed internationals between the Republic and England since the formation of the FAI) the Auld Enemy have only been defeated three more times.

Up to 30,000 crowded into Windsor Park to witness the historic occasion. It was the second successive international between the sides to be played this side of the Irish Sea after the English sportingly agreed to waive home advantage.

Close to the half-hour mark, the Irish inside-right McAuley was badly injured and was forced to leave the field, leaving Ireland to play with ten men for the remaining hour. Soon after, things went from bad to worse, when Sunderland's Buchan put the visitors in front on 36 minutes.

However, the ten men equalised on the stroke of half-time, when the English keeper only fisted a corner high into the air and Billy Gillespie looped a header into the far corner, which an English defender could only help to the net. Both sides struck the woodwork in a frantic opening to the second half, before Gillespie again struck for Ireland on 57 minutes.

For much of the remaining half hour it was a backs-to-the-wall defensive display from Ireland who frustrated the visitors time and again. It was a nail-biting finale, made worse by the premature pitch invasion prompted by a stray whistle 30 seconds before the real thing.

In an obituary tribute to Hannon, some 58 years later, the Westmeath Independent noted that it had been the achievement he had been most proud of during his lengthy career.

Such was the wave of joy that coursed through the Irish football scene that special medals were minted for the players to commemorate the occasion. They were feted, as the medals stated, "for bringing home the bacon".

Ironically, it was not one of Hannon's most impressive displays in the national shirt – but never mind, he had played his part in history.

Looking back on the game some 13 years later, one of Hannon's playing colleagues on the day, Val Harris, said: "Before the match, it was only a question of how many goals the great England side would score against us … I will never forget the outburst of cheering and excitement at the conclusion of the game. Belfast was absolutely wild with jubilation on Ireland's great victory."

Unfortunately, the victory was not enough to secure the Home Nations Championship as Ireland had lost the opening game of the series against Wales.

Strangely, the English match was Hannon's final time to play at this full international level under the IFA. He was not dropped for the remaining fixture of 1913, home to Scotland. In fact, he was chosen on the original line-up but cried off and was the sole absentee from that Windsor Park side which defeated England.

The following season saw the last internationals before World War One intervened and Hannon hardly featured at all for Bohemians, so it was no surprise that he wasn't chosen by the international selectors.

1913/14

The 1913/14 season appeared set to be a watershed year for Hannon as he took over the captaincy of his club.

Again he was selected for the amateur international but stood down due to unfitness. He had not played for Bohemians by the time of the annual test in November 1913.

In fact, despite his leadership role, Hannon hardly turned out at all for the Dubliners except in a few unimportant end of season contests.

And with World War One declared, the football calendar became obsolete. Although Hannon would go on to experience a hugely successful footballing career after the war, in 1914 he was 26 years old and entering what must have been his footballing prime.

If the war had not intervened it's almost certain that Hannon would have continued to rack up amateur and professional caps for Ireland.

1914/1915 – Hannon pulls on Athlone colours

Again Hannon was strangely subdued, playing less than a handful of games for Bohemians in the major cup competitions this season.

The war had not raged sufficiently at this stage to cause the cancellation of the Irish League – but Bohemians played appallingly, drawing just one of 14 games and finishing rock bottom with a single point.

However, this season was noteworthy in one major respect: the debut of Hannon in Athlone colours.

Despite his long footballing career, Hannon had never played for Athlone Town, having started as a young student with Bohemians.

And on January 23rd, 1915, he made his bow for Athlone in the Leinster Senior Cup victory over Frankfort. Interestingly, he was permitted to play with two different clubs at a similar level. Athlone went on to reach the semi-final of the competition but, unfortunately for Hannon, were unable to secure what would have been an intriguing final against his other club Bohemians.

Hannon's less than regular appearances in the past few seasons could be explained by the fact he was probably undergoing his solicitor's apprenticeship and studying for his final exams, which he subsequently passed in the middle of 1915.

1915 – 1918 – In time of trouble and war

The Irish League may have ceased due to the war, but the Irish Cup continued in 1915 and 1916 with Hannon featuring in some of the earlier rounds for Bohemians.

1915 was marked by his fourth Leinster Senior Cup medal when Bohemians defeated Shelbourne 3-2, thanks to a Hannon winner.

1916 was also notable as Hannon lined out for his native Athlone against Bohemians on Easter Monday in Athlone. Entry to the game at Athlone's Sportsground was priced at sixpence, but interestingly, on the day of the Easter Rising, it was still thought sensible to have a half-price admission fee for soldiers in uniform. His Bohemians colleague Johnny McDonnell also lined out for his home club, Athlone, in this friendly,

By this time, Hannon had also turned his attention to Gaelic football, and was chosen on an Athlone panel to play a friendly with Moate in September 1916. The match was used as a warm-up for Athlone's continued progression in the Westmeath Junior Football Championship.

Meanwhile, Hannon's career was progressing off the field and he was elected solicitor for Roscommon County Council late in 1916.

An involvement in the world of law and order during the turbulent times of the War of Independence and Civil War must not have been easy. And indeed Hannon was caught up in dramatic scenes in Athlone in September 1920 when the British authorities attempted to shut down the new Sinn Fein-organised Arbitration Court – a parallel judicial system established by the Republican movement to supplant the old imperial regime.

Hannon and two other solicitors were among 42 people arrested at the arbitration court sitting after the courthouse was taken over by the British Army. Hannon, the other solicitors and the members of the Arbitration Court itself were not released until late the following evening, after a preliminary investigation by the local army brass was concluded.

Hannon had been one of the first local solicitors to recognise the new Sinn Fein court system – a fact recognised by Sinn Fein members in subsequent memoirs.

1919 – 1921 – Final fling under old IFA regime

For the remainder of the war years, Hannon made irregular trips to Dublin to join Bohemians in key cup games – both in the Irish Cup and Leinster Senior Cup.

He also featured in friendly line-ups for both Athlone and Bohemians, particularly in 1919.

The ending of the war permitted the resumption of the amateur international series – and Hannon won his last cap under the IFA in Derby in November 1919 when he lined out for Ireland against England in a comprehensive 5-0 defeat. In Hannon's defence, he had seen little service that season.

With the Irish League back in operation after the ending of the Great War, Hannon rejoined Bohemians. He made only a handful of Irish League appearances for the Dubliners in 1919/20 and it appears his final appearance was in a local Dublin competition, the Metropolitan Cup, in the 1920/21 season.

Just as Hannon's career seemed on a slow fade out, it was destined for a dramatic revival.

Continued next chapter.

Chapter 20

Denis Hannon

The second coming

1921-1923

The formation of the Football Association of the Irish Free State in the middle of 1921 resulted in a major split in football on the island. Clubs south of the border rowed in behind the new organisation and Hannon was one of the prime movers in ensuring Athlone played its part in the development of the association.

As we have seen, the Athlone and District Association was one of only three to affiliate to the new body. Indeed, Hannon initially represented the local association on the council of the Free State Football Association.

Having severed his ties with Bohemians, Hannon lined out for Athlone for the first time in the new football era in the club's

Denis Hannon in 1922

historic first fixture in the FAI Cup in 1921 against YMCA.

The game, according to the Evening Herald, marked his reappearance on the field of play after a long absence.

Having overcome YMCA, Athlone were drawn away to Hannon's old alma mater, Bohemians. This time, Dinny featured at right-half back – probably to help staunch the attacking threat of the Dubliners. In any event, the tactic clearly did not work as Athlone succumbed by 7-1.

He opened his account for Athlone with two goals in the 4-1 victory at home to Brooklyn in the second round of the Leinster Senior Cup.

> **Clarence, 3; Athlone, 1.**
> At St. James's Park, Dublin. Hannon, the Bohemian and Internationalist, assisted Athlone. There was a poor attendance. A goal fell to Clarence early, Grant being the scorer. Hannon, who was in splendid form, equalised soon afterwards. In a scrimmage around Athlone's goal Grant piloted the ball through a forest of legs into the net. Athlone found the Clarence defence impregnable in the second half, despite much battering. Grant scored again for Clarence. and Weafer in goal stopped many well-directed shots from the Athlone forwards.

A newspaper report on Denis Hannon's first appearance in Athlone colours.

The 1922/23 season witnessed the arrival of Athlone on the League of Ireland scene, having been approved for membership by the league. Hannon, of course, was by now an instrumental figure in the club. He served as treasurer for some years in the 1920s.

He scored his first league goals for Athlone in the fifth match of the campaign with a brace at home on October 14th, 1922, to Olympia.

Hannon also assisted as Athlone reached the Shield final, their first senior decider under the new football administration.

Throughout his career, Hannon had an uncanny ability to produce the goods when it most mattered, on the big occasion. In the surprise Shield quarter-final defeat of Shamrock Rovers in 1922/23, Hannon played a major role. The Westmeath Independent remarked: "He was all over the field and many there were who said he never played better, even in the heyday of the Old Bohs."

The Evening Herald said Hannon was to be seen in defence and attack in equal measure. It was a sort of roving brief that he had regularly adopted for Bohemians but that would become his custom for Athlone in the next season's victorious cup run. In late 1924, the Sports Mail acknowledged: "It is no exaggeration to say that it is due to his unorthodox methods as a rover that the Athlone club are in the position they attained in the soccer world last season, the winning of the Blue Riband."

1923-24 – Cup glory

The 1923/24 season was to prove the pinnacle of Hannon's career with history beckoning in a multitude of ways. The old-stager would become the first man to win cup medals in both football jurisdictions on the island of Ireland.

He would score the winning goal for his native Athlone in the FAI Cup final and he would add two more international caps to his name, captaining his country for their first foray into international football as an independent nation.

For Hannon, the 1923/24 season commenced busily as he entered the new campaign as treasurer of the club. Hannon was also a member of the standard club committee; a member of the selection committee (in those days, there were no managers, simply trainers, and the task of picking the team fell on a special committee) and vice-captain.

On the field, he was a fixture on the starting eleven, mainly at inside-right but occasionally at right-half back.

However, Hannon appeared to focus himself particularly on the cup games. He used the Leinster Senior Cup contests in the first few weeks of January 1924 to fine-tune his shooting. He bagged two goals against St Paul's to warm up for the much more crucial cup quarter-final against Shelbourne a week later.

It was a pattern that would recur for the final, with Hannon keeping his eye in by scoring four in an 8-1 defeat of another Leinster Senior League side Inchicore Utd in the next round of the Leinster Senior Cup. It was noteworthy that Hannon had found his shooting boots in the last game before the cup final.

Indeed, Hannon pulled Athlone through the cup run with the elemental power of a force of nature.

Almost as if he felt the strength of his own will could catapult his team to cup success, Hannon strove to leave no stone unturned. His performance in the semi-final match against Bohemians was described by one paper as "tireless and ubiquitous".

In the replay, he again nominally lined out at inside-right, but spent much of the contest in defence assisting his hard-pressed half-back line. According to the Irish Independent, he was "really a half-back".

Hannon appears to have been the architect behind Athlone's successful tactics of a crowded, forceful, pressurised defence complete with swift attacking on the break. And he implemented the philosophy to the last detail.

The Evening Herald said he was "the star artiste at spoiling" in the semi-final clash with Bohemians.

In the quarter-final against Shelbourne, Hannon, nominally selected at inside-right, could constantly be found tracking back into defence to assist his beleaguered colleagues. His "wonderful energy" was noted by an impressed Irish Independent.

In the days before the cup final against Fordsons, Hannon must have been buoyed by his increased confidence in front of goal.

Hindsight can provide a falsely clear picture, but from this distance of years it appears almost inevitable that Athlone, and Hannon in particular, would triumph on St Patrick's Day, 1924. He had devised a philosophy of pressure tactics, forceful, physical play and swift counter-attacks based on sweeping moves to undermine the best teams in the land. He had displayed a steely determination to secure the cup – leading his charges from the front. And with the timely reappearance of his sharp-shooting instinct, it was set up for Hannon to hand Athlone its one and only cup day of glory.

Republic of Ireland's first captain

Of course, there were more stellar and historic honours to be conferred on Hannon that season as he prepared to travel to Paris in May to represent Ireland in the Olympic Games and indeed captain his country in its first foray as an independent nation on a football field.

If all that wasn't enough for one season, things were busy in his personal life too as he tied the knot with an Athlone woman, Molly Naughton, from another Connaught Street family, in late July 1924 at a ceremony in Westland Row, Dublin.

1924-1928 – Keeping the faith

Having reached the pinnacle of his career with Athlone, it would have been understandable if Hannon, in the wake of the cup glory and at the age of 36, had hung up his boots. But no, there was still more in the tank.

It may be that Hannon's sparing contributions in his early years with Bohemians helped to extend his career into his late 30s.

At the age of 36, the Sports Mail was referring to him as "a veteran of the game" but one who "shows little the worse for wear and is able to stay with the best either in defence or offence." After years of selective appearances for Bohemians and with the break of almost five years due to World War One, it's easy to understand how Hannon may not have had as many miles on the clock as his age would have suggested.

Still no-one can turn back time and as the seasons progressed Hannon's influence on the pitch began to wane in direct proportion to his growing prestige and control of Athlone's affairs behind the scenes.

Hannon may not have been the manager (no such position existed in those days) or indeed the captain, but he was the general.

It was Hannon who spotted the potential of probably Athlone's best player, John Joe Dykes. It was Hannon who encouraged Tommy Muldoon to join Aston Villa. And it was Hannon who was the on-field leader during the victorious cup campaign.

Hannon played the majority of league games in the 1924/25 season, some at centre-forward, scoring, at least, twice.

When Athlone attempted to retain the FAI Cup, Hannon featured at left-half in the semi-final defeat to Shelbourne. And as the campaign petered out in end-of-season Shield fare, run over a league basis, Hannon was still a regular fixture on the team sheet.

Come the 1925/1926 season, it appears as if he had opted to retire. However, he featured at least once, filling in for the injured Terry Judge at left-half in a league match against Brideville in October 1925. The Evening Herald seized on his appearance to state: "The suggestion that Dinny Hannon had retired had no basis in truth. He reappeared against Brideville and exhibited his customary cunning and cleverness from left-half."

Surprisingly, Hannon was back in harness for the following season, 1926/27, as he approached the age of 39. Starting as he obviously intended to go on, Hannon appeared in the season-opening league game against Bray Unknowns. In fact, of the 18 league contests, Hannon lined up in at least a dozen.

However, the season off had taken its toll at least in the early games of the campaign. It was then that the Football Sports Weekly voiced strong criticism of his conditioning. "Hannon found the pace too strong and especially because of the weight he is putting on …. Hannon is getting too fat," it remarked.

In the background, press reports were beginning to make more frequent references to Hannon's involvement in the management of the club. Football Sports Weekly in September 1926 noted that Hannon had taken a week's holidays (which coincided with an off week for the club). But it remained a working holiday to some extent. "He hopes to pick up some new talent for the Midland club," the paper commented.

As the season progressed, Hannon's early unfitness was becoming a thing of the past, and the same paper later noted how much work he got through in matches.

Hannon's influence, according to Football Sports Weekly, remained significant. Its writer, previewing the FAI Cup first-round clash with Shelbourne held in Athlone on January 8th, 1927, warned the Dubliners that there would be no roses scattered on the path that leads to the Midlands venue. "Denis Hannon will have his lads tutored to the needs of the moment and Dinny is a man who knows how to impart such advice. I can picture him emulating the village schoolmaster whom Goldsmith immortalised so long ago."

After defeat to Shelbourne and with the league concluded, the season finished with the tail-end Shield and Leinster Senior Cup competitions, with Hannon rarely if, at all, featuring. He did, fittingly appear on April 30th in the Athlone side which took on Bohemians in Dalymount Park in the second last game of the campaign.

There was no more appropriate opposition or venue for what may well have been his final competitive game – over 20 years after he made his senior debut. Athlone did have one last rearranged league fixture the following weekend, at home to St James's Gate, for which little details are available. It's not known if Hannon also featured in this contest, but, in a way, it would be nice to think he pulled down the curtain on a fantastic playing career against Bohemians in Dalymount Park.

The conclusion of his playing days, of course, did not mean the severing of his ties with Athlone. In fact, the opposite appears the case, as he threw himself into a reshaping of the Athlone side for the 1927/28 campaign.

And it was a daunting task as Athlone were facing almost insurmountable difficulties in the boardrooms of power. There was a real danger that threats to expel Athlone from the league due to the lack of proper ground facilities would be carried out. It was Hannon who took up the cudgel on Athlone's behalf, making an impassioned address at a meeting of the league's committee. It worked to an extent and at a price. Athlone had to commit to major investment in their ground facilities to secure admission for the 1927/28 season.

In the meantime, the focus of the club shifted entirely to the development of young local talent. All the Dubliners were shipped out and a team comprising some gnarled old veterans, youngsters plucked from the local junior scene and from the Mullingar ranks was pressed into service. Whether this was a tactic forced on the club for financial reasons associated with the ground development or a purely strategic decision is not known. What is known is the move did not work and Athlone finished marooned at the bottom of the table.

Hannon had been registered as a player for the 1927/28 season, but never took to the field of play. Instead, he was referred to as "manager" by the Football Sports Weekly later in the year.

The same paper darkly noted midway through the season that Hannon was having great difficulty in finding a new ground. As it transpired, Athlone had neither a new ground nor a berth in the League of Ireland for the following season and slipped out of the top rank of Irish soccer.

The rest

Of course, with Athlone's return to the local junior level, Hannon's involvement in football did not simply cease.

He was a constant fixture at Athlone games – and was noted for his patience and humility, rarely criticising the contribution of players who may not have matched his level of ability.

He was also chosen as Vice President of the Connaught Football Council in 1930. In January 1941, shortly after the Athlone Woollen Mills went up in flame, Hannon organised an Athlone Fire Disaster Relief Fund fund-raising friendly between an Athlone selection and Shelbourne in Dalymount Park.

The love of football ran through his family. His brother, Canon Patrick Hannon, for instance, defied then bishop John Charles McQuaid's call on Catholics to boycott Ireland's controversial game against communist Yugoslavia in 1955.

Although Dinny did not appear on the committee for some years after the club's departure from the League of Ireland, he was President from, at least, 1948, to some part of the 1960s. He was also a notable presence at major occasions in the club's history, speaking at the reception for the victorious FAI Junior Cup winners in 1935, and was instrumental in the purchase of St Mel's Park in 1936, carrying out the legal niceties free of charge.

When, in December 1967, Athlone travelled to Cork to play local side Crofton Celtic in the quarter final of the FAI Intermediate Cup, Hannon was amongst 300 supporters present. He was able to witness his hometown club qualify for the FAI Cup again after a gap of some 40 years.

When Athlone returned to the League of Ireland for the 1969/70 season, he was vice president of the club – ensuring a continuity from when Athlone last played in the league in the 1927/28 season.

Hannon was one of the directors in a limited company formed in 1970 to operate Athlone Town. According to his obituary, he stepped down from the board shortly after, before his death in August 1971, aged 83, to allow new blood into the club.

He was buried in Cornamagh Cemetery after a funeral mass in SS Peter and Paul's. Fittingly, the committee of Athlone Town formed a guard of honour for probably the greatest footballer ever produced in the town.

Denis Hannon's international caps

(Irish scores first)

AMATEUR CAPS IFA

December 7, 1907	V. England (a) 1-6
November 21, 1908	V. England (h) 1-5
November 19, 1910	V. England (h) 3-2 - SCORED
October 5, 1912	V. England (h) 3-2
November 15, 1919	V. England (a) 0-5

FULL CAPS IFA

February 15, 1908	V. England (h) 1-3 – SCORED
March 14, 1908	V. Scotland (h) 0-5
February 11 1911	V. England (a) 1-2
March 18, 1911	V. Scotland (a) 0-2
April 13, 1912	V. Wales (a) 3-2
February 15 1913	V. England (h) 2-1

FULL CAPS FAI

May 28, 1924	V. Bulgaria (Paris Olympics) 1-0 - CAPTAIN
June 2, 1924	V. Holland (Paris Olympics) 1-2 (A.E.T.) - CAPTAIN

Chapter 21

The FAI Cup final

Glory days

The gathering crowd

The gates of Dalymount Park were opened at 1.30pm and early-comers converged to gain a good vantage point. Those who filled the ground in the hours before kick-off were entertained by the St James Brass and Reed Band who presented a programme of music

By 3pm the sun had broken free of the few clouds in an otherwise crystal blue sky and shone gloriously down on Dalymount Park. The scene was set.

An estimated 14,000 had crammed into the ground a full 30 minutes before kick-off. By 3.15pm, the gates were closed and a capacity attendance of some 22,000, paying gate receipts of £1,100, had gathered. Interestingly, the practice was that the gate receipts would be divided in three; with each of the clubs and the FAI taking an equal portion.

It was a then record crowd for a cup final. And it shared with the attendance at the Free State League v. Glasgow Celtic game the record of being the largest crowd of the year.

The vast throng took every available vantage point. Some 250 stewards had been employed, but such was the scale of the crowd that they could do

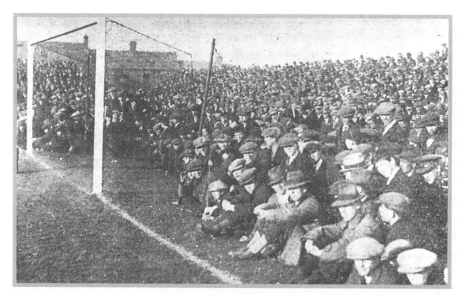

A scene from the cup final.

nothing to prevent the spectators crowding around both sets of goalposts and within touching distance of players along the endlines and sidelines.

A similar crowd at the Free State League v. Glasgow Celtic match a few weeks previously was described by the Evening Telegraph in a manner which also captured the atmosphere of cup final day perfectly:

"The crowd poured through the stiles faster and thicker and spread itself over the stands and slopes or took up positions by the rails or along the touchline seats in such numbers that by the time the usual photographic operations started, prior to the teams trotting onto the pitch, there did not appear to be a square yard of space unoccupied but still the stiles clicked and the latecomers elbowed their way to some place or other or squirmed themselves into the smallest openings amidst the five-deep row of standing spectators around the railings.

"They could not see much of the play but they had got in and trusted to luck to catch a glimpse of an occasional jerseyed player over the shoulders or heads of those in front as he flashed past their view.

"These back seaters or last-row spectators appeared to be quite satisfied at being there. If only to catch and enjoy the fever of the excitement and surrender themselves captive to the enthusiasm of those better situated to give audible expression to it.

"Every side of the pitch, rising to the highest point from where a view of the game could be got, was thickly dotted with faces. So closely were the people packed that their individual outlines were lost. One could see nothing but faces around, the sky above and pitch below."

Blue is the colour ...

Of the equally large crowd of March 17th, many were sporting the green and white of the Cork side; but equally, the colours of Athlone were everywhere to be seen.

Blue; on the self-styled Town mascot John McKervey, who was bedecked from head to toe in the Athlone colour.

Blue; on a little dog, whose collar of that same colour betrayed the affiliations of its owner.

Mascot John McKervey (left) meets local TD, Sean Lyons

214

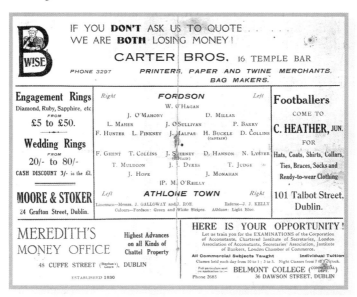

The Football Association of the Irish Free State
CHALLENGE CUP FINAL

Souvenir Programme

ATHLONE TOWN

FORDSON (CORK)

At Dalymount Park, Dublin,
St. Patrick's Day, 17th March

KICK-OFF 3-30 P.M.

OFFICIAL PROGRAMME, TWOPENCE

The front cover of the programme.

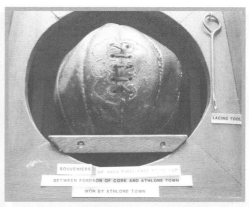

The match ball, preserved in the Athlone Castle Museum.

The precious FAI Cup final medal.

And blue in the heavens, the azure sky providing a lucky association with Athlone.

Having completed their photographic duties, Fordsons were first out on the pitch, led by their captain Harry Buckle. To a tremendous cheer, the Athlone eleven then entered the playing arena.

Buckle won the toss and elected to play down the slight incline in the first half with the warm sun on his team's backs. With adrenaline coursing through the 22 sets of veins and the impressive attendance roaring them on, both teams set into the game at a frenetic pace, particularly Athlone.

90 minutes of history

The midlanders attacked with a cyclonic fury which left the more thoughtful Fordsons badly perturbed. Indeed, Athlone's battering ram approach could have seen the game over as a contest within the first 15 minutes, bar a resilient display by the Fordsons rearguard and defence.

Hannon, in particular, was a menace in his roving role – and his extra focus on the attacking side of his game was noticeable.

Knowing the first goal would provide a crucial foothold in the match, the wily old campaigner was determined to propel his side into the lead early on. Indeed, it was Hannon who could and possibly should have opened the scoring after less than ten minutes. A fine combination between Collins, Sweeney and Lyster, led to the latter releasing Hannon, but he speared the effort narrowly wide, with O'Hagan spread-eagled on the turf.

Norman Lyster was playing a prominent part early on too and his right-wing centres were causing havoc for the Fordsons defence. It was another one of his deliveries, missed by the already pressurised O'Hagan, which provided the next in a series of clear opportunities for Athlone, but neither the in-rushing Hannon nor Sweeney could provide the necessary finishing touch.

Dykes was also joining the relentless forward march – and returned a couple of misplaced clearances from the harassed Fordsons defenders goalward to no avail soon after.

Then O'Mahony scrambled away a Hannon cross as the Fordsons backs defended desperately. They were at the pin of their collar to survive.

Fordsons attacks were rare; Frank Hunter over-running the ball when a half chance presented itself.

Although they had successfully rebuffed the first wave of Athlone attacks, Fordsons were to have little opportunity to attempt to regain the initiative as Athlone proceeded to once again steadily turn the screw. Ghent was now beginning to terrorise the Fordsons defence, linking with Collins to lethal effect, down the left. And he came close near the quarter-hour mark with a spectacular goal-bound half-volley which struck O'Mahony.

Although Fordsons cleared the ensuing corner they failed to snuff out the Athlone attack and a long-range Dinny Hannon strike whistled just over the bar. Two efforts from Hannon and each time he was getting closer.

The breakthrough came just before the 20th minute mark. Again the source of the danger was Ghent, the winger raced away down the left after Muldoon and Collins had combined to release him. Ghent rounded Millar, and despite the attentions of three opponents, delivered a dangerous cross into the goalmouth.

Sweeney racing in, smashed the ball goalwards, but it was blocked down by O'Mahony. O'Hagan, primed to react to Sweeney's effort, momentarily relaxed, fatally.

Hannon pounced on the loose ball, and despite having no clear view on goal, he instantly flashed a rising first-time shot through a small opening amidst a converging posse of three defenders.

The ball whistled through the gap. The keeper's frantic drive was a split-second too late and the net bulged.

It was Hannon at his opportunistic best. 1-0 Athlone.

Stunned into action by Hannon's strike, Fordsons attacked but were soon rebuffed and Athlone again pressed with Dykes and Lyster testing O'Hagan before Ghent's high drive struck the woodwork from an acute angle.

Soon after, Fordsons eventually threatened the Athlone goal. A poor clearance allowed Hunter to drop a dangerous cross into no-man's land between the defence and keeper. Pinkney failed to capitalise on the opportunity and Dykes got back to snuff out the situation. However, the danger was only momentarily averted as Fordsons quickly regained possession and Malpas, from Buckle's pass, was narrowly wide.

Athlone returned on the offensive and seemed to have been unjustly denied a second just before the interval when O'Hagan appeared to have scrambled Sweeney's header from a Lyster cross clear from behind the line. The ball curled up off the ground over O'Hagan's shoulder but he hooked it out from behind his body with his left arm.

After the break, Athlone were unable to sustain the remarkable pace they injected into the game in the opening half and as the contest progressed Fordsons were able to come more into proceedings, although they were never allowed to fully settle into their more cerebral style of play.

Although, the play was more evenly distributed, it was Athlone who were still in control, bar for the final quarter of the contest. Early in the second half, Athlone survived some Fordsons pressure, without ever being in serious danger, thanks to a hesitancy up front in the Cork eleven and some imperturbable defending from Hope and Monahan.

At the other end, Hannon came close before O'Hagan saved his side again when he scrambled a low drive from Tommy Collins clear from the goal line near the butt of his post.

Action from the final as Buckle attempts an acrobatic contact as Hope (left) and Monahan (right) prepare to intervene.

The Cork side should have levelled matters then when Denis Collins' left-wing cross left Malpas with only O'Reilly to beat but the centre-forward wastefully fired over. O'Reilly, who had effectively been a spectator in the one-sided opening half, now found himself paying full attention. The miss characterised Malpas' contribution. And indeed, the centre-forward was cast as the fall guy in many of the post-match newspaper reports.

Athlone, though, again pressed forward, and O'Hagan was lucky to deny Hannon. Soon after, Sweeney in characteristically forceful fashion, burst by three defenders and smashed an unstoppable shot past O'Hagan only to have the effort controversially chalked off for what match reports indicated was a breach of the offside rule. The incident summed up Sweeney's day: he had no luck in the game, according to the Irish Independent.

Soon after, O'Mahony saved his side when he bravely blocked down another Ghent effort.

Fordsons enjoyed more fortune down the flanks in the latter stages –and provided Athlone with a nerve-wracking final quarter-hour. Malpas was inches wide after a good passing move as Athlone's citadel endured a few narrow escapes.

But Fordsons had to wait till the final minute to produce a real danger moment of note when, with Athlone hearts in their mouths, Denis Collins had the chance from close range to snatch an undeserved replay. However, O'Reilly heroically parried the shot to secure the cup for Athlone.

When the final whistle went just seconds later, hundreds of fans swarmed onto the pitch and carried the triumphant Athlone heroes shoulder high from the playing surface.

Post-match presentation

For the first time in history, the FAI Cup was presented to the winning captain immediately after the game.

H.J. Brennan, the secretary of the Football Association of the Irish Free State, ascended to the balcony in Dalymount Park and introduced Sir Henry McLaughlin, Chairman of the Football Association of the Irish Free State, who said it was beneficial for the game and for the nation that Athlone should not only enter the ranks of senior football but also take possession of the cup.

When Jim Sweeney rose to collect the trophy, there was a deafening roar, that came in waves as Athlone fans allowed their joyousness to erupt.

Sweeney thanked the chairman of the Football Association and every member of the association and said he was delighted to receive the cup, for the first time in the history of Athlone. Concluding he called for three cheers for both the Football Association and for Fordsons.

This time around, Athlone finally reaped the credit their extraordinary cup run had merited.

There was unanimity that Athlone fully deserved the victory and indeed, a larger margin than a single goal, it was generally accepted, would have more justly reflected their dominance.

The Evening Herald noted: "Contrary to the expectations of those that witnessed Fordsons thrash St James Gate, Athlone Town made them look like a team of novices."

Despite the many warning lessons, Fordsons too were unprepared for Athlone's inimitable style. "They offered a poorer resistance to the dashing tactics of Athlone, than either Shelbourne or Bohemians," according to the Herald.

Then again, both Sport and the Irish Independent commented, to their amazement, that Athlone had actually intensified their activity levels and played "even harder and better" than in their matches with Shelbourne and Bohemians.

And of course that old reliable tactic of an early blitzkrieg on the opposition was utilised on cup final day too. "Their confidence was palpable from the start. They shaped like winners in the first five minutes' play," Sport said. Indeed, Athlone could have inflicted a severe hiding on Fordsons and won by a string of goals had the Cork defence wilted in the face of the early Athlone onslaught.

Sport said Athlone had given evidence of their invincibility as cup fighters. And although it again criticised the frequency with which the ball was in the air, the paper commended Athlone's unrelenting work rate and noted their unflappable confidence.

Some commentators were critical of the performance of the Fordsons full and half-backs but Sport was insistent on praising their unyielding defending against the early waves of Athlone attacks.

Nonetheless, it was clear Athlone's attacking five had the measure of their opponents and indeed, slicker finishing on the part of the Athlone forwards would have seen a more comprehensive victory.

The Irish Times believed Athlone were infinitely the better side and were full value for three or four goals.

Athlone again adopted the tactics which had served them so well throughout the campaign, swinging the ball about with carefree abandon and marking with ability and precision, that paper said.

Up front Fordsons were at sixes and sevens, their close-passing style easily snuffed out by the sentinels of the Athlone rearguard.

Indeed, there was general disappointment at the performance of the Cork side. The Irish Independent noted they had a fit of the Blues.

It added Fordsons' reactions resembled more the popular dance of the 1920s of the same name than their normal footballing style.

However, Sport felt that the real reason for Fordsons' off-colour display was Athlone's unique brand of football.

"It was the fierce dash and speed and the high and long kicking of Athlone which contributed mainly to their (Forsdons') undoing."

Sport also noted the "bewilderment of the Corkmen" at the spoiling work of the Athlone halves and fulls "who clattered the ball in all directions".

The large crowd may also have indirectly benefited Athlone, who after their three games against Bohemians and Shelbourne had grown accustomed to playing in such cauldrons. In contrast, Fordsons' display showed signs of a type of stage fright.

On the Cork side, only keeper O'Hagan came in for praise. Sport said: "The Cork team have him to thank that the scoring against them was so small."

And not for the first time, a premature obituary was penned for the career of veteran captain Buckle.

Eleven good men and true

Individually, the Athlone eleven performed heroically.

But as ever, there were some better than others. The Evening Herald selected Hope, Hannon, Ghent and Collins for particular mention.

O'Reilly had again been safe and reliable and had completed a remarkable feat of not having conceded a single goal in the cup campaign.

In front of him, Monahan and Hope were dogged and unyielding. "Cool, collected, resilient yet unbreakable, each in turn, first tackling and then clearing, in inimitable style," according to the Westmeath Independent.

They were equally well-protected by a half-back line, whose fulcrum was the unequalled John Joe Dykes.

Dykes' strength and direct play ensured he was ideal for Athlone's particular approach. He both quashed Fordsons attacks and initiated Athlone forward movements with the same simplicity and effectiveness.

Terry Judge had possibly the hardest task of the Athlone eleven in his duel with Fordsons' dangerman Denis Collins. But except for a late rally from the Cork winger, Judge easily overcame the outside-left whose reputation took a battering in the process.

At left-half, Tommy Muldoon was again the epitome of style. With a more cultured manner of play than many of his teammates, Muldoon stood out as an accomplished footballer, who also matched the determination and work rate of his colleagues. Muldoon was also a launch pad for much of Athlone's attacks. His regular feeding of Ghent and Tommy Collins helped Athlone to enjoy great success down the Fordsons' right and it was this trio who combined to create the winner for Hannon.

Hannon, as was now his wont, roamed freely, and could be found supplementing his defence as regularly as playing in his nominal position of inside-right. Noticeably though, Hannon focused more of his attentions on attack than he had in previous cup games with the end product of the crucial goal which brought the trophy back to Athlone.

Norman Lyster justified his inclusion in the unusual outside-right berth, particularly with a string of early crosses that helped Athlone take a foothold in the game.

On the other wing, Ghent and Collins enjoyed an instinctive understanding which left Fordsons' defence bedraggled. According to the Westmeath Independent, Frank Ghent completely overshadowed the Cork inside-left Denis Collins, on whom much of the pre-match attention had centred.

"Collins came up from Cork with fame and renown entwining him. He lost both and Ghent it was who took them away from Dalymount."

If Cork's Collins had disappointed, Athlone's namesake did nothing of the sort. In fact, Tommy Collins produced one of the games of his life availing of the space afforded by Fordsons decision to divert much of their attention to snuffing out the threat of Jim Sweeney. He struck up a connection with Ghent which had Athlone raiding with Viking-like impunity down the Fordsons right.

Captain Jim Sweeney received close attention from a number of Cork defenders, a move which limited his individual contribution to the victory but which created more space for the remainder of the forward line to exploit.

Despite the close attentions of a number of Fordsons defenders, Sweeney had two 'goals' controversially ruled out. The Evening Herald noted: "While the other two goals, one later in the first half, and in the second half, were disallowed, I am strongly of the opinion that both were legitimate."

The Herald journalist appeared to have been taken to task for his comments and a few days later offered this rather embarrassing climbdown.

"There was, we now learn, no ground for these statements, since in the first case the ball never crossed the line and in the second the ball was handled and was netted after the referee's whistle was blown."

The identity of the likely complainant to the newspaper may be become clearer from the paper's next paragraph.

"As proof of the referee's justice in disallowing the scores in these circumstances we are pleased to say that no complaints were made by any side in reference to the matter. The captains of both teams came to the referee after the match and expressed their entire satisfaction with his work."

This mini post-controversy was in reality an irrelevance.

As the Westmeath Independent remarked, joyously: "But of what consequence is it now anyway? Haven't we the cup? Isn't our captain there to fight another day? Hasn't he the proud and unique distinction of captaining the first Athlone eleven to bring the so-long desired trophy his native and historic town? Yes, all that and more."

Athlone Town team:
Paddy O'Reilly, Joe Monahan, Jimmy Hope, Terry Judge, John Joe Dykes, Tommy Muldoon, Norman Lyster, Denis Hannon, Jim Sweeney, Tommy Collins, Frank Ghent.

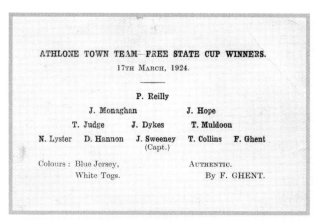

A commemorative postcard

The Cup final team

The grave of Jim Sweeney (Jim Sweeney inset).

Chapter 22

Jim Sweeney

Forgotten hero

An unmarked grave

As captain of the only Athlone Town team to win the FAI Cup final, Jim Sweeney's name should be immortalised in the pages of local sport history.

His deeds should echo through the years; his exploits remembered by future generations of sports fans.

Both his success and his exemplary dedication to football in Athlone deserve to be recognised.

Sweeney was an ambassador for Athlone and for his local football club since his introduction into the blue of The Town back in 1913. The Dundalk Democrat, at one stage, labelled him "The pride of Athlone".

An indomitable character, Sweeney's legendary grit and determination was at the backbone of the Athlone teams of the 1920s.

Despite playing much of his career at a variety of positions including in the half-back line, Jim Sweeney clocked up around 55 League of Ireland goals in five seasons. And almost 80 years from when he last pulled on an Athlone shirt, Sweeney remains the club's leading FAI Cup goalscorer; his haul of 10, eclipsing goal machines like Eugene Davis, Michael O'Connor and Noel Larkin.

In life, Sweeney may have answered the call and served his home town side loyally during Athlone's first stint in the League of Ireland.

Unfortunately, though, in death, Jim Sweeney has been forgotten. Having passed away unmarried and with no remaining family in the town to recall his sporting feats, it's somewhat inevitable that his story has faded from memory.

However, not only have his exploits been lost in the mists of time, but his final resting place in Cornamagh Cemetery lies unmarked.

No gravestone adorns his grave; no epitaph acclaims his sporting feats. The remains of forgotten hero Jim Sweeney lie in a lonely spot in the shadow of a solitary tree.

A Castlemaine Street upbringing

James Sweeney was born in Castlemaine Street, Athlone, in 1897.

The family owned a popular public house on the corner of Castlemaine Street and Retreat.

It had initially being held by the Gaffey family, but on the death of Jim's mother, Mary Sweeney (nee Gaffey), it passed into the hands of his father, James Sweeney senior, a former member of the RIC.

Castlemaine Street in the 1910s and 1920s was a relatively poor area and the pub's clientele came from the heavily populated Irishtown district.

With seven family rooms, as well as a number of outhouses, the pub premises was the largest building on Castlemaine Street.

Jim was one of three brothers. Tom moved to Mayo in the 1920s or 30s and worked as a plumber. The other brother John died unmarried in 1938 leaving Jim as the last of his family in Athlone.

Sport played a major part in the Sweeney family's life.

His father, James senior, was involved in Garrycastle Races and was also a keen football enthusiast. His brother, John, was a footballer of renown in his own right.

The early football years

Jim Sweeney first pulled on the blue of Athlone during the 1913/14 season.

It was an opportune time to became involved in football in Athlone, coinciding as it did with the Town's first real success of the 20th century. That season Athlone won the Leinster Senior League Division Two crown in their first year in the league. And while Sweeney was only in his teens, his contribution, mainly from the inside-right forward berth, was critical.

His instant impact attracted the attention of Bohemians, probably thanks to the watchful eyes of Athlone native and then Bohs player Denis Hannon. Indeed, Sweeney turned out for Bohemians on a handful of occasions in the 1913/14 and 1914/15 seasons, mainly in the Belfast City Cup – a cup competition run off on a league basis between the Irish League sides. He was joined in some of these games by another member of Athlone's Leinster League winning side half-back Johnny Begadon. Centre-forward Michael Coyle also represented Bohemians on a number of occasions in this competition, scoring for the Dubliners against Distillery. Jim Sweeney also had a couple of league appearances for Bohs in 1915.

However, it was in the hectic 1913/14 season that he made his mark.

Due to Athlone's busy schedule in the Leinster Senior League that year, they passed up on involvement in the Leinster Junior Cup.

Instead, it was local junior club St Patrick's League which represented Athlone in the competition. With Sweeney in their ranks, St Pat's lost out in the final to the reigning Dublin junior champions, Clarence.

Ahead of the 1914/15 season, Athlone were preparing to accept promotion to the top division of the Leinster Senior League. The Westmeath Independent reported the club intended to seek the services of Dinny Hannon for the new campaign. However, World War One intervened and football went into abeyance.

The war impacted on the careers of many footballers, not least Jim Sweeney, whose prime years in the early 20s were stolen by the conflagration across Western Europe. By the time competitive football returned in 1921/22, Sweeney was in his mid-20s.

Mr Versatility

A tall, rangy individual, with excellent heading prowess, Sweeney was Athlone's Mr Versatility, able to slot into numerous positions across the half-back and forward lines.

His favoured position was centre-forward, but it was as leader of the defence that Jim Sweeney shone during the 1921/22 campaign.

From centre back, Sweeney popped up with two goals in the 4-1 victory over Chapelizod in the Leinster Junior Cup final, thus compensating somewhat for his failure to win the same competition eight years previously with St Patrick's League.

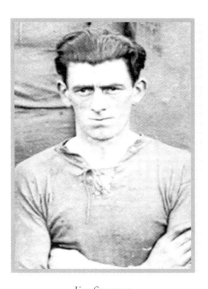

Jim Sweeney

And it was in that centre-half position that he featured in the club's historic first FAI Cup campaign that year against YMCA and Bohemians.

His role as natural leader and captain of the team had been usurped by his younger and promising brother, John, who also took over the centre-forward berth.

The following season as Athlone entered the League of Ireland for the first time, Jim, again, started off at centre-half in the opening handful of league games. When he did feature up front, it was often as inside-right, or indeed, outside-right, rather than in his preferred centre-forward role. Despite this, although details of the scorers in a number of Athlone games remain unknown, it's almost certain James Sweeney was the club's top scorer in the league that year, with over a dozen goals.

His reputation as a buccaneering centre forward was well established and it was in that role he scored in a 2-1 victory for Leinster in an interprovincial against Ulster during Christmas, 1922.

While Sweeney's career remained in full throttle, he was also keen to promote the game amongst the younger population. And in late 1922, James and his brother, John, donated a trophy for a new Athlone minor league. A committee to operate the league was composed of the Sweeneys, fellow players Hannon and Ghent and prominent referee Michael Broderick. It was the first of many occasions that Sweeney organised minor tournaments to develop young talent.

Back on the field of play, he continued to line out in a variety of positions for Athlone during the remainder of the 1922/23 season. That long first season for Athlone ended in passage to the final of the Shield competition, where Jim replaced his brother John as centre-forward for the decider.

Although, Athlone lost out, narrowly and possibly undeservedly, the game was notable for a typical Jim Sweeney moment. Embarking on a direct and forthright one-man assault on the Shelbourne goals, Sweeney was up-ended earning Athlone a spot kick. Although he was an established goal-scorer, Sweeney's ability to lead the line, take in possession and bring his team-mates into the game was negligible. Instead, he was a robust, battering ram of a centre-forward, who combined strength with pace and determination and who always headed directly for goal.

And while he may not have made an ideal linkman, his direct style was ideally suited to the helter skelter, frenetic game which Athlone adopted for the 1923/24 FAI Cup campaign.

Of course, this tendency to go it alone must also have frustrated his colleagues – and the many references to the lack of cohesion in the forward line and the players failed to work in tandem may well have been directed, in the main, at Sweeney.

This individualism was best summed up in the words of the supporter of the team whose assessment of the players over 40 years later cut to the bone. The writer simply remarked of Sweeney: "Give him the ball and go away and make a cup of tea for yourself."

In a time when goalkeepers were not the protected species they are at present, Sweeney was also an ideal exponent of the direct physical attack on the unfortunate goalkeepers who dallied with the ball in their hands that few seconds too long.

Cup-winning season

For the 1923/24 season, Sweeney was appointed captain, reflecting the respect in which he was held, and he was also on the team selection committee, along with Frank Ghent and Denis Hannon.

The arrival of John Joe Dykes had ensured the side now had a regular centre-half. But with his brother John or Dubliner Albert McLoughlin apparently favoured for the centre-forward spot, Jim played the early part of the 1923/24 season at outside-right.

However, tragedy was to strike in late September when John was seriously wounded in a shooting incident.

With McLoughlin having left the club, it was Jim Sweeney who was called in as centre-forward. And, again, back in his best position, he rowed in with eight goals in the next ten league games to help Athlone to a respectable fourth-placed finish.

Ironically, despite his rich vein of goal-scoring form, Jim Sweeney failed to find the net in Athlone's victorious cup run. However, his versatility and loyalty were shown in abundance when he again filled in at left-half in the FAI Cup quarter-final against Shels and at centre-half in the replayed semi-final when John Joe Dykes missed his connecting train from Sligo.

In three Leinster Senior Cup games played amidst the FAI Cup run, Sweeney rattled in seven goals, including four the weekend before the FAI Cup final against Leinster Senior League side Inchicore Utd.

In the final against Fordsons, Sweeney played a key role, despite again, frustratingly for him, failing to find the net.

Marked out as the danger man, Sweeney was patrolled by a posse of Fordsons defenders, thereby creating space for his forward colleagues.

Despite being so closely monitored, the centre-forward twice found the net, with both 'goals' being over-ruled.

The Westmeath Independent reported: "With all their marking and watching Fordsons could not prevent the tireless Jim from getting through to score in his best style. The Town supporters were simply appalled – bewildered - when the referee disallowed the point, because Sweeney had fairly and squarely beaten three Fordsons men before giving O'Hagan no earthly chance to save."

Nonetheless, despite his personal disappointment, it was Jim Sweeney who had the distinction of lifting the FAI Cup, becoming the first, and still the only, Athlone man to raise the trophy aloft.

The final also marked the inauguaral occasion the trophy was presented at the end of the game, allowing Sweeney to have the honour of being the first captain to receive the cup in front of his supporters.

In his role as captain, it was Jim Sweeney again who spoke on behalf of the team at a special concert to commemorate the victory held in the Foresters Club in Athlone a week later.

1924/25 - An anti-climax

As a club Athlone had always prioritised the cup. The expensive and tiring fortnightly trips to Dublin for league matches served to limit their chances of league success. And in the wake of the 1923/24 cup victory, the next league campaign failed to spark excitement in Athlone.

Indeed, captain Jim Sweeney effectively sat out the season, appearing in only two or three league games. His absence had a huge impact, as Athlone struggled to find the net, scoring only 15 times in 18 games – at a time when the goals-per-game ratio was much higher than it is now.

Of course, when he did feature, he found the back of the net, notably against Fordsons in November in the Sportsground. His personal frustration at not having registered a goal in the cup final a year previously may have sparked Sweeney to come out of his repose for this game. Later that season, he was back again for the FAI Cup campaign. The return of his brother John from the lengthy lay-off necessitated by his near fatal shooting may have also contributed to his reappearance.

Indeed, it was fortunate for Athlone that Jim Sweeney had readied himself for a return to the Town forward line for the FAI Cup first-round clash with Munster Senior League side Cork Bohemians on January 10th in the Sportsground. The Southerners provided a stiff test for Athlone who found themselves 3-2 down early in the second half. But two goals from Jim Sweeney, thereby completing his hat-trick, helped Athlone to a 5-3 victory.

Sweeney was Athlone's sole marksman, with two quick-fire first-half goals, in the 2-0 victory over Drumcondra in the next round. The five goals were the start of a cup spree for Sweeney, who had, strangely, failed to score in Athlone's eight previous FAI Cup ties across three seasons. However, for this year, his account was closed, as Athlone failed to find the net in a disappointing 4-0 defeat to Shelbourne in the semi-final.

The 1924/25 season petered out with James Sweeney continuing to feature in the end-of-season Shield games. However he had obviously regained his enthusiasm and was ready to grab hold of the 1925/26 season in spectacular fashion.

1925/26 – Back on track

The arrival of experienced striker Ned Brooks helped to free up Sweeney, who weighed in with an impressive 17 league goals, making him the fifth-highest scorer in a League of Ireland campaign for Athlone.

Only Andy Myler (29), Eugene Pooch Davis (23) and Michael O'Connor (22) and Noel Larkin (18) have scored more league goals in Athlone colours in a single season. His tally of 17 left him in third place in the goalscorers' list in the league that season, behind Billy 'Juicy' Farrell who netted 24 for the mighty Shamrock Rovers.

If goals had been in short supply the previous season for Athlone, there was no shortage in the 1925/26 campaign. Nonetheless, Athlone only finished seventh of the ten teams with their defence proving anything but water tight.

Back with a bang, Jim Sweeney rattled off ten goals in the first eight league games including a hat-trick against Jacobs in the Sportsground. A mid-season lull was followed up by another purple patch with seven goals in the final four league games including another hat-trick away to Brideville. He continued his strike rate in the FAI Cup, scoring in a 4-0 win against Brideville. A double in the next round at home to Fordsons wasn't enough to save Athlone from defeat in a five-goal thriller.

Sweeney scored many of his goals with flying headers from the pinpoint deliveries of Frank Ghent or trademark blasts after a powerful surging run through the opposition defence.

His revived form once again drew the attention of international and representative selectors and, as a result, in late February, he was one of four Athlone Town players chosen to attend preliminary trials ahead of the selection of the Irish team to take on Italy in Turin. Although he didn't make the cut, he did have the distinction of scoring for a Leinster Football Association XI which defeated the Free State League XI in the annual Evening Herald Hospitals Cup fundraiser during Easter. The victory was particularly impressive as Irish Free State League XI was the same as that which had beaten the Northern-based Irish League in the historic first-ever representative game between the two associations just four weeks previously.

All in all, Sweeney rattled up 24 goals across the 30 senior games in which Athlone participated in what was by far his most productive goal-scoring season.

1926/27 - *The utility-man role*

Although, there were continuous negative vibes about Athlone's existence as a League of Ireland club during the latter end of the 1925/26 season, Athlone ploughed on regardless into the next campaign.

The arrival of a regular centre-half, the vastly experienced Harry Leddy, and the retention of centre-forward Ned Brooks meant Sweeney slotted into a variety of positions during that campaign, including outside-right, left-half, right-half and inside-right.

Still, he weighed in with nine league goals,

Sweeney's more rounded contribution helped Athlone to a healthy league standing mid-season. However, an end-of-season collapse in which they took only three points (all draws) from their last seven league games undid much of the good work.

It meant attention focused once again on the FAI Cup but this time the effort was short-lived as Jim Sweeney's sole strike was more than matched by four from Shelbourne.

1927/28 – *The last hurrah*

Having served with Athlone since 1913, Sweeney opted out again in the 1927/28 season – as the focus turned more to young local players.

Indeed, in what was the most disastrous campaign in Athlone's history,

Sweeney didn't feature until almost the end of the league campaign at home on December 10th to St James's Gate.

With impeccable timing, it turned out to be Athlone's final home league game in League of Ireland football for 41 yeas as they dropped out of the league at the end of the season.

The Westmeath Independent reported earlier in the year that Sweeney had sustained an injured knee, which had kept him from rejoining the fray that season.

Football Sports Weekly noted his return to the playing fold and his involvement in club administration and optimistically remarked: "Now that he is back and taking a working as well as a playing interest in his local club we feel confident that everything will go right for the boys from the midlands."

However, with the traditional January FAI Cup game ahead, it's tempting to speculate that Sweeney linked up again with his old club, simply to have one more shot at the FAI Cup. Whatever the reason, Sweeney brought his FAI Cup goal tally to 10 when he scored in what remains Athlone's biggest cup defeat, a 9-3 thrashing at home by Drumcondra.

It was his first, and only, goal of the 1927/28 season – making him, one of only two players (the other was Frank Ghent) to score in each Athlone's six League of Ireland seasons.

He turned out once or twice more in Athlone colours in concluding Shield and Leinster Senior Cup campaigns before hanging up the boots.

Sweeney, and his club, Athlone, had sparkled briefly across the horizon illuminating the hitherto Dublin-centred game, before fading away into the darkness.

Although his playing career was over, Sweeney retained a keen interest in Athlone Town FC and was on hand eleven years later, when the Free State Junior Cup was brought back to the Shannon banks. In scenes reminiscent of those enjoyed in the wake of the senior cup triumph, the winning team was feted at a reception at the Ancient Order of Foresters' headquarters in Athlone. To wild cheers, Sweeney, as captain of the 1924 cup-winning team, reminded the attendance that Athlone was the first town to win both Free State Senior and Junior Cups.

The match ball

In later years, Sweeney settled down to operate the family business from Castlemaine Street.

To youngsters growing up in the area, he was part of the sporting folklore of the town.

One man who grew up in St Patrick's Terrace recalls: "There was a story told about him going into Mass with the ball, kicking it up into the air and catching it again on the way out."

Although a busy premises in the 20s and 30s, in later years the pub fell into disrepair and only opened irregularly.

A Scottish housekeeper Mary Kilroy lived with the Sweeneys for over 40 years and passed away in 1957.

Four years later, in March 1961, the premises was put up for auction. It had a seven-day licence and included a bar, taproom, store room, kitchen, scullery and bedroom on the ground floor as well as a sitting room and three bedrooms on the first floor.

Jim Sweeney entered St Vincent's Hospital where he died on June 26th, 1961, after a long illness. He had paid for his own grave four months previously. Money had also been left with the administrator of St Mary's parish to fund the funeral.

His obituary in the Westmeath Independent noted: "His feats in the heyday of Athlone football have been part of its tradition in the town". His former colleagues Frank Ghent, Norman Lyster and Denis Hannon all turned out for the funeral.

The Old Athlone Society rescued both the football from the 1924 Cup Final and Jim Sweeney's medal from the pub premises before the auction to ensure they were preserved.

The football is now displayed in the Athlone Castle Museum. However, Sweeney's medal has disappeared.

Chapter 23

The rest of the 1923/24 season

On a downer

The calm after the storm

The 1923/24 season may have come to a thrilling climax in the FAI Cup final of March 17th – but Athlone Town FC still had to see out the season to its conclusion by fulfilling their Leinster Senior Cup and Shield fixtures.

Three of the Leinster Senior Cup games against St Paul's, Jacobs and Inchicore Utd were peppered amidst the successful FAI Cup run. They had served a very real purpose by building confidence and helping to develop a winning habit as part of a 12-match unbeaten run.

The game away to then Leinster Senior League Division One leaders St Paul's on January 12th, came a week after the first-round FAI Cup defeat of Midland Athletic and a week before the shock victory over Shelbourne in the quarter-finals.

An away victory was not unexpected, but the facile manner (5-0) must surely have been a real confidence boost for Athlone, whose fast, open style of play was too much for the home side. Two goals within the first ten minutes from Denis Hannon set Athlone on their way.

After the victory over Shelbourne in the FAI Cup quarter-final, Athlone had a week off, before lining up against Jacobs in the Shield second round. This game was at home, and Athlone struggled somewhat to convert their superiority over the Dubliners into scores.

A headed goal from Jim Sweeney following a Tommy Muldoon corner was enough to secure victory but the Westmeath Independent warned: "The Town did not, as a whole, give of their best against Jacobs, and a much more determined attempt coupled with greater cohesion must be made when they meet Bohemians in the semi-final (of the FAI Cup)."

The victory qualified Athlone for the Leinster Senior Cup quarter-finals, where they met another non-league side, Inchicore Utd, on Sunday, March 9th. This game was their final warm-up before the FAI Cup final on St Patrick's Day.

An 8-1 triumph, of course, must have boosted morale but perhaps of more significance was Denis Hannon's four-goal haul. Hannon was never the most prolific of scorers and for him to find his shooting boots a week before the cup final was timing most propitious.

After the cup final, the action reverted to the Shield, which was played in a league format for the 1923/24 season.

The opening game away to Midland Athletic five days after the cup final win was bound to be an anti-climactic affair for Athlone. And indeed, the midlanders relinquished their unbeaten run and lost their first game in 12 matches away to a side they had easily accounted for on their three previous meetings that season.

Athlone did suffer a litany of injuries and absences; Muldoon missed the game with a flu, Collins had emigrated to London, Dykes received a significant injury during the game, Hope had to cry off at half-time leaving Athlone with just ten players, and Monahan was also suffering from injury.

But the reality may well have been, in the words of the Irish Independent, that Athlone "were suffering from the effects of fittingly celebrating their cup victory".

To make up the numbers, Athlonian Michael Coyle, who was probably based in Dublin at this stage and who had lined out with the side as far back as 1913, replaced the absent Collins at inside-left. Also present was the ever-loyal Barney Connaughton who had been jettisoned for the cup final.

The gate receipts for this clash were a paltry 12 shillings. The stark contrast to the £1,100 takings at the cup final a week previously was pointed out by the newspaper Sport which derided the "fickleness of the Athlone public".

In any event, despite the defeat in the first round of the Shield, Athlone still had the Leinster Senior Cup to concentrate on, having reached the semi-final stage.

The Westmeath Independent was enthusiastic. In its report on the cup final success, it noted that Athlone could look forward to the Leinster Senior Cup final on Easter Monday, conveniently overlooking the semi-final stage. However, it seemed as if this desire to take the success further was not reciprocated by the players.

Michael Coyle

Indeed, Athlone had reached a plateau – and it was downhill for the rest of the season from here on in. Of the remaining eight games in either the Leinster Senior Cup or the Shield, the club only won one and drew two.

The slide started with that Leinster Senior Cup semi-final. Brideville were Leinster Senior League Division Two winners and had, up to that stage, been undefeated across all competitions that season. They were also Leinster and Free State Junior Cup champions in 1923/34.

Athlone were understrength, without Dykes, who remained injured following the Midland Athletic game. Sweeney operated at centre-half, with Coyle again a recruit to the forward line. Remarkably, Collins returned from London for the game.

However, a scoreless draw, in which Brideville more than held their own, would been a real disappointment for those expecting Athlone to march gaily onwards to another cup triumph.

The Sunday Independent commented that Athlone exhibited semblances of staleness that were not surprising following the strenuous cup exploits. The Irish Independent said that only in physique were Brideville inferior to Athlone.

The replay on Wednesday witnessed the return of Dykes, while Paddy Flannery stood in for Collins, who had gone back to London. Flannery split his knee within the first few minutes and was forced to retire, leaving Athlone with just ten men for the vast majority of the contest. The Dubliners went ahead on 35 minutes, but Athlone equalised courtesy of Hannon midway through the second half. The Brideville winner came near the finish from the penalty spot.

Athlone were again off-form. The Irish Times said they had rarely given a poorer display.

The Evening Telegraph probably captured the feeling in the Athlone camp best. "Somehow having won their cup, they do not seem very keen on putting their heart into their matches now. It is to be hoped that they will pull themselves together and endeavour to do better."

Brideville were subsequently beaten in the Leinster Senior Cup final by Shelbourne, but two seasons later, were members of the League of Ireland. They reached the final of the FAI Cup in 1927.

Out of the Leinster Senior Cup, Athlone were forced to concentrate on completing their Shield programme which had been heavily delayed due to their prolonged run in both knock-out competitions.

On April 12th, for their third game in a week, a weakened Athlone succumbed 3-0 to Bohemians in Dublin. It was the fifth successive trip to the capital for Athlone and the seventh visit to Dublin in the last eight games.

The game on April 27th at home to Jacobs appears to have been abandoned due to the pitch being unplayable, although some records show a 7-1 victory for Athlone!

A week later, Athlone lost at home to Shelbourne by 2-0. The side was understrength (missing Hope and Judge) and included John Joe Dykes who was back from injury with one eye on the imminent Olympics but whose performance remained below par.

The following week, Athlone sustained a 5-0 home defeat inflicted by

Shamrock Rovers, in a game where they played the second half with one man short, following the half-time retirement of Hope, who had returned prematurely from illness.

Athlone did finally manage a draw away to St James's Gate on May 18th with Dykes and Sweeney finding the net in a four-goal game. It was a day after a pre-Olympics warm-up game in which four Athlone players had featured. The final Shield game a week later also saw an understrength Athlone, missing five of the senior players who were on duty in the Olympics, lose by 3-1.

The end-of-season games had been stale fare compared to the full-flavoured five-course spectacular served up during the FAI Cup run. The question now was whether Athlone, having had the taste of success, would remain hungry for more in 1924/25 season.

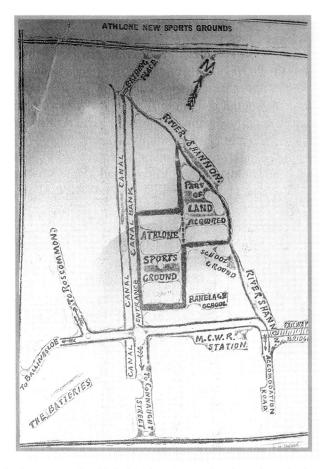

A map of the Sportsground published in the Westmeath Independent of July 25th, 1914.

The rise and fall of the Sportsground

The Sportsground located at Lakeview, close to the existing Athlone Leisure World site was purchased in July 1914 by Athlone Sports Company Ltd. This was a local enterprise with a nominal capital of £2,000, which was to be theoretically funded by the sale of 2,000 one-pound ordinary shares.

The Athlone United Trades sports committee, the Athlone GAA and a number of local dignitaries were among the main shareholders.

Thomas Chapman, owner of the Westmeath Independent and Athlone Printing Works, was managing director of the company and prime mover of the concept.

The Westmeath Independent reported in late 1917 that £500 had been paid for the ground and another £600 to £700 had been spent, by then, on improvements.

The ground was expected not only to fill a sporting need but to provide spin-off benefits to the local economy. The Westmeath Independent of July 25th, 1914, explained: "Because of its central location, Athlone is the natural meeting ground for many of the bigger athletic events hitherto held elsewhere.

"The advantages will not be exclusively to the sport-loving. It must also be felt among the business community in the large influx of people it is certain to bring into the district on the occasion of many future reunions.

"Once Athlone comes to be better known we believe our local attractions, including the Sportsground, are sufficient to keep up a constant stream of visitors for many months of the year."

However, hardly had the deal to buy the land been completed, than the British military authorities took over the Sportsground, sometimes known as Lakeview Park, as "accommodation ground". It may even have been used as a base to enlist soldiers into the British Army during the early part of World War 1.

The Sportsground was handed back to its owners sometime in 1915 – and was officially opened in conjunction with the hosting of the first event at the facility, the Athlone United Trades Sports of July 1915.

The Gaelic Athletic Association, which, in those days, considered athletics and cycling as part of its remit, sanctioned the Irish five-mile cycling championship and the Leinster half-mile track athletic championships to be held during the Athlone Sports. For the sports, a cinder track for cycling and athletics was laid around the pitch itself, spanning one third of a mile.

The football pitch at the centre ran on a roughly north-south axis. The Westmeath Independent said the banked track was "practically level" bar for a slight rise on the northern end.

Beyond the pitch itself, on the northern end, a hill sloped up gently, forming a natural grandstand with copses of trees providing some shelter. At the time, it was said "a substantial house", probably connected with the nearby Ranelagh School, provided dressing room facilities,

Entrance to the ground was from the east, in the direction of the canal bank, and via turnstiles. By that stage the ground had a small reserved seating enclosure. Both the pitch itself and the surrounding track were fully enclosed by "a substantial fence", theoretically, at least, preventing the encroachment of spectators onto the playing field.

When the military authorities surrendered the use of the grounds, the work of fitting it out as a sports facility had to be taken in hand.

The Athlone United Trades Sports in July 1915 may have come too soon for the Sportsground owners. The Westmeath Independent said after the athletics meeting that a lack of preparatory time had meant the track was not all that it should have been.

Although the event itself was a huge success, with, according to reports, 5,000 spectators turning up, the Westmeath Independent commented from the outset that further work would need to be done before the GAA would consider serious football or hurling championship events for the venue.

"Before we see championship football and hurling in Athlone, the pitch must be very considerably overhauled. The defects that were apparent are hardly worth bringing under notice for they have been recognised locally," it said.

Some effort was made to make the facility suitable for top class events. The limited company's annual meeting in February 1916 revealed that some £375 had been spent between raw material and labour. By April 1916, touchline seats had been added and a total capital of £835 had been issued. Among the initial subscribers were Athlone United Trades Sports Committee, Athlone GAA, JJ Coen (solicitor), Patrick Quinn, Robert Elder (solicitor), Thomas Hogan, Thomas Chapman, P. Henry, P. Macken, William Walsh, Thomas Mullins, M H Foy, H.W. Percy, Michael Duffy and Laurence Hogan.

All the effort seemed worthwhile when Athlone was chosen by the GAA to host an All-Ireland senior hurling and football semi-final in October 1916.

Up to 15,000 were expected for the matches between Cork v. Mayo in football and Tipperary v. Galway in hurling.

However, what should have been the biggest day in the venue's short history turned sour when the British military authorities moved to cancel trains destined for Athlone. As a result, only 1,000 people attended the games. The accounts of the Sports Committee for 1916 showed a loss of £9 18s and 5d, although the ground value had increased by £112, thanks to improvement work.

Plans to develop the facility further were constantly hindered by the British Army, who, at least twice, in late 1917 and early 1918, compulsorily acquired the ground for the training and recreation of troops.

The uncertainty over the usage of the ground affected its long-term development. But there were further issues dogging the project, not least the proximity of the Shannon which was causing major problems for the surface of the ground.

The sort of community-based ownership model employed also proved controversial with junior football clubs and Athlone GAA criticising the apparent priority given to Athlone Town FC by those in charge of the ground.

There were bigger problems afoot in May 1924 when the Westmeath Independent remarked that the company behind the Sportsground had now gone into liquidation. TP Chapman had died in April 1922 – and in his absence, the project faltered. The ground was likely to be sold to a private individual to be used probably as a grazing paddock, the local paper revealed.

This crisis was somehow overcome and the local limited company appeared to have continued in operation.

But the drainage remained a stumbling block. By 1924, the Westmeath Independent was regularly criticising the condition of the ground. Describing the site as being in a "muddy and flooded condition" in Autumn 1924, the paper said: "The majority of the players were treated to mudbaths … To make the ground playable some of the hollows should be filled and drainage work undertaken."

In late 1924, it appears some drainage work was carried out – but a lack of capital inhibited the development of the facility.

By early 1925, there was talk that the frequent cancellations of fixtures due to flooding in the Sportsground might force Athlone Town to hold some games in Mullingar.

In the background, administrative issues remained and in February 1926 the holding company was struck off the register of companies having failed to lodge any returns for five years.

And although it was subsequently reinstated by the High Court, the future was bleak. Three months later, the ground was sold for £1,000 to the military authorities; the Irish Army paying for what their British equivalent had compulsorily obtained during the war years.

The rest of the 1923/34 season

DATE	OPPOSITION	COMPETITION (Athlone score first in all scorelines)	SCORELINE	SCORERS
January 12, 1924	St Paul's (a)	Leinster Senior Cup	5-0	(Hannon (2), Jim Sweeney (2), Ghent)
February 2, 1924	Jacobs (h)	Leinster Senior Cup	1-0	(Jim Sweeney)
March 9, 1924	Inchicore Utd (h)	Leinster Senior Cup	8-1	(Jim Sweeney (4), Hannon (4))
March 22, 1924	Midland Athletic (a)	Shield	0-3	
April 5, 1924	Brideville (Dalymount Park)	Leinster Senior Cup semi-final	0-0	
April 9, 1924	Brideville (Dalymount Park)	Leinster Senior Cup semi-final replay	2-1	(Hannon)
April 12, 1924	Bohemians (a)	Shield	0-3	
*April 27, 1924	Jacobs (h)	Shield	7-1	(?)
May 4, 1924	Shelbourne (a)	Shield	0-2	
May 11, 1924	Shamrock Rovers (a)	Shield	0-5	
May 18, 1924	St James's Gate (a)	Shield	2-2	(Jim Sweeney and Dykes)
May 25, 1924	Brooklyn (h)	Shield	1-3	(?)

*Other sources indicate this match did not take place.

241

Chapter 24

Jim Kennedy

From out of left-field

Of all the sporting tales associated with Athlone's FAI Cup success in 1924, Jim Kennedy's is particularly unconventional.

Kennedy was a moderate goalkeeper – sometime full-back – who had played with Athlone from as far back as the mid 1910s.

Born in Bloomhill, Ballinahown, in 1892, he moved into Athlone in his youth and by the early years of the 20th century was working in the pub of his brother, John, in Mardyke Street. The premises are currently occupied by Liam McCormack's menswear.

According to Frank Egan's publication 'The Golden Mile of Athlone' this small grocery and bar was taken over by James Kennedy in the 1920s and operated until his retirement in the late 1940s. It was then run by Charles Quinn of Lecarrow. After Quinn's retirement, the premises passed into the hands of Paschal Hickey who, in turn, sold to a Mr Pollak who made extensive alterations, building a new bar and lounge. When he then left the business in 1979, the current owner opened up a drapery.

Jim Kennedy

Kennedy progressed into the Athlone side from the local junior scene. He featured between the sticks for the unimaginatively named United in a Leinster Junior Cup tie against another Athlone side, St Patrick's League, in 1912.

He made what's likely to have been his debut for Athlone Town in the last Leinster Senior League Division 2 (Saturday) fixture of the 1913/14 season against Dublin side Frankfort. Athlone had the division well and truly sown up in advance of this final game. With regular keeper Harvey absent, Kennedy was summoned to the front rank.

However, in what was one of only two defeats in the league that season, he was "not too sound in goal", according to the Evening Herald.

Indeed, throughout his career, Kennedy was to prove an erratic last line of defence, earning both strong criticism and lavish praise along the way.

Whilst unusual by today's standards, it was not unknown for goalkeepers to double on occasions as full-backs, and even half-backs. One of the skills associated with goalkeeping in those days was the ability to clear the ball under strong physical pressure from centre forwards. It required a skill set similar to that of the traditional clearing-the-lines full-back who was very much in vogue at the time. It meant that the interchangeability of full-backs and goalkeepers was more frequent that one would expect.

Kennedy made appearances in the half-back and full-back lines during the war years. But by the start of the 1919/1920 season, the first proper campaign after the war, Kennedy was back mainly in goal – lining out in the first two rounds of the Leinster Senior Cup, before missing the next round through illness. It was a costly absence as Athlone were disqualified, despite a 9-0 win, after the club secretary failed to register a substitute keeper for Kennedy in time.

1921/22 represented Athlone's first foray into senior football under the new Free State regime and Kennedy featured at full-back in many of the club's main games in the FAI Cup, Leinster Junior Cup and Leinster Senior Cup.

In the Town's first senior game, an FAI Cup tie against YMCA, he lined out at right-full, although he didn't make the side for the next round against Bohemians.

Later that season, he earned a Leinster Junior Cup winner's medal at left-full.

By the time the 1922/23 season arrived, Kennedy was still playing his part in local sporting history, lining out in Athlone's first-ever League of Ireland game against St James's Gate.

This was to be Kennedy's most active season, as he appeared in 13 of the first 14 league games for which team selections were available. When full-back Joe Monahan joined the squad that season after a half-dozen games, Kennedy moved to the half-back line, appearing mainly at right-half, and, once, at centre-half.

When regular netminder William Bracken was occasionally absent, Kennedy was the first-choice back-up keeper.

He produced a spectacular display between the posts in February 1923 in a league match away to Shamrock Rovers, topping it off with a penalty save against the deadly Bob Fullam who was renowned as having the most powerful shot in Irish football.

Legend has it that an Italian defender once begged Fullam, who was preparing to take a free-kick, not to strike him with the ball. Another Fullam blast from a free-kick had already knocked out another unfortunate Italian earlier in that 1927 clash between the countries in Lansdowne Road.

It was also in the goalkeeping capacity that Kennedy lined out in the Shield competition later that season. In the final against Shelbourne, comments on his display were less complimentary, with the Evening Herald labelling him "a laggard".

The Evening Telegraph was equally critical of his semi-final display in the same competition. "Kennedy was not too safe on a couple of occasions. I think he is on the lazy side. He is big enough for anything and has a powerful kick."

He was still guarding the Athlone net at the start of the 1923/24 season, although the eventual arrival from Dublin of Paddy O'Reilly effectively drew the curtain on his Town career.

He was to have one final performance, a swansong of epic proportions, when three months later, he was plucked from nowhere to fill the troublesome outside-left position in the FAI Cup quarter-final clash with Shelbourne.

A heavy injury list and a reshuffle necessitated by the non-arrival of John Joe Dykes by train from Sligo meant Kennedy was called up to the forward line.

Although, generally deemed a disappointment, Kennedy did scamper free to smash home the crucial second goal in the 2-0 victory and he also hit the post soon after.

It was a remarkable feat for a player utterly out of his comfort zone. His unsuitability for the role was evident, though, when he did not feature in the next round against Bohemians, despite his goal-scoring contribution.

In fact that glorious moment may well have been Kennedy's last game for Athlone Town, as there are no further references to him in the admittedly unsatisfactory details culled from newspaper reports for the remainder of the season.

During his bit-part career with Athlone, Kennedy also remained active on the local junior scene with St Patrick's. By 1925/26, he was lining out with a new local junior club called The Emeralds. It was probably his last playing involvement in a mixed career that, in its autumn years, had that glorious and unexpected golden moment in Shelbourne Park in February 1924.

Jim Kennedy died in February 1973 in Sir Patrick Dun's Hospital in Dublin and was buried in Cornamagh Cemetery. His wife, Annie (nee Burke), had predeceased him.

They had lived on Retreat Road for some time. During his later years, Jim had enjoyed a strong association with many charitable organisations in the parish including the Ren Club, of which he was a founder member.

Chapter 25

1924/25 season

A year of rebuilding

Flight of the stars

The success of a small club automatically brings the vultures circling and Athlone had some of the meat picked from their bones by the time the 1924/25 season had begun.

Goalkeeper Paddy O'Reilly had been snapped up by Shamrock Rovers, whilst Tommy Muldoon had secured a deal with Aston Villa in England. The newspaper Sport said he would represent a big loss not only to Athlone but to Free State football in general.

Tommy Collins had also departed for a new life in England, and some of the more senior players, including Jim Sweeney, were slow to turn out for the club at the start of the 1924/25 season.

The cup-winning squad of just six months previous had been torn apart. And it was clear that Athlone would face a difficult start to the season.

"Retirements through injury and other causes are predicted while the departure of O'Reilly will leave a difficult vacancy to fill," the Evening Herald said in a preview of the new campaign.

Ironically, all this was taking place at a time when Athlone were hosting a reception for the 1924 cup winners. The AGM of the club was held on Friday, August 29th, and the cup medals were formally presented to the players. The following night, they were guests of honour at a function organised by the Ancient Order of Hibernians.

Already, Athlone could well have been accused of living on past glories.

An ill-prepared beginning

Athlone had been due to play Shelbourne United away in the opening contest of the season, but the Dubliners were unable to find a home ground and were expelled from the league a day after the season started. Fordsons, whose initial application to join the league had been inexplicably refused, were elected in their stead.

In what was then the first game of their season the following weekend, Athlone played host to Shelbourne in the Sportsground. The extra week's preparation seemed to have had no impact, though, as the Sunday Independent noted that Athlone had difficulty in fielding a team. Athlone were also palpably unfit, according to the Evening Herald. In contrast, Shelbourne were "in the pink of condition".

A new goalkeeper, Davis, appeared, one of at least five to feature between the posts that season. A number of players taken from the junior ranks also lined out for Athlone, including Billy Blackwell and Joe Glavey.

Billy Blackwell

Blackwell was born in Ballymahon, Co. Longford, but moved to Northgate Street, Athlone, at a young age.

Although later to make his name as an international class boxer, Blackwell was also a fine footballer.

He appeared for Athlone in each of the final four seasons of their League of Ireland membership, although he was rarely a first-team regular. Indeed, for many of those years, he combined his stint with Athlone with a more regular involvement with Mullingar in the Leinster Senior League.

Blackwell first graduated to the Athlone Town line-up in the opening game of the 1924/25 season against Shelbourne. He linked

Billy Blackwell

up with Mullingar for the first time the following season, while also retaining his connection with Athlone, with whom he scored in a 5-2 League of Ireland victory over Bray Unknowns.

However, it was probably with Mullingar Town that he was most associated. During a six-year stint with the North Westmeath club, he played on the losing side at outside-left in the 1926 Leinster Junior Cup final.

For Athlone he featured in a variety of positions; in both attack and defence and in both right and left-sided roles.

However, it was as a defender that he was best suited – and it was in the left-full role that he won a Leinster Junior Cup medal with Mullingar in 1927.

He continued to be seen with both Westmeath clubs throughout the late 1920s. And he played a part in the final chapter of Athlone's first stint in senior football when he lined out in the club's swansong – a Shield clash away to Bray Unknowns at the end of the 1927/28 season.

In 1930, Blackwell was also present for a piece of Mullingar sporting history when he was on the only Mullingar side to play in the FAI Cup. That season the Evening Herald described Blackwell as "a consistently loyal player for the Midlanders through good and bad".

When Mullingar Celtic collapsed at the end of that season, Blackwell then joined Shamrock Rovers, and was a member of their reserve team in the Leinster Senior League during the 1931/32 season.

Meanwhile, his boxing career, which began with Athlone Boxing Club, flourished when he was approached to join An Garda Siochana in 1928.

At the time, boxing was a major sport within An Garda Siochana and police forces across Europe regularly met in representative contests. Having spotted Blackwell's fighting abilities, the Gardai moved quickly to secure his sevices.

By 1929, W.G. Blackwell was making a name for himself nationally in the field of boxing. The newspaper Sports Mail profiled the tough fighter late that year stating that he had improved significantly since joining An Garda Siochana and was "now showing progress in his boxing ability". Only a couple of months before, the same paper had said Blackwell liked nothing more than "a scrap".

As a middle-weight, Billy Blackwell represented the Gardai in a number of inter-police boxing tournaments, winning two European Police Championships in the process.

He also represented Ireland at full international level against Scotland, England, Germany, Norway and the United States among others. He won a Tailteann Games silver medal in 1928 in the unusual surrounds of Croke Park and also fought in the Royal Albert Hall in London.

In the most unusual incident of his career Billy Blackwell also shook hands with Adolf Hitler when he was the sole Irishman to compete in an international police tournament in Berlin in May 1933.

Back home Blackwell won Connacht and Leinster titles in the middleweight category but lost out in five national senior finals. The middleweight level in Ireland at the time was dominated by Garda Jack Chase who won seven national titles in a row.

When his own fighting career concluded, Blackwell turned to administration and was manager of the Irish national team which won the Golden Gloves competition in America. The squad included two future Olympic medallists, Freddie Gilroy and Johnny Caldwell.

His sporting interests were not confined to football and boxing. In fact, he was an all-round sportsman, who played rugby and was an excellent swimmer.

By the mid-1930s, he was stationed in Portlaoise where he became active in Laois boxing circles. He also served as President of the Leinster Council of the Irish Amateur Boxing Association. As a physical trainer, he helped the Laois Gaelic footballers to reach the All-Ireland senior final in 1936.

His interest in football remained undimmed and he was a founder member of Portlaoise AFC. A love of football remained in the family too as his nephew Billy Brett is a former chairman of Athlone Town and grand-nephew Gordon, a former player with Athlone and Galway Utd.

In 1963, Garda Blackwell received the Scott medal for bravery having disarmed a mentally unstable man who had discharged shotgun shots into houses near Portlaoise.

Trial and error

A 1-1 draw at home to Bray Unknowns the following week at least put a point on the board. That game was played in a quagmire as heavy rain the previous night had turned the always-vulnerable Sportsground into a mudbath.

Athlone's sole strike came from Dubliner Bill Charles in what was almost certainly his only game for the club. Charles had joined from the Dublin junior ranks. He moved on to Bohemians the following season, before returning to the junior ranks within three months due to work commitments. He was back in the League of Ireland as captain of Bray Unknowns in 1929 and, in 1931, lined out with Brideville in the FAI Cup final.

Ahead of the next game, again at home, to Jacobs, the Westmeath Independent reported that the services of several prominent city players had been secured.

A new goalkeeper, P. Hughes was among the newcomers and became almost a fixture in the team for the remainder of the league campaign. Hughes had played at one stage with Pioneers and would later feature in the Leinster Senior League.

Athlone tried out another couple of players - O'Connell, Carroll and Mick Henry - for the same game, but the promised city stars had not yet materialised.

Carroll was a Mullingar native who was now working in Athlone. A talented hockey player, he featured both at club and interprovincial level alongside Norman Lyster. Athlone man Mick Henry was to make the biggest impact of the newcomers.

John Joe Dykes, Jim Sweeney and Paddy Flannery also made belated seasonal reappearances for this game but to no avail as Athlone went down to a comprehensive 3-0 defeat. The Westmeath Independent bemoaned the "complete reversal of last year's form".

Mick Henry

Mick Henry was a native of Chapel
Street who had marked himself out, along
with Joe Glavey, as being among the most
talented of the next generation of
Athlone players.

Son of Michael and Susan Henry, he was
born in 1903 and was followed into
Athlone Town's ranks by two brothers, Pa
and John.

Mick Henry captained St Patrick's
League to the 1924 Athlone Junior Cup
and League double. He had made his
Athlone debut the previous season, at the
age of 19, at Christmas 1922 in a league
game against Rathmines Athletic.

But it was not until the 1924/25 season
that he would feature again. However, his
appearances were sporadic.

Mick Henry

Having featured in that third game of
the season for Athlone against Jacobs, Henry plied his trade for the majority of
the season with Mullingar in the Leinster Senior League instead.

Later that campaign, at the tender age of 21, he lined out at centre-half for
Mullingar in the 4-3 defeat to Talbot Utd in the Leinster Junior Cup final.

He only reappeared for Athlone for the last two games of the campaign and
scored in both the Shield victory over Shelbourne in Athlone and a league defeat
to Fordsons in Cork.

Henry was highly regarded throughout his career, but appeared not to have
fully realised his promise. He was content to alternate between the Leinster
Senior League and the League of Ireland, lining out on and off for both
Mullingar and Athlone at their respective levels during the same season.

His astonishing versatility may also have hindered his development. During his
time with Athlone, he was used at various times at full-back, centre-half, right-
half, left-half, inside-forward, outside-forward and centre-forward.

When, in 1925/26, he largely focused his attentions on Athlone, he reaped the
benefits. Having been a regular throughout the league campaign, mostly at
centre-half, Henry's form had caught the eye of media pundits and selectors
alike. The specialist football newspaper, Football Sports Weekly, in February
1926, said he was "winning additional admirers among the critics" each week he
played in Dublin.

He contributed nine goals that campaign, four in the league, one in both the
FAI Cup and Leinster Senior Cup and three in the Shield.

And at the age of just 23 he was among four Athlone players selected for a
preliminary trial as part of the selection process for the Irish international side to

play Italy in Turin in March 1926. Henry lined out at right-half with the possibles in a game against the probables in Dalymount Park but failed to make the cut.

This improved form – and the presence of his brother-in-law Tommy Muldoon in Villa Park – secured him a two-month trial with Aston Villa in the early months of the 1926/27 season. Midway through the trial, Football Sports Weekly said he had impressed during a number of games with Villa's reserves. However, the adventure ended unsuccessfully and Henry returned to Athlone in mid-November. He opted out of renewing his association with Mullingar that season.

However, despite his undoubted ability, Henry never made the step up from promising youngster to key senior player.

And whilst he continued with Athlone during the 1927/28 season, he, again, could also be found in the Mullingar colours on occasions that year.

After Athlone pulled out of the league, Henry turned out occasionally with Mullingar during the 1928/29 and 1929/30 campaigns. This involvement culminated in another FAI Cup appearance when Henry, at centre-forward, scored Mullingar Celtic's only goal in a 5-1 defeat by Dolphin.

He had also been pursued by Dundalk with whom he played two or three times in the League of Ireland in the last few weeks of 1928.

In 1930, he was to be found with Sligo Rovers during the FAI Cup qualifying rounds. Sligo were defeated by Rossville in the second round in November 1930, with Henry scoring the only goal from a free-kick. The Sligo Independent described him as "the one great man for Sligo" and as "a fine player, notwithstanding his years in the game". It was a Sligo side which also featured John Joe Dykes and Mickey Dowling.

In later life, Henry returned to Birmingham and secured work in the automotive industry. He is believed to have remained in England for the rest of his life.

His brother Pa continued to live in Athlone and only died in the last dozen years while John was a cinema operator who moved to Ballina, Co. Mayo.

Pa was a goalkeeper who made league and cup appearances in the later years of Athlone Town's first League of Ireland stint. He also played on the losing side for Mullingar in the 1925/26 Leinster Junior Cup final.

John was full-back on the Athlone Town side which won the Free State Junior Cup in 1935 and lost out in the Leinster Junior Cup final of the same year.

Finding their feet

A number of ex-Shelbourne United players, whose club had gone to the wall, were finally added to the squad ahead of the fourth game against Shamrock Rovers.

Mick Hanlon was a half-back who had featured for Shelbourne United over the previous three seasons. Redmond was a right-sided forward while the third player Mick Keegan went on to have a significant involvement with Athlone over a number of seasons.

Their arrival helped Athlone to settle on a more consistent side. And slowly the results began to improve with the first win of the season coming three games later in the sixth match of the campaign against Pioneers on October 18th.

However, the immediate impact of these new players was negligible as Athlone succumbed to an embarrassing 6-0 away defeat to Shamrock Rovers in the first game after their arrival. After four games Athlone lay rock bottom of the league. They had conceded 13 goals and scored only one.

A 0-0 draw at home to Brooklyn was nothing to write home about particularly as Athlone were fortunate to escape without defeat. But, at least, it steadied the ship. There were obviously difficulties up front. Athlone had only found the net once in their five league games to date.

Matters, admittedly, were set on a more even keel with the victory over Pioneers. The 3-1 away triumph was achieved courtesy of goals from Glavey, Keegan and Hannon. Having experimented with various line-outs, Athlone, through a trial and error process, had finally hit on a settled eleven.

The only real weakness now was the need, in the continuing absence of Jim Sweeney, for a natural centre-forward. By the end of the season, Athlone's top league goalscorer with just four goals was 18-year-old inside-left Joe Glavey, who was only in his first League of Ireland campaign.

Joe Glavey

Glavey was an inside-left who had emerged as the cream of the crop of young football talent in Athlone. Born in the Canal Banks area of Athlone's westside, Glavey's family later moved to Patrick Street.

Glavey was a stylish player whose delicate touch and easy-on-the-eye approach won him many admirers. His grand-nephew Padraig Dully displayed many of these qualities to great effect during his own career with Athlone and Shelbourne among others.

Aged just 18, Glavey made his debut in the opening game of the 1924/25 season and he went on to feature for Athlone for the remaining four seasons of their League of Ireland existence.

Joe Glavey

Towards the end of Athlone's time in the league, Glavey was switched to defence and it was a position he was to adopt in his later career.

A talented ballplayer, Glavey's inexperience told against him in the early years, particularly as the lack of a potent strikeforce left a heavy responsibility on his young shoulders.

After Athlone collapsed, Glavey signed for Shelbourne in time for the 1928/29 season and he made a decent impression during his three seasons there.

The undoubted highlight was the Championship victory in his first season at the club, during which he played on the left-wing of the attack for at least a half dozen league games. When not featuring with the first team, he lined out with the reserves in the top division of the Leinster Senior League.

The following season, he, again, alternated between the club's two sides, appearing in the half-back line some ten times or so in the league as well as in a number of Shield games. Shels were second in the league that season and Glavey was also in the side defeated by Shamrock Rovers in the Leinster Senior Cup final.

The 1930/31 season got underway with Glavey again a sort of standard twelfth man. Indeed, the Irish Independent couldn't understand why he was not first-choice centre-half.

His league appearances that year were curtailed although he featured in the Shield at the end of the season. After three years he bowed out, on a high, winning a Metropolitan Cup medal with the Shels B team.

For the 1930/31 season he initially linked up with Bray Unknowns, making an immediate impression with two goals in a league clash with Jacobs in September 1931. However, he then moved to Brideville a few months later, and featured occasionally with the Liberties club before being injured near Christmas.

Joe Glavey (centre, bottom row) in an unidentified team later in his career. Anthony Dowling is pictured third from left back row.

He left the League of Ireland the following season, playing instead with Strandville in the Leinster Senior League Division Two. In other years, he lined up with other Leinster Senior League sides including Dolphin and Queen's Park. Even by 1938, he was still a force to be reckoned with, lining out with Mullingar in the Athletic Union League.

Throughout his career, it was clearly evident that Glavey enjoyed his football. His on-field demeanour was always relaxed and friendly.

One paper, reporting on his successful conversion of a penalty, captured this philosophy well: "The smiling Glavey gave Collins no chance with his spot kick and the scorer would probably have grinned if he missed it too."

Outside of football, the army played a significant part in his life. His own father Patrick had been tragically killed in 1915 at Gallipoli whilst serving as a cook with the 5th Connaught Rangers during World War 1.

Newspaper reports at the time explained that Glavey went to his death after responding bravely to a major's request for volunteers.

"When he heard a major ask "Who was next to get over the parapet?" even in the teeth of a storm of shot and shell, he answered gaily: 'I have three sons fighting in France and one of them has won a DCM, let's see if the old father cannot get one now.'"

The Westmeath Independent poignantly reported: "He sprung to the top of the trench but a shell struck him and he did not return to answer the roll call."

Joe followed in his father's footsteps when he joined the British Army during World War 2. He later spent some time in England and the Middle East, before returning to Ireland in his 50s to work in the British Embassy in Dublin. Joe Glavey died in 1976.

Grounds for concern

The improvement continued away to St James's Gate the following week, when the same eleven eked out a share of the spoils, courtesy of another Glavey goal.

Whilst matters were slowly turning positive on the field of play, the field itself was increasingly becoming an issue.

Before the fifth match of the season against Brooklyn, the Westmeath Independent described the Sportsground as "very much cut up and in a muddy and flooded condition". Noting that the majority of players had been treated to "mudbaths", the paper said there was a need to fill hollows and undertake drainage work.

In the run-up to the planned game against Bohemians three weeks later, on November 1st, the Westmeath Independent revealed that the club's committee was undertaking much-needed drainage.

Whether the work was ever carried out, was yet to be undertaken, or simply did not work, it's not clear. In any event, the Bohemians visit was cancelled, due to "the flooded condition of the pitch".

The hiatus didn't appear to impair Athlone, who extended their unbeaten run to three games, with a narrow 1-0 victory over Fordsons in Athlone the following weekend. Jim Sweeney returned to the fray for this contest, perhaps powered on by a sense of injustice over his controversially ruled-out 'goals' in the cup final eight months earlier. Inevitably, his reappearance was marked with the only goal of a high-tempo game in which Athlone franked their cup final victory over the Cork side. Credit for the victory was mainly attributed to an impregnable home defence which withstood some sustained pressure.

The Evening Telegraph took confidence from the win. "This performance by Athlone marks a profound improvement in the cup winners' team which may yet accomplish great things. They are timing to a nicety their condition for the big struggles in the immediate future and with a couple of matches in hand in the league may yet overtake some of those already in front of them. But I think the cup is their sole objective at the moment."

Up and down

After putting together a run of two wins and two draws in their last four matches, Athlone then gathered only a single point from their next four fixtures.

The lacklustre sequence began with a 4-1 away defeat to Shelbourne, in which army officer John W McVeigh was included for his first start. Another defeat on their travels to Bray followed, in a match which featured the debut at inside-right of Jimmy Harvey, a Dubliner who had lined out with Shelbourne and Jacobs previously.

After two defeats on the trot, Athlone secured a share of the spoils, again in Dublin, against Jacobs. That was followed by a 5-0 home defeat to Shamrock Rovers, one of the worst performances of the season.

Fortunately, just as quickly as Athlone's form had dipped, it picked up again and the Town reeled off three successive wins to finish off the year on a high. The six points propelled them up the table and they finished seventh of ten teams. A 1-0 away victory against Brooklyn started the ball rolling, before a similar scoreline saw Athlone prevail at home to Pioneers. This game witnessed the return to Athlone colours of John Sweeney who had been missing since his horrific shooting some 14 months previously. A local junior player, Curley, was also brought in to fill the vacancy created by the departure of the regular netminder Hughes. The Town then overcame St James's Gate on St Stephen's Day (3-2) again at home.

Athlone had failed to fulfil their home and away fixtures against Bohemians. As a result, they forfeited the points, and incurred a hefty, and controversial, £25 pound fine.

The 2-1 defeat in April away to Fordsons meant the completed league table showed that, despite an horrendous start to the season with just one point from the first five games, Athlone finished seventh of ten. A paltry goals-for tally of 15 told its own story – while a cumulative 11-0 defeat to Shamrock Rovers indicated that Athlone were a long way off top level.

The mighty Rovers had swept all before them, winning the League, FAI Cup and Shield. They were unbeaten in 31 games across three competitions, winning 24 and drawing 7.

Chasing another FAI Cup

Athlone's late season run was interpreted in many quarters as representing a typical heightening of interest ahead of the cup.

As holders, Athlone were, naturally, more keen than ever to focus their energies on the competition. They were drawn at home to Munster Senior League side Cork Bohemians in the first round on January 10th, 1925.

The game had been expected to be played the previous weekend, but flooding had meant the Sportsground was unplayable. This time around, Ranelagh School was made available and the tie went ahead. Although Athlone prevailed, the 5-3 victory proved more difficult than they would have anticipated. In fact, Cork Bohemians led 3-2 shortly after the interval, before tiring.

The Sweeney brothers put Athlone two up early on but the visitors had halved the deficit by the interval. A period of intense Cork pressure saw the non-leaguers edge in front early in the second half with two early goals, but then Athlone took firm control and strikes from Ghent and James Sweeney (two – thereby completing his hat-trick) ensured victory.

Before Christmas, Athlone had signed up goalkeeper J McCabe who had performed wonders for Brooklyn a few weeks previously against the Town. McCabe made his debut in the St Stephen's Day game against St James's Gate in the league but was ineligible for the opening-round cup clash against Cork Bohemians on January 10th as he had not been a member of the club for a month prior to the cup fixture.

McCabe was a talented youngster who had only joined Brooklyn in November, having been on Jacobs' second string before that. He went on to play for Athlone for two more seasons, before jumping ship at Christmas 1926 to join Shelbourne. McCabe was first team regular for Shelbourne for two years until losing his place and joining Bray Unknowns in February 1928.

J. McCabe

Sport regarded him as a keeper "of a quiet and unassuming disposition with a great eye and an intuition to dive where the ball is coming for". His ineligibility for the cup game meant Curley continued between the posts for that 5-3 victory.

The draw was again kind to Athlone in the next round as they were pitted against Leinster Senior League side Drumcondra in Dublin. Dinny Hannon sat this one out, although McCabe was now safely installed as keeper. Monahan and Hope were, as ever, paired at full-back, Dykes was positioned at centre-half, with Terry Judge and Mick Hanlon on either side. Up front, Jim Sweeney led the line with Glavey and Ghent forming a left-sided partnership and John Sweeney and Jimmy Harvey on the right.

Two quick-fire strikes from Jim Sweeney before half-time were enough to give Athlone a 2-0 victory. However, on the balance of play, Drumcondra deserved to earn a replay and a squandered penalty after the interval hampered their attempts at recovery.

And so holders Athlone were back in the semi-final of the cup, and were paired against Shelbourne.

Before that game took place, Athlone began their Shield campaign, with a 1-1 draw at home to Bray Unknowns, followed by a 2-1 away defeat to Pioneers.

Shels' revenge

And so on February 15th, 1925, the stage was set for the cup semi-final in Dalymount Park.

Athlone's surprise 2-0 victory at Shelbourne's home ground in the previous year's cup quarter-final had heightened expectation ahead of this game.

The Evening Herald gave a good sense of the level of interest in the contest: "To suggest down Athlone way that the cup might be given up is tantamount to inviting personal danger. The efforts of the management and the players for the past time has been directed to preparations for retaining it. Nothing else matters. Which by implications means that their league form is to be ignored."

The same paper explained too that Athlone had been rebuilding during the year. "Athlone have lost many players who were valuable factors in their past success. The filling of their places has caused much worry and trouble. But the process is said to have given satisfaction."

The two victories by Shelbourne in the league clashes between the sides should be disregarded, the Herald argued "Athlone don't attach importance to them and have concentrated their aim and energy on the retention of the (cup) trophy."

The Westmeath Independent was more cautious in its pre-match build-up. "Will history repeat itself at Dalymount today. Few will forget the titanic struggle last year when Athlone Town conquered the famous Reds. Can they do it again? Perhaps. In any case, their chances will be ever so much brighter if the forward line part with the ball every time instead of trying the gallery stunt. No individual on the Athlone team is capable of walking through on his own."

Athlone fielded seven of the side which had won the cup the previous year. Young McCabe was between the posts and the Evening Herald said the inexperienced keeper would face "an enormous task" in a game of this nature. That doughty duo of Monahan and Hope again staffed the full-back line, with Judge, Dykes and Hannon in the half-backs. John Sweeney and Jimmy Harvey formed the right-wing partnership, with Glavey and Ghent on the left and Jim Sweeney leading the line at centre-forward.

In many of their games in the previous year's cup run, Athlone had blitzed their opponent from the off, grabbing an early lead goal which they defended stoutly.

On this occasion, the forward line displayed the worrying lack of cohesion that had been pinpointed beforehand by the Westmeath Independent.

Indeed, had they shown more teamwork and coolness, they would have taken a lead in the first few minutes, as John Sweeney (in particular) and Glavey both had early chances before Harvey hit the side-netting. The

Herald admitted: "With more efficiency they should have had a couple of goals in the first ten minutes."

But Shelbourne escaped and hit back with the opening goal after which Athlone's play deteriorated. According to the Herald's post-mortem: "That settled it. Athlone, for all practical purposes, were beaten then. They seemed to have banked their prospects on getting first blood."

Shels added a second before the interval following a goalmouth melee.

Athlone again rallied in the opening minutes of the second half and Jim Sweeney was twice denied by full-length saves from the Shels keeper. Having thwarted Athlone's early pressure, the Dubliners proceeded to ease through the second half, adding two more goals to run out comprehensive 4-0 victors.

Of the Athlone players, only the tireless Dykes and Jim Sweeney emerged with reputations enhanced. The heavy ground appeared to handicap Hope and Monahan, who were badly exposed by the nimbler Shelbourne forwards.

Some 13,000 attended the contest in Dalymount, but as the Herald said: "It did about everything but what it was expected to do – provide a strong, strenuous struggle."

Shelbourne were prepared for Athlone's shock tactics – and when Athlone couldn't force an opener, they settled into a passing rhythm that Athlone simply couldn't handle.

The shield

The cup had been yielded up, the season's focus was gone, but to their credit, Athlone did not simply collapse over the remaining Shield games.

In the midst of their shield commitments, Athlone were stunned when details emerged of the explosion at Custume Barracks on March 30th which left star centre-half John Joe Dykes hospitalised and badly injured.

Nonetheless, they were victorious in three of the five Shield matches contested, including a two-goal home victory over Shelbourne.

Their good work was undone when they were forced to concede the points to Fordsons and St James's Gate after renewed flooding on the Sportsground meant further fixture cancellations.

The Shield game against Fordsons was due in mid February but fell victim to the weather while Athlone were planning to move their Shield fixture against St James's Gate to Mullingar, although that game, too, never materialised.

The cancellations were not surprising as the winter of 1924/1925 witnessed some of the worst flooding on record in the town.

In early 1925, then Canon Crowe of St Peter and Paul's Church in Athlone, wrote to the Minister for Agriculture drawing attention to the calamitous state of affairs in his area. He said the water height was some nine feet above summer levels.

The Westmeath Independent commented: "Not within the memory of the oldest inhabitant have the dwellers along the banks of the river experienced anything like the hardship and suffering occasioned by its continuous inundations. For the past hundred years there is no record of the floods having reached such an enormous height as at present."

The susceptibility to flooding of the Sportsground, located as it was on the banks of the Shannon, was becoming a real difficulty for Athlone. And the condition of the ground reached crisis point in March when it was being suggested that Athlone play some home games in Mullingar, in order to eliminate a backlog of fixtures.

Sport reported in the same month that the Sportsground was "under several feet of water" due to the bursting of the adjoining canal banks.

Elsewhere off the pitch, fundraising continued to be a key focus. Dance nights were held in the Longworth Hall on Northgate Street each Monday to meet the club's running costs.

It didn't help that Athlone were not in any way compensated for the financial and logistical difficulty of having to travel every fortnight to Dublin. Instead, if anything, the club seemed to be the victim of unfair treatment.

In April, Athlone failed to travel to Dublin to play a long-outstanding league match against Bohemians. As a result, the council of the Free State League inflicted a £25 fine on the club.

However, a letter to the Westmeath Independent from an angry supporter noted how two years previously, Athlone had travelled to Dublin on a Saturday to play Shelbourne.

"The Town team then waited over to meet Olympia the following day (Sunday) at considerable expense," the letter-writer said.

When the team arrived on the field, they found that Olympia had not arrived nor had they even put up the goalposts. The game, of course, had to be abandoned though Athlone had to bear all the expenses.

The letter continued: "When the matter was brought before the council, Olympia were fined the modest sum of 40 shillings. Compare with this with the fine of £25 now sought to be imposed on Athlone."

The correspondent pointed out that 40 shillings was also the fine imposed on Brooklyn the previous season when they did not play Fordsons in Cork.

This begged the question: "If two pounds are considered sufficient to fix for two Dublin teams, whose actions had no semblance of justice, whereas the Athlone team had a genuine defence – why treat the matter as if the only idea prevalent in Dublin was to get them out of the football world entirely."

The writer said this approach augured badly for the future of the game for "which Athlone had played a more prominent part than 99% of those who rule the roost and who were unheard of when the deeds of Athlone were being proclaimed all over Ireland".

The sense of a Dublin-elite keen to shed its troublesome country cousins from the league was one that would build in the following years.

1924/25 season round-up

DATE	OPPOSITION	COMPETITION	SCORELINE	SCORERS
			(Athlone score first in all scorelines)	
September 13, 1924	Shelbourne (h)	League	0-3	
September 20, 1924	Bray Unknowns (h)	League	1-1	Charles
September 28, 1924	Jacobs (h)	League	0-3	
October 5, 1924	Shamrock Rovers (a)	League	0-6	
October 11, 1924	Brooklyn (h)	League	0-0	
October 18, 1924	Pioneers (a)	League	3-1	(Glavey, Dykes, Keegan)
October 25, 1924	St James's Gate (a)	League	1-1	(Glavey)
November 8, 1924	Fordsons (h)	League	1-1	(Jim Sweeney)
November 15, 1924	Shelbourne (a)	League	1-4	(Keegan)
November 22, 1924	Bray Unknowns (a)	League	1-3	(Hannon)
November 30, 1924	Jacobs (a)	League	1-1	(Glavey)
December 7, 1924	Shamrock Rovers (h)	League	0-5	
December 13, 1924	Brooklyn (a)	League	1-0	(Keegan)
December 20, 1924	Pioneers (h)	League	1-0	(Hannon)
December 26, 1924	St James's Gate (h)	League	3-2	(Glavey, Hannon, Sweeney*)
January 10, 1925	Cork Bohemians (h)	FAI Cup	5-3	(Jim Sweeney (3), John Sweeney, Ghent)
January 17, 1925	Drumcondra (a)	FAI Cup	2-0	(Jim Sweeney (2))
January 24, 1925	Bray Unknowns (h)	Shield	1-1	(Jim Sweeney)
January 31, 1925	Pioneers (a)	Shield	1-2	(Jim Sweeney)
February 14, 1925	Shelbourne (Dalymount Park)	FAI Cup S/F	0-4	
March 7, 1925	Bohemians (a)	Shield	0-5	
March 21, 1925	Brooklyn (h)	Shield	4-1	(?)
March 29, 1925	Jacobs (a)	Shield	2-3	(?)
April 4, 1925	Shamrock Rovers (a)	Shield	0-1	
April 18, 1925	Shelbourne (h)	Shield	2-0	(Henry, Glavey)
April 25, 1925	Fordsons (a)	League	1-2	(Henry)

*Not known which Sweeney
** Neither league game against Bohemians was played. Points went to the Dubliners.
*** Shield games against Fordsons and St James's Gate were also not played. Points to opponents.

Chapter 26

Barney Connaughton

"One of the cleanest backs in the Free State"

A slow apprenticeship

Born in Kiltoom in April 1900 to Thomas and Brigid (nee McDermott), Bernard Connaughton, or Barney as he was better known, spent his formative years in the town's urban westside.

He resided in High Street, College Lane and Patrick Street, among other locations, during his time in Athlone.

Aged 22, Barney Connaughton made his Athlone debut at full-back, on St Stephen's Day, 1922, in a 4-2 victory over Rathmines Athletic in the Sportsground.

Barney Connaughton

In those early years of the 1920s, Connaughton was a prominent figure in the local junior scene. In particular, he helped his side, St Patrick's League, to win the Midland League in 1923.

After his Yuletide introduction, it was to be over ten months before Connaughton would again feature in an Athlone senior line-out and when he did reappear it was mainly in the forward line at outside-right.

For a player whose defensive technique was later described as being "without polish", it appears strange that he would have been deemed a fitting outside-right, a position usually associated with fleetness of foot and delicateness of touch.

With team details sketchy, it's not known when Connaughton first appeared for Athlone in the 1923/24 season. However, he did line up in the away game against Pioneers when only six players travelled and the club, embarrassingly, were forced to secure reinforcements from the crowd.

Between then and the end of the league campaign on December 30th, 1923, Connaughton was regularly in the line-up and nearly always at outside-right.

Helping to pave the way to the final

When Athlone embarked on a run of nine successive victories culminating in the FAI Cup final in 1924, Connaughton was on the team in the first six of these games, before losing his place at the most inopportune time.

This was a crucial period as Athlone built up a head of steam which came to a boil when they blew the lid from football in the State by winning the FAI Cup.

The winning streak began at home to Brooklyn in the final game of the league campaign with Connaughton filling in at centre-forward. For the first round of the cup the following week against Midland Athletic, Connaughton retained his place, but was named at outside-right. In fact, he was to play in three of the five cup games en route to victory.

His first goal for Athlone, in a 5-0 away defeat of Dublin side St Paul's in the first round of the Leinster Senior Cup, probably ensured he retained his place the following weekend for the FAI Cup last-eight tie with Shelbourne. Again, he lined out at outside-right but was switched to centre-forward after the break probably to allow a fitter and speedier Tommy Collins exploit a weary Shels full-back who had sustained a first-half injury.

Connaughton continued his unbroken run in the team the following weekend at home to Jacobs in the Leinster Senior Cup and then at outside-right for the crunch FAI Cup semi-final cash with the all-powerful Bohemians.

This time, though, there was to be no hiding place and although Athlone secured a commendable draw in Shelbourne Park, Connaughton was pinpointed as the weakest link.

The Westmeath Independent was unusually scathing and trenchant in its comments. "Hannon was ubiquitous but was handicapped by not having a partner. If he had a good winger with him, the result would have been an outright win to Athlone. This solitary defect in the team must be remedied before the replay. The loss of a good right-wing may give the other forwards too much to do, while it makes the task of the Bohemians halves proportionally easier."

Having been dropped for the FAI Cup semi-final replay, Connaughton missed out on the final itself, although, along with the stricken John Sweeney, he was named as a reserve.

As no substitutes were allowed during the game this appears primarily to have been a cosmetic gesture. But, at least, it served to highlight that his contribution to the success had been valued.

Ironically, he was back in the starting eleven for the game after the cup final and appeared regularly throughout the final matches of the season in both the shield and Leinster Senior Cup.

Developing as a full-back

Strangely, for a player who had effectively nailed down a first-team berth, Connaughton was entirely absent the following season. There is no record that he featured with Athlone at all.

However, he returned from the outset of the 1925/26 season, although those in charge of Athlone appeared to have failed to learn the lessons of the past as they again attempted to slot Connaughton into the outside-right berth.

Eventually, Athlone learned how best to utilise his talents and he was switched to his favoured full-back position, although he also played at half-back on occasions during that season.

A regular starting berth in defence helped Connaughton to fine-tune his game, so much so that he began to develop at a rapid rate.

The 1925/26 campaign was one of his busiest seasons for Athlone and he continued to feature throughout the end-of-season Shield and Leinster Senior Cup competition.

By 1926/27, with time gradually catching up on the more established members of the 1924 side, Connaughton was among a new wave of local players who were now the backbone of the team. During this season, he was a mainstay of the side, playing throughout the 31-game season.

By now, he had also attracted the attention of some of the game's analysts. Football Sports Weekly said he was "one of, if not, the best, backs in the Free State and the cleanest".

The magazine Sport lobbied for his inclusion in a League of Ireland representative side to play both the IFA and Welsh Leagues in 1926/27. However, it admitted that Connaughton "though a greatly improved player, may have to wait a little longer before securing the selectors' confidence".

In November 1926, Athlone travelled to Dublin to take on Bohemians in a league clash, and although coming out on the wrong side of a 3-1 scoreline, Connaughton's performance was deemed worthy of comment. His "unhesitating style of tackling and his lusty kicking made him a prominent figure", it was reported.

In a crunch game with Shamrock Rovers during May 1927, Connaughton was deemed the best player on the pitch, heady praise given the presence of a full-strength Shamrock Rovers side which clinched the Shield trophy with a narrow victory.

By 1927/28, Connaughton, like many others, was beginning to spread his wings, playing on a few occasions for Mullingar in the Leinster Senior League Division 1, whilst retaining his link with Athlone.

In a trying season for Athlone, Connaughton was also a regular in the full-back line including in the 9-1 defeat by Shelbourne early on. According to the newspaper Sport, he was one of a few Athlone players to come out of this contest with any degree of credit.

Despite Athlone's defence being far from resolute, most press reports during this dismal season seemed to reserve their criticism for Athlone's attacking players.

In Athlone's concluding home league game in what was their final league campaign for many years, the Irish Independent, referring to the 0-0 home draw with St James's Gate, remarked: "They (Athlone) did well, as usual, in defence, but once more their forwards failed, especially at close quarters, to make the most of their opportunities." Connaughton, ever the dependable defender, along with keeper Pa Henry was credited, in particular, with keeping out the St James's Gate attackers.

Even in that demoralising season during which Athlone conceded 61 goals in 18 league games, Connaughton retained some form. Earlier in the season, Sport had noted: "Connaughton seldom plays a bad game and only a lack of polish prevents him from being compared with the best. He is one of our most consistent fulls."

Mullingar and Dundalk

With Athlone not fielding a team the following season, Connaughton initially switched allegiance to neighbouring Mullingar, where he lined out at full-back. Alongside him was a familiar face, Mullingar native Jimmy Hope, his old Athlone full-back partner from the 1927/28 season.

However, Connaughton was soon back in League of Ireland action having linked up with Dundalk, who were then in their third year in the league.

He made five first-team appearances for Dundalk in November and December 1928. His arrival coincided unfortunately with a spell of disappointing results and he was not retained.

That same season, Athlone fielded a representative junior side to take on Sligo in a friendly in the north west. Connaughton was right-full on the team which also included Billy Blackwell, Joe Glavey, Mick Henry, Mick Dunican and Michael and Anthony Dowling.

He returned to Leinster Senior League action with Mullingar Celtic the following season, 1929/30, playing at half-back in a team that also regularly included Billy Blackwell, Mick Henry and Jimmy Hope. With the North Westmeath side qualifying for the FAI Cup proper that year, Connaughton enjoyed one further taste of the premier knock-out competition.

However, it ended badly as Mullingar went down 5-1 to Dolphin in Dolphin's Barn.

Final years with Athlone

By 1931/32, he was back in the Athlone fold featuring in some of the earlier rounds as the team triumphed in the Leinster Junior Cup.

He made irregular appearances for Athlone throughout the early 1930s culminating in the hectic 1934/35 campaign in which the Town won the Free State Junior Cup and Sunday Alliance League as well as losing out in the final of the Leinster Junior Cup.

Connaughton did not appear on the Free State Cup winning-side. However, at the age of 35, he was centre-half in the team that lost the Leinster Junior Cup final against Emorville. Having drawn 0-0 in St Mel's Park, Athlone were beaten in front of 8,000 spectators in a Tolka Park replay.

Connaughton married a Dundalk woman Teresa McGeough and moved to Dublin. The couple had one son, who died tragically at a young age in a traffic accident.

Barney Connaughton passed away on September 17th, 1982, and is buried in Haggardstown Cemetery outside Dundalk.

Barney Connaughton
in 1935

Chapter 27

1925/26 season

Unfulfilled promise

After the disappointments of 1924/25, the only way was up.

To those looking in from the outside, Athlone was still a real cradle of football talent. Its multitude of junior clubs would have been expected to produce the necessary players to staff Athlone's ranks.

As Football Sports Weekly put it: "If they are not stronger this season, the time is near at hand when they will once again be a very formidable opposition as no town in the country for its population can boast so many junior clubs as Athlone."

Indeed, Athlone Town B was one of ten clubs entered in the local junior league that season.

If this was an optimistic outlook, if fitted neatly with the prevailing atmosphere of the day. The new season also brought with it a major revamp of the off-side law, prompting a heightened sense of anticipation at the feast of attacking football ahead.

Up to that point, an attacker could only be off-side if there were two or less opponents between him and the defending goal-line. Now, that had been reduced to one.

The changes were necessitated by the frequent stoppages for off-side which were bedevilling the game. Under the previous ruling, teams were able to leave just one back in the full back line and push other defenders well up the field.

They were safe in the knowledge that the last attacker could only remain level with the second last defender.

The change, brought into effect in the Free State League on the first day of the new season, was expected to favour forwards.

"Heavier scoring will accrue as a result of the new rule and faster play will be seen," one paper predicted.

For their part, Athlone prepared for the fresh campaign with a friendly in Galway against the pick of the local clubs in mid-August.

Off the field, the AGM elected the following committee for the 1925/26 season: Chairman: M.J. Lennon; Treasurer: D.J. Hannon; Hon Sec: W.J. Tormey; Assistant Hon Sec: P. Boushell. Committee: J. Galvin, M. Molloy, J. Martin, G. Gaylard, T. Browne, J. O'Donnell, T. Ghent, D. Hannon, F. Ghent and J. Sweeney.

The season proper got underway on August 30th with Athlone hosting Pioneers in the Sportsground.

Action from the second match of Athlone's 1925/26 season away to Bohemians in Dalymount Park. The Bohemians goalkeeper is pictured clearing upfield.

Three up after 15 minutes thanks to goals from Ghent, Glavey and James Sweeney, Athlone still had to depend on a late John Sweeney goal to secure the points after Pioneers had fought back to level by the interval.

The predictions of a goal glut appeared to be borne out when Athlone's second league game the following weekend yielded nine goals. Unfortunately, though, six of the nine were netted by the home side, Bohemians.

Athlone weren't helped by yet another injury sustained by Paddy Flannery, resulting in him missing the entire second half.

The club had fielded an experimental line-out including a number of players from junior clubs. The concession of three penalties, the legitimacy of two of which were queried by national newspapers, served to unsettle the inexperienced side.

Goals from Mick Henry from the penalty spot and Jim Sweeney had left Athlone trailing 3-2 at the interval. Unfortunately, the numerical disadvantage told in the second period and a John Sweeney goal was scant consolation.

The impressive McCabe, in goal, saved the third penalty while ex-Cowdenbeath player Flynn lined out as centre-half for his only appearance in Athlone colours, alongside Billy Blackwell.

The tests were coming thick and fast as Shamrock Rovers were the visitors to Athlone the following weekend.

The previous season the Hoops carried off an amazing clean sweep, winning every competition they entered, the league, FAI Cup and Shield, without losing a single game. It was no surprise that Athlone were swamped, losing 5-1 with Frank Ghent registering the only score for the home team.

Athlone had now conceded a staggering 14 goals in their opening three games. But after this tough opening to the campaign, they reeled off four successive wins.

The sequence commenced away to Bray Unknowns. For this one, in an effort to stem the flow of goals conceded, Terry Judge returned to the side at full-back, beside Hope, while Barney Connaughton and newcomer ex-Bohemians player Willams (in his only game) filled the half-back berths, either side of Mick Henry, who at a young age had been installed in the crucial centre-half berth.

Goals from John Sweeney, Jim Sweeney (2), Henry from the spot and Blackwell helped Athlone to a 5-3 victory.

If the defence had been buttressed somewhat, it was now time to strengthen the attacking unit with the introduction of one of Ireland's most celebrated players, Edward A. 'Ned' Brooks.

Ned Brooks

Ned Brooks was one of the premier strikers in Irish football of his time.

He had been capped by the old IFA against Scotland in Glasgow in 1920, while a Shelbourne player.

He had spells too with Drumcondra and Linfield but was most associated with Bohemians, with whom he initially appeared in the mid-1910s.

Brooks was a tricky, speedy and clever player who was able to knit play well as a centre-forward and who would always grasp a half chance at shooting.

Left-footed, Brooks was a snappy shooter who seemed to revel in wet conditions. Football Sports Weekly said of him: "He loves playing on a soft pitch or on a wet day."

Ned Brooks

One of Brooks' first introductions to Athlone was as a stranded Bohemians player during Easter 1916. The Dublin club had travelled for a regular festive friendly against The Town on Easter Monday. But when the Easter Rising erupted in Dublin that morning, the Bohs team were stranded in Athlone for some days after all Dublin-bound trains were stopped.

Brooks subsequently transferred to Shelbourne, with whom he earned an Irish League representative cap in 1919 against the Scottish League. He then joined Stockport County for some of the 1920/21 and 1921/22 seasons.

Ned rejoined Bohemians during the first League of Ireland campaign in 1922/23 but missed all of the 1923/24 league campaign having switched to Gaelic football.

Indeed, he only returned to the Bohemians colours in the FAI Cup semi-final replay against Athlone. He was Bohemians' top scorer with 14 goals the next year before he moved to Athlone a few games into the 1925/26 season.

He remained with the Athlone side for that campaign and all of the next season, before joining Brideville ahead of the 1927/28 campaign. Brooks also served in the 1928/29 season with the Inchicore club before dropping out of the league.

During his stints with various clubs he clocked up 63 League of Ireland goals in total.

Undoubtedly, Brooks' finest hour was in June 1924 when he became the first player to score a hat-trick for Ireland.

Brooks had been prohibited from travelling to Paris with the Irish Olympic team due to his time as a professional with Stockport County. But when the Irish officials invited the US Olympic team back for an international friendly against Ireland in Dalymount Park, Brooks was no longer ineligible.

And the dashing forward seized his opportunity, scoring all the goals in Ireland's 3-0 win. According to FIFA rules, that game is regarded as a full international – thus making Brooks the first scorer of a hat-trick in the green shirt. At the time, he was a Bohemians player.

Brooks also made an impact at representative level, scoring, as an Athlone Town player, for the new Free State League in a grudge match against the IFA in front of 20,000 spectators in Windsor Park in March 1927. He was also a regular in interprovincial matches.

In fact, Brooks was a real big-time player; always ready to step up a level under pressure.

When Blackburn Rovers, crowned FA Cup winners a week or two before, came for a friendly game against Bohemians at the end of the 1923/24 season, the surprise Bohemians victory was most remembered for a Brooks wonder goal. He picked up possession near the halfway line and beat defender after defender before spearing a rising drive past the visiting keeper.

Brooks was a goalscorer supreme – a player whose dashing, exuberant style was evidence of a deep passion for the game. During his time in Athlone, he scored 24 league goals in two seasons.

However, it was his goal-scoring feats during the full 1926/27 season which secured Brooks a place in the Athlone history books.

His record of 29 goals in all senior competitions in that campaign puts him alongside Eugene 'Pooch' Davis, Andy Myler and Michael O'Connor in the ranks of the most prolific strikers to play for Athlone.

A scoring streak

In the 1925/26 season, Brooks made his first appearance for Athlone in the fifth league game of the season, at home to Jacobs.

Despite not being fully fit, Brooks characteristically scored on his debut, helping Athlone to a 4-2 victory which also included a hat-trick from Jim Sweeney.

His arrival helped to improve Athlone's immediate form and Brooks also brought out the best in Jim Sweeney, whose 17 goals in the 1925/26 league season was his best haul.

The Evening Herald noted: "The Sweeney brothers flank him on the right and Ghent and Glavey on the left in an attacking formation that will shake the best of opposing defences from any tendency to somnambulism."

Brideville were the next foes to fall during Athlone's four-match winning run. Brooks and Sweeney were again on the scoresheet, accompanied by an unattributed effort as a result of an almighty melee.

In the midst of the winning series, Monahan had returned to the Athlone fold and lined out in his customary full-back role, releasing Terry Judge to his more normal half-back berth. Judge though sustained an injury against Jacobs and didn't return to the fold for the remainder of the season.

Hannon filled in for Judge at left-half in the Brideville game in what was possibly his only appearance of the year.

Carroll, an accomplished hockey player, featured at half back in the victory over St James's Gate in Dublin. In that game, although 2-0 down, Athlone rallied with goals from Brooks (2) and Jim Sweeney to seal the victory. This was the third in a streak of seven successive games in which Brooks found the net.

A sickener at home

The victory ensured that Athlone were just two points off joint league leaders Fordsons and Shelbourne, who incidentally were the next two sides the Town were due to meet.

As it transpired the Fordsons game, played in front of a huge attendance in the Sportsground, turned into something of a disaster. Athlone fought back from a 3-1 interval deficit and had a chance to level the game at 3-3 from the penalty spot, but Mick Henry skied his shot. Fordsons took full advantage and extended their lead before a bizarre own goal by Joe Monahan, who walked from the field in the same match, sealed a 5-2 victory for the Corkmen.

Worse was to come in the following game, away to joint league leaders and eventual champions, Shelbourne. Backs against the walls, Athlone defended solidly and nicked an early goal in the second half when Brooks converted a sublime Frank Ghent cross. Thanks to the superb defending of Hope and

Connaughton and the brilliant goalkeeping of McCabe, with ten minutes remaining it looked as if a shock was on the cards.

However, the concession of three goals in just three minutes changed the entire complexion of the game, leaving Athlone distraught and shattered.

The Evening Herald said Athlone's tendency to retreat into a defensive shell had cost them dearly.

"Attack is the best defence. Had Athlone put the axiom to practical test, they might now be glorying in the glamour of victory over the league leaders."

Athlone's commitment to the league was always fragile, particularly because of the onerous travelling regime required to Dublin almost every fortnight. Having geared themselves up for an assault on the championship, Athlone's morale had been badly dented by the two successive defeats.

It seemed as if Athlone then effectively wrote off the league, as they only managed to win one of the next six games.

That victory came the following weekend away to eventual bottom club Pioneers, who earned only two points that season and were not re-elected. Harling, a former Dublin United and Olympia player, made his debut in that game.

There followed four defeats on the trot. During this pointless sequence, the Football Sports Weekly remarked: "Somehow Athlone appear to have gone wrong since they lost to Fordsons. Up to that point, they had been doing splendidly … From what has reached us that game ought never to have been lost and the team has never completely recovered for its efforts. Pull yourselves together, Athlone!"

The losing sequence prompted a major reshuffling of the playing staff with locals like Norman Lyster, Johnny McManus and Dan Sullivan, a couple of Dubliners and a number of juniors all getting chances. Among those tried was Tommy Connor, a young outside-right who had featured in the local junior scene in Athlone and was then playing with Mullingar in the Leinster Senior League.

Johnny McManus

Johnny McManus is one of a handful of Athlone men to captain Ireland at international level.

The Connaught Street native earned the honour in 1931 when he led an Irish junior international team against Scotland.

At that time, McManus was Sligo Rovers' captain, but it was almost ten years previously when he first emerged onto a football field at the tender age of just 16.

In January 1922, McManus featured in Athlone's first-ever FAI Cup game against YMCA at outside-right. He played just one further game that season, scoring against Pioneers in the Leinster Senior Cup.

It's easy to imagine the youthful McManus hanging around the predominantly Connaught Street-based team looking for a game.

Johnny McManus

And indeed, when Athlone won the Leinster Junior Cup title a few months later, the traditional post-match photograph shows the team, officials and older supporters and the youthful McManus – more than a mascot but not a player.

McManus made intermittent appearances for Athlone in the coming years, featuring at least once in the 1925/26 season.

In the tail end of the 1927/28 league season when Athlone were at their lowest ebb, he again played a handful of games including in the final League of Ireland game played in Athlone.

Like many footballers before and since, McManus was forced to showcase his skills away from his home-town club. And it was with Mullingar and Sligo Rovers that he forged a notable career.

For fringe Athlone footballers who couldn't avail of a regular place in the local League of Ireland team, there were no regular football opportunities available in Athlone beyond the local junior club scene.

And while McManus featured prominently in the junior ranks, including on a combination side, Athlone Utd, in the Leinster Junior Cup in 1924/25, it wasn't long before he too made the short journey north to Mullingar to experience football at a higher level than the local junior club scene in Athlone.

Mullingar were in the Leinster Senior League and offered the chance of a regular weekly game at a decent level. 1926/27 appears to be the first season McManus lined out in Mullingar colours and he helped the Westmeath side to their third successive Leinster Junior Cup final.

Having been beaten in the two previous deciders and in the semi-final stages the two years before that, there was a frenzy of excitement in Mullingar that the long search for silverware would finally be ended.

Featuring at full-back, a position he had by now adopted, McManus scored from the spot in the semi-final and again converted a penalty in a 3-1 victory over Vickers in Shelbourne Park.

Alongside him that day in the full-back line was another Athlone native and sometime Athlone Town player, Billy Blackwell.

Many of their colleagues were to go on to feature with Athlone during the 1927/28 season – taking the step up from the Leinster Senior League to the League of Ireland.

In 1928/29, two years later, McManus secured a Free State Junior Cup medal to go with his Leinster Junior Cup victory. This time though he was representing Sligo having moved to the North West with his employers, Liptons, with whom he had previously worked in Athlone. Two of his team-mates at Mullingar, James 'Guy' Callaghan and Anthony 'Gully' McKenna (both of whom had also played, albeit rarely, with Athlone) had also transferred their loyalties to Sligo Rovers at this time. They too were on the Free State Junior Cup side of 1928/29 with McKenna scoring two in the final victory over Grangegorman.

A meeting in Athlone in late 1928 had resulted in the formation of a Connaught Football Association (including Athlone) and the Connaught Cup, a new junior competition for teams in the province, was created.

McManus, McKenna and Callaghan were all on the Sligo Rovers team to claim the cup in 1929/30, the second year of its existence.

McManus was steadily growing in stature and in April 1931 he captained Connaught in a friendly against a visiting Scottish junior team. But better was to come when, in October that year, he skippered Ireland's juniors when they travelled to take on Scotland in Falkirk. His former Athlone and Mullingar colleague Guy Callaghan was also capped in that game.

Sligo Rovers had progressed through the ranks of junior football and in 1932/33 were admitted to the top division of the Leinster Senior League.

They also qualified for the FAI Cup proper and McManus featured in the team that overcame League of Ireland side Brideville in the first round before succumbing to Shelbourne in the second round. His FAI Cup appearances came eleven years after he had first featured in the competition for Athlone against YMCA.

The following year, 1933/34, Sligo enjoyed a remarkable campaign, winning the Leinster Senior League and FAI Intermediate Cup, with McManus a regular at full-back. Callaghan and McKenna also contributed to the successes with Callaghan scoring twice in the Intermediate Cup final.

It was enough to ensure Rovers were elected to the League of Ireland in 1934/35, but by that stage McManus had left to join Mullingar after six hugely successful years with Sligo.

Guy Callaghan continued to feature periodically for the first two years of Sligo Rovers' League of Ireland tenure, scoring in both campaigns.

Eight years previously, he had been on the League of Ireland scoresheet for Athlone Town in the club's final league campaign.

Picking up the pieces

Another to join Athlone was well-known defender Matt Armstrong, who made his debut against Shamrock Rovers in Dublin in mid-November.

Armstrong had been out of the game for a year and according to the Football Sports Weekly: "He was not of the least assistance and the puzzle was to find out what he was doing on the field."

Armstrong was a Northener who had featured with Distillery before joining Dublin Utd, the team for Ulster exiles in the southern capital.

He did eventually settle into the side, scoring in a 4-1 defeat against Jacobs, the last of the four successive losses.

And he continued to feature regularly, although not weekly, for the next four or five months right up to the end of the campaign.

Having regained his match fitness with Athlone, Armstrong went on to play in an FAI Cup final the following season with Dublin club Brideville. He was reckoned to be Brideville's outstanding player in the final, which the club lost in a replay.

Another to move to Athlone, albeit very briefly, on the same path via Distillery and Dublin Utd was Eagleson, who had also signed with Bohemians but never played.

However, it was a return to goalscoring form by Jim Sweeney which finally roused Athlone from that terrible series of defeats.

The old reliable struck a hat-trick away to Brideville to snatch a draw before weighing in with two more the following weekend as Athlone easily accounted for St James's Gate, winning 5-1.

The season concluded with two further defeats, a narrow, and by all accounts undeserved, 6-5 loss in a thriller in Cork against Fordsons and a final 4-1 home defeat to champions Shelbourne on St Stephen's Day. Athlone had raced into a 3-0 lead after 20 minutes in Cork before being pegged back.

By the end of the season, Mick Keegan had returned from Shelbourne to Athlone, having gone in the opposite direction at the conclusion of the previous campaign. Shelbourne's victory in the Sportsground on St Stephen's Day ensured they were crowned champions after a tight struggle with Shamrock Rovers.

Athlone had finished seventh of ten teams, with 15 points. Their goals for column alone would have seen them finish fifth, but their number of goals conceded was the second highest in the league.

With the league campaign concluded, Athlone focused on their main aim of each and every season, the cup.

In the words of the Evening Herald in its preview of the first-round game against Brideville: "The Midlanders' league record does not convey true evidence of their potentialities. In this case, the cup's the thing. It inspires them to a higher pitch of enthusiasm and effort."

With doubts over Athlone's continued membership of the league lingering, this season the cup took on particular importance.

"At this particular time, their fortunes and future is intimately bound up with their advancement.

"Failure may have a fatal effect beyond mere departure from the trophy," the Herald continued.

In the first round, Athlone drew Brideville, a Liberties-based Dublin team, which had just completed a debut season in the League of Ireland.

Athlone were at full strength with Connaughton and Hope forming the defensive line in front of McCabe. Lyster, Henry and Armstrong comprised the half-back line with the front five of the two Sweeneys, Brooks, Glavey and Ghent.

It was a busy weekend for Norman Lyster, who had previously only turned out possibly once during that season for Athlone. The prominent businessman had spent the previous day representing Midlands in a hockey interprovincial match against Ulster.

Athlone had the victory sown up by the interval, with goals from Brooks, Ghent (a remarkable individual effort) and Jim Sweeney ensuring a three-goal half-time cushion. Despite Brideville pressure after the break, including a missed penalty, Athlone retained their advantage and indeed added a fourth late on through a Mick Henry penalty.

Fortunate Fordsons

The victory qualified Athlone for a quarter-final berth against their old rivals Fordsons of Cork. Fordsons had defeated Shelbourne in the first round after a replay in Dublin and were eager to have the cup tie against Athlone switched to the capital too.

However, Athlone would not consent despite the lure of larger crowds – and resultant financial dividends – at a Dublin location.

"The Midlanders prefer to retain their ground advantage instead of bartering it for an attractive financial consideration and a greater prospect of defeat," one paper explained.

Some 4,000 turned out in the Sportsground including about 600 from Cork for the contest on Sunday, January 24th.

As was now customary, the Sportsground was sodden and not in a condition conducive to good football; "a switchback pitch", according to the Evening Herald.

Again, misfortune dogged Athlone who dominated the opening period without availing of a couple of gilt-edged opportunities. And so it was that the visitors grabbed the opener through Billy Hannon after goalkeeper McCabe had poorly parried a shot. Jim Sweeney applied the finish to a

Frank Ghent cross five minutes later for an equaliser that was greeted with "thunderous applause".

McCabe again failed to clear a cross convincingly soon after, allowing Fordsons to add another courtesy of Dave Roberts.

Athlone had what appeared a clear penalty claim waved away before Fordsons registered a third before the interval from the boot of Paddy Barry.

Despite the 3-1 interval lead, Fordsons were under pressure for most of the second half. Goalkeeper Bill O'Hagan in the Cork goal pulled off a string of saves and was particularly fortunate when he parried a Joe Glavey shot onto the post.

Athlone contrived to twice miss penalties with the normally reliable Mick Henry having both of his spot kicks blocked by O'Hagan.

Later in the second half, Jim Sweeney converted yet another penalty as Athlone piled on the pressure in search of an equaliser.

Their prospects were not helped by the sending off of Jimmy Hope for a second bookable offence 20 minutes from the end. But despite the sending off, the final minutes were "one long attempt by The Town to equalise".

It was a harsh dismissal which if it had occurred in Dublin, according to the Football Sports Weekly, would have "sparked a riot".

The Evening Herald agreed: "Hope, realising Kelly's cleverness and effectiveness, tackled him strenuously but not dangerously, and appeared to have been harshly dealt with in being sent to the pavilion."

It later transpired that the flexibility of Athlone keeper McCabe had been severely limited as he had not shaken off the impact of a bout of lumbago. He had in fact played despite doctor's orders.

Despite all the mitigating circumstances, the Westmeath Independent was unusually critical of the team and its performance.

"It is somewhat disappointing to realise that after having broadcast "We are after the Cup and the Cup only" since the opening of the season, Athlone were not able, although provided with many golden opportunities, to beat the mediocre Corkmen."

And though the tame performances in 1924/25 had suggested the cup win of the previous season may have affected the players' mentality, for the first time there was the outright suggestion of such in print.

"It appears that the winning of the cup, at any time, has its disadvantages, particularly so when the heads concerned are unable to contain the success with becoming modesty and equilibrium."

The impact of the defeat must have only been magnified when, some four weeks later, the victors triumphed in the replayed cup final against Shamrock Rovers. Fordsons, vanquished by Athlone in the 1924 decider, finally had their hands on the cup.

Leaving Athlone that Sunday in January, the Cork supporters may have been happy – but they were also hungry – as no meals were available in the town.

Whatever shops did open may have engaged in a bit of profiteering from the captive audience as Football Sports Weekly reported: "From the prices we were charged, Athlone must be a dear place to live in."

The season peters out

Having suffered the hammer blow of losing in the cup in these trying circumstances, Athlone's season understandably petered out.

The following weekend they exited the Leinster Senior Cup away to Drumcondra and the Shield held little interest, bar as a crucible for experimental line-outs.

Setting off on their journey to Dublin for the Drumcondra game, Athlone left without Frank Ghent and only noticed his absence close to Mullingar.

As the Westmeath Independent put it: "The "Town" must have been sure of beating the lads from Drumcondra on Saturday last, because they elected to travel without an outside-left. There was a time, however, when the public felt that the senior team was composed of about one player - the outside-left."

The Shield competition was run off between all ten league clubs, with each team playing all others once. The club did at least fulfil all of its nine Shield fixtures – but it was noticeable that only three were at home as the fixtures seemed to be tweaked to avoid Dublin teams having to travel to the Midlands.

The record of one win, one draw and seven defeats says it all.

Although Athlone lost 5-1 to Shelbourne in Dublin in the Shield, the game was significant for keeper McCabe's "superb performance", which even had the home supporters applauding him time after time. A year later the Ringsend outfit signed the Athlone netminder.

Similarly, when Athlone dispatched Pioneers by 5-0 in the Shield, the vanquished Dubliners' keeper, Jimmy Murray stood out as exceptional, saving a penalty in the process. Mindful of the last time a Pioneers goalkeeper (Paddy O'Reilly) had produced such a display against Athlone and that his subsequent signing proved to be a masterstroke, Athlone were keen to try out Murray the following season too.

Among those who featured in Athlone's ranks towards the end of the season was Patrick 'Patsy' Gallagher, a teenager from Derry, who was on trial.

Gallagher signed with Glenavon the following year, had a short spell with Bohemians, before spending a season with Dundalk in 1927/28. Subsequently, he played with Belfast Celtic, Newry Town and Cork

Bohemians, in the League of Ireland, before lining out for a season in the English League with Southport in Division 3 North in 1933/34.

After his falling out with the club, Monahan did return for the Shield campaign while up to six juniors, many of them from Cork, played for Athlone in the Shield game away to Fordsons in May.

Trials and tribulations

Athlone's renewed standing in the game was reflected by the fact that four of the squad was chosen among 22 players for a trial to select the Irish team to meet Italy in Turin in late March.

The trial was a Probables v. Possibles affair, and a squad to travel to Italy was to be chosen afterwards. The squad was not finally confirmed until after another match against a Munster selection. However, as the key Munster players were all included in the Probables and Possibles sides, the subsequent game against Munster was more of a training exercise ahead of the Italian trip than a second trial.

Ned Brooks was chosen as centre-forward for the Probables side, while Frank Ghent (outside-left), Jim Sweeney (inside-right) and Mick Henry (right-half), all turned out for the Possibles.

Brooks, though, was the only one to make the final squad and he was pencilled in to start against Italy as centre-forward.

The lack of further representation from Athlone sparked anger locally with one letter writer to the Westmeath Independent claiming the new Dublin board of selection was as biased as the ill-fated Belfast-based committee in the days of the Irish Football Association.

The letter writer called for a trial between the best of the Dublin combinations and a selected eleven from Cork and Athlone. And he sought equal representation on the international selection committee from Cork, Athlone and other provincial centres.

Whilst the letter writer could easily be dismissed as a crank, it was evidence of growing frustration within Athlone circles at the difficulties the club had in competing in a Dublin-based league.

In any event, the Athlone contingent was reduced to zero when Brooks was forced to cry off the Italian trip following the tragic death of his son, Harold.

The seven-year-old from Rathmines was killed in a traffic accident the weekend before the Italy match and was rushed to hospital. Despite a blood transfusion given by his father, he died later.

Meanwhile, there were persistent rumours in national newspapers that some of Athlone's regular players were set to relocate to Dublin.

Football Sports Weekly cited speculation that Frank Ghent was set to join Shelbourne along with Ned Brooks.

It cited the burden of travelling to Dublin on successive weekends as a factor in Athlone's uncertain future.

Constant newspaper talk regarding the club's existence must also have been a destabilising influence.

However, Football Sports Weekly said when it came to rumours of Athlone's demise the possibility was that the wish was father to the thought.

"Athlone are too long established to go down and out for want of a little stimulus to their eleven." It suggested that "a few minutes' serious contemplation of their record and a business-like spirit to get it right" was all that was needed.

The Evening Herald speculated on Athlone's possible resignation in February 1926 but remarked: "Those entitled to speak for the club say they won't. They admit they have difficulties in carrying on but expect to surmount them and come up again in the new season."

A month or so later, the paper reported: "Athlone are not going out of the game for quite a long time – if ever. Their spirit is strong, their enthusiasm ebullient and their will unbreakable. They simply must be in the thick of it. They'll carry on."

Mullingar's junior final defeat

The Athlone footballing scene remained strong, of course, and there was no shortage of local talent.

That was exemplified by Mullingar's feat, for the second year running, of reaching the Leinster Junior Cup final. There was a strong Athlone connection to the team, with Pa Henry, brother of Athlone Town's Mick, in goal.

At outside-left was another Athlone native Billy Blackwell, who had already scored for Athlone Town in the Free State League earlier that same season. Henry was in the thick of the action as Mullingar lost 4-3 to Dublin side Strandvilla in the final in Shelbourne Park.

Sligo man Frank Tiernan, who had featured for Athlone in the 1923/24 season, scored twice while Tommy Connor, the young outside-right from Athlone, completed the Mullingar scoring.

Pa Henry

Henry, who would appear on the Athlone teamsheet during the following two seasons, was a potentially brilliant but dangerously erratic keeper. Both sides of his personality were on display in Shelbourne Park in a game in which he featured due to the ineligibility of the regular goalkeeper. Mullingar also reached the Free State Junior Cup semi-final that season but were defeated by Dublin side Brunswick in St James's Park in a game for which a special excursion train was organised from Athlone.

Overall, it was a disappointing season for Mullingar, who had started so promisingly and were top of the table in the Leinster Senior League Division Two around Christmas time.

They had also enjoyed a three-year unbeaten record at home in the Horse Show Grounds, located in the former Newbrook racecourse where in more recent years the Tarkett factory was located. This proud boast was to come badly unstuck when they qualified for the Leinster Senior Cup and drew Shamrock Rovers. Some 2,800 people came to witness the famous Hoops dismantle Mullingar by 7-0.

The defeat seemed to demoralise Mullingar, who began to lose their form. Their sticky patch coincided unfortunately with a fixture pile-up caused by Dublin teams finding plenty of excuses to avoid travelling to Mullingar during the winter time.

The decline in confidence and a glut of home games in quick succession saw them slip from the top of the table before the season's end.

However, the Green and Amber striped side did enough that year to catch the attention of Athlone's officials.

Within two years, many of the team would feature in the League of Ireland in Athlone colours.

Ranelagh to the rescue

Meanwhile back in Athlone, another major problem had emerged - the Sportsground, the club's home ground since the foundation of the Football Association of the Irish Free State in 1921 was no longer available.

The local limited company which owned the ground had effectively collapsed and in May 1926, the ground was sold to the Irish Army, leaving the club without a home pitch.

However, to the rescue came Robert Baile, headmaster of the private Ranelagh School, and a figure long associated with the game in Athlone.

The Westmeath Independent of July 17th, 1926, revealed the important development. "It has been learned that Mr Robert Baile, MA, Principal of Ranelagh School, has granted the use of the Ranelagh Grounds for the cup and league matches to the local senior football council."

Baile's uncle, also Robert, had previously been headmaster of the school, and was one of the key figures in the development of the game in Athlone.

He had provided the Ranelagh School Grounds as the first venue for the club after their foundation in 1887. It was here Athlone played their first-ever game.

Now, some 39 years later, the Ranelagh School connection and the Baile family's football involvement were to again throw Athlone a lifeline.

1925/26 season round-up

DATE	OPPOSITION	COMPETITION *(Athlone score first in all scorelines)*	SCORELINE	SCORERS
August 30, 1925	Pioneers (h)	League	4-3	(Ghent, Glavey, John Sweeney, Jim Sweeney)
September 5, 1925	Bohemians (a)	Laegue	3-6	(Jim Sweeney, John Sweeney, Henry)
September 12, 1925	Shamrock Rovers (h)	League	1-5	(Ghent)
September 19, 1925	Bray Unknowns (a)	League	5-3	(Jim Sweeney (2), John Sweeney, Henry, Blackwell)
September 26, 1925	Jacobs (h)	League	4-2	(Brooks, Jim Sweeney (3))
October 3, 1925	Brideville (h)	League	3-0	(Brooks, Jim Sweeney, Hannon)
October 10, 1925	St James's Gate (a)	League	3-2	(Brooks (2), Jim Sweeney)
October 17, 1925	Fordsons (h)	League	2-5	(Jim Sweeney, Brooks)
October 24, 1925	Shelbourne (a)	League	1-3	(Brooks)
October 31, 1925	Pioneers (a)	League	2-1	(Brooks, Henry)
November 7, 1925	Bohemians (h)	League	1-2	(Brooks)
November 15, 1925	Shamrock Rovers (a)	League	0-3	
November 21, 1925	Bray Unknowns (h)	League	2-3	(Glavey, Jim Sweeney)
November 28, 1925	Jacobs (a)	League	1-4	(Armstrong)
December 6, 1925	Brideville (a)	League	3-3	(Jim Sweeney (3))
December 12, 1925	St James's Gate (h)	League	5-1	(Jim Sweeney (2), Glavey, Brooks, John Sweeney)
December 20, 1925	Fordsons (a)	League	5-6	(Jim Sweeney (2), Keegan, Brooks, Henry)
December 26, 1925	Shelbourne (h)	League	1-4	(Jim Sweeney)
January 9, 1926	Brideville (h)	FAI Cup	4-0	(Brooks, Ghent, Jim Sweeney, Henry)
January 17, 1926	Brideville (h)	Shield	2-3	(Henry, John Sweeney)
January 23, 1926	Fordsons (h)	FAI Cup	2-3	(Jim Sweeney (2))
January 31, 1926	Drumcondra (a)	Leinster Senior Cup	2-4	(Henry, Keegan)
February 20, 1926	Shelbourne (a)	Shield	1-5	(Jim Sweeney)
March 6, 1926	Pioneers (a)	Shield	5-0	(Keegan (2), Glavey, Jim Sweeney, Henry)
March 20, 1926	St James's Gate (a)	Shield	1-7	(Glavey)
March 27, 1926	Jacobs (h)	Shield	0-2	
April 5, 1926	Shamrock Rovers (h)	Shield	0-2	
April 11, 1926	Bray Unknowns (a)	Shield	2-2	(Jim Sweeney, ?)
May 2, 1926	Fordsons (a)	Shield	2-8	(Jim Sweeney, Henry)
May 8, 1926	Bohemians (a)	Shield	0-3	

Chapter 28

Frank Ghent

The flying winger

Pace and strength

Frank Ghent was the creative dynamo of much of Athlone's FAI Cup success.

An Athlone native, Ghent's relentless stream of crosses provided the ammunition for the team's snipers to pick off the opposition.

An outside-left of pace and determination, Ghent was the antithesis of the modern twinkle-toed winger. Strong, fiercely determined and fleet of foot, Ghent was a physical match for the burly full-backs who were the fashion of the day. Indeed, the shoulder charge was a weapon he deployed with maximum effect

Born in 1897, one of six children to Patrick and Mary Ghent, Frank was brought up in Brideswell Street, before in later life residing in St Mary's Place.

One of his three brothers, Tom, also played football, mainly at junior level, and was a prominent club member. Another brother, Christy, was a

Frank Ghent in his Irish strip

founder member of the Labour party in Athlone – before moving to England where he lived the remainder of his life.

Their father, Patrick, was the principal of St Mary's National School.

In his final years, Frank, who was unmarried, resided with his sister Margaret Macken (nee Ghent).

Ghent's footballing prime coincided with Athlone's arrival on the scene of the new era of football in Ireland. Aged 25 when Athlone entered the League of Ireland, Ghent was ideally placed to be a cornerstone of the club's development.

When Athlone were admitted to the League of Ireland in 1922/23, they faced a huge challenge. The club had been catapulted from playing a handful of cup games at junior ranks straight to the top level, without even having the weekly rigours of football in the Leinster Senior League.

But the ability of players like Frank Ghent, Jim Sweeney and James Hope to take that giant leap forward was crucial to Athlone's ability to survive in the League of Ireland.

Ghent's deliveries from the left-wing were a regular source of goals for the likes of Jim Sweeney. Crucially too, he was no stranger to finding the net himself. Indeed, he weighed in with two goals during the 1924 FAI Cup campaign.

Athlone's cup-winning team of 1924 had a particularly strong left flank where Ghent and his wing-partner, Tommy Collins, were backed up by Tommy Muldoon at left-half and Jimmy Hope at left-full. It was possibly the club's strongest unit – and one to be envied by many other outfits who struggled to overcome the dearth of naturally left-sided players.

The early competitive years

Ghent appears to have first lined out competitively for Athlone in the 1919/20 campaign at the conclusion of World War One, having previously appeared in friendlies against military sides.

Having been unsuccessful in their attempts to secure the Leinster Junior Cup in both 1919/20 and 1920/21, Athlone finally succeeded in 1921/22, with Ghent, in his third season with Athlone, also contributing to the triumph.

He was a fixture in the Athlone side that season, featuring mainly at inside-left. He scored in the second replay of the Leinster Junior Cup semi-final against St Patrick's. The final of the junior cup itself saw Ghent in his inside-left berth earning his first football medal of note.

Athlone also qualified through a preliminary regional competition to take part in the FAI Cup that year and Ghent had the honour of scoring in Athlone's first senior football game under the new FAI.

That goal came against then league club YMCA and the following week Ghent added another against Pioneers in the Leinster Senior Cup.

Putting his stamp on the league

When Athlone were accepted to membership of the League of Ireland in 1922/23, it was Ghent more than most who made the step up with ease. In that historic season he found his goalscoring boots, netting at least seven times in the league; the highest return of any league season in his career. And with history failing to record the scorers of 13 of Athlone's league goals that season, it's likely he bagged a few more into the bargain.

He lined out in the forward line in the first League of Ireland game against St James's Gate in the Sportsground on September 16th, 1922.

Ghent was a fixture in the team in the league, nearly always at his favoured position of outside-left. He also scored in the third league game, a home draw to Shelbourne Utd, helping to earn Athlone's first point in the League of Ireland.

Athlone had to wait until the fifth match, at home to Olympia, to record their first league win. And although Ghent didn't score in that match, he knocked in four goals in the next three games to propel Athlone to three further wins on the trot. A double against Midland Athletic came during a rare appearance at centre-forward.

Ghent's contribution for much of the remainder of the season was as a provider rather than as a goalgetter. Whether on the scoresheet or not, Ghent was one of Athlone's most consistent players; a crucial element in the club's armoury.

Indeed, when reporters concluded their reports with comments on the quality of the various players, Ghent was rarely excluded from the pick of the Athlone bunch.

It wasn't until the turn of the year that Ghent found his scoring boots again – this time netting in three successive games against the mighty Shamrock Rovers. Rovers ended Athlone's Leinster Senior Cup challenge after a replay before the sides met again the following week in the league.

Strangely, over the years, Ghent appeared to reserve his best performances for jousts with Shamrock Rovers.

His goal in the Leinster Senior Cup game came in trademark fashion and was described thus: "Ghent, with one of his usual runs, ran right through the defence." Indeed, most of his goals came at the end of such typical sorties, where he used his searing pace to outsprint the defence, before lashing in a powerful drive.

In the league game in Dublin, Athlone went two up courtesy of Ghent, both scored after he skipped past his marker, raced in and banged unstoppable shots to the net.

Although Rovers somehow rescued the game, scoring four times without reply in the last 17 minutes, Ghent's performance, this time at inside-left, was one of the sort which prompted the Evening Telegraph to say that he and his team-mate Paddy Flannery were sure-fire crowd drawers.

"Many will report this weekend to see Ghent and Flannery, two of the visiting side who have made good with the Dublin public," the paper said, in its preview of the Rovers league game.

The 1922/23 season concluded with Athlone reaching the Shield final in which Ghent earned his first senior medal, albeit a runners-up memento.

With the arrival of Tommy Collins as a regular in the Athlone eleven towards the end of the 1922/23 season, Ghent moved to inside-left with the nippy Moate man on his outer.

However, by 1923/24, the partnership had been reversed and it was Ghent whose flying runs were best suited to a touchline berth, who played at outside-left.

Over the years, it appeared to be Ghent's prime position, but Athlone's selectors seemed determined to shoehorn his talents into the inside-left spot.

It was in this position that he played in the opening five or six league games of the 1923/24 season and even occasionally throughout the remainder of the league schedule.

A pair of crucial cup goals

During the famous cup run, Ghent filled in at inside-left against Shelbourne following the switching of Tommy Collins to centre-forward.

His two goals in the FAI Cup campaign were both vital; the first against Shelbourne put Athlone two up while the second in the replayed semi-final versus Bohemians gave Athlone the vital breakthrough in a tightly-fought encounter.

His performance in the quarter final against Shelbourne was particularly impressive; the Dublin Evening Mail described him as the best forward on view.

Whilst not shining so brightly in the games against Bohemians, Ghent's ability still stuck out amidst the helter-skelter nature of Athlone's game plan.

And of course, in the final, it was his wing wizardry which provided the material for Hannon to mould that famous winning goal.

His performances earned him a call up for the Olympic trials and subsequent selection to travel to Paris.

And although he was not chosen for Ireland's first international game against Bulgaria, he was the 12th man as shown by the official photograph where he is the sole squad member seen flanking the selected eleven ahead of their Olympic debut.

He was recalled for the second round against Bulgaria, filling in at inside-left for Joe Kendrick; the outside-left berth had been nailed down by Bohemians' Johnny Murray.

288

Fire and loss

That Olympic international cap was one of Frank Ghent's prized possessions. Athlone man Jimmy O'Connor recalls how Ghent, as a barman in the Irish National Foresters, would quietly listen to a football-related discussion, before whipping his international cap out from under the counter as a sure-fire argument-settler.

Unfortunately, the cap went missing when the family home in St Mary's Place was being renovated after the death of his sister.

Frank himself had died many years earlier, having previously lost many of his own prized footballing possessions.

He had worked for many years in the Athlone Woollen Mills and kept his medals, trophies and other memorabilia for safe-keeping in his company locker. Unfortunately, they were to be lost in the famous woollen mills blaze of 1948.

His nephew Paddy Macken recalls that Frank Ghent had little interest in football in his later years – and suggests the loss of these items may have contributed to his disenchantment from the sport.

He retained his Olympic parchment, a signed scroll given to each participant at the Paris games.

Frank Ghent with his Olympic cap

The reliable Ghent

The following season, Ghent was back in harness for Athlone. While some of his cup colleagues such as Jim Sweeney and John Joe Dykes turned out on notably fewer occasions than normal, Ghent remained a permanent feature of the Athlone attack.

Without the intuitive play of Tommy Collins beside him, with the majestic Tommy Muldoon absent from the left-half berth behind him and with nobody of the like of Jim Sweeney to convert his numerous crosses, Ghent had one of his poorer seasons in an Athlone shirt. He failed to score in the league, although he was on target in the FAI Cup against Cork Bohemians in the first-round victory.

Nonetheless, during that season, Ghent earned the following plaudits from the Sports Mail: "A clean clever player with a fine turn of speed. Ghent is a source of worry to defenders and has turned down many an offer to leave Athlone but prefers to render service to the cup holders."

Although his form, like the team's, may have fluctuated in later years, Ghent remained a regular creator of goals from the left-wing. He was also useful from deadball situations, particularly corners.

Staying local and loyal

The 1925/26 season saw a return to his best from Ghent. He found the net twice in the league and, for the third successive season, he was also on target in the cup. That goal, against Brideville, was a typical Ghent strike - an individual effort in which he scampered past the challenges before finding the net.

In fact, the Dubliners must have been sick of the sight of the Athlone winger as he also created mayhem in the league game between the sides in Dublin, setting up two of Jim Sweeney's three in a 3-3 draw.

It was that renewed zest for the game that saw him earn a call up to trials for the international against Italy in April 1926.

His revitalised form also attracted the attention of Dublin clubs that season. Football Sports Weekly speculated late in 1925 that he was soon to change his jersey. It appeared that Shelbourne or Shamrock Roves were the suitors.

At the time, Ghent was in flying form. In the December 1925 home league clash with Shelbourne with Athlone lost 4-1, Ghent was described by Sport as "the finest forward on the field", "rarely has he played so well".

However, he remained commendably loyal to Athlone, and indeed was probably the most regular name on the teamsheet over the seven years of senior football. He, alone, of all the FAI Cup players had no gaps of any significant length in his service.

Indeed, Ghent and Jim Sweeney were the only two players to score in each of Athlone's seasons in the League of Ireland.

During his playing career, he also took an active interest in the running of the club, sitting on the committee and helping to select the team.

On occasions, Ghent was prone to flashes of temper and he found himself on the receiving end of a handful of red cards during his career. His buccaneering style also attracted robust attention from defenders and won his side many a penalty kick.

The slow fade out

In 1926/27, Ghent was still campaigning relentlessly as a fully-subscribed member of the wingers' union.

The constant criticism of Athlone's forward line during their later years was the lack of cohesion.

Ghent, in particular, as a winger, was a player who depended on his inside-forwards to bring him into the game.

During the last three or four years, Frank's regular partner at inside-left was Joe Glavey and while Glavey was a fine player in his own right, the two never appeared to click in quite the same manner as Ghent and Collins had previously.

By the end of the 1926/27 campaign, Ghent was a pale shadow of his former self. Sport noted he had "gone off completely".

Nonetheless, by 1927/28, despite playing in an evidently unsuitable team, Ghent was back producing his wing magic. Athlone's main problem that season was inexperience and a lack of goalscoring talent.

Football Sports Weekly said of the game against Shamrock Rovers in Dublin: "Ghent kept prancing merrily along the Athlone left and he dropped in a few centres in front of the Rovers' stranglehold but there was no real finisher in the Athlone ranks."

Having enjoyed the high points, Ghent was unfortunately there too for the doldrums. He was one of just two survivors of the FAI Cup team of 1924 to play in the 9-1 defeat by Shelbourne in the 1927/28 season, the worst league defeat in the club's history.

Maintaining his impressive appearance statistics, Ghent was again a regular feature in the 1927/28 season, scoring twice in the league for a struggling outfit.

Fittingly, when Athlone bowed out of senior football on April 8th, 1928, with a 4-1 Shield defeat to Bray Unknowns, it was Ghent who notched Athlone's only goal.

Having scored in Athlone's first senior game under the new association in the FAI Cup against YMCA more than six years earlier, Ghent, and Athlone, had come full circle.

Although only 30, Ghent resisted any temptation to further his footballing career outside Athlone and stepped down from the game.

After his football career, Ghent, who was always immaculately dressed and maintained, remained a familiar figure in Athlone, working firstly in the Woollen Mills and later as a barman for the Foresters and in the Prince of Wales Hotel.

He died in October 1965 and is buried in Cornamagh Cemetery.

None of the Ghent brothers had male heirs and the family name, for long so prominent in Athlone, has died out.

Chapter 29

1926/27 season

Bringing in the heavy guns

For the new season, Athlone appeared to have opted to speculate in order to accumulate.

A strong Dublin contingent was enlisted to help restore the glory days of 1924. Among them were former international Harry Leddy and later in the season added Charlie Jordan, while fellow Dubliners Brooks, Keegan and McCabe were retained.

Otherwise the team was pretty much all local with the likes of Monahan, Hope, Connaughton, Glavey, Ghent, Hannon and Jim Sweeney joined by more young Athlone talent, including half-back John Conway who had made the step up from the local railway side, All Blacks.

Problems at Ranelagh

On the administrative side, there were ongoing difficulties to address.

The move to Ranelagh did not solve Athlone's ground problems; in fact, if anything, as the season went by, it became clearer that the difficulties had simply been exacerbated.

A decision to move even closer to the Shannon seemed illogical particularly as the previous pitch in the Sportsground had been so prone to flooding. In the press, there were references to Ranelagh being a temporary home, while plans for a new home were progressed. Whether there were ever such plans is open to question.

In any event, if there had been mutterings about the condition of the Sportsground, there was a howling cacophony of voices criticising the Ranelagh School grounds.

This constant sniping could only eat away at Athlone's morale as the incisive Sport was able to point out.

"Athlone have surmounted many troubles in their rather crowded career and the spirit of enthusiasm that keeps the game alive in the midlands has been their strong weapons in these annual battles.

"But these continuous blows are bound to have some effect and are probably the reason why Athlone do not always give of their best.

"Their latest trouble concerns their playing pitch. The old one has been closed to them and their preparations for a new one are progressing. Meanwhile they will occupy a temporary home."

While there had been a number of notable arrivals, there were also a few critical personnel missing.

Mick Henry, the talented centre-half back, had been attracted cross-channel for trials with Aston Villa, the club where his brother-in-law Tommy Muldoon was plying his trade. John Sweeney had retired from the game and centre-back Matt Armstrong had moved on to Brideville. It was in his stead that Harry Leddy was signed.

Harry Leddy

Harry Leddy was an intriguing figure. Capped for the Irish amateur side in 1911 – in the days when amateur internationals were almost as highly-regarded as the full equivalent - he was one of the most prominent footballers of his age.

A Dubliner, Leddy had enjoyed a moderately successful footballing career cross-channel and would have been a household name to most football fans at the time.

His career had begun with Dublin team Frankfort before he joined the famous Belfast Celtic. He also had spells with Glenavon, Shelbourne and Clyde in Scotland.

After the war he returned to the north with Distillery and Glenavon.

Soon he had been enticed cross-channel to line out with Tranmere Rovers before signing for

Harry Leddy

top division outfit Everton. Only a squad member there, he then moved to Division Three north side Chesterfield for a fee of £1,000.

It was here where he created his own piece of football history.

At the time he joined, Chesterfield were lingering in the bottom section of the division. They offered Leddy the then maximum wage allowed of £9 pounds per week for the reminder of the 1921/22 season and all of the following season.

His transfer to Chesterfield came at a time when football clubs were experiencing significant financial losses and in an effort to stabilise the situation the Football League moved to cut the maximum wage to £8 a week and £6 in the summer.

It left the club in a Catch 22 scenario. They could either ignore the legally-binding contract they had signed with Leddy or risk the wrath of the Football League by breaking its wage ceiling.

The club chose to take what they must have thought was the line of least resistance – paying Leddy the maximum allowed. Leddy signed the new contract but did so without prejudice to further action. Indeed, he promptly sued Chesterfield for a total of £99 in lost wages.

His case was assisted by the players' union, which at that stage was poorly regarded and believed to be ineffectual.

Such was its weakness that the Professional Footballers Association (PFA) was required to seek the permission of the Football Association to take the case.

Litigation dragged on for much of the 1922/23 season but Leddy continued playing with Chesterfield, performing excellently at centre-half.

Finally, in the High Court, Leddy won his case, establishing players' rights to be paid at the contracted rate notwithstanding the Football League's attempt to change existing agreements by lowering the maximum wage. The ruling had obvious implications for hundreds of players across the existing league clubs at the time.

But it also reenergised the PFA, giving it much-needed credibility and rescuing it from near oblivion. Leddy's case didn't, however, challenge the maximum wage rules, which remained in place for almost 40 more years.

In many ways, Leddy was the Jean Marc Bosman of his age. A journeyman footballer who challenged the status quo.

The following season he moved on to captain Grimsby before returning to Ireland, and briefly to Shamrock Rovers and his first love, Leinster Senior League side Frankfort, before linking up with Athlone.

Aged 38, he joined the midlanders at the start of the 1926/27 season, playing most of the league matches.

His business as a bookmaker meant Saturday matches were rarely suitable and there were numerous hints in the sporting newspapers that he intended to retire from the game to concentrate on his business career.

However, he saw out most of the season with Athlone, only dropping away during the concluding Shield games.

The following season he became player-coach of Bendigo, another Leinster Senior League side with a long and illustrious history.

And just as his main contribution to English football may have been as a result of action off the field in Chesterfield, so too did his most important role in Irish football lay outside his playing career.

It was Leddy who first drafted the legendary Paddy Moore, often described as the Republic's answer to George Best, into adult football while with Bendigo.

Primarily remembered for a four-goal second-half haul in a World Cup match against Belgium for Ireland in 1933, Moore was the most skilful and famed player of his era.

Tragically, at the age of 41, Paddy Moore passed away, ravaged by alcoholism.

A bright start

Athlone's first home match on August 28th, 1926, was against Dundalk, who were newly elected to the League of Ireland.

However, it was the condition of the pitch which grabbed some of the headlines. The Dundalk Democrat noted that hay had only been removed from the pitch the previous day leaving "a thick, stubbly thing that is almost painful to walk on".

Whatever the condition of the pitch, it was Athlone that emerged victorious on a 3-1 scoreline.

Combined with the impressive 5-2 victory against Bray Unknowns in Wicklow in the opening game the previous weekend, it appeared Athlone were on the right track. Having struck up a fine understanding the previous season, Jim Sweeney and Ned Brooks picked up where they had left off, banging in seven goals between them in the opening two games.

Brooks scored a hat-trick in the season-opener against Bray – kick-starting a campaign that was to be a personal triumph for the centre-forward.

Local youngster John Conway made his first senior start at right-half in this game.

Jimmy Hope was back to his best at full-back, and indeed, his partnership with Barney Connaughton proved solid in the early stage of the campaign. Later, due to the return of Joe Monahan, Hope played the remainder of the season in the half-back line. At centre-back Leddy was a crucial stabilising factor, too, and his style of play which involved sweeping possession wide to the wingers from his pivotal central role suited the likes of Frank Ghent and Joe Glavey.

The revamped back-line functioned well and ensured Athlone's goals against column was beginning to show an improvement.

Meanwhile, doubt was being cast on the suitability of the Athlone grounds and there was speculation that the fourth game of the season against Bohemians, could be held in Mullingar.

However, the match went ahead in Athlone and the Westmeath Independent reported "improvements recently carried out in the grounds were favourably commented on".

The Ranelagh school pitch was unfortunately too often the subject of negative comment from reporters. It was criticism which Athlone Town answered in forthright fashion.

Commenting to the Football Sports Weekly, an Athlone official said: "The Athlone pitch seems to give a certain scribe a bit of trouble. When the visiting team does not take any of the points, he harps at the ground. For his information, a deputation of the Free State Council inspected the ground and that's that. I don't believe this individual would eat an egg laid in Athlone."

The press, always ready to criticise when it came to their own facilities, also regularly highlighted the absence of any press accommodation at the ground.

Before hosting Bohs, Athlone travelled to Brideville for the third game of the season and came away with a share of the spoils following a goalless draw that was due, in no small part, to the wonderful form exhibited by goalkeeper Paddy Sherlock.

Paddy Sherlock

Paddy Sherlock, a Dubliner who worked with the Midland and Great Western Railways in Athlone, was also on the squad list that season.

Born in 1901, he had moved permanently to Athlone sometime in 1925 or 1926 and lived in a house where the current railway station is located.

While in Athlone he was probably better known for his involvement in the Friary Choir and local musicals than for his goalkeeping with Athlone Town.

Sherlock had initially played with the railway team Midland Athletic based in the Dublin depot of Broadstone. He had held down the goalkeeper's jersey for the side from the early part of the 1920s until the end of the 1923/24 season.

Paddy Sherlock

Sometime in early 1924, he obtained an exciting move to Bohemians. It was a sign of his burgeoning talent. Indeed, Sherlock's growing reputation in the game was franked by his selection to compete in the trials for the Olympic Games in 1924.

However, his dream move to Bohemians turned sour almost immediately when he broke his leg in a collision with a Shamrock Rovers forward during a game in Dalymount Park a month later.

The newspaper Sport said he had been considered one of the best goalkeepers seen in the league in some years before his accident, but he had never the opportunity to fulfil the potential afterwards.

Having spent some time in hospital, Sherlock returned to the football field with Athlone in a Shield match against Brideville in January 1926. However, it wasn't until the 1926/27 campaign that he featured regularly for Athlone.

It seems he never really shook off the effect of that broken leg and he was unfortunately dogged by injury afterwards.

Having played some five or six successive games for Athlone early in the 1926/27 season – and earning rave reviews in the process – Sherlock again succumbed to injury. It effectively ruled him out for the remainder of the season.

He was ushered back from the treatment table as an emergency keeper for the FAI Cup clash with Shelbourne in January, but didn't return again until the third last game of the season, an unimportant affair against Jacobs in the Shield. Even then, he was hurt during the game and remained out for the rest of the campaign.

In Athlone's final season, 1927/28, Sherlock was one of at least six different goalkeepers tried out between the posts.

His enthusiasm for the game appeared to have waned a little at this stage. There was talk during the early part of that season of Mullingar attempting to coax him back into activity. However, nothing came to pass.

He moved back to Dublin in the 1930s but retained his links with football and indeed was trainer to the Irish senior team in 1954.

Self-inflicted wounds

The draw against Brideville left Athlone as joint league leaders and optimism was obviously growing as Football Sports Weekly noted that Denis Hannon was on holidays from Athlone seeking to add to the squad.

Maybe, he was looking to replace himself as the now 38-year-old was "too fat" for the game according to the blunt reporter from Football Sports Weekly.

However, Athlone's promising start faded somewhat. A 3-3 home draw against Bohemians was not by any means a disaster. The game was notable for some fine corner kicking by Frank Ghent which led to two of Athlone's goals.

However, a less satisfying feature was the extent to which both sides indulged in rough play.

The Westmeath Independent claimed the fouls committed by Athlone had denied them what would have been a deserved victory. The paper blamed a lack of fitness.

"This must cease and it will cease when every individual player on the Athlone team is thoroughly trained and fit, which they are not at present."

Still well in contention for league honours, Athlone then made the bizarre choice to concede home advantage in the next game. Possibly stung by the criticism of the Ranelagh ground, Athlone travelled to Dublin to meet Shamrock Rovers in what had been fixed as a home league clash.

Maybe the fact it was the second ever competitive match in the new Glenmalure Park was part of the attraction. Who knows? Whatever the reason, Athlone slumped to a 5-2 defeat, their first loss of the campaign.

After the Rovers defeat, the committee men, anxious to divert the blame away from themselves, chose to announce their intention to bring in new players.

The two that were signed were Cahill, from Leinster Senior League side St Paul's and Charlie 'Spid' Jordan, a diminutive, nippy outside-right from another Dublin side.

This was a further addition to an already extensive coterie of Dublin players – an indication that Athlone were committing themselves to hefty expenditure this season.

Although Cahill played in the following league game against St James's Gate, he was judged not to up to the required standard and soon returned to Dublin.

On the other hand, Jordan didn't feature for a number of games, but when he did he made an instant impact.

Originally a GAA player, Jordan switched sports to football, joining Brooklyn during their stint in the League of Ireland. Halfway through the 1924/25 season, he transferred to Shamrock Rovers to fill the outside-right berth.

Only two seasons before, Charlie 'Spid' Jordan had won an FAI Cup medal with Shamrock Rovers with a man-of-the-match display in the final against Shelbourne. He appeared again for Rovers in the cup final defeat to Fordsons the following year.

Despite playing in both FAI Cup finals during his two years at Rovers, his second season, in particular, was marked by infrequent starts.

Soon, he slipped out of the league to play for a local Dublin junior club before being picked up by Athlone.

Charlie Jordan

Described by the Sports Mail as the "smallest and lightest winger in the league", Jordan had an explosive turn of pace and enjoyed an impressive League of Ireland career.

The introduction of Jordan was an immediate success and he scored twice in his debut later on in the season in a 5-1 win at home to Bray Unknowns. His arrival meant Jim Sweeney was shuffled into an unaccustomed inside-right role.

Jordan remained with Athlone for a single season before joining St James's Gate, Fordsons, and St James's Gate again.

Maybe the committee men's decision to travel to Milltown for the home game against Shamrock Rovers had deflated the players as Athlone fell to a second successive 5-2 defeat, away to a poor St James's Gate side who, up to then, had not registered a victory that season.

Thankfully though Athlone stopped the rot at home to Jacobs the following weekend this time coming out on the right side of another 5-2 scoreline.

That Athlone had shot themselves in the foot was now increasingly clear. Indeed, the Evening Herald admitted as much when it said: "There was joy in the Athlone camp at the handsome victory over Jacobs. There had been a feeling that their (the players) enthusiasm was waning."

Brooks was the star of the show, according to the Westmeath Independent, in what was an impressive all-round team display.

By the time of the trip to Cork to play Fordsons, Paddy Sherlock had sustained the injury which kept him out for most of the season and McCabe returned between the posts.

Visits to Cork were a logistical nightmare for Athlone, who on this occasion left the midlands on Saturday morning and arrived back in town on Sunday night, having travelled via Dublin on train.

It was no surprise then that they had a reserve battalion of players in the Southern capital ready to pull on the blue if required.

301

The Athlone team from the 1926/27 season. Back row: Joe Monahan, PJ Boushell, Barney Connaughton, Jimmy Hope, J. McCabe, WJ McVeigh, Harry Leddy, Jim Sweeney Senior and George Gaylard (trainer).
Front row: Charlie Jordan, Jim Sweeney, Frank Ghent, Joe Glavey and Ned Brooks.

W 'John' McVeigh, the former Athlone player, who was now on army duty in Cork, regularly lined out with his old club on their journeys south. And on this occasion, he had also enlisted the services of a talented outside-right, Burke.

Burke was a fixture in the Munster Senior League scene playing with a number of clubs. And he was to score on his Athlone debut against Fordsons. It wasn't enough to overcome the Cork men, who were victorious by the odd goal in three, although Athlone's Mick Keegan sent a last-minute penalty wide of the posts.

Fordsons were a huge draw and in fact attracted 10,000 spectators to another home game around the same time when Shamrock Rovers came visiting to Cork. Burke also featured throughout the following 1927/28 season for Athlone.

Back to winning ways

After their dip in form, Athlone quickly got back on track and reeled off three successive wins in the league, starting off with that 5-1 victory against Bray in which Jordan made his scoring debut and including an away victory over new boys Dundalk.

The Louth men in their first season in the league had hitherto remained unbeaten at home. And indeed their undefeated run on home soil stretched back for over a year. The 3-2 win was memorable for a spectacular Jim Sweeney goal, when he burst onto a pinpoint Joe Glavey cross to power a header to the net. Athlone's pace and power was too vigorous and sustained for a shell-shocked Dundalk, according to the Evening Herald.

The final game of the winning sequence was at home to Brideville when Ned Brooks ran riot in a mud-splattered Ranelagh grounds, bagging his second league hat-trick of the season.

Worryingly the Westmeath Independent described the ground in the first week of November as "drenched in mud and slush". At least, it meant that soft-ground mudlark Ned Brooks was in his element. During that three-game run, McCabe had also impressed between the posts, saving a penalty away to Dundalk.

Eleven games in and Athlone had clocked up 14 points. It left them in fourth place in the league, just four points off joint-leaders Shamrock Rovers and Bohemians. However, that victory over Brideville was to be the last league win of the season as Athlone embarked on a seven-game run without a victory.

Athlone travelled to Dalymount Park the following weekend and lost 3-1 in a game where their forward line was disjointed and lacking cohesion, although it was only in the last 15 minutes that Bohemians took control. A home game to Shelbourne was due to follow but the Ranelagh pitch was underwater so the fixture switched to Shelbourne Park the following Wednesday.

Athlone welcomed back Mick Henry, whose lengthy trial with Aston Villa had ended without success, while former Pioneers full-back Tom Moore also featured. Four months later, Moore won a cup final medal with Drumcondra.

The visitors took Shels by surprise by their fine first-half exhibition and were unfortunate to be only level early in the second half. However, the pace finally told on Athlone who lost out on a 4-2 scoreline. The performance of McCabe in the Athlone goal was obviously a revelation to the Shelbourne Park outfit who promptly snapped him up.

Out of contention

Having opted to make a concerted effort to challenge for league honours that season, Athlone now found themselves out of the running and destined for a mid-table spot. With the prize out of reach, players who had travelled up and back to Dublin, Cork and Dundalk were now becoming weary. A number of the veteran campaigners opted out of the next trip to Dublin to play Shamrock Rovers. When one of the listed eleven, John 'Jack' Murray of Mullingar Town, failed to materialise, Athlone were left with only ten men. A 6-0 hammering in the circumstances was not unexpected.

A home match against St James's Gate was postponed the following weekend as the Ranelagh Ground was still unplayable. It was not played until the following May and resulted in a 3-0 victory for the Gate.

Athlone salvaged some self respect with three successive draws as the league came to a close. The sudden departure of McCabe and the injury to Sherlock left Athlone without a regular keeper and young Pa Henry, brother of Mick, was drafted in from the junior ranks for his debut in the home game against Jacobs on December 11th.

From Chapel Street, Henry was one of three brothers who played for Athlone. On his debut, he performed impressively making some key saves as Athlone drew 1-1. However, it was only one side of his Jekyll and Hyde character between the posts. Henry also played towards the end of the season in the Shield games when it became clearer that his form was wildly unpredictable.

Football Sports Weekly criticised the young keeper for his performance against Brideville, in which he scored an own goal by slicing an attempted clearance into his own net.

"Henry failed to impress. He appeared nervy and uncertain and was betimes lucky in his clearances. He gave of his best however, what little was seen of it."

That Shield game at the very tail end of the season also featured the arrival of Anthony 'Duck' Dowling in the Athlone team. Dowling, a youngster who grew up on Abbey Lane, showed "remarkable promise" according to Football Sports Weekly, scoring in a completely undeserved 3-2 defeat to Brideville.

Back to the league campaign, after the draw with Jacobs former Pioneers keeper Jimmy Murray was signed up to fill the gap between the posts.

Since the departure of Pioneers from the League of Ireland the previous season, Athlone had snapped up a couple of their former staff and Murray's brothers Charlie and Tommy also wore the blue of Athlone later that season. The link between the clubs took the form of J.S. Murphy, who was a Pioneers club man, but who took on the duty of representing Athlone Town on the FAI Council. In 1925/26, Murphy, representing Athlone, became the President of the League of Ireland.

His inside track on the Pioneers club may have been the reason why players like Paddy O'Reilly, Tom Moore and the Murray brothers, lined out for varying lengths of service and with varying degrees of success for Athlone. Incidentally, Pioneers FC was formed as part of the Temperance movement established by Matt Talbot and subscribed to the concept of teetotalism.

Murray was in goal again on New Year's Day for a potential championship decider against Shelbourne.

Shels were a point behind leaders Shamrock Rovers coming into the final game of the league and needed to win at home to Athlone. They also required Rovers to stumble in a difficult tie away to Bohemians to leave the door open for a Reds' league victory.

In a lion-hearted defensive display, Athlone, having nicked a first-half goal through Mick Keegan, held out against a tide of Shelbourne attacks. Although the home side levelled matters after the break, they couldn't force the winner against an Athlone defence who for "four fifths of the game underwent a terrific gruelling".

As it transpired the result was incidental for Shels as Rovers managed to eke out a 2-1 victory in Dalymount Park and secured the league crown by their own hands.

Cup revenge for Shelbourne

However, it did set up a grudge rematch just a week later in the FAI Cup when both Athlone and Shels were due to meet again, this time in Ranelagh.

Ironically both Murray and McCabe were ineligible for their respective teams, probably not having signed before the cup registration deadline. The same applied possibly to Pa Henry, so Athlone were forced to summon the injured Paddy Sherlock.

Keegan and Glavey were not named in the team line up meaning that old veteran Dinny Hannon continued at inside-right making up a forward line that was completed with Jordan (outside-right), Sweeney, Ghent (inside and outside-left) and Brooks (centre-forward), while Henry, Leddy and Hope made up the half-back line ahead of full-backs Connaughton and Monahan.

This time, Athlone couldn't match a majestic Shels performance, which was kick-started by two quick-fire early goals. Jim Sweeney replied for a battling Athlone, who "stuck to their work with sheer guts". However, Shels were too slick. "Athlone were opposed by a team that rarely played so well," said Football Sports Weekly.

Both the league and cup dreams were dashed for another year.

Brooks' 29-goal season

Despite the poor end of league form, Athlone finished fifth of the ten teams. However, having been in touch with the main contenders with 11 of the 18 games concluded, it was disappointing to finish a massive 15 points behind the winners Shamrock Rovers. Considering home advantage had been conceded to the top two teams, Shelbourne and Shamrock Rovers, the league position is slightly misleading.

On the scoring front, Ned Brooks had banged in 14 league goals, but it was in the Shield and Leinster Senior Cup that he was to enjoy more bountiful days.

Athlone played nine Shield fixtures, again bizarrely suffering the disadvantage of having been allotted just three of the games at home.

That number was reduced still further when the game against Fordsons set for January 30th had to be switched to Shamrock Rovers ground in Milltown as the Shannon had again flooded the pitch.

Sport noted in its review of the Shield game against Fordsons: "At no time during the game did Athlone display the virility and snap that we are accustomed to expect from them, and as in seasons gone by, their enthusiasm seems to wane when their interest in the cup ceases."

Of the nine games, Athlone won just two, the first, the opening Shield contest at home to Bray Unknowns. This game was notable for another Ned Brooks' hat-trick. Towards the end of the season, he notched up a phenomenal twelve goals in eight games. The dozen goals included a five-timer in an 8-2 home victory in the Leinster Senior Cup clash against non-league Dublin side Strandville.

However, at times during the 1926/27 season, the old lack of interplay up front which had bedevilled Athlone struck again.

On paper, the Athlone attack seemed razor sharp. However, towards the end of his first season with Athlone, the Evening Herald commented: "Brooks does not fit effectively into the Athlone attack. He has to do all of his own foraging and never gets the ball as he likes it down the centre where he can chase it past the defences. With helpful partners he should be getting bags of goals with the new offside rule."

And despite a whopping 29-goal haul in the 1926/27 season – there was still a semblance of truth to this suggestion.

For Athlone, Brooks had often to drop deep foraging for possession, effectively acting as an inside forward. The likes of Jim Sweeney and Mick Keegan were often pressed into service as inside forwards during that season – and in the words of Sport displayed no knowledge of how to play this position.

Denis Hannon's wanderlust often left him out of position too, forcing Brooks to provide his own ammunition regularly.

Brooks scored the only goal in the next round of the Leinster Senior Cup away to Jacobs to bring Athlone to the semi-final stage against Shamrock Rovers.

That game took place on April 3rd, 1927, in St James's Park and again, Athlone, while impressive, fell just short. Rovers prevailed on a 3-2 scoreline, but were deemed to be fortunate to escape with the win. In the second half, Athlone attacked persistently but couldn't find a way past their old keeper Paddy O'Reilly, who most reporters attributed the victory to.

Barney Connaughton played brilliantly and was described as the best player on the pitch – a remarkable compliment considering the quality of some of the Rovers players. Rovers went on to win the Leinster Senior Cup after a replayed final against Bohemians.

Athlone and the Shield winners

Athlone did have another opportunity to thwart the Milltown side in the final game of the Shield a month later. The home side needed a victory to secure the trophy.

Again, Athlone almost pulled off a surprise, but couldn't finish the job, despite debutant goalkeeper Eddie Broderick saving a penalty from the famous Bob Fulham.

Leading 2-1 midway through the second half, they were pegged back by one of the best goals ever scored at Glenmalure Park. Standing on the touchline, midway between the central line and the corner flag, William 'Sacky' Glenn, who would later be capped for Ireland, dispatched a low-flying rocket which struck the ground inside the goal line with such force that it caused the earth to shatter like a burst of shrapnel.

Despite the defeat, Athlone were commended for the vigour and fight they put into a game which had little meaning for them.

Lining out for Athlone that day was Ernie Crawford, a 30-times capped Irish rugby full-back, who captained his country on 15 occasions. He was later president of the IRFU and a selector for the 1948 Grand Slam-winning side.

Crawford was one of the legends of Irish sport at the time – a man to whom the honour of coining the derisory term alickadoo for freeloading rugby officials is attributed. It was his third successive game to fill in at full-back for Athlone.

A northerner, he played his rugby with Malone and Lansdowne and dabbled in soccer with Bohemians – a fact that possibly allowed his former team mate Denis Hannon to coax him into playing for Athlone.

A Tongan stamp issued in 1999 with Ernie Crawford pictured

Of course, it hadn't helped that Athlone had been forced to play a meaningless rearranged league game at home to St James's Gate the day before what was effectively a Shield decider.

Season in review

With five or six top class Dubliners in their ranks, Athlone had gone for broke in the 1926/27 season, aiming to build on signs of promise from the previous year.

It was probably somewhat of a financial gamble but despite the presence of quality players like Brooks, Jordan, Leddy, Keegan, McCabe and others, the investment had clearly not been worth it.

Following an impressive start, the season had tapered away and the Town had finished with just two league points more than the previous campaign. Their cup run had ended abruptly in the first round too.

And, as usual, when the cup campaign - the annual focus of Athlone's interest - had ended, the Town found their interest hard to maintain.

In its end-of-season review, Sport again noted that Athlone had endured a hard fight just to keep the flag flying and said in the circumstances it was little cause for surprise that their play lacked a lot of the snap that usually characterised their endeavours.

It noted that despite a creditable performance in finishing joint fourth in the league, they were not a dangerous force in the cups or shield campaign.

With storm clouds gathering once again on the ground front, there was a clear need for a reappraisal of strategy ahead of the new 1927/28 season.

And it appears Athlone opted to pursue a local policy for the following campaign based on a clutch of promising Athlone juniors, along with members of Mullingar's all-conquering Leinster Junior Cup campaign.

The Athlone junior scene was still rich in talent. Connaught United had reached the 1926/27 Free State Junior Cup 6th round before being controversially eliminated by Sligo Town.

The team included seven who had already or would, in the following year, line out in the senior team's colours.

Another local junior club, Park Rovers, was beaten in the semi-final of the Leinster Junior Cup. Among them were bit-part Athlone players Carroll, Dan Sullivan and Mick Dowling.

Mullingar's Leinster Junior Cup win

It was a competition which was finally won by Mullingar after their third successive appearance in the final. Again, there was a strong Athlone connection. This time Johnny McManus played at right-full alongside Billy Blackwell. McManus scored from the spot during a 3-1 victory over a Dublin shipyard club Vickers.

The victory was a huge boost for Mullingar, who had lost the two previous finals and gone out at the semi-final stage of the competition in each of the two years before that.

The 1926/27 Leinster Junior Cup campaign had caught the imagination of the Mullingar sporting public and the catchphrase 'Never Let It Be Said' became the club slogan. It was to signify their determination not to leave the cup behind them again.

The Westmeath Examiner report of the final captured the mood perfectly with its headline: "It has not been said!"

The Athlone connection though could have backfired badly on Mullingar when Vickers objected to their line out, claiming two of their players had represented Athlone in the league and/or Leinster Senior Cup.

They may, indeed, have been right as certainly Blackwell and probably John Murray had featured with Athlone during that season. However, it clearly wasn't in breach of the rules as the result stood.

Of the other nine players who lined out in the final for Mullingar, five played for Athlone at some stage during the 1927/28 campaign. They were right-half Frank Harvey, centre-half and captain, John 'Jack' Murray, left-half, Sam Macken and forwards Anthony 'Gully' McKenna and Guy Callaghan.

The first three were all Mullingar natives while McManus, McKenna and Callaghan would enjoy further success as teammates with Sligo Rovers in the future.

Athlone's decision to pin much of the hopes for the 1927/28 season on purely local talent, supplemented by the core of the Mullingar Leinster Junior Cup winning side, was fraught with danger. This was particularly so as most of the Mullingar players continued to play with their original club, meaning they often faced two matches over the weekend.

Although Athlone had made the step up from Leinster Junior Cup success in 1921/22 to the League of Ireland the following season, the team included players of considerable experience such as Denis Hannon and Jim Sweeney.

The Mullingar Leinster Junior Cup winners 1926/27.
Back row: Billy Blackwell, William Whelehan, Christy Walsh, Johnny McManus,
Gabriel Callaghan. Front row: Sam Macken, Frank Harvey, Jack Murray, John Lalor,
Anthony McKenna, Patrick Grant.

Not being a member of any league in that 1921/22 season, Athlone had no yardstick to judge themselves by. But the fact remained they fitted quickly and reasonably successfully into the League of Ireland.

It was asking a lot for the Mullingar outfit to do likewise in 1927/28. In contrast to Athlone six years previously, this team played its football in the Leinster Senior League Division Two and had been unable to steer a course to the top division over the past few years.

Time would tell if the gamble would pay off, but for the moment financial considerations dictated it was on local talent that Athlone was to depend.

Players like Mick Henry, Joe Glavey and Barney Connaughton would be crucial as they took over the mantle from the now ageing battalion of 1924 FAI Cup heroes.

Could they lead this all-local side to success?

1926/27 season round-up

DATE	OPPOSITION	COMPETITION (Athlone score first in all scorelines)	SCORELINE	SCORERS
August 21, 1926	Bray Unknowns (a)	League	5-2	(Jim Sweeney (2), Brooks (3))
August 28, 1926	Dundalk (h)	League	3-1	(Jim Sweeney, Brooks, Ghent)
September 5, 1926	Brideville (a)	League	0-0	
September 11, 1926	Bohemians (h)	League	3-3	(Glavey, Jim Sweeney, Brooks)
September 26, 1926	Shamrock Rovers (h)	League	2-5	(Brooks, Jim Sweeney)*
October 2, 1926	St James's Gate (a)	League	2-5	(Leddy, Keegan)
October 9, 1926	Jacobs (h)	League	5-2	(Glavey (2), Keegan (2), Brooks)
October 16, 1926	Fordsons (a)	League	1-2	(Burke)
October 23, 1926	Bray Unknowns (h)	League	5-1	(Jordan (2), Brooks (2), Glavey)
October 30, 1926	Dundalk (a)	League	3-2	(Glavey, Jim Sweeney (2))
November 6, 1926	Brideville (h)	League	5-0	(Brooks (3), Keegan (2))
November 13, 1926	Bohemians (a)	League	1-3	(Brooks)
November 24, 1926	Shelbourne (h)	League	2-4	(Keegan, Jordan)**
November 28, 1926	Shamrock Rovers (a)	League	0-6	
December 11, 1926	Jacobs (a)	League	1-1	(Brooks)
December 18, 1926	Fordsons (h)	League	2-2	(Jim Sweeney (2))
December 27, 1926	Bray Unknowns (h)	Shield	5-1	(Brooks (3), Jordan (2))
January 1, 1927	Shelbourne (h)	League	1-1	(Keegan)
January 8, 1927	Shelbourne (h)	FAI Cup	1-4	(Jim Sweeney)
January 15, 1927	St James's Gate (a)	Shield	2-4	(Jim Sweeney, Glavey)
January 30, 1927	Fordsons (h)	Shield	0-3***	
February 6, 1927	Dundalk (a)	Shield	2-3	(Jim Sweeney, Brooks)
February 12, 1927	Strandville (h)	Leinster Senior Cup	8-2	(Brooks (5), Keegan, Glavey, Jim Sweeney)
March 19, 1927	Jacobs (a)	Leinster Senior Cup	1-0	(Brooks)
April 3, 1927	Shamrock Rovers (a)	Leinster Senior Cup	2-3	(Ghent, Jordan)
April 9, 1927	Shelbourne (h)	Shield	2-7	(Brooks, Blackwell)
April 17, 1927	Jacobs (a)	Shield	2-1	(Brooks, Jordan)
April 24, 1927	Brideville (a)	Shield	2-3	(Brooks, Dowling)
April 30, 1927	Bohemians (a)	Shield	2-4	(Brooks (2))
May 7, 1927	St James's Gate (h)	League	0-3	
May 8, 1927	Shamrock Rovers (a)	Shield	2-3	(Jordan, Henry)

* Home advantage conceded, game played in Milltown
** Home advantage conceded, game played in Shelbourne Park
*** Game played in Milltown

Chapter 30

Jimmy Hope

On a Sunbeam from Mullingar

A well-known business family

Jimmy Hope was one of two Mullingar natives to feature in Athlone's cup final triumph of 1924.

Hope's contribution to Athlone Town's ascent to cup glory was immense. If the entire edifice of success was founded upon a rock-solid back line, Hope was the cornerstone on which that defensive bulwark was based.

Versatile, equally adept with both feet, reliable, determined and effective, Hope was the dam upon which innumerable waves of opposition attacks foundered over his six seasons with Athlone.

Jimmy Hope

Born on August 3rd, 1894, to James and Mary Hope, he was the youngest of four sons and two daughters.

Jimmy and his brothers were well-known figures in their time in Mullingar. A quartet of talented mechanics, they operated the first garage in the town from a prominent Dominic Street premises.

Beginning in an era when bicycle trade outnumbered motor vehicle business, the garage continued under the managership of Jimmy and another brother, Ned, right into the 1960s.

Advertisements for the business in 1924 listed Humber, Swift, Maxwell and Coventry among cars stocked for hire.

Jimmy Hope was also one of the very first hackney drivers in Mullingar. It was a trade he continued in tandem with the garage in later years.

Jimmy Hope married Margaret P. Smith in Mullingar on April 21st, 1936. They had one son, Fergal.

A sporting life

Sport was an all-consuming passion for Jimmy Hope. His first love was football and as a teenager he became involved in the game with local junior club St Mary's Mullingar as early as 1913.

Jimmy Hope, though, was a master of many sporting trades. He was a rugby player of note, an inter-county Gaelic footballer and a champion swimmer.

With football in abeyance during the war years, Hope tried his hand instead at Gaelic football, partaking in local street leagues in his native Mullingar in the closing years of the 1910s. His involvement in the sport culminated in him winning a county junior football medal with Mullingar Irish National Foresters in 1918, beating Moate in the final.

The Mullingar Irish National Foresters team which won the 1918 Westmeath Junior Football Championship. Hope is third from right in middle row.

This performance earned him a call-up to the county senior team and he was one of two subs named for the first-round Leinster Championship game in 1919 against Offaly in June. The following month he made his debut for Westmeath from the bench as they succumbed to Kildare in the second round of the Leinster Championship.

However, the infamous ban on GAA members playing football inhibited his progression in this game.

Hope also proved himself a skilful exponent of rugby and was present when Mullingar Rugby Club was founded in September 1925. He subsequently featured at full-back for the team, often playing football for Athlone and rugby for Mullingar on alternate weekend days.

The Mullingar rugby team in the later years of the 1920s.
Hope is fourth from right on back row.

At home as easily on water as on land, Hope won the Westmeath swimming championships in 1923.

His talents and success were recognised in 1967 when he was conferred with the Westmeath Sportstar Award for soccer. And seven years later, he was the first person to be inducted into the Westmeath Sports Hall of Fame as part of a countywide awards scheme organised by Mullingar GAA club.

A short stay with Bohemians

Despite his sporting ecumenism, it was in football that he was to really make his mark, albeit not until the relatively mature age of 27.

In April 1921, his football career finally began to blossom into full bloom when he was snapped up by Bohemians in a move which had generated much enthusiasm within the Dublin club. At the time, the newspaper Sport noted: "The Dalymount club have got hold of an Athlone lad named Hope in whom they have great expectations."

He made his debut in his customary full-back role for Bohemians B team in the Leinster Senior League Division Two game against Bray Unknowns on April 30th, 1921. Partnering Hope in the full-back line that day was Irish rugby international captain Ernie Crawford, the most high-profile Irish rugby player of his era.

However, whatever ambitions Bohemians had for the Mullingar man were quickly quashed when the relationship ended over the issue of the payment of travel expenses for Hope to games.

Jimmy Hope's only child Fergal Hope explained that Bohemians' amateur status was so strict that the club baulked at covering Hope's train expenses.

With Hope unable to bear the costs of travelling to and from Mullingar, the relationship petered out very quickly, limiting his appearances with the Bohs to possibly that single game.

Bohemians' loss was to be Athlone's eternal gain as the Midlands club who were on the alert to his talent moved quickly to snap him up ahead of the 1921/22 season.

Linking up with Athlone

Such was Athlone's rate of progress in the next six years that Hope's career, despite that late start, marks him out still as the most successful footballer ever to emerge from Mullingar.

The reality when Hope joined Athlone was much different. At the start of the 1921/22 season, Athlone were not affiliated to any league. Their annual focus tended to be the Leinster Junior Cup campaign and even that was unavailable to Hope in 1921/22 as his brief foray at senior level with Bohemians had rendered him ineligible for Athlone's triumphant campaign in the lower ranks that year.

Fortunately for Hope, Athlone did come through Midlands qualifying rounds for the FAI Cup and reached the competition proper. Thus on January 14th, 1922, the Mullingar man took to the field at left-back for Athlone's first-ever FAI Cup game against YMCA.

The names Monahan and Hope were peas in a pod in the Athlone full-back line throughout the 1920s but the partnership did not come into being until the next round of the cup in which Athlone were easily dismissed by Bohemians.

The Leinster Junior Cup success had also secured Athlone a place in the Leinster Senior Cup in which Hope was eligible.

The two senior cup competitions at least provided Hope with some on-pitch experience with Athlone in his first season with the Bit of Blue.

The League of Ireland

By the following season Athlone had been elected to the League of Ireland and Hope had the distinction of being the only non-Athlonian in the first side which took on St James's Gate in the Sportsgrounds on September 16th, 1922.

He was virtually ever-present during that tough formative year for Athlone Town and his extremely rare absences tended to coincide not with injury or unavailability but with his continued connection with his native Mullingar.

He played with the North Westmeath town side in the FAI Cup qualifying competition, including matches against Athlone junior team St Patrick's and Sligo Celtic in the regional final. That debarred him from featuring with Athlone in the FAI Cup that season. His absence was only for one match as Shamrock Rovers travelled to the midlands and knocked out Athlone at the first-round stage.

Athlone's impressive debut season, in which they finished sixth of twelve teams and just two points off fourth place was mainly attributed to a strong defence.

His first medal with Athlone came at the end of that inaugural season in senior soccer when he was on the side vanquished by Shelbourne in the Shield final.

By the start of the 1923/24 season, Hope was a permanent fixture, bringing a sure-hearted dependability to his sporting passion.

When only six players turned up for the trip to Pioneers at the lowest ebb of Athlone's league campaign in that year, it was no surprise that Hope was one of the half-dozen stalwarts present.

And his loyalty was be rewarded later that same year – when he earned an FAI Cup medal.

An FAI Cup medal

During the cup run, Hope and Monahan were an ever-present pairing in front of keeper Paddy O'Reilly. This trio could boast of having secured the cup without conceding a goal in 450 minutes of football.

Hope played his part in the shut-out with starring performances against Shelbourne and against Bohemians in the replay.

In the final, Hope formed a left-side quartet completed by Muldoon, Collins and Ghent which ruled the roost. Indeed, it was this unusual feast of high-quality natural left-footed players which was one of Athlone's secret weapons during the cup success.

Although a modest man, Jimmy Hope, according to his son Fergal, was immensely proud of the fact that Athlone had lifted the FAI Cup without conceding a goal.

According to family information, a bout of pneumonia scuppered his chances of an Irish selection. That's likely to involve the Paris Olympics of 1924 in which five of Hope's colleagues from that triumphant cup-winning breakthrough side featured.

The week after the cup win, Hope cried off midway through a Shield game against Midland Athletic. He was to miss seven weeks of football ruling him out of possible Olympics selection, despite a recommendation for his inclusion from no less an authority than the newspaper Sport. When he did return for Athlone, a week before the Olympic trials were due to take place, he was forced to cry off at half-time during the Shield match against Shamrock Rovers on May 11th, 1924.

A defensive lionheart

By the start of the following league campaign, he was back in the fold and renewing his partnership with Joe Monahan at the heart of the Athlone defence.

However, the 1924/25 campaign was characterised by a real sense of anti-climax following the lofty heights of the previous year. Athlone's interest in the league seemed limited. But they did make a creditable attempt to retain their FAI Cup crown, bowing out at the semi-final stage to Shelbourne.

Hope and Monahan were unable to cope with heavy conditions and were outfoxed by the slicker and nimbler Shelbourne forward line.

As the years progressed, and with changes in the off-side rule favouring swift attackers, Hope was less sure-footed.

Still, he soldiered on with Athlone throughout the 1925/26 and 1926/27 seasons, making the long journeys from Mullingar to Athlone and other venues.

During the 1925/26 season, Hope began to concede a number of penalties and was becomingly increasingly error-prone.

As his career moved into its twilight years he began to feature occasionally at left-half or indeed at centre-half, where speed was not such a prerequisite. Here his in his early 30s, his defensive qualities of physical strength, agility and anticipation could be better showcased.

However, it was in his customary left-back role that he featured in the 1925/26 FAI Cup quarter-final against Fordsons, a rematch of the 1924 Cup final.

It was a game that Athlone could, and possibly should, have won. Their prospects were diminished when Hope was harshly dismissed for a second yellow-card offence with 20 minutes remaining.

Football Sports Weekly remarked on the injustice of the decision. "Had the dismissal of Hope occurred in Dublin, there would have been a riot."

Back to the beginning

Jimmy Hope played one of his last games for Athlone not in defence, but, bizarrely, in goal, on April 30th, 1927. He had taken over temporarily between the sticks two matches previously following a mid-game injury to the first-choice keeper. When the sub goalkeeper sustained injuries in the following game, it was to Hope that Athlone turned again to fill the breach.

Ironically, this was in a Shield game in Dalymount Park against Bohemians, bringing him back to the beginning of his senior football career. And even more coincidentally, the game occurred six years to the very day from his debut for Bohemians.

Playing with Hope in the colours of Athlone that day was a certain Ernie Crawford, the Irish rugby international captain who had featured alongside Hope for Bohemians in that lone appearance.

Hope re-emerged for Athlone for just the opening game of the 1927/28 season at home to Dundalk in August but failed to feature again that year.

The Westmeath Independent noted later that year that Hope had been ill and it was not until late November that he returned to the fray, this time for Mullingar in the Leinster Senior League.

He remained with his home-town club, making irregular appearances during the 1928/29 and 1929/30 season in the Leinster Senior League.

A final cup bow

In January 1930, Hope made one final bow in the ranks of senior soccer, at the age of 36, featuring for Mullingar Celtic in the first round of the FAI Cup.

Mullingar Celtic, then a Leinster Senior League Division One side, had reached the cup, but were drawn away to another non-league outfit Dolphin in Dublin.

The club was on its knees at that stage and there was even talk of Mullingar not fulfilling the fixture. In the end, it went ahead and Hope was one of the few Mullingar players to impress in a 5-1 defeat.

However, he was forced to leave the field in the second half following an injury sustained before the interval.

Recalling the great enthusiasts

Throughout his career with Athlone, Hope rarely missed a match, despite the difficulties that travelling to and from Mullingar for both home and away games must have presented.

Interviewed by the Westmeath Independent in October 1975 ahead of the legendary visit of AC Milan to St Mel's Park, Hope made light of his travel commitments, recalling: "I had a Sunbeam Huber and I had the road to myself."

He said he had followed the fortunes of Athlone with close interest over the years. And his continuing dedication to football in Athlone was displayed by his frustration at being unable to attend the game against AC Milan, having just emerged from hospital after a serious operation.

According to Hope, his interest in football was reflected by all the members of the 1924 team.

"The lads of the 1924 team were really marvellous players and were great enthusiasts about the game. They were all so keen on the game that they were glad to play a match anywhere and the night's social activities never came into issue at all," he said.

Jimmy Hope died in 1976 and is buried in Ballyglass cemetery, Mullingar.

His sporting talents lived on in the family; son Fergal played Gaelic football at a decent level, while his grandson Brian won a British Universities football title with the Scottish Universities representative side.

Chapter 31

1927/28 season

The end is nigh

Grounds for complaint

While financial restrictions meant Athlone faced a stern test of their credentials on the pitch, there were even stiffer hurdles to cross for those involved in the club's administration.

In June 1927, three months before the new season was due to start, Athlone's very existence hung by a thread, once again due to the thorny issue of their home ground.

If the Sportsground had induced its share of knockers, then Ranelagh Ground was attracting them in droves.

There appeared to be some just cause for criticism of the condition of the pitch. The playing of rugby there on and off since 1922 by the relatively new local club obviously didn't help. However, there also appeared to be an undercurrent of Dublin bias to the controversy.

At a key meeting of the Free State League management committee during the close season, one official claimed that manure had been used to fill holes containing water during one of the matches played there at the end of the previous season.

The Athlone representative at the meeting was forced to slowly explain that it was in fact bog mould that had been utilised in order to soak up excess rainwater.

That meeting gave Athlone until June 14th to comply with specific league rules relating to ground requirements.

Later, Football Sports Weekly noted that a forthcoming meeting of the league would represent "a fateful night for the Athlone club as they have been asked to give assurances as to their ground".

"Should Athlone be unable to comply with the demands of the league certain actions may follow which will cause surprise in football circles."

The tone of this and other press coverage suggested that the footballing public was being prepared for the shock decision to expel Athlone.

With their backs to the wall, it was to that old stalwart Denis Hannon that Athlone turned to save them from the abyss. Hannon may have only been the treasurer of the club, having finally hung up his boots at the end of the 1926/27 season, but he seems to have been the real driving force behind the scenes.

And it was Hannon who addressed the league's management committee in late July regarding Athlone's ground. According to Football Sports Weekly, he stated that "certain alterations and improvements would be carried out in regard to the pavilion etc".

Although the offer was not considered sufficient, the committee agreed to write to Athlone seeking again that the club comply with the terms of the specific league rule governing the provision of ground facilities. Athlone were given another short period of time to meet the league demands.

In advance of that second deadline, there was renewed speculation as to the club's future and predictions that the Town would be thrown out of the league.

Football Sports Weekly in a comment piece said: "We hope that the league will not be guilty of another crowning act of folly by getting rid of Athlone Town." However, it added, darkly: "We hear that Athlone Town is likely to get the order of the boot."

Eventually in early August, the league rowed back from the brink and readmitted Athlone to membership for the coming season.

Although Athlone were deemed to have complied with the regulations governing ground requirements, political realism may have simply dictated that the issue be fudged and a final decision deferred.

Football Sports Weekly sagely noted: "We could not afford to do without a club in the midlands who are the means of expanding the game there and in the west."

That the league would even contemplate eliminating one of its by then three provincial clubs (Dundalk and Fordsons being the others) was evidence of a blinkered nature to the development of the game outside Dublin. That limited vision was further highlighted when around the same time the Athlone issue was being hammered out, the league refused to either extend its membership or to create a second division.

The vote to create a second division was beaten narrowly when the Dublin clubs voted en bloc against the proposal. This, according to the Football Sports Weekly, proved that "the Dublin monopoly is the dead hand that is holding back and slowly but surely killing interest in the game".

Although Athlone had been granted a reprieve from football's death row, the noose was still dangling dangerously overhead.

In order to secure membership for the 1927/28 season, Athlone were forced to commit themselves to substantial expenditure on ground improvements in advance of the 1928/29 campaign.

An all-Dublin league

After the issue of league membership had been settled, Football Sports Weekly, in its preview of the new season, said that Athlone's ground difficulties would remain a significant stumbling block.

"If the committee cannot find a way out, the very existence of the club may be threatened."

And it effectively accused the league of making life all but impossible for Athlone.

"It appears as if they want to turn the Free State League into a Dublin league. The town of Athlone is off the beaten track as viewed by the other clubs which comprise the league but it is no argument why it should be ostracised and left to repine in its solitude," the paper said.

"It would be regrettable if this ambitious club be driven to extinction through no fault of its supporters or its own."

It also called for the league – and the richer Dublin clubs – to take cognisance of Athlone's difficulties.

The writer compared the financial health of both the IFA and the FAI, noting that the latter had made around £1,000 profit the previous season, compared to the £750 loss sustained by their northern counterparts.

The IFA's loss was due to funding given to Distillery to help replace a stand lost in a storm. Contrasting the IFA's benevolent treatment of Distillery to the FAI's handling of Athlone, Football Sports Weekly said: "And we here in the Free State pride ourselves as the great sports we are and pass no comment at the order sent to that splendid team Athlone Town, soccer's hope in the West and Midlands of Ireland, re their ground requirements."

The paper said Athlone had very little chance of funding the desired improvements – unless assistance was forthcoming.

It suggested that Shamrock Rovers, Shelbourne and Bohemians operate excursion trains for their supporters to away games in Athlone to help boost the gate returns for the home side.

While there was obvious anger in some quarters at the manner in which Athlone was being treated, up in Dundalk, there was similar disquiet at the treatment meted out to their favourites by the league authorities.

Jim Murphy's monumental book: "The history of Dundalk FC – the first 100 years" also outlines how Dundalk insiders felt their club was similarly unwanted in the corridors of the Free State League in the same period.

After Dundalk had been fined a whopping £100 following disturbances at a home match, the Dundalk Democrat's football reporter, Sideliner, commented: "Nothing will ever convince us that it was inflicted for any other reason than that Dundalk is not wanted in the Dublin competition… You couldn't very well put Dundalk out in the way that Athlone went. But you took another (and perhaps equally effective way) of hitting the team in the pocket."

All of this administrative intrigue and political subterfuge meant nobody was in a position to assess Athlone's potential ahead of the new season.

Football Sports Weekly asked: "What sort of figure will Athlone Town cut in the new season?" Answering its own question, it went on to remark: "Nobody outside of the centre cares to even make a guess and I am wondering whether the natives are not in as deep a state of perplexity."

Changes galore

Ahead of the 1927/28 season, PJ Boushell had taken over as honorary secretary from the long-serving William J. Tormey. Boushell was then manager of the Palace Bar – a pub long connected with football in Athlone and now owned by Paddy McCaul, the Vice President of the FAI and a former chairman of Athlone Town FC.

There were changes in the playing ranks too, most notably the absence of Denis Hannon, who had bowed out of football at the end of the previous season. All of the Dubliners had gone elsewhere; Ned Brooks and Mick Keegan linked up together again with Brideville; Charlie 'Spid' Jordan went to St James's Gate and Harry Leddy took the role of player-coach with a Dublin Leinster Senior League outfit called Bendigo.

Of the local stalwarts, Jim Sweeney opted out for most of the season, but Joe Monahan and Frank Ghent were still lining out in the blue of their home town.

Mick Henry, one of the more experienced of the younger players, threw in his lot with Mullingar for much of the season, only lining out with Athlone midway through their league campaign.

It signalled a drastic change in strategy by Athlone with the club now relying entirely on local players with the intention of encouraging young new talent. It was a policy that Sport deemed to be "praiseworthy"

As we have seen Athlone also attempted to integrate the best of Mullingar's crop of footballers who had just triumphed at Leinster Junior Cup level the previous season.

However, even after the first game of the season, commentators were warning it was already apparent that Athlone would need to strengthen their side.

After all the furore, the opening game of the season went ahead in Ranelagh, but, according to the Westmeath Independent, Athlone fielded "a very moderate team" against a seasoned Dundalk side which included many with cross-channel experience.

Anthony Dowling and Joe Glavey scored Athlone's goals in the 5-2 defeat. The match was also notable for Jimmy Hope's final appearance in the blue of Athlone.

A record league defeat

Worse was to follow the following weekend when Athlone suffered their heaviest league defeat in their history - a 9-1 thrashing – away to Shelbourne.

The team, on paper, should never have sustained a defeat of such magnitude, featuring as it did the likes of Barney Connaughton, Joe Glavey, Frank Ghent and Joe Monahan, players who had survived the test of League of Ireland football over the last few seasons.

Maybe some were getting by their sell-by date. Obviously, the new blood such as John Conway, Anthony Dowling and goalkeeper Eddie Broderick – son of the then Dáil deputy, Harry, and nephew of referee Michael, were obviously not reaching the required standard quickly enough.

The remainder of the side that was thrashed by Shelbourne had been culled from the ranks of Mullingar's victorious Leinster Junior Cup-winning side of the previous season.

Jack Murray and Sam Macken lined out in the half-back line while Frank Harvey and Guy Callaghan, who recorded Athlone's sole strike, were outside and inside-right respectively.

Murray, a railway employee, was captain of the Leinster Junior Cup winners of 1926/27 and had been involved from the start of the five-year search for the trophy.

In the 1925/26 season, Macken had caught the attention of the respected newspaper Sport which praised his role in Mullingar's progression.

The left-half, it said, "possesses much dash, is very speedy, has good recovery powers and a limitless capacity for hard work". Macken subsequently emigrated to America.

Gabriel 'Guy' Callaghan later starred with Sligo Rovers, winning an Irish junior cap as well as earning FAI Junior Cup and Intermediate Cup medals. After Rovers were elected to the League of Ireland, he scored in both of their first two campaigns.

Jack Murray

Sam Macken

Guy Callaghan

Gully McKenna

His later Sligo colleague Anthony 'Gully' McKenna was a more regular starter for Athlone in this final season.

These players were not inexperienced having played with Mullingar for the previous couple of seasons. Unfortunately, though, they may have been thrown in the deep end with Athlone, in some cases, at a very young age – rather than being gradually introduced to League of Ireland football.

After the Shelbourne fiasco the Sunday Independent noted that the decision to play local players meant Athlone "fielded what was more or less an experimental side and included a number of juniors whose lack of experience also explains the heavy defeat the team sustained".

It probably didn't help too that many of the Mullingar footballers and indeed some of Athlone's regulars from previous years often mixed League of Ireland football with Athlone and Leinster Senior League football with Mullingar on successive weekend days.

The day after the Shelbourne game, Joe Glavey, for example, was on the scoresheet for Mullingar away to Shamrock Rovers B in a Leinster Senior League Division One contest.

Even though Athlone were to endure a horror season in the league in 1927/28, the 9-1 defeat was of a scale and nature far beyond the results of the rest of the dismal campaign.

The Football Sports Weekly proposed one possible theory when it said Athlone were "comparative pygmies" to the physically stronger Shelbourne.

But even it was somewhat baffled by the collapse – indicating that Athlone should simply try to put it behind them. "The boys from the midlands must learn to forget this day. It should be to them but a dream."

Sport, which had lauded the all-local experiment as praiseworthy, was now singing a different tune. It said the material at hand in Athlone was very raw and expressed the fear that Athlone would be in "Queer Street" before it was properly developed.

It was much the same team - bar one or two changes - that lined out against Brideville in Athlone, the following weekend, only to again succumb, this time by 5-2. For this game, 1924 FAI Cup winner Terry Judge was recalled after an absence of over a year.

In a trend that was to unfortunately continue for much of the year, Athlone and Brideville were level (2-2) at the interval, before the home side collapsed after the break.

Football Sports Weekly argued that the Athlone youngsters "possess football ability and skill but they lack experience".

Athlone finally broke their duck, recording what was to be one of only two league wins that season, in the fifth game, at home to Bray Unknowns on September 17th.

Athlone won 2-1 despite playing much of the game with ten men, after centre-forward Anthony Dowling dislocated his shoulder.

Anthony 'Duck' Dowling was one of the real stars of the Athlone junior scene at a young age. He progressed from his club, Connaught United, and quickly worked his way into the senior ranks, making his debut for Athlone in the closing games of the previous season.

He was then billed by the Football Sports Weekly as "a young man of remarkable promise".

For the 1927/28 season, Dowling took centre stage in Athlone's revamped line-up, featuring regularly at centre-forward, although, occasionally too at outside-right.

He got off to a flying start, scoring three times in the first four games, but his goal contribution then dried up.

Anthony Dowling

Nonetheless, he finished the season as Athlone's top league scorer with five league goals. Like many of his colleagues, he too represented Mullingar in the Leinster Senior League that season.

Although regarded as an exciting talent at a young age, Dowling's footballing career never fulfilled its initial promise. His development was obviously not helped by having to carry a disproportionate goalscoring burden at an inexperienced age in a mediocre team.

He was reported to have signed for Fordsons in the mid-1920s but nothing seemed to come of the proposed switch.

In later years, Dowling appeared for a number of Dublin junior clubs and joined up with Mullingar.

His older brother Mick probably didn't feature in Athlone's ranks in their League of Ireland days. However, he was a stalwart of the club for many years, featuring right up to the 1937/38 season.

Dowling was on the victorious Athlone Town team which won the Leinster Junior Cup in 1931/32 and was a squad member of the Free State Junior Cup winners of 1934/35. He also lined up with Sligo Rovers in 1930/31 for a short period.

Mick Dowling, a plumber by trade, was also a member of the committee of Athlone Town for many years, as well as being a prominent referee.

After the victory over Bray, Athlone travelled to Dublin to meet Shamrock Rovers. By this stage Athlone were using at least their third goalkeeper of the season in the shape of Bill Kaine, a Londoner, who had played for both West Ham Utd and Spurs in the English top flight, while also being on the books of Arsenal.

27-years-of age, Kaine was a skilful custodian, who in his first game for Athlone "rose to dizzying heights of excellence", according to the Westmeath

Mick Dowling

Examiner, which due to the influx of Mullingar players with Athlone had taken a sudden interest in the fortunes of the South Westmeath club.

In Athlone colours, Kaine proved himself, according to the Evening Herald, to possess "resources and cleverness of a high order" although he was "a trifle slow in his clearances". Kaine lasted only four games before returning to London for "business reasons" and signing up with Bradford City.

Miserable mid-season

That defeat to Rovers started a five-game losing streak. Despite the miserable mid-season run, Athlone rarely embarrassed themselves.

In the game against Shamrock Rovers in Dublin, Athlone went in front and were level at half-time, before the home side ground out a 3-1 win with two second-half goals.

The following week, Athlone lost by a single goal in three at home to Bohemians, although Anthony Dowling missed a sitter in the final moments. The young forward shot into the arms of the keeper from four yards, though the by-now perennially abysmal conditions of Ranelagh may have had something to do with it. The Westmeath Examiner, in mitigation of Dowling, reported that as he shot "the ball had got stuck in a pool of water and was not easily dislodged".

The Athlone goals against both Dublin teams, Rovers and Bohemians, were scored by Paddy McGuirk, another Mullingar Town player, who threw in his lot with Athlone for a brief period. McGuirk, who was not from the midlands, later lined out with Drumcondra in the League of Ireland.

Against Bohemians, the ground conditions favoured Athlone as the lighter Dubliners could not pass their way through the greasy conditions which better suited the sweeping style of Athlone.

Athlone then proceeded to come out on the wrong side of tightly-contested games against Fordsons and St James's Gate. "Had Fordsons left with a point instead of taking two, the impartial observer would have been better pleased," commented the Westmeath Examiner.

Johnny 'Pongo' Malynn, only 20-years-old, made his debut for Athlone in this game. He was a stalwart for Athlone in the next era of success in the early to mid 1930s, captaining the Free State Junior Cup winners of 1935.

After more defeats it became clear that an inability to maintain the pace of the game throughout the 90 minutes, due to a lack of fitness, and the absence of cohesion in the forward department were costing the team badly.

Sport noted during this part of the season that there should be nothing amiss with the side's defence, considering the calibre of players there.

It added that despite the fine wing play of Ghent and Dowling, Athlone's inside-forwards were manifestly unable to turn the chances into scores.

After the Fordsons game, the same paper said Athlone felt that by cup time a decent side which could hold its own might evolve from the material at hand.

After another decent performance but demoralising defeat against St James's Gate, the Football Sports Weekly remarked: "It cannot be

Johnny Malynn

said that the lads from the midlands are a helpless band. They are not. Perhaps the sun will beam on them one of these fine days. The real root of the evil is forward."

Seeking answers cross-channel

With the lack of clever inside-forwards now a major problem, three cross-channel players, Floyd, McQuaid and Heaney, were signed up in late October.

Heaney and McQuaid came from Scotland while Floyd was Welsh. Heaney from Falkirk had been playing with a junior club St Anthony's as had McQuaid, who the previous year was reported to have been on the books of Glasgow Celtic. Floyd had spent time with Cardiff City, but came to Athlone from another local club, Mid Rhondda.

The trio had to wait for two weeks for their debut after a proposed away trip to Dundalk was deferred due to a death and then a home game to Shelbourne called off due to flooding. The league authorities refused to allow Athlone's request the week before the Shelbourne game to forfeit home advantage and to play in Dublin. In any event, flooding made Ranelagh unplayable and the contest was finally held two weeks later in Athlone on Tuesday, November 15th.

The newcomers finally made their debut in a 3-1 away defeat to Brideville. The introduction of all three forwards resulted in a huge reshuffling of personnel. To make way, Joe Glavey, normally inside-right, was switched to right-back while Burke, who had predominantly played up front, lined out in the half-back line.

A week later, Athlone recorded just their second win of the league campaign, at home to Jacobs, on a 2-1 scoreline, though it appears none of the three imports featured. Glavey and Burke accounted for the Athlone goals. The game was notable for the return of Paddy Sherlock between the posts, after Kaine had gone back to England.

Athlone played the first 15 minutes with only nine men as Mick Henry and Barney Connaughton had not arrived in time for kick-off.

Rather than heralding an upsurge in form, the win represented a high point which Athlone would not reach again that league season. Indeed, it was to be Athlone's last victory in league football for over 41 years with the club failing to record a victory in the remaining six league games.

A 7-2 thrashing to Shelbourne in the rearranged midweek clash followed with Burke scoring a brace for the home side. Again, there was wholescale experimentation in an increasingly frantic attempt to improve matters on the field of play.

Sport also noted the versatility of the Athlone players, citing four or five who were playing out of their normal positions – a move smacking of desperation.

Just short of a year after his debut, Pa Henry was back between the sticks for the next game against Bray – a 4-2 away defeat in which Heaney and McQuaid featured, although by then Floyd had returned home.

Heaney impressed, beating four opponents before being taken down for a penalty, which was sent wide by Joe Glavey. Glavey subsequently struck a second spot kick off the bar. However, Ghent netted the rebound.

Bar the next game, which he missed, Henry was the first-choice custodian for the remaining dozen games across all competitions in Athlone's final season.

The mystery final scorer

Three more new players were introduced for the home game against Shamrock Rovers – a Cork-based goalkeeper, Jerry O'Mahony, and two Belfast juniors, O'Callaghan and a player named as Devlin, who was apparently associated with a Northern club, Belfast Bohemians. Heaney and McQuaid had followed Floyd back across the Irish Sea.

The reinforcements clearly failed to shine with Shamrock Rovers winning 4-0, although it was noted that the Dubliners had been hard-pressed for most of the game.

O'Mahony and O'Callaghan were gone again and only 'Devlin' remained for the following trip to Bohemians on Saturday, December 3rd. Although, Athlone had three more league games on the schedule, the Dalymount Park game was marked by Athlone's final league goal for close on 42 years.

Among the line out was Ernie Crawford, in another of his cameo appearances. Johnny McManus, who had appeared in Athlone's first eleven as a 16-year-old six seasons previously, made one of his handful of annual appearances too.

Athlone pushed Bohemians all the way and led into the second half, before two goals in as many minutes gave the home side a 2-1 victory. The visitors' sole strike came from Devlin, who converted a low Glavey cross-shot.

The Sunday Independent noted that Athlone's tireless tackling had reduced Bohemians' scoring opportunities to a minimum.

According to Football Sports Weekly, the credible performance was proof of the paper's belief that Athlone did not deserve to be rooted at the foot of the table.

And with the ground issue still hanging over Athlone, Football Sports Weekly was still acutely aware of the threats to Athlone's existence: "We cannot afford to oust them unless of course the powers that be want to destroy the game in the midlands." It predicted for that reason that Dinny Hannon would not have much difficulty in having Athlone re-elected to the league.

The performance against Bohemians was all the more commendable considering the disarray enveloping the club – with the team only chosen once it became clear who was in the dressing room before the match.

The scorer of the final league goal was Devlin, who was described as a diminutive figure, whose feet, however, could "twinkle a merry tune". However, Football Sports Weekly corrected the record the following week, stating: "There was no Devlin in the Athlone attack. We understand that no player of that name played for Athlone against Bohemians."

One can only assume that Devlin was a pseudonym for an illegal or unregistered player. In a way, it was a fitting finale to what had been a chaotic season.

It means the real identity of Athlone's final League of Ireland goalscorer will be forever shrouded in doubt.

The last league game

Even at this late stage in the season, the Evening Herald was continuing to insist that it was now "more or less an admitted fact" that Athlone would occupy a more respectable position on the league table if they could contrive to hit on an attacking formation that would work.

The following fixture on December 10th, 1927, was Athlone's final home league game of the season. St James's Gate were the visitors and the game ended in a frustrating 0-0 draw. By this stage, it was becoming clear that supporters too were growing increasingly frustrated at the impotent attack. According to the Westmeath Independent, the forwards' displays were frequently the subject of uncomplimentary references by spectators, "who were worked to a high pitch of excitement at this point and they railed against the home forward line"

Back after a knee injury, for the first time that season, was old warrior Jim Sweeney, who understandably failed to show his usual form. Frank Ghent's "helpful centres" were again not being properly utilised, one newspaper noted.

The scale of the ground difficulties confronting Athlone was also made clear by the Westmeath Independent report which said the pitch was almost unplayable. "Players frequently fell in the mud and two bedraggled teams left the pitch with almost resembled a village plot."

Athlone missed a series of chances, particularly in the final minutes and brought down the curtain on their home pitch with a scoreless draw.

Two away ties completed Athlone's league campaign, the first on December 17th against Fordsons in Cork.

With Athlone already beyond redemption at the bottom of the table, it was no surprise that they succumbed to a 5-0 defeat in Cork, with their old player McVeigh among the home scorers.

And their final League of Ireland fixture for over 41 years came on New Year's Day, 1928, when they were forced to endure a horrendous trip in dire weather conditions to Dundalk.

The Dundalk Democrat report on that game told its own story. "Football on a day like Sunday was more a test of endurance than of skill ..."

"It was a dreadful day with sleet and rain, bitterly cold and a stepmother's blast that chilled one to the marrow."

To make matters worse Athlone had been delayed en route by the weather. "An Athlone man told me that on the long motor journey for the Midland team, the team had twice been held up by sleet and blinding snow... He preferred either to the rain and hail we gave him in Dundalk."

The Evening Herald noted that the Athlone motors had "literally to plough their way" to Dundalk and on their arrival both sides agreed to a 30-minute-a-side contest.

"It had become necessary to cut the game to an hour in order to avoid a finish in darkness. But the wicked weather of wet and wind intervened to prevent even this plan being carried out.

So deep down in a slough of ill-luck were Athlone that even the full points would not have saved them from having to apply for re-election.

"They will have formidable opposition but I hope they get back for they are a sporting lot and are doing their best under great difficulties," said the Dundalk Democrat.

Even in the teeth of the fierce wind, Dundalk, in the first half, did most of the attacking and led 1-0 at the break. So it was no surprise that shortly after the interval, Athlone threw in the towel. The Democrat explained: "It transpired that the Athlone side had seen the futility of holding out further and had given Dundalk a walkover."

The weary reporter concluded: "Sensible men they were too for the downpour was getting worse ... The ending was just as satisfactory as could have been wished for."

The newspaper Sport disagreed arguing that this could not and would not have happened earlier in the season and should be looked into by legislators.

Technically, the game was null and void as both sides had agreed to play for less than the regulation time. However, there is no sign of the result having been struck from the record.

Including this fiasco, during the entire 1927/28 league campaign, Athlone had managed just two league victories, one draw and 15 defeats.

The conceded a massive 61 goals in 18 games, an average of just under three and a half goals per game.

They finished bottom of the ten teams with just five points, albeit only one point behind ninth-placed Bray Wanderers and four behind Jacobs.

Both Athlone and Bray were thus required to apply to retain their membership of the league. The omens were not particularly favourable. Already there had been warnings in the media that the applications for re-election would not be a matter of form, with other strong candidates waiting in the wings for admission to the league.

Scraping the bottom

In the meantime, though, there was the FAI Cup, the Leinster Senior Cup and the Shield to contend with.

However, there was to be no fairytale improvement in form. Instead, there was further embarrassment ahead, even if Athlone's league agony was well and truly concluded.

The cup had always coaxed a battling response from Athlone and the visit of Drumcondra to the midlands, on paper at least, provided an opportunity for Athlone to redeem their fallen reputation.

Drumcondra, though a Leinster Senior League side, were the FAI Cup holders having become the first and only side from that league to win the trophy the previous season.

The game on January 7th was an unmitigated disaster for Athlone as they lost 9-3 on home soil. Athlone were totally out of sorts and two of their three goals were scored after Drumcondra had completed their haul.

The dismal showing left Sport to predict: "I would not be surprised if they do not seek readmission to the league."

The Shield was equally unfulfilling for Athlone, with just one win from the six completed fixtures. Indeed, the Town were fined for failing to fulfil their schedule and Bohemians, Shamrock Rovers, and Shelbourne were awarded the points for the respective games. At least two of these contests were due to be played at Ranelagh, but the riverside pitch, even in April, remained underwater.

The trip to Cork on January 28th to play Fordsons was always likely to be unpalatable. Athlone needed to call on the services of five Cork junior players in a game which they lost 10-1, with Charlie Heinemann scoring seven for the home side. It was yet another low point in a season of nadirs, and is almost certainly the highest individual tally scored by a player in a single game against Athlone.

But worse was to come when a complaint was lodged with the league claiming that Athlone side had used false pretences to encourage junior players in Cork to break their status by lining up in the senior league game. The outcome of the complaint is not known. However, it is not inconceivable that Athlone would have been guilty of such an offence.

Compounding their problems was a growing inability for players to secure time off work to travel to the increasing number of away games. The vulnerability of the Ranelagh Grounds to flooding had forced Athlone to increasingly concede home advantage and caused a glut of away fixtures.

In a break to the Shield schedule, Athlone lined up in the Leinster Senior Cup which was blessedly played on a knock-out basis that season, saving the club a plethora of further morale-draining defeats. Instead, they had to endure just one when they lost to Dundalk in Dalymount Park by 5-2 having again ceded home advantage when Ranelagh was unplayable once more.

Athlone did secure a Shield win eventually against Jacobs at home on March 3rd thanks to two goals from newcomer Mick Dunican in a 3-2 triumph.

Two weeks later, there were indications that Athlone had something up their sleeve. Football Sports Weekly reported that the club was very optimistic about the new season.

The following weekend, they were on the move to Wicklow to take on Bray Unknowns in what ended up as Athlone's final senior game for some years.

Again, it was a low-key affair with the Wicklow People noting that the game had been organised on short notice leading to a failure to advertise the attraction and a consequent small crowd. Athlone lost by 4-1 with Frank Ghent the sole scorer. The only other players mentioned in reports of this final game were Glavey, Dunican, keeper Pa Henry and Blackwell.

The curtain had been drawn on Athlone's involvement in senior football in a slipshod fashion that mirrored the entire season.

The rubber stamp

The AGM of the football league occurred on June 28th, 1928 at which Athlone's departure became official.

Drumcondra were elected in Athlone's stead, whilst Bray, whose record was only marginally superior to Athlone's, survived.

Bray had gathered just six points and had a negative goal difference of 41. Athlone had five points and a goal difference tally of –42.

In Athlone's case, the clock had run down on the year's grace given to resolve their ground difficulties.

And with no progress on securing a premises, Athlone were forced to concede defeat and yield their place in the League of Ireland.

The abysmal showing in their final campaign could only have inhibited efforts to find a solution to their ground difficulties.

The optimism that Hannon and his compatriots could pull another rabbit out of the hat was misplaced.

As it was, it took another six years before the club secured a new permanent home in St Mel's Park.

Athlone's departure was met with genuine regret. Sport, which had always backed the club, said: "There is something wrong somewhere. Such splendid players as Dinny Hannon, Johnny McDonnell, Enright and Muldoon were introduced to soccer by Athlone. No club is producing players like that anymore."

The Sports Mail referred to the "almost practical impossibilities" that had forced Athlone to pull up the shutters.

"Athlone is the oldest club playing the game outside Belfast and in the years gone by, before most of our present city clubs were even thought of, produced players who made history."

The team of 1924 had run its course. The practical problems of operating a League of Ireland team from a small town like Athlone in the 1920s had finally overwhelmed the club.

However, the exploits of the team of 1924 will be forever written in the annals of Irish football.

From their midst came five Athlone players who proudly flew the Irish flag aloft for the first time amongst the football nations of the world.

The Olympic Games in Paris in 1924 provided a fitting epitaph to a great team.

1927/28 season round-up

DATE	OPPOSITION	COMPETITION (Athlone score first in all scorelines)	SCORELINE	SCORERS
August 20, 1927	Dundalk (h)	League	2-5	(Dowling, Glavey)
August 27, 1927	Shelbourne (a)	League	1-9	(Callaghan)
September 3, 1927	Brideville (h)	League	2-5	(Dowling, McKenna)
September 10, 1927	Jacobs (a)	League	1-4	(Dowling)
September 17, 1927	Bray Unknowns League (h)	League	2-1	(Glavey, Gibbons)
September 24, 1927	Shamrock Rovers (a)	League	1-3	(McGuirk)
October 1, 1927	Bohemians (h)	League	1-2	(McGuirk)
October 8, 1927	St James's Gate (a)	League	1-3	(Ghent)
October 15, 1927	Fordsons (h)	League	0-2	
November 5 1927	Brideville (a)	League	1-3	(Dowling)
November 12, 1927	Jacobs (h)	League	2-1	(Burke, Glavey)
November 15, 1927	Shelbourne (h)	League	2-7	(Burke (2))
November 20, 1927	Bray Unknowns (a)	League	2-4	(Ghent, Dowling)
November 26, 1927	Shamrock Rovers (h)	League	0-4	
December 3, 1927	Bohemians (a)	League	1-2	('Devlin')*
December 10, 1927	St James's Gate (h)	League	0-0	
December 17, 1927	Fordsons (a)	League	0-5	
December 26, 1927	Dundalk (a)	Shield	1-3	(Henry)
January 1, 1928	Dundalk (a)	League	0-1**	
January 7, 1928	Drumcondra (h)	FAI Cup	3-9	(Jim Sweeney, Henry (2))
January 14, 1928	St James's Gate (h)	Shield	0-1	
January 22, 1928	Brideville (a)	Shield	1-4	(Glavey)
January 28, 1928	Fordsons (a)	Shield	1-10	(Wade)
February 23, 1928	Dundalk (Dalymount Park)	Leinster Senior Cup	2-5	(Blackwell (2))
March 3, 1928	Jacobs (h)	League	3-2	(Dunican (2), Glavey)
April 8, 1928	Bray Unknowns (a)	Shield	1-4	(Ghent)

*   "Devlin" was a pseudonym for an unknown player

**   Game played in Dalymount Park

***   Shield games against Bohemians, Shamrock Rovers and Shelbourne did not take place. Points awarded to opponents.

Chapter 32

1924 Olympic Games

History-makers

Out of the darkness

The 1924 Olympics represented the defining moment when Irish sport came blinking out of the darkness and into the bright lights of the international stage.

It was in the Paris games that Ireland, as a free country, registered its first involvement in the Olympic Games. It was to 16 footballers plucked from four League of Ireland clubs (including five from Athlone) that history granted this unique honour.

Leaving Dublin's Westland Row station in late May 1924 on their way over land and sea to the French capital, this nondescript group were badly prepared, under-funded and ill-informed of what lay ahead, but they were making history.

They ventured forth to Paris as true ambassadors of a proud new State which was ready to take its place among the sporting nations of the world.

They were blazing a trail too for their football association which was charting a steady course through the choppy waters of international sporting politics.

And quite literally they were flying the flag for Ireland on the Olympic stage as the tricolour hitherto had not been exhibited at an Olympic Games.

In short, these men were both Ireland's first Olympians and Ireland's first international football team.

They are the starting point for two rich traditions of Irish sport that brings together names like Ronnie Delany and Liam Brady, Sonia O'Sullivan and Roy Keane, Paul McGrath and Michael Carruth.

The first Olympians

Ireland's involvement in the Olympic movement prior to its development as an independent nation has been well documented.

Athletes both from Ireland and from the Irish diaspora competed under an array of flags in the seven Olympics that preceded the 1924 games.

But Paris was the first occasion that athletes could unfurl the green, white and gold or enjoy having the word 'Ireland' appear after their names in the official literature of the games.

In 1924, Ireland entered 37 competitors across four disciplines but with football preceding the main tournament, the honour of leading the new Free State nation into the Olympic movement fell on the shoulders of the football team.

As the governing body of football in the Irish Free State, the FAI bore the responsibility to select and manage the team of players. But it was the Olympic Council of Ireland which submitted the application to participate in the Olympic football tournament and which carried out all the administrative work.

How the Olympics bedded down the FAI

From the perspective of 85 years later, it's readily apparent why the Olympic movement held such an attraction for football officials.

The FAI had fought a long, complex and deeply political battle to carve out a niche for itself on the world stage.

With the might of the four 'home' nations as they liked to view themselves (the IFA, the FA, the Scottish FA and the Welsh FA) bitterly opposed to the development of the FAI, the Irish were forced to exploit the growing divide in the game's governance internationally.

The four UK associations were part of their own governing body of the game, the International FA Board (IFB). FIFA joined the IFB in 1913 and was given one vote in five. However, the FA resigned from FIFA in 1920 when the latter, in the wake of World War One, refused to expel those whom the English considered as 'enemy nations'.

It was in this backdrop that the Irish sought to curry favour with FIFA in an attempt to end the international blacklisting under which the FAI, its league and clubs laboured.

A FIFA convention in late 1923 eventually agreed to sanction the FAI's application for membership - thus ensuring that football in the Free State had a solid platform from which to develop.

When invitations to take part in the football tournament in the Olympic Games came winging their way from FIFA headquarters soon after, the FAI officials sensed a valuable opportunity to stamp their identity on the world game.

Keen to exercise their new powers and imbued with the first flush of youthful enthusiasm, the new kid on the block by late 1923 had already signed up to enter a football team in the games.

At the time, the matches against Bulgaria, Holland and Estonia (in Paris) and the US (back at home) were regarded as full internationals. However, over the years, the games have been downgraded to amateur international status.

In 1999, FIFA ruled that all Olympic Games match from 1908 to 1940 be regarded as full internationals. For Ireland, it simply means restoring the forgotten internationals to their original place on the front rank.

Trial and financial error

Finance, though, was a major stumbling block to the FAI's aspirations to send a team to Paris.

An official from the FAI wrote to the Irish Independent pointing out that: "To send this team to France will cost more money than the Football Association possess, but it has issued an appeal to every footballer and ex-footballer in the country to contribute to a fund specially created for this purpose."

Initially, it was intended to send 22 players and a squad of that number was officially nominated but only 16 were eventually selected to travel – a decision that may have been dictated by the absence of sufficient funds.

By late April, it was estimated that the fund had reached £450 with another £50 expected.

The visit of Glasgow Celtic had been a key part of the fundraising strategy. The massive crowd of some 22,000 people paid gate receipts of over £1,200. However, once the payment to Celtic (£480), an entertainment tax payment to the Government (over £300) and sundry expenses were deducted, the game yielded just £250 to the fund.

The Entertainment Tax was a legacy from British rule. It required sports clubs to pay 25% of total gate receipts to the Government as a levy. Always hugely controversial, it became doubly so when for a period the tax did not apply to Gaelic games but remained for football.

Even though, the fundraising was not immediately favourable, the football association had let it be known that they would not back down.

They said they were determined to put a team into the arena for the honour and glory of the country even it it meant bankruptcy. Other nations were liberally furnished with funds. The Belgium team, which had won the previous Olympics, had a war chest of one million francs.

The preparations were not helped by the disorganisation which prompted the Irish Olympic Council to hurriedly submit an ad hoc squad of 22 players. They were mistakenly under the impression that a deadline for putting forward a list of players was approaching fast.

This list, which was subsequently revoked, has not been reproduced, although a report by the Westmeath Independent in April announcing that seven Athlone players including Joe Monahan and Jimmy Hope would be selected for Paris may have emanated from this source.

It later transpired that the deadline for sending final squad lists to the

French Olympic Committee was May 4th and changes could be made up to and including May 15th.

The news was met with relief and allowed a series of trials to be held, the first of which took place in in Shelbourne Park on Thursday, April 24th.

The trials also doubled as a fundraising initiative, although their returns were paltry.

Three Athlone players, took part in the first trial. Muldoon lined out at left-half for the Reds, while O'Reilly and Hannon filled their customary roles for their opponents, the Whites.

Hannon was on the scoresheet as his side prevailed by the odd goal in five.

Four days later, another trial was held in Dalymount Park. Nine of the original 22 returned and were supplemented by 13 newcomers, including Athlone's Frank Ghent who was the sole local representative on this occasion.

Although, Sport said there was little to be gauged from the two trial games, it did admit that the first contest in Shelbourne Park had been the more revealing.

The paper said O'Reilly's performance in that game should mark him down as a certain starter.

The writer was equally clear-cut about his preference for the left-half berth.

"We have not seen anyone who is eligible to travel that can compare with Muldoon of Athlone. He is the most improved half-back in the country and a real good one."

In attempting to pin down the remaining squad members, the paper was less insistent. It went on to propose Dinny Hannon for either inside-left or centre-forward.

"Hannon should make a good centre-forward. What he doesn't know about the game isn't worth knowing … I fail to see how he could be left off."

Later, when assessing possible replacement full-backs, Sport suggested both Hope and Monahan as worthy options.

During the second trial, young Joe Kendrick from lowly Brooklyn impressed and secured his place on the boat.

In early May, the final sixteen was chosen. It included five players from each of Athlone Town, Bohemians and St James's Gate along with Kendrick. The squad was: Paddy O'Reilly (Athlone Town), Bertie Kerr (Bohemians), Tom Murphy (St James's Gate), Jack McCarthy (Bohemians), Ernie McKay (St James's Gate), John Joe Dykes (Athlone Town), John Thomas (Bohemians), Tommy Muldoon (Athlone Town), Michael Farrell (St James's Gate), Joe Kendrick (Brooklyn), Paddy Duncan (St James's Gate), Frank Ghent (Athlone Town), Charlie Dowdall (St James's Gate), Denis Hannon (Athlone Town), Christy Robinson (Bohemians) and Johnny Murray (Bohemians).

Dykes was the only player to have made the cut without participating in a trial match.

The players were given two weeks to have their passports ready and to present themselves for departure at Westland Row on the evening of May 24th.

The sixteen players were to be accompanied by a group of officials (R. F Murphy L. C. Sheridan, J. S. Smurthwaite, J. L Brennan, J. T Kelly and M. Redmond).

The official list sent to the French Olympic Committee also included six other players who did not travel. These were Ernie Crawford (Bohemians), Bob Cowzer (Shamrock Rovers), John Healy (Bray Unknowns), Frank Heaney (St James's Gate), John Lea (Shelbourne) and Tom Aungier (St James's Gate). Each of these players took part in one or other of the trials.

The squad then completed its preparations with a challenge match against a Shelbourne Utd selection in Dalymount Park on May 17th.

Eleven of the Paris-bound group were expected to make up the Free State Olympic side while the remaining five, along with six others, were to appear as a Shelbourne Utd XI. However, again Dykes did not appear. The game drew a respectable gate, with receipts of £100 before various deductions including entertainment tax were made.

Farrell scored two of the Olympic-bound team's goals in this final trial. The Evening Herald noted that Hannon's reputation had taken a battering with a poor performance.

One of the selectors' more difficult decisions was whether to select Bohemians' Johnny Murray or his Athlone counterpart Frank Ghent for the outside-left spot in the starting eleven.

Ghent's prospects of dislodging Murray were badly dented with a poor performance for the Shelbourne Utd selection in contrast to the latter's excellent display.

The Irish Times said of Murray: "He repeatedly beat the defence and had his inside partners utilised the openings made for them the score must have been much larger."

After the game, the players were also requested to report on the following Tuesday and Thursday for training under team manager and Bohemians official Charlie Harris.

By then, Sport was able to inform its readers that Ireland would line up in blue jerseys, white knickers and black stockings with blue tops. A spray of green shamrocks would be worn on a white shield on the breasts of their jerseys.

There was little fanfare surrounding the footballers' adventure outside the restricted columns of the specialist football sections of the daily newspapers.

One paper, though, seemed acutely aware of the significance of the occasion.

Sport's football correspondent, Viator, advised the departing players to "battle on to the last gasp, as though life and death depended on their efforts, even to the risk of never being fit to play another game in their lives".

"Such an opportunity as this, in all probability, will never come the way of those Irish players again.

"To be the first Irishmen to compete in the Olympiad is great. To be the first Irishmen to win would be infinitely greater. They must not think of themselves. Their uppermost and inseparable thought must be of their country.

"Their country expects them to do their duty to play as Irishmen, to win as Irishmen and if the worst comes to the worst, to lose as Irishmen fighting unflinchingly to the last."

The Parisian adventure

The adventure began on Saturday, May 24th, 1924, when the players and officials gathered in Westland Row for a brief meal. They then travelled to Dun Laoghaire from where they caught a boat to Holyhead. A mid-morning train to London followed. They were then given a short break to catch up with some sleep before continuing their journey to France via Dover.

When they eventually arrived in France on a boat to Calais in the early hours of Monday, they headed directly to their base, the Prince Albert Hotel, in central Paris.

Although many of the 22 teams that took part resided in the Olympic Village for the duration of their participation in the tournament, the FAI had opted to lodge in a city hotel.

Later on Monday, the squad visited the Cenotaph and laid a wreath, in the shape of a harp composed of roses and other flowers, on the tomb of the the Unknown Soldier.

They were accompanied by the French Under Secretary for Foreign Affairs and by Mr M. J. Bailey, the representative of the Irish Free State Consul in Paris.

The ceremonies concluded with the formal unfurling of the tricolour at the Arc de Triomphe – the first time the Irish Free State flag had been flown in Paris.

That evening the players took in the Uruguay v. Yugoslavia game, in which the South Americans displayed their array of skills in a 7-0 demolition.

The performance left the players and officials spellbound.

One witness recorded the reaction: "The feeling was that if the other contestants were anything like the Uruguayans we might as well come home right away."

On Tuesday, the entire team and officials, along with those from Holland, Belgium and Bulgaria, were formally welcomed to the Olympics by Count Clary, the President of the Olympic Games Executive Committee

The travelling contingent had initially been under the impression that they would enter the Olympic fray on Tuesday, May 27th but their game with Bulgaria was deferred to Wednesday.

With an extra day's preparation, the squad on Tuesday, under the supervision of trainer Charlie Harris, underwent what was described as "some perfunctory practice". How perfunctory it was became clear when it was revealed that the 16 players were joined by the six middle-aged officials to comprise two teams.

A view of Stade de Colombes.

Beating the Bulgars

The game against Bulgaria took place on Wednesday 28th at 4pm in the Stade de Colombes, the main football stadium which would host the Olympic final the following month.

Both sides had received a bye in the opening round – and the winner of this second-round clash was therefore guaranteed a quarter-final spot.

Nervous tension filled the air as the Irish eleven lined up behind the tricolour and paraded in front of the main stand at Stade de Colombes.

There was naturally surprise when the marching band launched into Let Erin Remember, rather than the national anthem. The FAI would later argue that the Irish Olympic Committee had chosen that piece of music.

Nonetheless, it was an emotional and nerve-wracking moment. The infant nation of Ireland was taking its first baby steps in both the Olympic

The Irish team which played Bulgaria.

movement and international football.

At their helm was captain Athlone's Denis Hannon – at 36 years of age the oldest player among the 22 squads at Paris. With O'Reilly, Dykes and Muldoon also in the eleven, the line out against Bulgaria featured four from Athlone Town.

Bohemians had three representatives in the shape of full-backs Jack McCarthy and Bertie Kerr and outside-left Johnny Murray. St James's Gate also provided three players; half-back Ernie McKay and forwards Mickey Farrell (outside-right) and Paddy Duncan (centre-forward).

One of Denis Hannon's Olympic caps.

A ticket for the game against Bulgaria.

Togged out in their blue jerseys, the Irish players nervously went through the preliminaries. The referee would later comment that he had never seen a more tense bunch of players.

The significance of the occasion may have been, to a large part, lost on the media and football world back home in Ireland, but here in Paris, there was no mistaking the sense of history in the air.

The sporting ambassadors of a proud new nation were about to present their credentials to the world.

Unfortunately, though the world seemed disinterested as only 522 paying spectators were present to witness this momentous occasion in Irish sporting history.

With the sparse crowd spread out in the cavernous stadium, the atmosphere was eerily surreal, more akin to a training session than a country's international debut.

The official attendance was 1,659, with the 500-odd paying customers joined by 1,137 complimentary ticket holders– although it's not clear if these free tickets were utilised or simply distributed.

From the crowd, the words of old Gaelic songs could be heard on the pitch. Indeed, the few hundred supporters that were present made light of the vast cavernous surrounds to roar their approval throughout.

The game itself was dwarfed by the sense of occasion.

The Bulgarians were a young side including many players who had learned the game from the more experienced football nations of Austria and Hungary.

Previously, Bulgaria had mainly played fellow Central European countries and, in common with Ireland, were an unknown factor on the wider stage.

What passed as previews of the game in French newspapers in many cases were little short of exercises in national stereotyping, the Bulgarians were that Eastern European standard 'scientific' while the Irish apparently combined the practical English game with a spontaneity that was characteristic of the Latin countries.

With the sun and wind against them, Ireland started poorly and only settled into the game midway through the opening half.

They had thrown themselves into the heat of battle in a haphazard fashion as their enthusiasm threatened to spill over.

Duncan in the opening minutes became a victim of Ireland's over-robust style when he was injured in a clash with the Bulgarian centre-half. The combative St James's Gate stalwart left the field but with the help of Charlie Harris subsequently recovered to restore his side to their full complement.

In a tough physical game, there were numerous stoppages, and in the second half, off-side rulings, as both teams attempted to deploy the one-back game.

The Bulgarian team

It was Ireland that threatened first with Duncan hitting the post. Bulgaria's centre-forward whizzed an effort just wide of the Irish goal soon after.

Just before the interval, Hannon slipped whilst in an ideal position and then Johnny Murray banged a Farrell centre straight at the Bulgarian keeper

The city daily Le Petit Parisien noted that the Bulgarian half-back line was dictating the flow of the game but the Eastern European forwards were unable to take advantage.

The Bulgarians enjoyed a height and weight advantage over the smaller Irish, who displayed, according to one French newspaper, a more incisive and cohesive style of attack.

After the break, Ireland's determination began to wear down the Bulgarians. The unstoppable force began to erode the not-so-immovable object.

The unorthodox Bulgarian goalkeeper who had already raised laughs when he saved a shot with his head was penalised three times for over-carrying the ball. All three free-kicks inside the penalty area were taken by Hannon but without success.

In quick succession, Murray shot over, whilst Kendrick, Farrell and Hannon all struck woodwork as the Bulgarians came under intense pressure. It seemed as if Ireland were now destined not to score. Then a cross from Murray was thumped home by the re-energised Duncan for the winner. Most French newspapers remarked that Duncan appeared to be clearly offside

The lead goal demoralised Bulgaria who faded away badly in the final minutes.

Despite this, Ireland were unable to convert a plethora of chances. Late on, Duncan again found the net from a Hannon cross, but this time, the effort was ruled out for off-side. Hannon brought a fine save from Ivanoff in the Bulgarian goal while Dykes struck the angle of post and crossbar.

However, Bulgaria were still alert enough to bring a decent save from O'Reilly in the final minutes. The French papers selected Muldoon as the most impressive player in the Irish team.

Overall, though, Ireland had failed to live up to their own expectations. The newspaper Sport said Ireland moved sluggishly and did not seem able to accustom themselves to the strange conditions and unfamiliar tactics of their opponents. It added that rarely had so many chances being missed in a representative match.

"The score does not represent the true run of the game nor the superiority of the winners," Sport reported.

Post-match analysis concentrated on Ireland's missed chances, although there was a belief that Ireland were the better side over the game.

Le Petit Parisien commented that Ireland's backs were powerful although their clearances too often found the touch-line.

Their half-backs and forwards insisted on long sweeping balls in the air. On the contrary, the Bulgarians indulged in short passing and always retained possession for too long.

Ireland's lethargy was unsurprising, considering their recent arrival in Paris following the lengthy sea and rail journey.

It was only later in the week that the Evening Telegraph reported that the players had fully recovered from the effects of their journey. The same paper said many of the other nations had domiciled in Paris for weeks, and in some cases, months, before their first engagement. Ireland, in contrast, arrived very late on Sunday night for a Wednesday match.

The paper too stressed that the heat conditions were "well nigh unendurable" for the Irish.

Quarter-final

The squad trained daily from Thursday to Sunday, ahead of their quarter-final on Monday, June 2nd, against Holland. The game was set for the Stade de Paris, a smaller stadium than Colombes and far less inspiring.

In the days after the Bulgaria clash, Holland, who were staying close to the Irish quarters, issued an invite to their next opponents for dinner on Monday evening.

Holland had hit six without replay against Romania in the second round, and were warm order to overcome Ireland, who had not generally impressed in defeating the Bulgarians.

The game kicked off at 5pm on Monday night and this time the official

The Irish team before the Holland game.

attendance (1,506) was even smaller than for the Bulgaria clash. Almost 900 paid in, but there were only 613 availing of the complimentary tickets.

In fact, the attendances at the two Irish games were the lowest in the entire football tournament. History was in the making but there was practically no-one there to see it.

One who was present though was the Irish rugby international Ernie Crawford, who was one of the unfortunate six to have been pared from the original squad when its number was reduced to 16.

Crawford, though, made the journey as a supporter, although he found himself in hot water when a revolver was found in his luggage by custom officials en route.

His explanation: he had it for his own "peace of mind".

Meanwhile, there were fireworks of a sort on the pitch too as Ireland's Olympic dream was dashed by the Dutch in a tightly-contested encounter that was only settled after extra time.

Frank Ghent replaced Joe Kendrick at inside-left bringing the Athlone representation to five players. Not since then, has any one club provided more than four players to an Irish international side in a single game.

In an encounter in which both sides had opportunities, the Dutch forward line appeared to have a principled objection to shots at goal.

"Time and again, they threw away easy chances in front of the goal," said the Evening Telegraph.

In an astonishingly open game, both sides attacked throughout. Ireland, equally, had their fair share of goal opportunities, but failed to capitalise.

The Dutch raced into an early lead when OK Formenoy, a striker from Feyenoord, struck after just seven minutes.

However, Ireland had the better of the remainder of the half, and Murray came close before his corner was converted by Ghent for the equaliser on 38 minutes.

Holland dominated the second half of normal time, but Ireland defended stoutly.

Formenoy struck the underside of the crossbar early in that half and the rebound was sent wide by a wasteful Dutch player.

Mickey Farrell then came close, having jinxed past a whole posse of defenders on a slalom run from near the halfway line. At the other end, Formenoy was denied by O'Reilly while Ireland thought they had scored after a melee. Despite the strong belief of the crowd and the Irish players, the referee ruled the ball had not crossed the line.

Ireland did all the attacking in the first period of extra time, but it was just before the half-time interval that Holland struck for the winner courtesy of Formenoy.

The second period of extra-time represented one long struggle for Ireland to equalise, but the Dutch held on to make the semi-finals where they were eventually knocked out by Uruquay.

By running Holland so close, Ireland's reputation had soared. But that was no consolation to the heart-broken players, whose desolation in the dressing room later prompted captain Denis Hannon to comment that he had never seen such a disappointed team.

Ireland knew that they had been within touching distance of a medal, something they would never have thought possible.

Estonia calling

Later that night, the vanquished Irish broke bread with the victors, but there was little time for social interaction as Ireland were in action the next day in a friendly international with Estonia, who were also out of the Olympics at this stage.

The selectors opted to bring on the four players who had yet to experience action: Thomas, Dowdall, Robinson and Murphy.

Hannon was rested for the friendly and the armband as captain was transferred to another Athlone player John Joe Dykes. The club had produced Ireland's first two skippers.

Frank Ghent retained his position at inside-left as did O'Reilly between the posts. Muldoon also featured and scored along with Duncan and Robinson in a 3-1 victory.

Strangely, 3,000 witnessed this friendly encounter played in the Stade de Colombes.

Whilst in Paris, Ireland renewed acquaintances with the members and officials of the local club Cercle Athletique de Paris, which had twice visited Ireland.

They were the original boycott-breakers, the starting point in a long journey that had culminated in Paris.

The club hosted a formal dinner on Wednesday evening and as the proceedings turned informal later on, the Soldier's Song could be heard lustily delivered. Present at the dinner was one Jules Rimet, then president of FIFA, and later the man whose name adorned the original World Cup trophy.

Indeed, in a way the Olympics were the major world football championships in the years before the World Cup.

However, ongoing battles over the definition of amateurism prompted FIFA to establish its own competition, particularly after the 1928 football tournament at the Amsterdam Olympics was badly hit by withdrawals.

Of the 1924 Olympics squad for Uruguay, seven won the initial World Cup six years later.

The Paris Olympics was significant as it was the first occasion that countries from outside Europe travelled to take part in international matches. The tournament was an unqualified success with 50,000 people watching the final between Uruguay and Switzerland.

Learning lessons

Travel, they say, broadens the mind and the Evening Telegraph predicted that the experience of the Olympic footballers would extend their sporting horizons too.

"After their visit to Paris, it is most improbable that any of the Free State footballers will ever again look towards England or Scotland as the centre of what has been considered the best in football. Their outlook has been radically changed.

"What they have seen and learned in France was not only amazing but defies verbal description and they are all returned to Dublin on Friday convinced that in football we in Ireland are solely behind most other countries and hopelessly in the rear of several".

Robert F. Murphy, one of the six officials to accompany the players, wrote

Frank Ghent's official Olympic Scroll

in the Irish Independent later that the overall standard of play was very high.

"In general the players were quick in getting the ball under control – no simple task on the hard grounds.

Contrary to what was the fashion in Ireland and Britain, "short low passes seemed to be the favourite mode of progression".

"Goalkeeping was of a particularly high standard and we noticed that all the Continental defenders made frequent use of back passes to the custodian when in difficulty," he added.

In his assessment, Murphy made the point that the interaction with Continental styles could only benefit the game in Ireland and help to bring it from under the guiding influence of England.

"It would be well for many of our insular spirits here if they could observe how this worldwide game has softened the asperities that arise between different peoples and what a part it is destined to play in bringing about a common understanding."

If the players had learned from the experiences, so too had the officials.

The complex administrative processes within the Olympic movement have regularly spawned bitter rows between individual sporting bodies and the Olympic Council of Ireland in more recent years.

The uncertain relationship was evident 85 years ago too

More than a year after the Olympics, the Football Sports Weekly commented that it would hope that others would not meddle in the Olympic football sector and that the FAI would have "the deciding voice on such details as the colours to be worn by the footballers, the music to be played on entering the arena and the qualifications of the players chosen".

"Some dreadful things happened last year. To avoid a repetition the FSFA should take steps to be represented on the Olympic Council. They can trust no one but one of themselves to have things done properly."

At its AGM in August 1924, the FAI said that it had been given no encouragement from the Olympic Council of Ireland, who had even refused to process visa applications for the footballers.

The Olympic adventure had one further postscript; a visit by the US Olympic team to Dalymount Park on June 14th.

For this one, Tommy Muldoon was the sole remaining Athlonian. O'Reilly had been replaced, while Dykes, who had been originally selected at centre-half, was unavailable.

Three players who did not fit the narrow definition of amateurism were included for this game; Frank Collins in goal, Tony Hunston up front and Ned Brooks as line-leader.

Brooks was the star of the show grabbing a hat-trick in a 3-1 victory.

The Americans paraded onto the Dalymount pitch carrying both the Irish flag and the Stars and Stripes. This may have earned the respect of the 4,000

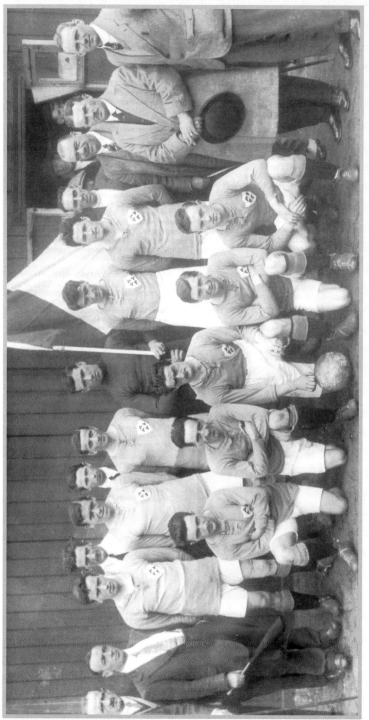

Ireland USA

attendance but the actions of the US players in gathering in the centre circle before the game to enact a battle cry sparked only humour.

The captain of the USA team addressed a post-match dinner in Clearys thus: "I guess we are proud to be in Ireland. I guess we enjoyed a good game. I guess we thought we would win. I guess we were beaten and that's all that's to it."

Muldoon, Johnny Murray and Paddy Duncan were the only players to have featured in each of the first four internationals. Muldoon had carried off the honours in Paris, attracting positive comment from Continental analysts and reporters.

But there was a greater legacy for the nation as a whole.

The Irish Free State, as it was then officially known, had staked out its reputation as a football nation of some consequence. It had also embarked on an Olympic adventure that continues to great acclaim to this day.

And Athlone's quintet of football pioneers was at the very heart of this double achievement.

Athlone sport fans can always proudly remember the days when we were kings.

.